PEOPLE, PRACTICE, POWER

PEOPLE, PRACTICE, POWER

DIGITAL HUMANITIES OUTSIDE THE CENTER

Anne McGrail, Angel David Nieves,
and Siobhan Senier

EDITORS

DEBATES IN THE DIGITAL HUMANITIES

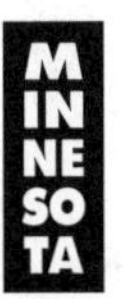

University of Minnesota Press
Minneapolis
London

Published by the University of Minnesota Press
111 Third Avenue South, Suite 290
Minneapolis, MN 55401-2520
http://www.upress.umn.edu

ISBN 978-1-5179-1067-9 (hc)
ISBN 978-1-5179-1068-6 (pb)
Library of Congress record available at https://lccn.loc.gov/2021023189.

Printed in the United States of America on acid-free paper

The University of Minnesota is an equal-opportunity educator and employer.

30 29 28 27 26 25 24 23 22 21   10 9 8 7 6 5 4 3 2 1

PART III

Pedagogy: Vulnerability, Collaboration, and Resilience

ANNE McGRAIL, ANGEL DAVID NIEVES, AND SIOBHAN SENIER

Our volume's title, *People, Practice, Power: Digital Humanities outside the Center*, intends to foreground the *human* side of digital humanities (DH) infrastructure. For most people, *infrastructure* calls to mind things including hardware, software, storage capacity, funding, and facilities. But the writers collected in this book ask us to *humanize* infrastructure—to consider what the sociologist Susan Leigh Star called those "invisible layers of control and access" that undergird any scientific or scholarly work.[1] Data visualization tools and content management systems are, after all, designed by people, people in very specific social and economic locations, and they are used by groups of people in still other, often heterogeneous and contradictory social and economic positions. They are deployed, shared, and repaired in a tangle of institutional protocols, disciplinary conventions, and systemic inequalities. It is these everyday, deeply felt, and sometimes disenfranchising practices and relations that most concern the authors featured in this book.

Two other sociologists, Walter Powell and Paul DiMaggio, once observed that "institutions are not necessarily the products of conscious design."[2] From its very first volume, the *Debates* series has taken up some of the often unconscious designs that have characterized the emerging field of digital humanities. Indeed, as DH has become institutionalized, the social and disciplinary relationships that constitute it have arguably come to govern "what has meaning and what actions are possible" within it, as Powell and DiMaggio might say.[3] Steven Brint and Jerome Karabel, who write about the history and economic promise/dispossession of community colleges—a subject near and dear to Anne McGrail's heart—put the matter this way: "organizations may make their own history, but they do not make it just as they please," because the development of institutions takes place "within larger fields of power and social structure."[4] When we drew up our initial call for papers, we wanted to zero in specifically on some of these larger fields of power and social structure. We wanted to gather, under one big tent, some of the scholars, students, and practitioners who have been thinking deeply about and indeed are living with and working around some of the power dynamics and social structures that now seem baked into DH.

In the current crisis in higher education, it is easy to be pessimistic about the ways that institutional power and resources shape and stymie us. However, institutional arrangements are also shaped by participants' agency, and many of our authors undertake what Thomas B. Lawrence would call "institutional biographies" that complicate that overdetermination. "Good biography," Lawrence and his colleagues write, "portrays the social structural influences, the opportunities for agency, and the successes and failures of the individual to shape their world."[5] Our ability—our human ability—to reflect on our embeddedness within distinct power structures provides a direction for action in the field, what Pamella Lach and Jessica Pressman in this volume call "infrastructural imaginaries." On some fundamental level, as Patrik Svensson and David Theo Goldberg have suggested, infrastructure is ultimately "about imagination and connecting deep conceptual ideas with material manifestations."[6]

Meanwhile, as we sat down to write this introduction to over twenty outstanding essays about digital humanities and its institutions and infrastructures, we found ourselves interrogating the old English nursery rhyme, "This is the House that Jack Built":

> This is the horse and the hound and the horn
> That belonged to the farmer sowing his corn
> That kept the rooster that crowed in the morn
> That woke the judge all shaven and shorn
> That married the man all tattered and torn
> That kissed the maiden all forlorn
> That milked the cow with the crumpled horn
> That tossed the dog that worried the cat
> That killed the rat that ate the malt
> That lay in the house that Jack built.

The rhyme itself is called a *cumulative tale* or *chain tale*, a form that depends on reiteration and layering for its effect. The original builder, Jack, and even his house ultimately seem less important in the end than the dizzying chains of relationships they prompt—relationships sometimes productive, sometimes fraught, often marked by differences in social position and resources. "Jack's house" means different things to different people: the very title of this song has been reset and reinterpreted across a wide range of places and times, from the lyrics in a mournful tune by Aretha Franklin, to the name, more recently, of a creepy Lars von Trier film, and back, somewhat presciently, to "The House that Jack Built," an episode from the cult British 1960s television show, *The Avengers,* where the protagonist, Emma Peel, finds herself trapped in a maze-like, digitally controlled sci-fi apparatus, itself secreted within a seemingly traditional country house.

If we think about the enterprise of digital humanities as being a little like Jack's house, we might observe that it is inflected, practiced, and hosted by an ever-widening circle of constituencies beyond those present solely at its founding. It is embedded within a variety of other structures and institutions, some small and seemingly insignificant (like the cat or rat of the rhyme), others much larger with structures and practices of their own (like civil law or global agriculture). DH likewise accrues its value and complexities chiefly from its situatedness in other institutions, generally in institutions of higher education, although the "global humanities research infrastructure" that James Smithies posits points us far beyond that to government and nongovernment and commercial and noncommercial sectors as well.

In recent years, we have seen the values and complexities of DH dramatically shift with explosions of new funding opportunities (and their attendant reporting and deliverables requirements), new job advertisements (and the redesign of old tenure lines to include digital foci), and new publications that reflect new understandings of DH, its institutions, and its infrastructures. Like Jack's house, DH is now a contact zone where phenomena such as humanistic deliberation, aesthetic inquiry, and aspirations for institutional and social justice collide with the star system, the supplanting of tenured labor forces with contingent ones, neoliberal management and market ideologies, and the sheer acceleration of digital technologies themselves. Infrastructure, in its most rudimentary definition, comprises the facilities and structures that a house or a university or a society require to maintain basic operations. It *costs*, indisputably: money, labor, and human capital. However, it is also profoundly relational. Seeing digital humanities infrastructure in this way—as a set of evolving relations and dependencies and not merely static resources—supports a critical digital humanities practice that acknowledges institutional constraints and engages in purposeful, reflexive action.

In our academic institutions, we find ourselves increasingly unable to talk about even the smallest daily tasks without running up against institutional and infrastructural challenges and inequities. This is perhaps especially true of DH precisely because it presents today as so resource- and infrastructure-intensive. Many of our colleagues and students fail to imagine some of the tools, teams, and *time* that DH seems to require, even as digital literacy becomes the sine qua non of professional and civic life. And even those in the most privileged and amply funded spaces know that infrastructure is always vulnerable. Storage is often insufficient. Platforms require continual maintenance and updating. Things *break*—and as Steven J. Jackson has suggested in an earlier essay, "Rethinking Repair," the repair involved requires additional and perhaps even more expensive outlays than all the shiny innovations in our path. Overriding all our work, administrators at higher and ever more remote levels are making major decisions about digital infrastructure that affect our research and pedagogy in ways of which we are unaware or unable to determine.

When we think about *infrastructure* in this context, we are thinking of the inescapable infrastructural dependencies: shifting and unstable labor requirements, grant-funding exigencies, spatial and other physical requirements, and version control and lapse. The authors in this volume see infrastructures beyond the technical, hardware, and financial needs of their own institutions, programs, and centers. They are keenly interested in political, social, and economic factors including promotion and tenure processes, student research support, pedagogical development, and even extra-institutional instruments such as project charters and memoranda of understanding. These authors call attention to the ineluctably human side of DH infrastructure, and insist on rethinking infrastructure in *human* terms, which is perhaps one of the more radical things that DH can do.

We hope that our volume builds on the installed base of the textual infrastructure established by the *Debates in the Digital Humanities* series. Earlier volumes have tracked conversations and controversies around DH's *big tent* metaphor, and how (and whether) DH can be fruitfully practiced outside the digital humanities center (DHC) and large institutions with their considerable resources. Echoed in this volume are Amy Earhart's earlier call for mechanisms to welcome DIY digital projects into the institutional canon; Moya Bailey, Anne Cong-Huyen, Alexis Lothian, and Amanda Phillips's insistence on the essential role of "nontraditional output" such as activist social justice work to create a transformed field that extends beyond the academy; and Anne McGrail's ongoing advocacy for meaningful digital humanities work for students in open-access community colleges. More recently, the themes organizing Jacqueline Wernimont and Elizabeth Losh's *Debates* volume, *Bodies of Information* (2018)—materiality, values, embodiment, affect, labor, and situatedness—anticipate the relational quality of DH infrastructural dimensions with which our authors engage here.

A great deal, if not the vast majority, of DH work today is actually being conducted outside of dedicated DHCs. It is happening in a variety of institutions that might never before have imagined conducting digital research and teaching, including small liberal arts colleges, community colleges, teaching-intensive institutions, historically black colleges and universities (HBCUs), and Hispanic-Serving Institutions (HSIs). We accept the decentralization and diffusion of DH as a welcome development and intend to fill a gap in the literature available to practitioners who, at DHCs and at underresourced institutions alike, are now confronting and dealing with unexpected infrastructural challenges. Such issues as contingent labor, soft money funding, academic hierarchies, and state politics at a variety of institutions (from the underresourced to the generously endowed) require practical response and theoretical guidance on how and whether to proceed with digital initiatives.

Although we did not necessarily intend to include essays in what is now called critical infrastructure studies, many of the pieces resonate with issues raised in this emerging field. Alan Liu, as a member of the Critical Infrastructure Studies Collective, defines infrastructure as "the social-cum-technological milieu that at once enables the fulfillment of human experience and enforces constraints on that experience."[7] In this definition, infrastructure comprises more than just the transportation, electrical grids, internet, and other media and hardware through which and upon which culture happens: it *is* culture, or at least it operationalizes our experience of it. To Liu, "the word 'infrastructure' can now give us the same kind of general purchase on social complexity that Stuart Hall, Raymond Williams, and others sought when they reached for their all-purpose word, 'culture' . . . and critics will need to attend to "that cyborg being whose making, working, disciplining, performance, gender formation, and hybridity are increasingly part of the core identity of late modern culture."[8]

If Liu is right (and he is), then humans can no longer leave discussions of infrastructure to the technocrats. We witness this truth daily around the globe with evidence including water supply contamination, pipeline explosions, and structural failures. In the face of extreme weather and the resulting evacuations and population dispersals, we are starting to look more closely at the physical materials and engineering systems that are failing us. We inevitably begin to pose questions involving the *human,* and regarding *power.* Who decided, for instance, to divert Flint, Michigan's drinking water? Why did National Grid lock out its union laborers before its gas lines began exploding across northeastern Massachusetts? Who benefits from the privatization of Puerto Rico's electricity authority? In academic institutions that are witnessing (and too often replicating) similarly grievous inequalities, the questions are no less urgent. Which students are afforded the opportunity to *practice* digital humanities? Under what labor conditions and power differentials do adjunct, library, and technical staff create digital projects? How do underfunded groups sustain their collaborative projects over the long haul—or can they? With these kinds of vulnerabilities and precarities in mind, to think about *infrastructure* and about human struggles to build communities of care that can respond to these dilemmas is to bring a social justice orientation to bear on our humanities disciplinary practice.

We believe that many of our authors respond, at least implicitly, to the call to consider infrastructure much as we used to think about *culture.* In the first section of this volume, "Beyond the Digital Humanities Center: Historical Perspectives and New Models," our essays respond explicitly to the call. James Malazita, who teaches DH at Rensselaer Polytechnic Institute, describes what he calls an "epistemic infrastructure" in the form of technological instrumentalism. This epistemic infrastructure, he determines, seeks to cordon off technical expertise from critical inquiry. This practice does not occur only in STEM disciplines; it threatens to take over our universities wholesale, he warns, if DH does not bring its humanistic tools to challenge it. By exploring the tensions among multiple epistemic regimes, DH scholars can subvert this subversion. In a similar vein, Erin Glass issues a clarion call for digital humanists to question academic institutions' wholesale and passive adoption of capitalist digital technologies in an educational technology market with hundreds of billions of dollars at stake. Focusing on what she calls the "invisible discipline" of pervasive campus digital technologies, she surveys early twenty-first-century classroom instances of what Shoshana Zuboff calls "surveillance capitalism" as they operate in the digital classroom.

Elsewhere in "Beyond the Digital Humanities Center," several essays reexamine the very premise of large-scale, collaborative DH projects dependent on a lab or center. Weighing in on the DH *lab* definitionally, Lauren Tilton and Taylor Arnold maintain that it is not so much a question of whether or not labs or DHCs are preferred infrastructures for DH work; instead, it is how labs are described and situated that best informs how DH work is sustained in our distinct, institutional contexts. They describe how resources prove a double bind for the social symbolic work of digital humanities: the lab—a new space in humanities—offers great opportunities for digital scholarship but can also paradoxically foreclose some possibilities. With its differentiated spaces, roles, and staffing hierarchies and its growth in infrastructure, Tilton and Arnold suggest that the lab simultaneously enables and limits the "experimentation, collaboration, and access" that are hallmarks of the field's development.

Urszula Pawlicka-Deger, writing from Aalto University in Finland, similarly considers the idea of the laboratory, arguing that from her standpoint DH has pivoted from an "isolated, discipline-based center, to an interdisciplinary laboratory," to a series of dispersed, virtual practices and collaborations occurring in various platforms such as Slack and DH Commons. Pawlicka-Deger's history traces the lab's institutionalization from scientific to social space and evolving function as a support for humanities research, as well as physical space to host equipment and people, a service and display space, and a platform for global networking and experimentation.

Laura Braunstein and Michelle Warren theorize DH's infrastructural and discursive formations as *stacks*. Which uncanny categories, they ask, lie beneath disciplinary declarations of openness, collaboration, and innovation? They direct us to three versions of the stack as metaphor and offer an intervention in the two-dimensional agon of *hack* and *yack*, making visible the social-symbolic disciplinary labor of engaging with past, present, and future. The authors help us to comprehend the infrastructure that tracks our own achievements, whether through built archives, shared method and pedagogies, or digital translations on the web.

Reading Quinn Dombrowski's excursion through a brief history of digital directories reminds us all why taxes on infrastructure are necessary—and often resented. Because infrastructure is visible only upon breakdown, supporting its ongoing function while it is still working can appear to be supporting nothing at all.[9] What might a tax on directory infrastructure, and all common goods in DH infrastructure, look like? Dombrowski's history fits well within what Steven J. Jackson calls "broken world thinking" with its emphasis on an ethos of care and sustainability.[10] Her history illuminates the paradox of a "successful failure" in the digital research tools (DiRT) directory: "the fact that grant funding is available for development, but institutions may or may not step in to provide ongoing support for operations" explains the infrastructural gap for projects such as DiRT. Institutional commitment and affiliation (as Geoffrey Rockwell of the University of Alberta has for TAPoR and Liu has for the DH Toychest) are ultimately essential to the long-term survival of digital projects (even if they are stewarded mainly by one person) but they are elusive.

In another case study, Maria Sachiko Cecire and Susan Merriam describe how a local and specific institutional culture can shape DH projects. They call for a flexible, "one size does *not* fit all" approach, which "can develop original programming, maximize existing resources, and have institution-wide positive effects." Cecire and Merriam's account of work at Bard College's Center for Experimental Humanities resonates with the theme of naming *as* infrastructural element. While in some circles the name *digital humanities* has become as welcome and understood as an aging teenager, Cecire and Merriam optimistically respond by forming their project in alignment with their institutional culture rather than against it. These authors provide a clear example of how, as Lawrence, Suddaby, and Leca suggest, "individuals actively engage in processes of institutional maintenance, disruption, and change."[11]

We close "Beyond the Digital Humanities Center" with a piece by Christina Boyles that foregrounds and reflects on urgent cries to elevate issues of race, gender, sexuality, class, and other forms of power in our DH work. Boyles surveys early DH projects that responded to the need, as Roopika Risam has put it elsewhere, to "carefully privilege diversity, multiplicity, and plurality."[12] Boyles notes that a robust intersectional infrastructure is still necessary to stem the loss of important sites that have disappeared from the internet through neglect and insecure funding. She offers strategies that resist the marginalizing of difference that scholars such as Risam, Amy Earhart, and Dorothy Kim have shown persists in reproducing narrow canons and inequitable power structures inherited from analog contexts. Lost projects by people of color reveal potholes in the infrastructure of critical digital humanities and demonstrate how the social justice frameworks espoused by the field in theory can be neglected in practice. Because neglect is a distributed phenomenon, it requires institutional and infrastructural response.

Our second cluster of essays is titled "Human Infrastructures: Labor Considerations and Communities of Practice." This section includes alternatives to the DHC, even for institutions lucky enough to have robust DHCs in place. For instance, Kelsey Corlett-Rivera, Nathan Dize, Abby Broughton, and Brittany de Gail have worked outside the purview of the University of Maryland's MITH (Maryland Institute of Humanities and Technology) to produce the smaller, low-tech but highly important digital primary source reader, *A Colony in Crisis,* which examines a grain crisis on the eve of the Haitian revolution. The authors recount a deep synergy between the powerful university infrastructure and the "fast prototyping" and incubations possible within their low-tech project housed in their university's French department. However, a project's strengths can also demonstrate its weaknesses; issues such as personnel changes and students' inevitable departure again show that maintenance and continuity are infrastructural necessities without which the show will not go on. While they value some of the basic project management and technical support they gained from proximity to a large DHC, they also find that the

DHC model tends to marginalize a smaller-scale, iterative project such as theirs—a project that may be otherwise valuable precisely because of its focus on pedagogy, service, and marginalized histories.

Brennan Collins and Dylan Ruediger explain how Georgia State University has instituted a Student Innovation Fellowship (SIF), which trains graduate students as well as honors undergraduate students in a variety of skills on digital projects. It brings together faculty and students from a range of disciplines with heavy orientation toward computer science and the humanities, and it has progressively become more focused on projects devoted to understanding urban space and experience in and around Atlanta. Collins and Ruediger draw on multiple and contingent resources in labor, space, and funding, in effect "building a network of student specialists capable of playing significant roles in the development of long-term DH projects." Like many authors in this volume, they emphasize how they exploit extant infrastructures to realize their digital humanities aims. Accessing networks as a means of developing DH projects shows what Corlett-Rivera and her colleagues describe as an "opportunistic willingness" that allowed for their success. Noticing "cracks" in the foundation, these authors are able to provide "cement" in the form of #alt-ac labor and "squatted on resources" to support DH pedagogy.

Elizabeth Rodrigues and Rachel Schnepper consider DH infrastructure issues within the small liberal arts college (SLAC), offering a thought-provoking set of findings that demonstrate how DH librarians and staff can leverage faculty content expertise and initiative while also breaking down some of the institutional hierarchies and caste systems that ultimately mitigate against successful and sustainable collaborations. The authors focus on the "sedimented history of higher education's hierarchies, reward structures, and expectations." They ask whether the division of labor that comes with reduced/constrained resources at SLACs can coexist with collaboration. Like many other authors in the field, they show that digital humanities sometimes does what textbook publishing and brick-and-mortar archives could not do: expose the labor hierarchies in humanities work. The deep interdependence and emotional labor that may have been occluded in less collaborative and resource-intensive settings are everywhere visible in the collaboration required of digital projects. Noting the "affective consequences . . . embedded in hierarchy," the authors reframe service as learner-centered collaboration.

Eduard Arriaga writes about DH in community organizations and service-oriented universities, arguing that even as DH has become more capacious epistemologically and conceptually, infrastructure continues to be understood as "digital devices and institutional resources." Without discounting the real need for material resources, Arriaga points the reader to examples of vibrant grassroots DH activities that "do not aim to study the impact of digital culture or to implement a technique to preserve cultural heritage as a practice that extends an exclusive world order," but rather "use tools to pursue social justice agendas that question conceptions of humanity, development and inclusion." Resonating perhaps with Alex Gil's powerful notion of "minimal computing," Arriaga calls for a "humane digital" infrastructure that is positive and productive and includes community relationships and nonnetworked technology such as computers and electricity itself. This can be compared to the persistent challenges the academy is finding in trying to leverage predigital economies of value—, that is, unrecognized contributions and hierarchies.

Similarly, Pamella Lach and Jessica Pressman, writing from San Diego State University, an HSI, determine that DH in a service institution requires working with people at the local level with a focus on pedagogy and social justice. Lach and Pressman claim collaboration as feminist practice and offer their initiative *SD/DH* as a model for interinstitutional collaboration. As with other authors in this collection (Cecire and Merriam, Rodrigues and Schnepper and others), Lach and Pressman's work makes visible the emotional and affective infrastructures required of digital humanities in ways that traditional humanities practices could never do. The authors recount their process of creating an initiative driven by local, situated practices they liken to Lisa Parks's "infrastructural imaginaries"—those "ways of thinking about what infrastructures are, where they are located, who controls them, and what they do."[13] By creating an "area of excellence" within their university context, these authors also demonstrate the importance of leveraging the infrastructure of resources, including cultural capital of prestige, in the larger institutional context.

Ashley Sanders Garcia, Lydia Bello, Madelynn Dickerson, and Margaret Hogarth describe their efforts at the Claremont Colleges to build a transdisciplinary, *transrank* community of practice centered in the library, in which librarians are genuine project partners rather than simply facilitators. One of the key debates constituting the *Debates* series is around access—who needs it, who has it, what are the obstacles to it, and even what is meant by it. By looking at what they call "hard" and "soft" infrastructure, Sanders Garcia and her colleagues show how the constraints imposed by large conventional funders such as Mellon can have downstream impacts on collaboration at institutions. They call for major funders and other influential institutions to work for inclusion of multiple recognized roles and professionals within DH projects, including librarians and #alt-ac professionals. While they stress the importance of reaching across disciplines, positions, and ranks when creating their communities of practice, they caution that emphasizing the "digital" at the expense of the "humanities" can dilute the prominence of humanistic values and critical method.

All these writers are theorizing infrastructure as communities of practice, with all the attendant relationship building (and relationship *care*) that such communities require. In the 2012 *Debates* volume, Tara MacPherson identified a "lenticular" organizational principle that governed both computational design principles and racist power dynamics in mid-twentieth-century America. Lenticular logic provides an indispensable critical tool for examining interstitial, infrastructural effects that isolate and render invisible the interdependent functions of power and oppression. One could fruitfully extend the isolating logic of the lenticular view to the separation in higher education of issues of quality in research and teaching from those of labor and precarious faculty conditions. The two final essays in our section on human infrastructures, by Jana Remy and by Kathi Inman Berens, reflect on the human risks and costs of DH work by considering the need for protecting DH work in the promotion and tenure process, and on the need for protecting adjunct laborers, respectively.

Previous *Debates* volumes have noted the persistent marginalization of pedagogy in DH scholarship, and so our third cluster of essays, "Pedagogy: Vulnerability, Collaboration, and Resilience," turns to that topic. Margaret Simon begins this section with a compelling rumination on the haptic and sensory affordances of digital texts. For her, they raise issues of access, insofar as digital texts invite "both scholarly inquiry and participation in larger conversations about media change." She wants to attend to "the human infrastructures that underlie even seemingly straightforward digital pedagogies, revealing the institutional hierarchies that can determine how new methodologies enter the classroom." Simon witnesses students' development of empathy through the "interpretive potentials of remediation" brought by digitized primary texts. Simon is aware that even the accessibility of the Folger archives to her students relied on the research networks to which she was privy. This kind of upstream access to special collections, which she enjoyed as a scholar in a networked community, reveals hidden "market-driven economies of professional connection and prestige that function as shadow infrastructures in fostering digital learning and research."

Continuing this attention to access and inequity from a graduate-student perspective, Chelsea Miya, Laura Gerlitz, Kaitlyn Grant, Maryse Ndilu Kiese, Mengchi Sun, and Christina Boyles offer a manifesto calling for alternatives to DH-focused graduate programs that might "better support students and encourage collaboration and experimentation." If graduate programs are where "the system reproduces itself," as Louis Menand would have it, attention to the experiences of our graduate students is essential. Like our other essays, this manifesto calls for an ethos of care in programs where the next generation's digital humanists are apprenticed. The perceived need to "do double duty" as skilled coders and inventive critical thinkers threatens to undermine the health of the discipline's future. The authors call on their fellow students to self-organize and step into leadership roles, to "reimagine the field from the bottom up."

Next we have two calls (and two practical agendas) for offering DH to first-generation college students. Jamila Moore Pewu and Anelise Hanson Shrout provide another institutional biography, one that reveals the affective and emotional infrastructure required for successful knowledge transmission in digital humanities. Through the inclusion of culturally relevant curricula, culturally relevant use of tools, and clear pedagogies that build DH skills, these authors intend to "push [the extant DH community] toward a more expansive, and less infrastructurally limited conception of DH." They examine how first-generation students learn and how their digital fluencies manifest, and they also intentionally revise the exclusionary founding narratives of digital technologies, "(re)inserting . . . living and nonliving role models . . . to increase feelings of self-confidence, belonging, and inclusion within the discipline."

Roopika Risam demonstrates how digital humanities can intervene in institutional stratification by responding to "immediate, local, geographical" communities in regional comprehensive universities and reframing "limitations . . . as affordances" rather than as deficits. At Salem State, writes Risam, neither students nor the institution itself were prepared for DH. Meeting these students' needs "underscores the role of social justice in our work." Risam provides a playbook for colleagues at similar institutions, calling for digital humanists to be "digital stewards of place."

Our volume concludes with a kind of coda by Matthew Applegate, who makes a salutary pitch for putting DH in greater dialogue with critical university studies (CUS), a field that now attends specifically and fervently to neoliberal discourses of scarcity, abundance, efficiency, productivity, and speed. Applegate argues that we must refuse common organizational models and that a DH/CUS conversation could help us better imagine "infrastructure as autonomous iterations of global and local education." This is not dissimilar to Liu's metaphorical call to arms, in his book in progress, *Against the Cultural Singularity,* where he highlights the tendency of business corporate institutions to monopolize all our other institutions, remaking them in their image. Scholars and students might be forgiven, we suspect, for believing that *that* particular horse has already bolted from the barn. Applegate encourages us to get past deficit/scarcity thinking and calls for a "coalitional standard for educational infrastructure that foregrounds difference." He points out Liu's "antifoundationalist" and tactical interventions as strategies for this coalition, and he sketches a pairing of Risam and Mohanty that encourages tactical linking of struggles across institutional spaces.

We admit that we were profoundly disappointed that, in the end, we were unable to secure submissions from scholars and practitioners at community colleges, HBCUs, and tribal colleges for this collection, despite outreach to colleagues and friends at such institutions. What does the failure to locate this work signal about the impact of the institutional stratifications that our field inherits and deploys? We are reminded of Mary Douglas's suggestion that institutional classifications say a great deal about how we understand ourselves.[14] We are also reminded of Deb Verhoeven's insistence that omissions from the archive are themselves archived; silences in a field must be critically examined as an inherited affordance of the infrastructure itself.[15] However, silence, like absence, is more difficult to examine than active debate. "The more opaque the mode of transmitting inequalities," write Brint and Karabel, "the more effective it is likely to be in legitimating these inequalities," and nothing is more opaque than absence.[16] DH is a discipline perhaps exceptionally localized in its sites of privilege and disadvantage. Contrast, as all our authors do implicitly, the advantages of a Texas A&M or Northeastern University–style dedicated digital humanities lab against activities in a cash-strapped community college's adjunct's classroom. With these seemingly intractable infrastructural chasms in place, how can we continue our work identifying privilege and raising critical awareness of the conditions of the field's knowledge production?

Community colleges sit between two institutional models—one of the *school* with its focus on transmitting agreed and accepted knowledge and the other of the *university* defined by *wissenschaft* (scholarship). Universities find their justification "always and only" through engagement with "problems and issues yet to be resolved, whether in research or teaching."[17] Community colleges and other colleges whose justification is to serve *students* and not only abstract *knowledge* are structurally excluded from some of the most important developments in the humanities today. However, because the field of DH is still evolving, developing, and morphing—in response to technology and in response to its own discoveries and impasses—what is agreed and accepted knowledge and what is *wissenschaft* are questions still in play. Perhaps this provides an opportunity for community colleges to bridge this gap between agreed and accepted knowledge and *wissenschaft.*

Along with Paul Edwards, we might ask how we can "enable or generate translation across entrenched practices and institutions."[18] One mechanism could be through curriculum as boundary object. In their edited collection in the *Debates* series, *Bodies of Information: Intersectional Feminism and Digital Humanities* (2018), editors Jacqueline Wernimont and Elizabeth Losh use keywords as "boundary objects" to organize their volume's intersectional intervention in the field of DH. Developed by Susan Leigh Star and others, the concepts of "boundary objects" and "boundary infrastructure" might help us intervene with respect to the silence of community colleges and other institutions. Boundary objects "both inhabit several communities of practice and satisfy the informational requirements of each of them." Able to "travel across borders and maintain some sort of constant identity," they "can be tailored to meet the needs of one community" and "have common identities across settings."[19] How might we construct boundary objects to "generate translation across entrenched practices and institutions"?[20]

Digital humanities curricula may provide some trans-institutional mechanisms for building a boundary infrastructure of DH at community colleges, HBCUs, tribal colleges, and other institutions in higher education.[21] Responding to this issue is *Digital Pedagogy in the Humanities: Concepts, Models and Experiments,* edited by Rebecca Frost Davis, Matthew K. Gold, Katherine D. Harris, and Jentery Sayers, organized around keywords that articulated a common vocabulary for the community of practice of DH. One idea for DH practitioners is to build on the base of keywords and agree on threshold concepts as a mechanism for engaging institutional subalterns. Jan Meyer and Ray Land describe threshold concepts as the key moments in learning that represent a "transformed way of understanding, or interpreting, or viewing something."[22] A model of this kind of work is Linda Adler-Kassner and Elizabeth Wardle's edited collection, *Naming What We Know:*

Threshold Concepts and Writing Studies, where more than twenty writing studies scholars articulated key understandings of major concepts in that field of English. The classroom edition of the text is itself a boundary object between scholarly and student audiences. As both boundary and portal, thresholds are an ideal infrastructural metaphor. Perhaps future practitioners across the higher education spectrum of institutions would undertake this work and create a boundary infrastructure that would bridge the silences in the field.

Until then, the essays in the volume at hand give us hope that, at least in some places, scholars, librarians, teachers, and students are working together, *tactically* as Liu might say, to create intelligent, *humane* projects and paradigms. Sadly, outmoded and even inoperable reward systems continue to demonstrate a lack of consensus about how best to support the intellectual work of DH. Elsewhere, successful and influential projects stand as high-water marks in a young field, while other highly admired and prized projects are abandoned for lack of reliable, systemic support. These examples highlight the lingering tensions between the demands of digital knowledge production and the support that variously positioned institutions are able (or willing) to provide today. Issues such as these are just some of the infrastructural hazards featured in *People, Practice, Power: Digital Humanities outside the Center* that continue to characterize the ongoing project of the house that DH built.

Notes

1. Star, "Got Infrastructure?," 3.
2. Powell and DiMaggio, *New Institutionalism,* 8.
3. Powell and DiMaggio, *New Institutionalism,* 9.
4. Brint and Karabel, "Institutional Origins," 346.
5. Lawrence, Suddaby, and Leca, "Institutional Work," 55.
6. Svensson and Goldberg, "Knowledge Production," 330.
7. Liu, "Drafts for *Against the Cultural Singularity* (book in progress)."
8. Liu, "Drafts for *Against the Cultural Singularity* (book in progress)."
9. See Star and Ruhleder, "Steps Toward an Ecology," 113.
10. Jackson, "Rethinking Repair," 232.
11. Lawrence, Suddaby, and Leca, "Institutional Work," 53.
12. Risam, "Navigating the Global Digital Humanities," 364.
13. Parks, "Media Infrastructures and Affect."
14. Douglas, *How Institutions Think.*
15. Verhoeven, "As Luck Would Have It," 7.
16. Brint and Karabel, *Diverted Dream,* 224.
17. Watts, *Public Universities,* 50.
18. Edwards, "Understanding Infrastructure," 19.
19. Star, "Got Infrastructure?," 16.
20. Edwards, "Understanding Infrastructure," 19.

21. We should note that there are many HSIs that remain outside of the disciplinary circle of DH, including HSIs that are also community colleges.

22. Meyer and Land, "Threshold Concepts," 53.

Bibliography

Adler-Kassner, Linda, and Elizabeth Wardle. *Naming What We Know: Threshold Concepts and Writing Studies.* Logan: Utah State University Press, 2015.

Bailey, Moya, Anne Cong-Huyen, Alexis Lothian, and Amanda Phillips. "Reflections on a Movement: #transformDH, Growing Up." In *Debates in the Digital Humanities 2016,* edited by Matthew K. Gold and Lauren F. Klein. Minneapolis: University of Minnesota Press, 2016.

Brint, Steven, and Jerome Karabel. *Diverted Dream: Community Colleges and the Promise of Educational Opportunity in America, 1900–1985.* New York: Oxford University Press, 1989.

Brint, Steven, and Jerome Karabel. "Institutional Origins and Transformations: The Case of American Community Colleges." In *The New Institutionalism in Organizational Analysis,* edited by Walter W. Powell and Paul J. DiMaggio. Chicago: University of Chicago Press, 1991.

Douglas, Mary. *How Institutions Think.* Syracuse, N.Y.: Syracuse University Press, 1986.

Earhart, Amy E. "Can Information Be Unfettered? Race and the New Digital Humanities Canon." In *Debates in the Digital Humanities,* edited by Matthew K. Gold. Minneapolis: University of Minnesota Press, 2012.

Edwards, Paul N., Steven J. Jackson, Geoffrey C. Bowker, and Cory P. Knobel. "Understanding Infrastructure: Dynamics, Tensions, and Design: Report of a Workshop on 'History and Theory of Infrastructure: Lessons for New Scientific Cyberinfrastructures.'" Arlington: National Science Foundation, January 2007. https://deepblue.lib.umich.edu/handle/2027.42/49353.

Gil, Alex. "The User, the Learner, and the Machines We Make." *Minimal Computing* (blog), May 21, 2015. https://go-dh.github.io/mincomp/thoughts/2015/05/21/user-vs-learner/.

Jackson, Steven J. "Rethinking Repair." In *Media Technologies: Essays on Communication, Materiality, and Society,* edited by Tarleton Gillespie, Pablo J. Boczkowski, and Kirsten A. Foot. Cambridge, Mass.: MIT Press, 2014.

Kim, Dorothy. "Teaching Medieval Studies in a Time of White Supremacy." *In the Middle.* August 27, 2017. https://www.inthemedievalmiddle.com/2017/08/teaching-medieval-studies-in-time-of.html.

Lawrence, Thomas B., Roy Suddaby, and Bernard Leca. "Institutional Work: Refocusing Institutional Studies of Organization." *Journal of Management Inquiry* 20, no. 1 (2011): 52–58.

Liu, Alan. "Drafts for *Against the Cultural Singularity* (book in progress)." *Alan Liu,* May 2, 2016. http://liu.english.ucsb.edu/drafts-for-against-the-cultural-singularity.

Macpherson, Tara. "Why Are the Digital Humanities So White? Or Thinking the Histories of Race and Computation." In *Debates in the Digital Humanities,* edited by Matthew K. Gold. Minneapolis: University of Minnesota Press, 2012.

McGrail, Anne. "The 'Whole Game': Digital Humanities at Community Colleges." In *Debates in the Digital Humanities 2016,* edited by Matthew K. Gold and Lauren F. Klein. Minneapolis: University of Minnesota Press, 2016.

Menand, Louis. "The English Department: Imagined Futures." *ADE Bulletin* 151 (2011): 9–17.

Meyer, Jan, and Ray Land. "Threshold Concepts and Troublesome Knowledge: Linkages to Ways of Thinking and Practicing within the Disciplines." Enhancing Teaching Learning Project, May 2003. http://www.etl.tla.ed.ac.uk//docs/ETLreport4.pdf.

Parks, Lisa. "Media Infrastructures and Affect." *Flow: A Critical Forum on Media and Culture* May, 19, 2014.

Powell, Walter W., and Paul J. DiMaggio, eds. *The New Institutionalism in Organizational Analysis.* Chicago: University of Chicago Press, 1991.

Risam, Roopika. "Navigating the Global Digital Humanities: Insights from Black Feminism." In *Debates in the Digital Humanities,* edited by Matthew K. Gold and Lauren F. Klein. Minneapolis: University of Minnesota Press, 2016.

Smithies, James. "Interrogating Global Humanities Infrastructure." Modern Language Association, January 6, 2018. New York. https://jamessmithies.org/blog/2018/01/06/interrogating-global-humanities-infrastructure/.

Star, Susan Leigh. "Got Infrastructure? How Standards, Categories and Other Aspects of Infrastructure Influence Communication." The 2nd Social Study of IT Workshop at the LSE ICT and Globalization, 22–23 April 2002. https://citeseerx.ist.psu.edu/viewdoc/download?doi=10.1.1.19.7523&rep=rep1&type=pdf.

Star, Susan Leigh, and Karen Ruhleder. "Steps toward an Ecology of Infrastructure: Design and Access for Large Information Spaces." *Information Systems Research* 7, no. 1 (1996): 111–34.

Svensson, Patrik, and David Theo Goldberg. "Knowledge Production, Learning, and Infrastructure." In *Between the Humanities and the Digital,* edited by Patrik Svensson and David Theo Goldberg. Cambridge, Mass.: MIT Press, 2015.

Verhoeven, Deb. "As Luck Would Have It: Serendipity and Solace in Digital Research Infrastructure." *Feminist Media Histories* 2, no. 1 (2016): 7–28.

Watts, Rob. *Public Universities, Managerialism and the Value of Higher Education.* London: Palgrave Macmillan, 2017.

Zuboff, Shoshana. *Surveillance Capitalism: The Fight for a Human Future at the Frontier of Power.* New York: Hachette, 2019.

PART I

BEYOND THE DIGITAL HUMANITIES CENTER

Historical Perspectives and New Models

Epistemic Infrastructure, the Instrumental Turn, and the Digital Humanities

JAMES MALAZITA

In his essay "How Not to Teach Digital Humanities," Ryan Cordell outlines some of the pedagogical and institutional challenges of integrating digital literary methods into the classroom, and in structuring those classroom experiences into broader humanities institutional curricula. Cordell's advice for digital humanities (DH) instructors includes scaffolding skills in classes and across the curriculum, not smothering undergraduates with the layers of metacritique of the humanities embedded within DH work, and recognizing undergraduates' skepticism of *the digital* in classroom settings due to poorly deployed digital learning strategies such as massive open online courses (MOOCs). Importantly, Cordell argues that successful digital humanities pedagogy must always take into account local institutional and infrastructural contexts, and he notes how his structuring of classes to allow students' leveraging of campus archival collections.[1]

Although I agree with and applaud Cordell's arguments, particularly his advocating "the local," his illustrations of local pedagogical and infrastructural context— "libraries, museums, research centers, or other campus-level initiatives"—invoke particularly material notions of space and place.[2] The material situatedness of any given institutional space is of course important in thinking pedagogically about the digital humanities. Material infrastructures inflect contexts of teaching and scholarship. However, digital humanists must also account for the ideological and epistemological structures that shape our institutional contexts. Ideological structures run deeper than institutional mission statements and tenure review boards; they serve as axiomatic epistemological frameworks that underpin the decision-making processes, value judgments, curricular strategies, and normative and political orientations of the university. They give justification to the construction, maintenance, neglect, or destruction of material infrastructure and campus initiatives. In addition, as I argue in this essay, the pervasiveness of these epistemic infrastructures enables these frameworks to subsume and consume alternative knowledge-making practices and normative orientations within the institution.

This essay is not meant as a criticism of Cordell. Cordell's focus on material and institutional infrastructure as the context of digital humanities work is an exemplar of the DH genre of calling for engagement with the wider structures that enable DH work. Other contemporary examples include Matthew Kirschenbaum's "Digital Humanities Is/As a Tactical Term," the allusion to anticorporate publishing models in the Manifold project, and invocations of "critical infrastructure studies" from Alan Liu and from Lisa Parks and Nicole Starosielski, among others.[3] The highlighting of the material systems and institutions that underpin digital technologies can provide crucial insights into the hidden labor and material translations that shape DH institutions. However, this kind of highlighting can serve to make invisible the ideological-epistemological structures that also undergird digital practices.

I write this essay in an attempt to broaden our imaginations of where DH work takes place and where it could take place; to broaden our conceptions of what infrastructures are and of the multiple ways in which they structure our discourse and (de)legitimize our practices. Digital humanities practitioners must be keenly aware of the epistemological and ideological infrastructures of our institutions and the ways in which those epistemic regimes structure our students' educational experience. These infrastructures do important boundary work for students and for researchers: they define what kinds of knowledges and experiences are legitimate— which kinds are worthy of consideration in a discipline and which are not. They work to limit the social and technical spaces in which DH research and pedagogy are constructed as relevant. They shape the demographics, cultures, pedagogical strategies, and teaching tools of every classroom.

I am a faculty member in the Science & Technology Studies (STS) department at Rensselaer Polytechnic Institute (RPI), an engineering-centered institute. In the context of the STEM educational apparatus, institutional epistemological frameworks can be especially influential, manifesting as an emphasis on technical expertise, presumably at the cost of the kinds of critical knowledge work that humanities faculty claim to encourage in our research and teaching. At face value, this may not be particularly surprising to other humanities scholars. In advocating for the need for DH faculty to resist overplaying *the digital*—and thus *the technical*—card in our classrooms, Cordell describes the orientation of the kinds of students that we find enrolled in humanities majors:

> Many of our students honestly, truly, really choose literature or history or art history or religious studies because they wanted to read and think deeply rather than follow what they perceive as a more instrumentalist education in business or technical fields. To do so they often resist substantial pressure from family and friends pushing them toward "more practical" majors, which are often perceived to be more technical majors.[4]

Cordell's characterization fits the standard narrative of where DH takes place: in English departments and humanities classrooms in which computational methods are used to augment "traditional" humanities education.[5] These students, the story goes, are of a different sort from students in more "instrumentalist" programs and majors—usually stereotyped in DH scholarship as STEM students interested in quantification, technology, and the ability to get a job.[6] This narrative is so widely shared among DH scholars that William Pannapacker has argued that the *digital humanities* should really be called the *digital liberal arts.*[7]

This narrative, however, limits imaginations of where DH can make meaningful interventions. DH need not operate only as an interdisciplinary bridge that brings computers and data into English classrooms and research.[8] Rather, DH may act as a force to resolve and heal the constructed divides between computational/technical practices and interpretive/critical scholarship. In order to use DH to do so, we must begin to take seriously the kinds of epistemic-infrastructural contexts in which academics and students across disciplines are embedded, as well as understand the ideological histories that have shaped those contexts. We must reach out to students and scholars in educational contexts the opposite of which Cordell outlines in the previous quotation: in engineering-centered institutions, polytechnics, and other instrumentalist educational contexts.[9]

The instrumentalist epistemic regime cuts two ways. First, instrumentalism operates by tacitly encouraging quantitative, technological, and metric-based forms of knowledge making over the interpretive and critical scholarship privileged in the humanities. Polytechnics, in concert with other neoliberal educational institutions, often advertise themselves as pragmatic educational centers that train students to have "real-world impact" through technological, scientific, and economic innovation. Administrators at these institutions tend to be quite excited about the digital humanities, which they understand as *applied* humanities practice that centers technical work (and generates funding), leading to the potential for well funded but narrowly intellectually supported DH initiatives on campus.

This first cut—the tension between quantitative/technical method and humanities scholarship—has been well documented and critiqued in DH scholarship.[10] In this essay, I want to talk about a second cut: instrumentalism not as pragmatic practice but as ideological-epistemological apparatus. This second form of instrumentalism is more dangerous to DH pedagogy and scholarship than the first because it not only resists the kinds of nondeterministic scholarship practiced in many humanities spaces but also is designed to account for, consume, and subvert the impacts of critical perspectives on technological systems.

This subversive power is not an accident. The rise of instrumentalism in U.S. higher education was a conservative response to efforts to bridge the humanities and engineering education in the late 1960s. Through a tracing of this history, I argue here that the ideological apparatus of instrumentalism both encourages technical students to marginalize humanities—including digital humanities—scholarship and at the same time works to colonize humanities work (especially digital humanities) to bring humanities knowledge-making practices into adherence with the dominant sociotechnical epistemic regime.

Because of our willingness to explore the tensions among multiple epistemic regimes, digital humanities scholars find ourselves in a unique position to subvert instrumentalism's subversion of humanistic knowledge-making practices and to encourage students to break down the bracketing of technical expertise and critical inquiry.[11] However, tackling the challenge of bridging "the two cultures" requires more than bringing computers into humanities classrooms.[12] It requires a better understanding by humanists of the intellectual and political histories of contemporary structural instrumentalism, as well as pedagogical and interpersonal strategies for navigating the instrumentalist university as epistemic infrastructure and for connecting with STEM students and others enmeshed in the instrumentalist epistemic regime. Therefore, this essay also offers two tactical frameworks for engaging with and subverting this regime, drawn partly from my own experiences in teaching critical DH work at an engineering-centered institution: Scaffold *Everything*—Politically; and Build Interdisciplinary Connections for Social Capital.[13]

The Instrumental Turn in STEM Education

In a (perhaps prescient) forecasting of DH's own history, contemporary institutional instrumentalism manifests during a moment of self-perceived disciplinary crisis. Before the Crisis of the Humanities served as a backdrop for digital humanities writing in the early 2010s, U.S. STEM education's crisis moment coalesced in the late 1960s. As Matt Wisnioski has documented, it was in the late 1960s, amid the calls for greater pollution control, the growing evidence of the detrimental impact of industrialization and globalization on the natural environment, the launch of Sputnik, and the subsequent intertwining of the aerospace/aeronautical sectors and military funding in the shadow of the Cold War that members of the engineering profession began to lose faith in the narratives of science and technology's march toward social progress.[14]

Engineering education did not always have an antipolitical or anticritical epistemic culture. During the period immediately following the Second World War, technology, which was understood as a natural extension of humanity's recursive adaptation to its environment, was framed as a driver of both mental and material change in human social networks.[15] Thus, technological development was constructed as the moral imperative of engineers and other STEM practitioners: the creation and proliferation of new, global cybernetic infrastructures would allow humanity to better predict, control, and optimize both the Earth and human social development. Engineers thus constructed themselves in the role of philosopher-builders. Engineers had a normative vision of the ideal shape of human society and imagined themselves as possessing the technological and infrastructural where-withal to design that world into being, unlike their humanist and social scientist colleagues.[16]

Notably, humanities texts were adopted in STEM education in the early twentieth century. Corporate interests in the 1920s and 1930s had already begun recommending that engineering students be exposed to philosophy and analytic social theory. In the corporate view, liberal education allowed engineers to better predict and control human behavior.[17] It was fairly common for polytechnics and other technical schools to establish liberal education and humanities departments, and for engineering students to read texts like Plato's *Republic* and Hobbes's *Leviathan*. These texts were often read by engineering students rather shallowly and interpreted as justifications for the imposition of technological regulations on social life.[18]

Whereas the postwar era was dominated by the rhetoric of a rapid and guided natural progression of technology (and therefore of society), technological development during the 1960s' U.S. military aggression in Vietnam felt anything *but* predictable and controlled. Rather, Wisnioski argues that the techno-ecological-political crises of the late 1960s shook public confidence in the figures of the engineer and the technologist; cultural narratives of progress in the United States were replaced by narratives of technology out of control, of Sputnik, and of "men on the moon and children on fire."[19]

In response to this emerging public distrust, the late 1960s would see the rise of the New Engineers, practitioners from both industry and academia who advocated for the incorporation of critical humanities and social science texts into engineering curricula.[20] The New Engineering curriculum worked to identify literature and social theory that was critical of rapid, unchecked technological development and to *integrate* those texts into the engineering curriculum. New Engineering drew upon then-burgeoning Technology & Society literature, represented by writers such as Herbert Marcuse, Rachel Carson, Jacques Ellul, Lynn White, and Lewis Mumford. Rather than shunting social theory to separate humanities departments as the postwar engineering education model had done, New Engineering encouraged STEM faculty to teach critical texts directly, and it even produced Technology & Society textbooks for the STEM classroom that assumed neither that the students nor that the instructor were well versed in social theory.[21] The New Engineers broached the boundaries among engineering, the sciences, and the humanities through written scholarship, pedagogical and curricular strategy, the integration of humanists into engineering scholarly societies like the American Society for Engineering Education (ASEE), and the creation of new academic initiatives such as the Society for the History of Technology (SHOT) and its flagship journal, *Technology and Culture*.

Although the New Engineers represented only a small minority of engineering and STEM educators, they soon began to have a substantial impact on engineering education. Bolstered by educational initiatives sponsored by ASEE and helped by supportive engineering deans and school presidents, the curricular infrastructures of some major centers of STEM education were radically altered in the short period from 1965 to 1968.[22] At institutions like MIT, Dartmouth, Rensselaer Polytechnic Institute, UCLA, Harvey Mudd College, and Caltech, the postwar model of engineering education, along with its accompanying pedagogical infrastructure of core engineering classes supplemented by General Education and History of Western Civilization classes, would be supplanted by diverse instantiations of hybrid humanities-engineering education.

The early results of these models were varied and mixed and were not without problems. Many practical issues stemmed from the same conceptual incommensurability familiar to most digital humanists and critical makers: the difficulties of applying interpretive and critical humanistic inquiry to the design of new technologies and artifacts in STEM contexts.[23] However, it is difficult to judge what the potential longer-term impacts of these hybrid humanities-engineering programs would have been, because the programs were largely structurally and epistemologically dismantled by the mid-1970s due to the influence of the instrumental turn.

It was in response to the hybrid humanist-engineering curricular experimentations of the late 1960s that the contemporary instrumentalist turn of STEM education emerged. Upset by the growing impact of the New Engineers on engineering education and frustrated by what was constructed as the diluting of core engineering knowledge in engineering students, the conservative wings of engineering education worked to reframe the public concern over large-scale technological growth.[24] Wisnioski argues that the instrumentalist response to the social critics of technology was not to deny or dismiss those criticisms but rather to sideline them by differentiating them as a separate domain of knowledge.

Rather than returning to the cybernetic vision of the engineer as manager and controller of social progress, the engineering reactionaries instead depoliticized the technical practices and fundamental concepts of engineering by turning toward abstraction, instrumentalization, and management. The instrumental turn did not operate as a naive view that technological artifacts were simply socially neutral instruments to be wielded for good or ill.[25] Rather, conservative elements in engineering education countered the critical lens of the New Engineers not by denying the critical perspective on technical practice but by developing an ideology of "proximate instrumentalism."[26] The engineering curriculum removed any remaining liberal arts and critical humanities literature from the classroom while it shifted the focus of engineering expertise away from hands-on material construction and toward abstract mathematic and physical fundamentals. This dematerialized educational apparatus further divorced engineering students from the social contexts that their creations would once have constructed. Engineering students today spend the vast majority, if not the totality, of their technical education learning calculus, physics, thermodynamics, and managerial decision-making processes. Very few courses have students actually engaging in the development of technological systems, and those that do rarely deploy those designs outside of the engineering classroom setting, thus trapping students within a context of decontextualization.

If engineers were responsible for the social impacts of technology, it was only in a limited, abstracted way. It became the engineer's function to design systems to specifications given by a client. This client, presumably, had included in the definition of the specifications considerations for managing the social effects of the system. The engineer's role, then, was to use his or her apolitical technical expertise to bring these managed designs into being. These designs presumably contributed to some sort of social good or at least did not actively contribute to harm. Wisnioski characterizes this shift in the fundamental normative orientation of engineering away from social shapers and toward technical experts as an "ideology of technological change." To quote Wisnioski:

> An ideology of technological change posited that technology was neither good, nor evil; neither was it neutral. Technological change was a semi-autonomous force that was accelerating rapidly, outracing the ability of social institutions [to] adjust. It produced tremendous opportunities, but also social dislocations, alienation, and the threat of nuclear holocaust. Through rational management, however, technology's negative *unintended consequences* could be *minimized* and its positive capacities *maximized (original emphasis).*[27]

In the instrumental turn, social concerns of technology became demarcated as either (1) elements that can be rationally, systematically, and first managed and optimized—given enough technical expertise; or (2) elements that are outside the purview of engineering knowledge. Social concerns were placed into one of these two categories on the basis of how easily they could be transformed into questions of technical expertise and incorporated into a managerial decision-making process.[28]

One need not look further than the Accreditation Board for Engineering and Technology's (ABET) requirements for engineering curricula to see how social and political concerns have been included, and yet also systematized and compartmentalized, in engineering education. Among the eleven "student outcome" criteria engineering programs must meet, social concerns are addressed in only two: students must have "an ability to design a system, component, or process to meet desired needs within realistic constraints such as economic, environmental, social, political, ethical, health and safety, manufacturability, and sustainability" and must also have "the broad education necessary to understand the impact of engineering solutions in a global, economic, environmental, and societal context."[29] The first criterion labels social concerns as one of many "constraints" on technical design decisions. The second clearly demarcates engineering "solutions" from the social and ecological contexts in which they exist. Not even the calls for "broad education" should give humanists comfort: that specific student outcome is likely to be removed in the upcoming revisions to ABET's accreditation requirements, as it is perceived as too burdensome for accreditors to measure and evaluate.[30]

Digital Humanities in/as Instrumentalist Epistemic Infrastructure

The diminished normative orientation of STEM practices has become naturalized in the construction of technological methods as apolitical. As Amy Slaton writes, this conservative ideology of technological change is now so dominant that it serves as an unspoken axiomatic underpinning of broader STEM education, even beyond engineering-centered institutions.[31] Not only do these infrastructures influence the kinds of projects that get funded, the availability and quality of lab equipment, curricular decisions, and the presence or absence of humanities faculty, graduate students, and undergraduate students; they also produce the epistemic frameworks of those individuals who are a part of the apparatus. Anecdotally, I can say that many of the neoliberal and corporatist initiatives and restructurings that we see foisted upon state-funded universities are first developed and prototyped by private engineering institutions.

I thus want to inflect the concept of *infrastructure* differently from Alan Liu, who defines infrastructure as "the social-cum-technological milieu that at once enables the fulfillment of human experience and enforces constraints on that experience."[32] Rather than enabling and constraining the activities of users, I argue that infrastructures operate epistemically, as "machineries of knowledge," to *produce* those users themselves.[33] I borrow from STS scholar Karin Knorr Cetina in arguing that infrastructures of scientific and technical production, including those relevant to the digital humanities, should be understood less as "knowledge structures" and more as "epistemic structures." For Knorr Cetina, the term "knowledge structures" implies that material-social practices work to produce *what* we know. The term "epistemic structures," in contrast, highlights how those practices instead work to produce *how* we know, by producing and legitimizing the discourses, tools, spaces, and boundaries of knowing and of knowable objects.[34] Machineries of knowledge thus produce "epistemic subjects" and "epistemic objects": practitioners and their always-in-negotiation objects of study.[35] While Knorr Cetina largely bounds her analysis to the practices and cultures of scientific knowledge workers, we should extend our understanding of epistemic structures to material-cultural infrastructures as well. I argue that it is in epistemic infrastructures—the tools, institutions, and apparatuses that undergird and produce knowledge practices—where the ideologies and politics of knowledge become externalized and concretized, where they are made durable.[36]

If we take seriously the epistemic infrastructures of STEM education, it would be wrong to think of students as instrumentalist persons who enter STEM in order to be filled with narrow technical expertise or of engineering instructors as conspiratorial antipolitical agents. Rather, the instrumentalist epistemic infrastructures of STEM education *produce* students and teachers who are technical practitioners: experts who through their mastery of the fundamentals of math and physics practice the production of "nonpolitical" material systems. Simultaneously, although engineering students generally understand that technology "in the world" has social dimensions, engineering's epistemic infrastructures produce technology as an *epistemic object*—Technology as abstract and ideal, methodological and *apolitical*—and define the boundaries of STEM's knowledge domain as the exploration of that epistemic object of Technology. Again, even ABET's call to "understand the impact of engineering solutions in context" explicitly demarcates engineering expertise from the social, political, and material world. It is thus imperative for humanists to learn that engineering students are not taught to build what we might understand as technological systems but rather are taught to practice apolitical Technology.

Instrumentalist epistemic infrastructure is frighteningly effective at producing antipolitical practices. Erin Cech's longitudinal study of engineering students at four different universities showed that engineering students' interest in public welfare, social concerns, and the political impacts of technological systems steadily *declines* over the course of their education.[37] This takes place despite that in most engineering programs, what little hands-on design, making, and human-interaction work that students do engage in almost always occurs toward the end of their coursework. This heavy declination of interest in social and political good should be especially concerning given that early outreach programs, particularly at the grade-school level, combine building activities with "use technology to change the world" rhetoric to recruit students into STEM career paths. These programs, which include activities like *Lego Mindstorms* workshops and hands-on hackathons and may be considered similar to the celebrated *making* pedagogies in the digital humanities, even consciously recruit women and underrepresented minorities, ostensibly in an effort to diversify the STEM workforce. Upon entering STEM higher education, however, students are subjected to a double "bait-and-switch": as making and building activities are immediately sidelined in favor of math and science foundations courses, so too are political and ideological concerns systematically excised from the epistemic object of engineering.[38] This double bait-and-switch is coupled with a systemic administrative devaluing of interpretive humanities and social science courses. Although engineering students in the United States are currently required to take "broad educational" courses, in my experience engineering students are often encouraged by their academic advisors to take "easy" humanities courses that they can mostly ignore in order to concentrate on their core educational work and simultaneously boost their GPA. Instrumentalist infrastructures thus practice the double move of simultaneously *accounting for* and *defanging* the political ramifications of humanities scholarship.

Unlike Cordell's students who, for various reasons, approach technologically centered humanities classes with reticence and suspicion, technical students who want to take seriously their humanities classes are often attracted to classes such as economics or philosophy of technology that appear to fit in with or dovetail with their technical education, or to classes such as digital arts that allow them to apply their technical skills in the hands-on, self-directed ways that they are unable to pursue in their core coursework. The technological inflection of the digital humanities thus offers a unique incentive for STEM students as well as a pathway for critical humanities and social sciences faculty to productively engage with those students. Ideally, the digital humanities could begin subverting the instrumentalist epistemic infrastructures of STEM educational models and the neoliberal university in general.

However, digital humanities pedagogy is also in a unique position to reinforce instrumentalist epistemological infrastructure. This comes partly from the difficulty of teaching technical skills and critical thought to undergraduates at the same time, due in no small part to the epistemic infrastructures erected in the university postinstrumental turn. Ian Bogost has opined that humanists have to bracket criticality in order to get our grounding in technical skills.[39] I certainly sympathize with the pragmatic difficulties of teaching undergraduates code and close reading at the same time, particularly in our contemporary instrumental episteme. However, bracketing technological practice into apolitical skills and social impacts, even in the context of a humanities course, only continues to produce Technology as apolitical epistemic object, as something that can be learned apart from the social and political world. As Tara McPherson suggests, the ontology of brackets is particularly pervasive in digital culture and can actively undermine critical perspectives on technology and ontologies of difference that emerge from feminist, queer, and postcolonial positions.[40] Thus, DH's relative lack of attention to the epistemic practices of Technology can encourage students to assume the instrumentalist stance and, worse, to pretune students to the rejection of politics of difference.

Too often, digital humanists treat digital and technical methods as instrumental tools that can be applied to humanities inquiry or that can be used to disseminate research, as opposed to epistemic and therefore ideological and political positions that researchers assume. Again, a digital-as-method approach reproduces the instrumentalist turn in STEM by positioning technologies as apolitical material that has social implications upon its entering the real world. Edward Vanhoutte implicitly invokes the instrumentalist stance when he attempts to summarize the vast arrangement of activities that make up DH:

> For the moment, we know that Digital Humanities tries to model the world around us through success and failure in order to arrive at a better understanding of what we know and don't know about humankind, their activities, artefacts, and record. And this can maybe serve as a definition of the field.[41]

Here, digital methods are thus framed as tools that output accumulative data rather than epistemic frameworks that generate ideological—and at times, contestational and incommensurable—positions and knowledge, or as abstract arguments that advance knowledge about the world, rather than actions that benefit some persons and cause harm to others. For digital humanities teachers to seriously engage with and counter the instrumentalist epistemic infrastructure of STEM education, we must use our class time to help students frame their technical education as epistemic positions heavy with political weight, or else run the risk of allowing instrumentalism to frame the humanities criticism as an interpretive realm that floats, disconnected, above and apart from technical expertise.

Digital Humanities as Tactical Epistemic Infrastructure

It is a common refrain for the digital humanities to self-identify as a "tactical" set of practices; as Matt Kirschenbaum has remarked, "digital humanities" as a term can and should be tactically deployed by scholars to "get things done" in the contemporary university.[42] In this spirit, DH as tactical practice references the ability to capture funding streams, faculty lines, and administrative attention in an era of increasingly tight institutional budgets and in an epistemic infrastructure that demarcates humanities and social sciences from "high-impact" technical STEM departments on campus. However, the digital humanities can also be tactical in the politically resistive manner that de Certeau employs the term.[43] For de Certeau, "tactics" are the small-scale, ever-evolving, everyday practices that those not in power use to disrupt the hegemonic strategies of those in power. Tactics "from the bottom" involve persons on the ground navigating geographic, epistemological, and political spaces in manners that are unthinkable in designing systems of control "from above." De Certeau himself cites the shortcuts that walkers take when navigating strategically planned urban spaces as a subversive act that allows urban inhabitants to reassert their own agency in spaces largely designed to direct their everyday actions.

Tactical digital humanities can be used to assert the humanities in spaces that are not "our own" and to explicitly challenge the antipolitical epistemic strategies of computing and STEM education. A DH imagined as tactical infrastructure can help students grapple with, and ideally subvert, the very real political and normative entanglements of computing infrastructure. Practically, it is important to recognize that STEM students, particularly those in engineering, have relatively few credit hours to spend on humanities classes. Even engineering students who elect to minor or double-major in humanities or social sciences often find their plan of study weighted toward their technical majors. However, humanities classes can have a tremendous impact upon the educational outcomes of STEM students, particularly when those classes are designed to help STEM students frame and assert their personal and political experiences of their technical coursework.[44]

In the following sections, I detail two tactics that I have used in my own educational context to help resolve the divide between critical inquiry and technical expertise. Like all tactics in the Certeauean sense, tactical digital humanities infrastructure must be responsive, opportunistic, and flexible in the context of the larger strategic and epistemic infrastructures in which they exist. Responsiveness, opportunism, and flexibility may seem contrary to the language of infrastructure, which implies a certain rigidity and obduracy. But framing DH infrastructure *as* an epistemic and political position, as an obdurate commitment to a normative conception of computing, can help the development of tactical practices in computation by providing a ground for DHers to put our boots on. A tactical DH epistemic infrastructure can allow humanists to assert and direct computing practices from a critical ground rather than allow dominant computational infrastructures and their politics to direct our attention and actions.

Scaffold Everything—*Politically*

Ryan Cordell argues the need for digital humanities teachers to "scaffold *everything*" in our classrooms, both within a single course and across a cohesive curriculum. Cordell largely focuses on students' technical skills and discourages DH faculty from assuming that students have an innate understanding of coding or computational production simply because they have grown up with computers and social media. "Good digital humanities pedagogy," Cordell reasons, "must inculcate: not 'how to use x tool,' . . . but more 'understanding how x functions, delineating its affordances and limitations, and then imagining y or z.' "[45]

Again, I agree with the spirit of Cordell's suggestion—and it is certainly true that one of the most important tasks in learning the practice of *designing* technological systems is unlearning the practice of uncritically *consuming* technological systems. However, again, the frame of scaffolding as narrowly tool-centric plays into the instrumentalist demarcation of political/critical stance from technical tool/method. This demarcation is furthered by the narrative of tools as systems of affordances and constraints. Instead, digital tools produce and are produced by epistemic positions within their subjects. McPherson argues this point in her call for DHers to foreground critical inquiry in their computational projects:

> Participants [in DH] call on humanities scholars to learn to code or . . . to acquire advanced technological literacies. I agree, but I would also issue a reciprocal call for coding humanists to engage feminist phenomenology, postcolonial theory, and theorizations of difference. Gender, race, sexuality, class, and disability might then be understood not as things that can be simply added on to our analyses . . . but instead as operating principles.[46]

Similarly, digital humanities teachers must make efforts to more deeply integrate critical analysis, both of technology and of society, into our classrooms. These efforts are especially important for those teaching STEM students who are being actively divested of their interest in critical inquiry through their core curriculum.

As Cordell suggests with technical skills, however, care must be taken to scaffold ideological critique both in individual DH classrooms and across DH curricula. Humanities teachers will already be familiar with the challenges that can arise with teaching critical theory to undergraduates, due both to ideological resistance and to the difficulty of language in many critical texts. These challenges can be exacerbated in teaching digital humanities, where there exist more calls for ideological critique "within DH" than examples of doing that critique, to say nothing of the even greater challenges of teaching ideological critique through the digital humanities to STEM students, whose entire educational infrastructure actively undermines ideological critique.

Humanities and social science teachers need to help undergraduate students, particularly those in STEM, translate critical inquiry through their technological practice.[47] I have had the most success in my own classes by tightly bounding both the line of critical inquiry and the technological venues through which that inquiry can be explored. For example, Open Source Art, Music, and Culture, a freshman-only hybrid lecture-studio course cotaught by STS (myself) and arts (my colleagues Silvia Ruzanka and Shawn Lawson) faculty members, combines a basic introduction to politics of technology and queer theory with novice-level programming and craft skills. A class of ninety students represented a diverse set of RPI's majors but was dominated by computer science students. The "yakking" and "hacking" components of the course consisted of a once-a-week two-hour reading/discussion session and a once-a-week two-hour studio/making session, respectively, with concepts and critique discussed in the discussion section materially explored in the studio section. Importantly, although students were free to influence the direction of both class discussion and studio work, the integrated critical making project assignments were topically and technologically constrained enough to require students to explore the depth of connection between technological practice and critical theory.[48]

For example, students read queer theory, particularly texts that addressed heteronormative biases in computing, making, and craft cultures, such as Jack Bratich's "The Digital Touch" and Fiona Barnett et al.'s "Queer OS."[49] Students then considered those in light of open source software's particular cultures of collaboration and materially explored those critiques through the collaborative creation of open source project development. The projects were designed to redefine the boundaries of what students considered to be open source practice as well as to foreground critique. Projects included open source "Stitch 'n Bitch" sessions, in which students learned the basics of cross-stitching from instructors and online materials and discussed the role of craftwork and gendered notions about technical labor in digital society during collaborative stitching circles.[50] Another assignment directed students to expand on Barnett et al.'s Queer Operating System by having student groups conduct independent library research on LGBTQ activist movements, and to paper prototype apps and computational systems that foregrounded the experiences and knowledge practices of queer persons. One student group even went as far as to do some initial digital prototyping of their system using the Processing scripting language.

Although I would not argue that all the STEM students in the Open Source class were transmuted into radical queer theoreticians, the varied reactions to the course assignments were more positive than might have been anticipated. Although there were certainly some students who disengaged with the material and sought only a passing grade, other students became so engaged that they chose to minor or dual-major in STS or the arts. More importantly, many students in the middle reported, at the very least, more deeply questioning the lack of normative and political content in their CS courses. As we iterate the course in the coming years, we hope to more firmly encourage students to connect critical insights in the class to their educational experiences in their technical courses.

Tactical DH infrastructures can be epistemologically scaffolded beyond a single course and throughout curricula, as well. The 2017–2018 academic year at RPI included the prototyping of a new four-course humanities sequence titled *alt.code,* a minor that builds on the critical-technical foundations laid in the Open Source course. While the alt.code sequence is available to all RPI students, part of its goal is to serve as a consistent, critical humanities and social sciences experience for computer science and electrical engineering students. Following the model established in Open Source, alt.code students will continue to engage in humanities reading and critical making activities throughout the course of the minor. However, the potential strength of scaffolding tactical DH infrastructure through a series of courses is not merely enabling STEM students to continue exploring ideological frameworks of technology. Rather, these courses are intended to serve as a framing experience for STEM students by creating space for reflection on the politics and practices of their STEM majors—and their personal, political, and intellectual relationships to those majors—over the course of their education.

Build Interdisciplinary Connections for Social Capital

For all the debates, differences, and tribes in the "big tent" of the digital humanities, support for the need to build interdisciplinary connections and alliances has been a nearly universal refrain, and so it may be easy to take for granted interdisciplinarity as a tactic. However, what I want to reflect on here are the kinds of tactical connections that DH should build and to what purpose, particularly in teaching students within instrumentalist infrastructure.

One of the strengths of instrumentalist epistemic infrastructure is its resilience to ideological threats via the demarcation of those threats as external to the epistemic object of technical inquiry. As argued by McPherson previously, social context is often bracketed from technical practice in digital culture; this bracketing extends to the historization of computing and engineering technology. McPherson, for example, has traced responses to Travis Brown's online forum about Critical Code Studies, noting that many argued that "code" was an ahistorical and apolitical "byproduct of a software design" and that the rational mathematics of code and the social-cultural context of code are separate things. Such is the success of instrumentalist infrastructure that even humanities scholars are willing to abstract and depoliticize technical production.[51]

The willingness to bracket cuts deeply: not only can STEM students be resistant to arguments that explore digital technical practice as political phenomena (indeed, it may be more accurate to call instrumentalism *antipolitical* rather than apolitical) but that resistance can be doubled when those arguments come from a humanist or social scientist—someone not vetted into the epistemic culture of STEM and therefore an Other. In my own experience, even humanists who can demonstrate their coding chops are often seen, at best, as interstitial interlopers in technical practice. The firm boundaries of the epistemic object of Technology serve to undermine humanists' and social scientists' purchase among STEM students.

It is therefore important not only to reach out to STEM students through politically inflected technical practice but also to build interdisciplinary connections with supportive STEM faculty who can help reinforce critical and political perspectives from within the classroom. Although there have been previous calls to build alliances with faculty from computer science and IT, those calls have largely been framed in instrumentalist terms, that is, technical faculty are important because they have technical skills.[52] The alliances that DH needs to build, however, are not alliances based on skills but are alliances based on political commitment. Like the New Engineers of the late 1960s, a critical minority of STEM academics are working to mitigate some of the apolitical and instrumentalist ideologies they encounter in their practice. Their generated academic initiatives run the gamut from the American Society for Engineering Education's (ASEE) division of Liberal Education/Engineering & Society (LEES) to the *International Journal of Engineering, Social Justice, and Peace* to postcolonial computing talks at the Conference on Human Factors in Computing Systems (CHI).

Building alliances with critically minded STEM faculty provides valuable pedagogical and infrastructural weight. STEM faculty members have social and pedagogical access to their students that humanities and social science faculty do not have. Computer Science and Engineering faculty occupy epistemically authoritative roles in STEM curricula that allow them to reinforce the need for critical perspectives in the technical classroom and to actually bring humanists into those classrooms. The tactical alt.code initiative at RPI is made possible in part by collaborations with Computer Science faculty, graduate students, and undergraduate students in modifying Computer Science I, a core introductory class for CS students that teaches the Python programming language. Our new Critical CS1 teaches the same technical skills but through assignments and discussions that center the intersections of power, identity, and computationalism.[53] Importantly, these critical perspectives are taught with and through the technical skills that students would have learned during the original version of CS1.

The ultimate goal of the collaboration is to eventually redesign all the assignments and projects of Computer Science I in a politically foregrounded manner. The course serves as an interruption of the ontology of bracketing that CS majors encounter in many of their other technical classes. This course structure would not be possible without Drs. Barbara Cutler, Sibel Adali, Wes Turner, David Goldschmidt, Uzma Mushtaque, and Chuck Stewart, who in addition to intellectually supporting the project also provide the relatively underfunded humanities and social sciences indirect access to some of the infrastructural capital of computer science at RPI.

Importantly, building alliances with STEM faculty also affords digital humanities faculty the ability to be better teachers and mentors to STEM students. By learning the curricular structures of STEM students on our campuses, we can better identify places to tactically intervene in their epistemic development and better work with STEM academic advisors to encourage students to use their free electives and humanities credits to enroll in DH classes designed to frame and critique their instrumentalist educational experiences. Ultimately, building alliances with critical STEM faculty may allow digital humanists to build better alliances with STEM students themselves and to help students understand their own potential roles in the digital humanities not as pairs of hands that use their technical expertise to help complete projects but as full technological-ideological participants themselves in DH scholarship.

STEM classrooms and engineering-centered institutions do not generally come to mind when discussing interstitial spaces in the digital humanities. As mentioned, many of the conversations surrounding tactics in DH center on subverting the tightening budgets for the humanities at universities or strategizing ways to raise capital in a discipline that has not traditionally foregrounded lab work. While the humanities themselves may not receive large amounts of capital at engineering institutions, the access humanists have to equipment and lab space in STEM schools generally exceeds that of our colleagues at many community colleges, small liberal arts schools, and HBCUs. However, instrumentalist epistemic infrastructure has often relegated humanities and critical social science programs to interstitial spaces at STEM schools or has even quashed that type of inquiry outright by demarcating and divesting critical and political thought from the epistemic objects of Technology and technical practice. This *making interstitial* of the humanities in infrastructures of STEM scholarship has also crept into larger social infrastructures, from large state schools to the technocratic rhetoric of digital culture itself.

However, tactical and critical digital humanities at engineering institutes also provide a model of transformational resistance to technocratic culture. Rita Raley has argued that "the digital humanities should not, and cannot, bear the burden of transforming the technocratic knowledge economy."[54] But if not we digital humanists, then who? Who better to build material-epistemic infrastructures that subvert the bracketing of critical thought and technical practice, that challenge the very ideological tenets of instrumentalism, than digital humanists? By entangling ourselves in the apparatuses of STEM education and by building frameworks for STEM students to ideologically contextualize their own educational experiences, digital humanities pedagogy can make inroads into dismantling technocratic epistemic infrastructure by allying with the very persons in the best position to reproduce it.

Notes

1. Cordell, "How Not to Teach."
2. Cordell, "How Not to Teach."
3. Kirschenbaum, "Digital Humanities Is/As a Tactical Term"; Liu, "Drafts for *Against the Cultural Singularity*"; and Parks and Starosielski, *Signal Traffic.*
4. Cordell, "How Not to Teach."
5. Kirschenbaum, "What Is Digital Humanities."
6. Cordell, "How Not to Teach."
7. Pannapacker, "Stop Calling It 'Digital Humanities.'"
8. Biemann et al., "Computational Humanities."
9. Nieusma, "Conducting the Instrumentalists."
10. Allington, Brouillette, and Golumbia, "Neoliberal Tools (and Archives)."
11. McPherson, "Designing for Difference."
12. Snow, *The Two Cultures and The Scientific Revolution.*
13. de Certeau, *The Practice of Everyday Life.*
14. Wisnioski, *Engineers for Change.*
15. Wiener, *Cybernetics.*
16. Wisnioski, "Liberal Education Has Failed."
17. Noble, *America by Design.*
18. de Nevers, *A General Education Course on Technology.*
19. Winner, "Do Artifacts Have Politics?"; and Wisnioski, "How Engineers," 409.
20. Wisnioski, "How Engineers."
21. de Nevers, *General Education,* cited in Wisnioski, "How Engineers."
22. Wisnioski, "How Engineers."
23. Ratto, "Taking Things Apart/Making Things Together"; and Malazita, "Translating Critical Design."
24. Nieusma and Riley, "Mapping Engineering and Liberal Education Initiatives."
25. Kaplan, *Readings in the Philosophy of Technology.*
26. Newberry, "Are Engineers Instrumentalists?"
27. Wisnioski, "How Engineers," 410.
28. Bucciarelli, *Designing Engineers.*

29. *ABET Criteria.*

30. Slaton and Riley, "The Wrong Solution for STEM Education."

31. Slaton, *Race, Rigor, and Selectivity.*

32. Liu, "Drafts for *Against the Cultural Singularity.*"

33. Knorr Cetina, *Epistemic Cultures,* 3.

34. Knorr Cetina, "Culture in Global Knowledge Societies."

35. Knorr Cetina, *Epistemic Cultures.*

36. Latour, "Technology Is Society Made Durable."

37. Cech, "Culture of Disengagement in Engineering Education?"

38. Lachney and Nieusma, "Engineering Bait-and-Switch."

39. Bogost, "Comment on: Koh and Risam, 'Open Thread.'"

40. McPherson, "Designing for Difference."

41. Vanhoutte, "The Gates of Hell," 147.

42. Raley, "Digital Humanities for the Next Five Minutes"; Raley, *Tactical Media*; and Kirschenbaum, "What Is Digital Humanities."

43. de Certeau, *Practice of Everyday Life.*

44. Nieusma, "Conducting the Instrumentalists," 159–63.

45. Cordell, "How Not to Teach."

46. McPherson, "Designing for Difference," 181.

47. Malazita, "Translating Critical Design."

48. The "'critical making' project assignments" were inspired by Ratto, "Taking Things Apart."

49. Bratich, "The Digital Touch"; and Barnett et al., "QueerOS: A User's Manual."

50. The project was inspired by Pentney, "Feminism, Activism, and Knitting."

51. McPherson, "Designing for Difference," 180.

52. Pannapacker, "Stop Calling."

53. Malazita and Resetar, "Infrastructures of Abstraction."

54. Raley, "Digital Humanities," 40.

Bibliography

ABET Criteria, 2015–2016. Baltimore: ABET, 2014. http://www.abet.org/wp-content/uploads/2015/05/E001-15-16-EAC-Criteria-03-10-15.pdf.

Allington, Daniel, Sarah Brouillette, and David Golumbia. "Neoliberal Tools (and Archives): A Political History of Digital Humanities." *Los Angeles Review of Books,* May 1, 2016. https://lareviewofbooks.org/article/neoliberal-tools-archives-political-history-digital-humanities/.

Barnett, Fiona, Zach Blas, Micah Cardenas, Jessica Marie Johnson, and Margaret Rhee. "QueerOS: A User's Manual." In *Debates in the Digital Humanities 2016,* edited by Matthew Gold and Lauren Klein, 50–59. Minneapolis: University of Minnesota Press, 2016.

Biemann, Chris, Gregory R. Crane, Christiane D. Fellbaum, and Alexander Mehler. "Computational Humanities—Bridging the Gap between Computer Science and Digital Humanities." *Dagstuhl Reports* 4, no. 7 (2014): 80–111.

Bogost, Ian. 11 May at 8:39am, Comment on: Adeline Koh and Roopika Risam, "Open Thread: The Digital Humanities as a Historical 'Refuge' from Race/Class/Gender/Sexuality/Disability?" *Postcolonial Digital Humanities* (blog), May 10, 2013. http://dhpoco.org/blog/2013/05/10/open-thread-the-digital-humanities-as-a-historical-refuge-from-raceclassgendersexualitydisability (link is now dead).

Bratich, Jack. "The Digital Touch: Craft-Work as Immaterial Labour and Ontological Accumulation." *ephemera: theory and politics in organization* 10, no. 3 (2010): 303–18.

Bucciarelli, Louis. *Designing Engineers.* Cambridge, Mass.: MIT Press, 1994.

Cech, Erin. "Culture of Disengagement in Engineering Education?" *Science, Technology, and Human Values* 39, no. 1 (2014): 42–72.

Cordell, Ryan. "How Not to Teach Digital Humanities." *Ryan Cordell,* February 1, 2015. http://ryancordell.org/teaching/how-not-to-teach-digital-humanities/.

de Certeau, Michel. *The Practice of Everyday Life.* Berkeley: University of California Press, 2011.

de Nevers, Noel. *A General Education Course on Technology for the Non-Technological Student.* ERIC, Clearinghouse, 1970. https://eric.ed.gov/?id=ED179397.

Kaplan, D. M., ed. *Readings in the Philosophy of Technology.* Lanham, Md.: Rowman & Littlefield, 2004.

Kirschenbaum, Matthew. "Digital Humanities Is/As a Tactical Term." In *Debates in the Digital Humanities,* edited by Matthew Gold, 417–21. Minneapolis: University of Minnesota Press, 2012.

Kirschenbaum, Matthew. "What Is Digital Humanities and What's It Doing in English Departments?" In *Debates in the Digital Humanities,* edited by Matthew Gold, 3–11. Minneapolis: University of Minnesota Press, 2012.

Knorr Cetina, Karin. "Culture in Global Knowledge Societies: Knowledge Cultures and Epistemic Cultures." *Interdisciplinary Science Reviews* 32, no. 4 (2009): 361–75.

Knorr Cetina, Karin. *Epistemic Cultures: How the Sciences Make Knowledge.* Cambridge, Mass.: Harvard University Press, 1999.

Lachney, Michael, and Dean Nieusma. "Engineering Bait-and-Switch: K–12 Recruitment Strategies Meet University Curricula and Culture." *Proceedings of the American Society for Engineering Education* (2015).

Latour, Bruno. "Technology Is Society Made Durable." *The Sociological Review* 38, no. 1 (May 1990) Supplemental: 103–31.

Liu, Alan. "Drafts for *Against the Cultural Singularity* (Book in Progress)." *Alan Liu,* May 2, 2016. http://liu.english.ucsb.edu/drafts-for-against-the-cultural-singularity/.

Malazita, James W. "Translating Critical Design: Agonism in Engineering Education." *Design Issues* 34, no. 4 (2018): 96–109.

Malazita, James W., and Korryn Resetar. "Infrastructures of Abstraction: How Computer Science Education Produces Anti-Political Subjects." *Digital Creativity* 30, no. 4, Special Issue on Hybrid Pedagogies (October 2019): 300–12.

McPherson, Tara. "Designing for Difference." *Differences: A Journal of Feminist Cultural Studies* 25, no. 1 (May 2014): 177–88.

Newberry, Byron. "Are Engineers Instrumentalists?" *Technology in Society* 29, no. 1 (January 2007): 107–19.

Nieusma, Dean. "Conducting the Instrumentalists: A Framework for Engineering Liberal Education." *Engineering Studies* 7, no. 2–3 (2015): 159–63.

Nieusma, Dean, and Donna Riley. "Mapping Engineering and Liberal Education Initiatives: Approaches, Underlying Assumptions, and Conceptual Challenges." *Proceedings of the American Society for Engineering Education* (2017).

Noble, David F. *America by Design: Science, Technology, and the Rise of Corporate Capitalism.* New York: Penguin Random House, 1977.

Pannapacker, William. "Stop Calling It 'Digital Humanities.'" *Chronicle of Higher Education,* February 18, 2013. http://www.chronicle.com/article/Stop-Calling-It-Digital/137325.

Parks, Lisa, and Nicole Starosielski. *Signal Traffic.* Chicago: University of Illinois Press, 2015.

Pentney, Beth Ann. "Feminism, Activism, and Knitting: Are the Fibre Arts a Viable Mode for Feminist Political Action?" *Third Space: A Journal of Feminist Theory and Culture* 8, no. 1 (Summer 2008).

Raley, Rita. "Digital Humanities for the Next Five Minutes." *differences: a Journal of Feminist Cultural Studies* 25, no. 1 (May 2014): 26–45.

Raley, Rita. *Tactical Media.* Minneapolis: University of Minnesota Press, 2009.

Ratto, Matt. "Taking Things Apart/Making Things Together: A Critical Making Experiment." Talk given at the Royal College of Art/Imperial College, London, UK, April 22, 2008.

Slaton, Amy. *Race, Rigor, and Selectivity in U.S. Engineering: The History of an Occupational Color Line.* Cambridge, Mass.: Harvard University Press, 2015.

Slaton, Amy, and Donna Riley. "The Wrong Solution for STEM Education." *Inside Higher Education* (July 2015). https://www.insidehighered.com/views/2015/07/08/essay-criticizes-proposed-changes-engineering-accreditation-standards.

Snow, C. P. *The Two Cultures and The Scientific Revolution.* Cambridge: Cambridge University Press, 1959.

Vanhoutte, Edward. "The Gates of Hell: History and Definition of Digital." In *Defining Digital Humanities: A Reader,* edited by Melissa Terras, Julianne Nyhan, and Edward Vanhoutte, 119–56. New York: Routledge, 2013.

Wiener, Norbert. *Cybernetics, or Control and Communication in the Animal and the Machine.* Cambridge, Mass.: MIT Press, 1949.

Winner, Langdon. "Do Artifacts Have Politics?" *Daedalus* 109, no. 1, *Modern Technology: Problem or Opportunity?* (Winter 1980): 121–36.

Wisnioski, Matthew. *Engineers for Change: Competing Visions of Technology in 1960s America.* Cambridge, Mass.: MIT Press, 2012.

Wisnioski, Matthew. "How Engineers Contextualize Themselves." In *Engineering in Context,* edited by Steen Hyldgaard Christensen, Bernard Delahousse, and Martin Meganck. Copenhagen: Academica, 2009.

Wisnioski, Matthew. "Liberal Education Has Failed: Reading like an Engineer in 1960s America." *Technology and Culture* 50, no. 4 (2009): 753–82.

Reprogramming the Invisible Discipline
An Emancipatory Approach to Digital Technology through Higher Education

ERIN ROSE GLASS

Sleepwalking into surveillance capitalism, which is evolving into data and computation driven authoritarianism, one cool service at a time.

—Zeynep Tufekci (@zeynep) April 26, 2017

One of the things that built Apple II's was schools buying Apple II.

—Steve Jobs

It is no secret that digital technologies are posing profound questions regarding the protection and advancement of human freedom in a digitally mediated world. In the last several years, a string of highly publicized scandals—such as Edward Snowden's revelations of the global surveillance program in 2013, the fake news scandal of the 2016 U.S. presidential election, and the Facebook–Cambridge Analytica data scandal reported about in 2018—have tempered early enthusiasm for networked digital technology that was predicted to powerfully democratize knowledge, politics, and culture. Today, the democratizing rhetoric often employed by digital companies and boosters (such as manifest in Facebook's mission to "give people the power to build community and bring the world closer together" and in Google's mission to "organize the world's information and make it universally accessible and useful") sounds naive if not duplicitous given the way that digital tools (especially those provided by these companies) are used to exploit, surveil, manipulate, and deceive users on a global scale. However, as the treacherous aspects of these tools

---

Due to the COVID-19 pandemic, the use of educational technology has significantly expanded and intensified since the writing of this paper in 2017. Nonetheless, I believe that the emancipatory approach of student-governed technology sketched out here remains just as relevant, if not more urgent.

become increasingly apparent, it is less certain whether and how the academic, whose forms of knowledge production and dissemination are deeply dependent on digital practices, is obligated to respond to them.

In this chapter, I argue that the academic does in fact have the unique responsibility to fight the forms of surveillance and control that are increasingly imposed on individuals by corporate digital technologies. As part of the infrastructure that supports research and teaching, digital technologies are often adopted and evaluated by academics and institutions according to their practical value and professional or community norms. What I want to offer here is an analysis of digital technologies that instead focuses on the broader social and political realities that they reinforce, support, or create. This type of analysis may seem foreign to many academics because of the way higher education has long encouraged (or even *taught*, if you will) its members to passively accept digital technology within research and learning environments as predominantly natural, neutral, and inevitable. Although the university's tendency to reinforce technological complacency may be accidental, its effects have been politically disastrous; in teaching students to passively accept black-boxed, company-controlled technologies for research and writing—a technological attitude that they carry into their professional and personal lives—we miss the opportunity to turn them into critical digital citizens capable of demanding and building user-governed digital technologies that might resist market-incentivized surveillance and control. Elsewhere, I have called this unfortunate tendency in higher education the university's *invisible discipline* and have linked it to the mass helplessness we see in response to widely reported ethical infringements carried out by large digital technology companies. Here, I discuss what I see as current myths that continue to reinforce the presence of the invisible discipline within higher education and point to promising directions that academics can take to help "reprogram" this discipline toward a more critical and democratic culture of computing.

By academic, I mean anyone whose professional vocation is dedicated to preserving, producing, critiquing, and disseminating knowledge for the good of society regardless of that person's particular discipline or title. My comments here are specifically directed to those—whether as faculty members, teaching assistants, librarians, or IT workers—who have influence on what technologies are used in support of education, but I hope the arguments are useful to all those who consider themselves invested in the stewardship of knowledge. The academic, of course, like many other users of digital technology, is a social and professional being subject to the same pressures that make social media, search engines, smartphones, collaborative editors, and other forms of digital technology appealing or necessary in their professional and personal activities. Inarguably, these tools have been invaluable for enabling more individuals to participate in and benefit from knowledge production and knowledge-making communities while expanding the variety of forms in which types of knowledge and academic discourse are produced (such as the blog post or the social media discussion). These tools have also provided critical support for progressive movements within the academy today such as collaborative pedagogy, public engagement, and coalition building for groups marginalized within or by the academy.

At the same time, however, the continued use of these tools in the face of these companies' disregard for democratic principles (I subsequently describe this more fully) represents passivity on the part of the academic community in the shaping of our digital world. If we consider knowledge production and dissemination as a social good, then it seems we should consider the social effects of our academic technology practices as seriously as the intellectual products that they help us produce.

As it stands, the academy has been largely complacent in the formal and informal adoption of digital technologies from companies whose unethical practices, although perhaps less apparent a decade ago, are now regularly front-page international news. Although there is no study on academic perceptions of the politics of academic technology (which I would welcome from academic technology organizations such as the Coalition of Networked Information or EDUCAUSE), this complacency is readily observable in the continued and pervasive use of Google services (from Google Search to Google Docs), Twitter, and Facebook by academics (myself included) for research, teaching, and professional communications.

Such passivity may seem natural and inevitable given that a majority of academics are not in the business of technology making nor have the skills and resources to create or use alternative tools. However, what I will argue here is that in fact academics (even the most self-proclaimed "technophobes") have an exciting, unique, and above all *necessary* role in steering our digital age toward a more democratic future. Furthermore, the digital humanities, as a field that possesses the technical experience, expertise, and community as well as diverse interdisciplinary and cross-professional connections, can play a powerful part in leading the way.

One of the first steps that we can take toward overcoming academic passivity toward digital technology is understanding the perceptions that are often used to justify it. I have observed three general perceptions of digital technology among members of the academy, which I call *myths,* that contribute to a passive acceptance of unethical forms of digital surveillance and control in academic infrastructure. In the following sections I discuss each myth as a means of advancing three general arguments regarding the academic's relationship to digital technology. I first argue that political issues related to digital technology are serious and urgent. I then argue that these political issues are relevant to the academic's vocation. Finally I argue (and hopefully show) that the academic has the power to meaningfully address these issues in his or her own academic practices.

Myth #1: There Is Nothing to Worry About

The first myth I would like to discuss sounds so contrary to the general tenor of the news these days that it may seem hardly worth discussing. However, when I asked the audience during a talk at the Design@Large series at UC San Diego in February 2018 if any of them thought concerns over the political issues of digital companies like Facebook and Google were overblown, a number of hands shot up. Granted, this was only one room of people, and many folks in the room also raised their hands when I asked if anyone *did* feel concerned about these issues. Nonetheless, I think it is important to directly address the apathy expressed by the first group, especially as it reflects a broader apathy toward these issues embodied in many of our institutional partnerships with these companies. In this apathetic category, I'd like to include not only academics who are genuinely unconcerned about digital surveillance and control but also academics who may in fact be alarmed by these issues but not enough to believe that changes in their personal or institutional technological practices are warranted. Regardless of the origin of this lack of concern, it is often accompanied by the assumption that law, economics, experts, or some assumed form of inevitable progress will sort out any concerning features of these companies in due time without the need for individuals to change their technical practices or make political demands. It is also often mistakenly assumed that the main criticism of these companies is their disregard for conventional privacy norms, which can be dismissed as an obsolescent social value (such as claimed by Facebook CEO Mark Zuckerberg in the interest of his company[1]) or as a personal good that individuals have the right to exchange for the use of digital services on the basis of their own judgment of the risks and benefits.

Privacy infringement, however, is only the tip of the iceberg of the social and political harms caused by the unchecked power of these digital companies. Framing ethical issues in digital technology solely in the context of privacy concerns distracts us from the deeper issue at hand, which is that the ways in which we think, learn, debate, share news and information, shop, socialize, date, and elect political leaders are being shaped by and for private interest largely outside of democratic processes and often at the expense of the public good. The dystopian byproducts of this arrangement are widely documented. Rebecca Mackinnon, Jose van Djick, Christian Fuchs, Zeynep Tufekci, and David Lyon demonstrate how digital technologies and platforms enable corporate and state actors to surveil or censor users or shutdown services to control political unrest.[2] Tiziana Terranova, Trebor Scholz, and Fuchs show how these digital companies exploit the labor of their users, enabling them to grow ever more powerful while crowding out alternatives that might give users more democratic oversight of their digital tools.[3] John Cheney-Lippold, Lawrence Lessig, and Alexander Galloway demonstrate how many of these platforms manipulate or control user behavior while Tarleton Gillespie has pointed to the way they can be used to algorithmically control the circulation of information.[4] Jean Burgess and Ariadna Matamoros-Fernández argue that digital platforms such as Twitter, YouTube, and Tumblr inadequately suppress abusive activity, and Safiya Noble highlights the racial biases of Google Search and its contribution to reproducing racial inequality.[5] There are many more examples of ways these companies violate democratic and ethical principles, but what is perhaps most important to note is that privacy violation is not the sole critical political danger of these digital companies. Privacy violation, or rather the surveillance of personal data that it entails, is merely one of the exploitative mechanisms by which digital companies increase their corporate power while diminishing the agency of their users.

An earnest consideration of these issues should convince even the most enthusiastic supporter of digital media that there is at least room to improve the policies and practices of the most popular and powerful digital media companies. However, even when we acknowledge the need for improvement, it might still be difficult to understand that the issues raised by these critics are reinforced or intensified by digital technology. After all, many of the ills listed here, such as racism, misinformation, behavioral manipulation, and surveillance, existed long before the invention of computing technologies. Nonetheless, as these critics demonstrate, many of these issues are uniquely exacerbated by digital technology. This is not to say that digital technology in and of itself is responsible for intensifying these issues but rather the dominant current forms of digital technology that are shaped by an underlying economic logic. Shoshana Zuboff has called this logic "surveillance capitalism," which she describes as a form of capital accumulation in which personal data is collected to "predict and modify human behavior as a means to produce revenue and market control."[6] Under this logic, technology is often developed with an eye toward extracting the personal data of users. Maximum extraction, however, requires users to interact with tools as much as possible and not to abandon them for tools produced by competing companies. Thus, this economic logic incentivizes the production of digital technologies that covertly work to control users in ways that maximize user engagement, user data production, and ultimately, company profit.

Some might call this set of techniques good business strategy. I would like to suggest that these strategies can also be usefully understood as enacting forms of digital oppression. Although we might normally associate oppression with political realities that are far more visibly violent, degrading, and controlling of groups of people, Paulo Freire offered a definition of oppression that allows us to see how it can be carried out even in seemingly peaceful settings. For Freire, oppression was the systematic suppression of the right of individuals to collectively understand and transform their world.[7] As an educator working with Brazil's illiterate poor in the mid-twentieth century, Freire developed his concept of oppression to describe the way the ruling class prevented lower classes from comprehending and overcoming their domination. What is perhaps most surprising about Freire's work on oppression, however, is his argument that education, typically conceived of as an instrument of self and social betterment, is often a critical site for carrying out oppression. In his 1968 book *Pedagogy of the Oppressed,* he described how the many seemingly civil activities of education are in fact techniques of domination. Although there is not space here to thoroughly discuss those activities, we should note how well his definition of oppression describes the political reality of digital technology operating under the logic of surveillance capitalism. Like the type of education he condemns, dominant forms of digital technology production are designed to keep individuals uninformed and passive. If we accept Freire's definition of oppression, then we begin to see that the problem with digital technology is not simply the sum of the many political and social issues that have become more visible or more pressing with the rise of digital technology. Rather, the problem is that many of the decisions that shape powerful digital technologies are made without the oversight of the humans who are affected most. If the academic believes in democracy, then the academic should recognize that the digital status quo represents a serious threat to its development and survival.

Myth #2: The Politics of Digital Technology Are Irrelevant to the Vocation of the Academic

Even if we acknowledge that there are urgent problems related to the digital status quo, these problems may still seem ultimately beyond the concerns and capabilities of an academic and too abstract to have much consequence in one's scholarly activities. From this perspective, academic knowledge is academic knowledge regardless of the tools used to produce and transmit it and thus tools should be chosen solely according to their practical value in supporting academic activities. Other concerns, such as digital surveillance and control, are better left to the technologists and politicians.

In many ways, this is a reasonable point of view. We should not blame the academics for being more interested in their subjects of expertise than in the tools that they use to investigate and teach those subjects. Knowledge would never get very far if it were consistently required to examine the technological conditions of its production before making its claims. However, too little attention to the technological conditions of knowledge production inhibits us from appreciating the extent to which digital technology already shapes the form, reach, and argumentative structures of our academic practice. As Johanna Drucker and Patrik Svensson observe, everyday academic technologies such as word processing and presentation software "imprint their format features on our thinking and predispose us to organize our thoughts and arguments in conformance with their structuring principles—often from the very beginning of a project's conception."[8] Without critically assessing the influence of technology on academic practice, we leave both research and education vulnerable to technological logics that may be counter to our interests as both academics and citizens.

Some academics will protest that they are "not technical" and therefore these issues are outside the scope of their interest or capacity. What the self-proclaimed "Luddite" or "technophobe" academic fails to recognize, however, is that research and teaching—even in their more traditional forms—have been deeply shaped by digital technology for more than half a century. Those dusty, analogue books we so adore? The bountiful access to books across university libraries on which scholarly production depends is in no small part due to the fact that university libraries were among the very first sites of higher education to embrace the computer in the 1960s. The circulation, discoverability, and accessibility of massive numbers of books that may seem predigital in fact rely on innovative uses of the computer to automate aspects of library cataloguing work and to share books and catalogue information across library systems.[9] Word processing is another example of a digital technology whose ubiquitous presence has become nearly invisible but was reported to have greatly changed the pace and practice of scholarly production by academics who made the switch from typewriters in the early and middle 1980s.[10] Thus, even the most traditional forms of humanities research and teaching, such as the monograph or the research paper, have long been shaped by digital technology but often in ways that are no longer visible or have been largely forgotten.

How digital technology shapes the intellectual character of academic practice is an interesting research question that we have only begun to explore. One area in which the influence of digital infrastructure on academic practice is becoming increasingly clear is in the practice of student writing. A growing number of scholars have demonstrated how student writing can be positively enhanced when carried out on collaborative or public-facing digital platforms rather than learning management systems.[11] However, what I am more interested in here is the way that the invisibility of this relationship within the academy helps foster a broader disregard for the politics of digital technology within the university. Use of digital technology for educational purposes doesn't simply assist with a learning goal but also profoundly shapes students' consumer habits, expectations, imagination, and capabilities in regards to digital technology in general. Given that many academics take digital infrastructure for granted, students are rarely taught to question the ways that digital technology shapes their intellectual work or the complex set of interests and ideologies that these technologies serve.

At the beginning of this chapter I described this phenomenon of taught technological passivity as the university's invisible discipline. This style of adopting and promoting technology use in the university teaches students to become passive users with little expectation of collectively understanding or modifying the various digital technologies that mediate our world. Although it may be hard to imagine a world in which students are given the right to critically understand the technical processes facilitated by their software (such as surveillance in learning management systems and search engines) and the right to transform those technical processes according to their needs and values, many advocates and activists have argued for user rights and protections along these lines. For example, since its formation in the 1980s the Free Software Foundation has advocated for a form of software freedom that guarantees users the right to study, modify, and share software code. Many exciting and often voluntarily built free and open source software projects have been developed along these principles, such as the GNU/Linux operating system, the text editor

Emacs, the anonymous browser Tor, and social networks such as GNU Social and Mastodon. The history of computing and educational technology includes examples of experts who advocated for the educational, intellectual, and cultural value of giving ordinary users more control over the design and function of their computing environments. For example, Ted Nelson's 1974 manifesto *Computer Lib* presents a book-length argument on why "You Can and Must Understand Computers Now," and Alan Kay's 1972 proposal for the Dynabook highlighted the cognitive and practical benefits to be gained if students created and governed their computing environments. Today activist organizations advocate for greater user control and oversight over their computing and networked environments, including The Electronic Frontier Foundation, The Internet Defense League, Fight for the Future, Platform Co-op, and Unlike Us.

Although these ideas and organizations have all shone light on the possibility and value of more democratic forms of software production and oversight, they have not yet secured a genuine, popular, and sustainable alternative to surveillance capitalism technologies. Two challenges stand out as obstructing their progress: (1) insufficient financial support, and (2) the lack of mass adoption. Without capitalist business models designed to extract value from user activity, these initiatives have limited resources to develop competitive alternatives to capitalist digital media. And without mass adoption (which is in part a result of these limited resources), they are unable to offer interactive access to a networked population, one of the most valuable features of social platforms with massive user bases.

The challenges of cultivating these alternatives are significant. However, by investing its IT budgets and educational practices in ethical alternatives to surveillant and controlling forms of digital technology, the university could potentially play a powerful role in supporting more ethical digital practices and services. The university, after all, has been a long-term partner in developing a market for technology companies and acculturating student populations to certain products and brands. In the early days of computer science, companies such as IBM provided massive discounts to universities for use in computing courses with the hope of training the next generation of computer scientists on their systems.[12] With a broader focus, Apple pursued initiatives, partnerships, and political lobbying to bring its computers into every educational institution in the country with a vision of exposing all students to its products, of which the formation of the Apple Education Foundation in 1979 is one early example.[13] As Steve Jobs remarked in an interview, "One of the things that built Apple II's was schools buying Apple II."[14] In 1998, David Noble observed these commercial activities as part of a transformation of education into a market estimated to be around several hundred billion dollars, replacing health care as the focal industry in which companies would aim to sell their wares.[15]

Today, the importance of the educational market for digital technology companies remains as strong as ever, including more recent companies such as Google and Amazon and more recent products like e-textbooks, email services, and cloud storage. For example, Apple CEO Tim Cook credited students for a 21 percent increase in Mac sales in 2014.[16] In a 2007 article for Inside Higher Ed, Andy Guess observed that Microsoft and Google were providing free email services to universities with the hope that "they'll have won users for life."[17] Jeff Keltner, Google's enterprise specialist for collaboration products, is quoted in the article as saying, "We think students are going to take these tools out to their personal lives, their professional lives." In a similar vein, tech writer Brian Heater has observed that digital technology companies' intense interest in education is not as altruistic as they might want it to seem. "Fostering an entire generation of first-time computer users with your software and device ecosystem," he writes, "could mean developing lifelong loyalties, which is precisely why all this knock-down, drag-out fight won't be drawing to a close any time soon."[18]

The public-private partnerships between schools and technology companies reflect a broader trend of commercial activities carried out in and through schools (such as direct advertising, provision of corporate-sponsored educational materials and teacher training, and market research) that generate cash, equipment, or other types of assistance to private companies. Prior to 1983, only 17 percent of elementary and secondary schools in the United States were reported to have partnerships with private companies. By 2000, however, there were more than several hundred thousand partnerships between schools and businesses, contributing an estimated $2.4 billion in aid to schools.[19] Public-private partnerships with information technology companies however are qualitatively different than partnerships with other companies that have typically participated in these relationships, such as those in the publishing or food and beverage industry. For one thing, as Juneau and Jaron Lanier note, information technologies are capable of locking users (in this case, the institutions and the faculty and students they serve) into certain digital services and infrastructure because of the complexity, inconvenience, and sometimes impossibility of transferring individual or institutional data and network relations from one digital service to another or changing an entire institution's technological practice and habits.[20] These technologies also generate valuable user data, often without full consideration by the user, for the purposes of capitalist accumulation. On one hand, these collection practices potentially leave users, including students, vulnerable to future discrimination as personal data is increasingly used to make predictions about individuals' professional, criminal, consumer, or other types of behavior.[21] However, even barring such potential discrimination, this collection nonetheless represents a violation of student privacy and autonomy in and of itself.

Although academics may consider data surveillance and other forms of digital oppression as irrelevant to the subject matter of their research or teaching, these forms of oppression are nonetheless often facilitated and normalized through the digital practices that they use for research and teaching. Just as thinkers within the tradition of critical pedagogy argue that standard practices of education work in subtle or surprising ways to reproduce racial, social, and class-based inequalities, we should recognize that academic practices have unwittingly come to play an important role in reproducing an oppressive digital status quo.[22] Normalizing a passive acceptance toward software within the university reinforces a passive mentality toward software at large, reproduces the class division between technology users and technology makers, reifies an understanding of software as a neutral utility that need not and cannot involve the general user's participation in design and governance, and inhibits the cultivation of skills and organization that would enable users to collectively understand and modify software according to their diverse needs and interests. Altogether, this culture of software use in the university reinforces a broader culture of software use driven solely by private interest rather than governed and shaped by the needs and interests of a community of users. Although the academic may not be aware of it, that person is often a key facilitator in this process.

Myth #3: The Typical Academic Cannot Meaningfully Respond to These Issues

But what can the academic do, constrained by professional demands and limited technical capabilities, to actually resist digital oppression? In an academic culture submerged in the corporate ethos of speed, a rejection of popular digital tools and the important time-saving, collaborative, and networking affordances they offer may feel equivalent to professional suicide.[23] Additionally, some digital technologies are extraordinarily helpful for implementing progressive, collaborative, student-centered, and publicly engaged learning in the classroom as critical alternatives to institutional technologies that are often driven by management imperatives rather than educational principles.[24] Outside of the classroom, social networking tools are also essential for growing activist or research networks across institutional boundaries or simply connecting with a supportive community during the many solitary and anxiety-ridden stages of an academic career. Even though certainly not all academics consult the "hivemind" on platforms like Twitter or Facebook, use Google Docs to cowrite articles and conference proposals, or turn to Gmail as a personal or overflow email service (if it does not already power their university email service), it is unlikely that even self-described academic Luddites avoid using the tools of surveillance capitalism—be it a smartphone, an operating system, or a web search engine—in any of their working days. Thoroughly rejecting digitally oppressive tools is not only counterproductive to progressive aims, but it may well be impossible.

It is also unclear which tools represent more ethical alternatives. Although Facebook and Google are currently getting the most critical press, the logic of surveillance capitalism touches nearly the entire ecosystem of digital technology. University-provided digital services are not as free from forms of surveillance as we may like to think, especially as they become increasingly supported through partnerships with Google, Microsoft, or Amazon Web Services. Furthermore, as Estee

Beck et al., Audrey Watters, and Chris Gilliard have noted, forms of student surveillance have been thoroughly normalized by commercial learning management systems as a feature for instructors to keep track of students.[25] Faculty, too, along with the entire academic community, have come to discover that their universities may be secretly spying on them, as well. In 2016, it came to light that University of California president Janet Napolitano ordered the installation of computer hardware to allow surveillance of all online activity across the UC system.[26]

Third-party tools that are provider-described as *open* are not necessarily any better. In a critique of what she calls "openwashing," Audrey Watters cautions against trusting software options that the vendor describes as open but nonetheless are still guided too strongly by profit-seeking motives at the cost of educational values.[27] Even tools that have gained credibility in ethically oriented user communities are not immune from sudden change in practice and vision. Microsoft's acquisition of the version control system Github and Elsevier's acquisition of the open-access publishing company bepress are just two examples of how corporate behemoths can easily co-opt tools that many had considered ethical alternatives. The fact of the matter is that rejecting tools that enforce digital oppression would take an extensive amount of expertise, commitment, and sacrifice, if it were possible at all. The academic, many would agree, is simply not the person needed or able to solve the problems of digital oppression.

Certainly, it will take more than academics alone to work toward a more ethical digital future. However, as members of an institution designed to educate society, academics have a unique opportunity to help foster a critical and engaged technological consciousness in students and society at large. Rather than teaching students to unquestioningly accept academic technologies, we might train them in the practices and values of community-governed software and encourage them to consider how they might continue to shape digital tools according to their needs and interests. If we wish our digital world to reflect democratic values then it is essential that we educate all our citizens to critically participate in its making.

Developing the type of critical and participatory consciousness appropriate for our age is no small task. However, it is precisely the sort of task for which the social institution of higher education is designed. Although the road may not be easy or straightforward, we need to think hard about how we as academic individuals and communities can do a better job in showing students that the politics of digital technology matter. We also need to give students experience in working together to overcome digital oppression and negotiating the technical, social, and institutional challenges that come with that process. As Chris Gilliard has written, "if higher education is to 'save the web,' we need to let students envision that something else is possible, and we need to enact those practices in classrooms."[28] The cost of our complacency is not simply our individual privacy but is also the training of a generation to helplessly accept digital oppression as if there is no other choice.

Toward Student-Governed Technology

How do we develop this new form of participatory technological consciousness in our academic work? There are many different steps we can take as individuals and as institutions, but I would like to first recount a personal project that I hope further articulates what I mean by participatory technological consciousness. In 2014, as a graduate student in the English department at the CUNY Graduate Center, I began codeveloping the networked writing platform Social Paper with Matthew Gold, Jennifer Stoops (then a graduate student in the Urban Education department), and the Commons in a Box development team. As budding scholars in the digital humanities, we were not only inspired to apply our humanities scholarly perspectives to the digital infrastructure that supported our educational practices but were also connected to a community of digital humanities practitioners who could help us develop *new* infrastructure on the basis of our insights. The objective of our project was to create a digital hub for networking student writing and feedback across classes, disciplines, institutions, and academic terms that would help cultivate genuine and sustained publics around student writing. Jennifer and I were inspired to build Social Paper because we had experienced firsthand the positive effects of networked student writing environments, such as the course blog, but recognized a number of ways in which networked environments might be improved in order to more fruitfully support cross-institutional and cross-disciplinary student writing communities. Networked student writing environments were often hosted in one-off virtual spaces (such as a blog) and rarely had the opportunity to grow into a reflexive community of writers that transcended the class or the academic term. These virtual spaces also often lacked granular permission settings, robust social functionalities, and a larger network of users that had played important roles in user growth and engagement in digital networks like Facebook and Twitter. Our hope was that an easy-to-use networked writing hub would encourage a greater number of students to experiment with networked writing practices while it allowed for a community of student writers to grow over time. I, personally, was excited to see whether the growth of such a community might transform the way that students thought about their assigned writing and whether they might begin to dream up new social and political purposes for their writing that transcended its use as a demonstration of a mandated learning goal.

I was also excited about the political potential of Social Paper. Although its first round of development involved a small team of developers, I was hopeful that Social Paper might one day turn into a writing platform on which students played a key role in developing its policies (such as those related to user data collection and code of conduct), its design, and its functionality. A community-controlled platform would give students the ability to analyze data for self or community study in ways typically available only to corporate administrative entities. In both these respects, it would provide an opportunity for students to critically understand and transform the digital medium of intellectual production in the spirit of Freire's liberatory practice. Although these practices might seem unrelated to the objectives of student writing, I hoped they would provide the opportunity for students to better explore the extent to which our digital tools influence the way that we produce, circulate, read, and respond to writing. Students might begin to ask how educational technologies (such as Turnitin, Blackboard, Canvas, and Google Classroom) reflect certain ideologies about the purpose of student writing and in turn influence the character, economic realities, and social effects of that practice. A community-controlled platform would also offer the opportunity for students to experiment with its design and functionalities to see how different decisions in these areas might influence the intellectual and social character of their writing and intellectual exchange.

The idea for a student-run writing platform was partly inspired by the idea of a student newspaper. Just as the student newspaper has trained countless students in the role, methods, and complexities of one of the most important media institutions of the twentieth century, a student-governed digital platform would help train students in the challenges and opportunities of communication in a digital age. Not every student would need to be heavily invested in building the tool (that could be reserved for special student organizations, classes, and internships), but every student might have access to it and understand its mission. What if the university used these funds to build a community-governed platform for its students that might also be open to the public?

Such a utopian vision for educational technology may never come to pass. But even if a large-scale student-governed platform is unrealistic, there are still many opportunities for us to encourage and enable students to critically evaluate the technologies used to support their education and to push for opportunities to allow them to help shape and govern those technologies and their policies. At the very least, we should make sure to no longer allow forms of digital oppression to pass through the classroom invisibly. If we must use digital tools that are known to surveil or exploit user data for corporate or administrative use, we should make sure students are aware of these practices through the syllabus or class discussion. In this spirit, Autumm Caines and I published a reusable syllabus statement to help instructors alert students to these issues in the *EDUCAUSE Review*.[29]

There are also a number of exciting open source and community-driven tools that instructors can use in their teaching. While it is unlikely that a course would be able to entirely avoid forms of digital surveillance and control, incorporating alternatives in the classroom is a powerful way of showing students that different technical choices have different political, intellectual, and technical challenges and opportunities. One might simply try experimenting with a course blog as an alternative to learning management systems, such as many educators have written about in journals and on community sites like *Journal of Interactive Technology and Pedagogy,*

Hybrid Pedagogy, Kairos, and HASTAC, to name just a few. Although blogs are not neutral technologies (there is no such thing) and cannot be considered entirely free from digital surveillance and control, they offer much greater forms of user privacy and user autonomy than many other forms of educational technology. Blogs often allow for more collaborative and public-facing forms of learning and also give the instructor and students more autonomy around the privacy settings and design of the site. For example, in his dissertation project "My Digital Footprint,"[30] Gregory Donovan created a youth research group in which youth participants determined the privacy settings and design features on the blog space with which they communicated. Donovan's research suggests that giving the youth participants greater control over their privacy settings helped them develop a greater critical awareness of digital privacy issues more broadly, and it should encourage us to incorporate similar practices in education at large.

Blogs, of course, come with their own sets of considerations. When setting up a blog, one has to consider questions such as how it will be hosted, who will fund the hosting, and who will have administrative control. Though there is not space enough here to discuss the many different possibilities and the various benefits and setbacks entailed in different types of blog setups, I'd like to make a few recommendations for individuals whose institutions do not provide blogging services. One exciting option is the Modern Language Association's Humanities Commons, which provides free WordPress blogging tools and hosting for research and instructional use. On the MLA Humanities Commons, course blogs are not only free to host, but they are also embedded in a growing scholarly network that includes scholarly websites, group forums for discussing scholarly topics and building community, and an open access repository for hosting scholarly work. Use of the MLA Commons also represents a vote for community-driven academic software as opposed to for-profit academic platforms such as Academia.edu that have no user oversight.[31] More ambitious instructors may consider setting up a digital commons using the free and open source software Commons in a Box (CBOX) that powers the MLA Humanities Commons. Although setting up a CBOX for one's home institution involves a fair amount of work and often requires some form of institutional commitment, CBOX gives its administrators much more freedom to shape the space, functionality, and network as they like.[32] Domain of One's Own and Reclaimed Hosting are also great options for providing students and faculty with full control over their online environments, although they require institutional funding.

I have focused on blogging opportunities, but there are many other free digital tools and practices that can be experimented with in the spirit of digital liberation. The nonlinear publishing platform Scalar, the annotation platform Hypothes. is, and Wikipedia are just a few examples of these possibilities, and ideas for how to use these tools in teaching can be found in some of the journals and sites mentioned previously. What is important to note, however, is that digital liberation is not secured through the adoption of any one particular type of tool but rather through the fostering of critical technological consciousness in students. Any tool, as we have come to learn, can be co-opted for private interest. And even community-driven tools deserve our ongoing critical attention as a means to improve their capacity for serving our diverse educational goals, social and political values, and scholarly communities. Sometimes the most important questions to ask about technologies are social rather than technical. A critical understanding of our technological environments should also inspect the ways our organizations and cultural practices establish or impose technical norms on large communities. We should ask who gets to make these decisions, for what interests, and how might we make these decision-making processes more democratic.

It is my hope that the humanities, especially with the help of the community of digital humanities scholars, will recognize the extraordinary contributions that their educational and technological practices could make toward forging a more critical and participatory technological consciousness in students. History, philosophy, literature, the arts, and other humanities disciplines all have much to offer in consideration of the many issues arising from digital technology, and each discipline could in turn benefit from this technological engagement. Indeed, this sort of extra attention to the technologies used for educational purposes may feel difficult at times or irrelevant to the subject of study. But if the point of higher education is to prepare students to critically understand and act in our digitally mediated world, then it is nonetheless our duty.

Notes

I would like to thank panel organizer Jeff Alred and fellow panelists Lawrence Hanley and Jeremy Dean for the opportunity to present my then in-progress dissertation work in the form of this paper at the 2017 American Studies Association conference.

1. Johnson, "Privacy No Longer a Social Norm."

2. MacKinnon, *Consent of the Networked;* Van Dijck, *Culture of Connectivity;* Fuchs et al., *Internet and Surveillance;* Tufekci, *Twitter and Tear Gas;* and Lyon, "Surveillance, Snowden, and Big Data."

3. Terranova, "Free Labor"; Scholz, "Platform Cooperativism"; and Fuchs, *Digital Labour and Karl Marx.*

4. Cheney-Lippold, "A New Algorithmic Identity"; Lessig, "Code Is Law"; Galloway, "Protocol"; and Gillespie, "Relevance of Algorithms," 167.

5. Burgess and Matamoros-Fernández, "Mapping Sociocultural Controversies"; and Noble, *Algorithms of Oppression.*

6. Zuboff, "Big Other," 75.

7. Freire, *Pedagogy of the Oppressed,* 44–45.

8. Drucker and Svensson, "Why and How of Middleware."

9. Salmon, "LITA's First Twenty-Five Years," 15.

10. Moran, "Electronic Media," 113–15; and Case, "Processing Professorial Words."

11. Savonick and Tagliaferri, "Building a Student-Centered (Digital) Learning Community"; and Davidson and Goldberg, *Future of Learning Institutions*.

12. Chopra and Dexter, *Decoding Liberation*.

13. Juneau, "Reflection on the History"; and Lundall, "On-Line Data-Base Revenues to Pass $1 Billion."

14. Morrow, "Excerpts from an Oral History Interview."

15. Noble, "Digital Diploma Mills."

16. McCracken, "Apple Story."

17. Guess, "When E-Mail Is Outsourced."

18. Heater, "As Chromebook Sales Soar in Schools."

19. Kowalski, "Public-Private Partnerships."

20. Juneau, "Reflection on the History"; and Lanier, *You Are Not a Gadget*.

21. O'Neil, *Weapons of Math Destruction*.

22. hooks, *Teaching to Transgress*; and Shor, *Critical Teaching*.

23. Berg and Seeber, *The Slow Professor*.

24. Chu and Kennedy, "Using Online Collaborative Tools"; Stommel, "If bell hooks Made an LMS"; and Watters, "Beyond the LMS."

25. Beck et al., "Writing in an Age of Surveillance"; Watters, "Ed-Tech in a Time of Trump"; and Gilliard, "Pedagogy and the Logic of Platforms," 64–65.

26. Matier and Ross, "Cal Professors Fear UC Bosses."

27. Watters, "From 'Open' to Justice# OpenCon2014."

28. Gilliard, "Pedagogy and the Logic of Platforms," 64–65.

29. Caines and Glass, "Education before Regulation."

30. Donovan, "MyDigitalFootprint.ORG."

31. For a brief overview of the MLA Humanities Commons and its values, see an interview with its former director Kathleen Fitzpatrick in "Humanities Commons: Networking the Humanities through Open Access, Open Source and Not-for-Profit," in Scholarly Kitchen.

32. For instance, KNIT, the digital commons I direct at UC San Diego, has been opened to students and faculty at neighboring universities and community colleges to encourage more forms of cross-institutional collaboration and public engagement.

Bibliography

Beck, Estee, A. Crow, H. McKee, C. Reilly, J. deWinter, Stephanie Vie, Laura Gonzales, and D. Devoss. "Writing in an Age of Surveillance, Privacy, and Net Neutrality." 2016. https://www.semanticscholar.org/paper/Writing-in-an-Age-of-Surveillance%2C -Privacy%2C-and-Net-Beck-Crow/607af395b5d1cfa615e72bf533e631a02a6ac ebd.

Berg, Maggie, and Barbara K. Seeber. *The Slow Professor*. Toronto: University of Toronto Press, 2018.

Burgess, Jean, and Ariadna Matamoros-Fernández. "Mapping Sociocultural Controversies across Digital Media Platforms: One Week of #gamergate on Twitter, YouTube, and Tumblr." *Communication Research and Practice* 2, no. 1 (2016): 79–96.

Caines, Autumm, and Erin Glass. "Education before Regulation: Empowering Students to Question Their Data Privacy." *Educause Review,* October 13, 2019. https://er.educause .edu/articles/2019/10/education-before-regulation-empowering-students-to-question -their-data-privacy.

Case, Donald. "Processing Professorial Words: Personal Computers and the Writing Habits of University Professors." *College Composition and Communication* 36, no. 3 (1985): 317–22.

Cheney-Lippold, John. "A New Algorithmic Identity: Soft Biopolitics and the Modulation of Control." *Theory, Culture & Society* 28, no. 6 (2011): 164–81.

Chopra, Samir, and Scott D. Dexter. *Decoding Liberation: The Promise of Free and Open Source Software.* New York: Routledge, 2008.

Chu, Samuel Kai-Wai, and David M. Kennedy. "Using Online Collaborative Tools for Groups to Co-construct Knowledge." *Online Information Review* 35, no. 4 (2011): 581–97.

Davidson, Cathy N., and David Theo Goldberg. *The Future of Learning Institutions in a Digital Age.* Cambridge, Mass.: MIT Press, 2009.

Donovan, Gregory Thomas. "MyDigitalFootprint.ORG: Young People and the Proprietary Ecology of Everyday Data." (Ph.D. dissertation. Graduate Center, City University of New York, 2013).

Drucker, Johanna, and Patrik Svensson. "The Why and How of Middleware." *Digital Humanities Quarterly* 10, no. 2 (2016). http://www.digitalhumanities.org/dhq /vol/10/2/000248/000248.html.

Freire, Paolo. *Pedagogy of the Oppressed.* New York: Continuum, 1996.

Fuchs, Christian. *Digital Labour and Karl Marx.* London: Routledge, 2014.

Fuchs, Christian, Kees Boersma, Anders Albrechtslund, and Marisol Sandoval. *Internet and Surveillance: The Challenges of Web 2.0 and Social Media.* New York: Routledge, 2013.

Galloway, Alexander R. "Protocol." *Theory, Culture & Society* 23, no. 2–3 (2006): 317–20.

Gillespie, Tarleton. "The Relevance of Algorithms." *Media Technologies: Essays on Communication, Materiality, and Society* 167 (2014): 167.

Gilliard, Chris. "Pedagogy and the Logic of Platforms." *Educause Review* 52, no. 4 (2017): 64–65.

Guess, Andy. "When E-Mail Is Outsourced." *Inside Higher Ed,* November 27, 2007. https:// www.insidehighered.com/news/2007/11/27/when-e-mail-outsourced.

Heater, Brian. "As Chromebook Sales Soar in Schools, Apple and Microsoft Fight Back." *TechCrunch,* April 27, 2017. https://techcrunch.com/2017/04/27/as-chromebook -sales-soar-in-schools-apple-and-microsoft-fight-back/.

hooks, bell. *Teaching to Transgress: Education as the Practice of Freedom.* New York: Routledge, 2014.

Johnson, Bobbie. "Privacy No Longer a Social Norm, Says Facebook Founder." *The Guardian,* January 11, 2010. https://www.theguardian.com/technology/2010/jan/11/facebook-privacy.

Juneau, Karen R. "A Reflection on the History of Educational Technology and Evolving Pedagogies." In *Technology Integration and Foundations for Effective Leadership,* edited by Shuyan Wang and Taralynn Hartsell. Hershey, Pa.: IGI Global, 2013.

Kowalski, Theodore J. "Public-Private Partnerships, Civic Engagement, and School Reform." *Journal of Thought* 45, no. 3–4 (2010): 71–93.

Lanier, Jaron. *You Are Not a Gadget: A Manifesto.* New York: Vintage, 2010.

Lessig, Lawrence. "Code Is Law." *The Industry Standard* 18 (1999).

Lundall, Allan. "On-Line Data-Base Revenues to Pass $1 Billion." *InfoWorld* 3, no. 15 (July 27, 1981).

Lyon, David. "Surveillance, Snowden, and Big Data: Capacities, Consequences, Critique." *Big Data & Society* 1, no. 2 (2014): 2053951714541861.

MacKinnon, Rebecca. *Consent of the Networked: The Worldwide Struggle for Internet Freedom.* New York: Basic Books, 2013.

Matier, Phil, and Andy Ross. "Cal Professors Fear UC Bosses Will Snoop on Them." *San Francisco Chronicle,* January 29, 2016. www.sfchronicle.com/bayarea/matier-ross/article/Cal-professors-fear-UC-bosses-will-snoop-on-them-6794646.php.

McCracken, Harry. "The Apple Story Is an Education Story: A Steve Jobs Triumph Missing from the Movie." *The 74,* October 26, 2015. https://www.the74million.org/article/the-apple-story-is-an-education-story-a-steve-jobs-triumph-missing-from-the-movie/.

Moran, Charles. "Electronic Media: Word Processing and the Teaching of Writing." *The English Journal* 72, no. 3 (1983): 113–15.

Morrow, Daniel. "Excerpts from an Oral History Interview with Steve Jobs." Smithsonian Institution Oral and Video History, 1995. https://americanhistory.si.edu/comphist/sj1.html.

Noble, David. *Digital Diploma Mills: The Automation of Higher Education.* New York: Monthly Review Press, 2003.

Noble, Safiya Umoja. *Algorithms of Oppression: How Search Engines Reinforce Racism.* New York: New York University Press, 2018.

O'Neil, Cathy. *Weapons of Math Destruction: How Big Data Increases Inequality and Threatens Democracy.* New York: Crown, 2016.

Salmon, Stephen R. "LITA's First Twenty-Five Years: A Brief History." *Information Technology and Libraries* 12, no. 1 (1993): 15.

Savonick, Danica, and Lisa Tagliaferri. "Building a Student-Centered (Digital) Learning Community with Undergraduates." *DHQ: Digital Humanities Quarterly* 11, no. 3 (2017): 67–79.

Scholz, Trebor. "Platform Cooperativism." In *Challenging the Corporate Sharing Economy.* New York: Rosa Luxemburg Foundation, 2016.

Shor, Ira. *Critical Teaching and Everyday Life.* Chicago: South End Press, 1980.

Stommel, Jesse. "If bell hooks Made an LMS: Grades, Radical Openness and Domain of One's Own." Jesse Stommell, June 5. https://www.jessestommel.com/if-bell-hooks -made-an-lms-grades-radical-openness-and-domain-of-ones-own/.

Terranova, Tiziana. "Free Labor: Producing Culture for the Digital Economy." *Social Text* 18, no. 2 (2000): 33–58.

Tufekci, Zeynep. *Twitter and Tear Gas: The Power and Fragility of Networked Protest.* New Haven, Conn.: Yale University Press, 2017.

Van Dijck, José. *The Culture of Connectivity: A Critical History of Social Media.* New York: Oxford University Press, 2013.

Watters, Audrey. "Beyond the LMS." Hack Education, September 5, 2014. http://hackedu cation.com/2014/09/05/beyond-the-lms-newcastle-university.

Watters, Audrey. "Ed-Tech in a Time of Trump." Hack Education, February 2, 2017. http:// hackeducation.com/2017/02/02/ed-tech-and-trump.

Watters, Audrey. "From 'Open' to Justice# OpenCon2014." Hack Education, November 16, 2014. http://hackeducation.com/2014/11/16/from-open-to-justice.

Zuboff, Shoshana. "Big Other: Surveillance Capitalism and the Prospects of an Information Civilization." *Journal of Information Technology* 30, no. 1 (2015): 75–89.

What's in a Name?

TAYLOR ARNOLD AND LAUREN TILTON

"Labs Are for the Humanities, Too," asserted a July 2016 *Inside Higher Ed* headline over its reporting on an NEH-funded conference exploring alternative models for humanities research and teaching among institutions of higher education. Collaboration, the author noted, was a primary aim and could produce exciting interdisciplinary research. The lab, a physical space that facilitates collaborative scholarship by building on individual strengths, offered a promising organizational strategy worth pursuing and assessing.[1] Yet, less considered is how physical labs can foster as well as foreclose digital scholarship. Labs can be exciting spaces where collaboration and experimentation can lead to new avenues of scholarly inquiry and knowledge. However, the costs of the lab expansion movement for digital humanities can be challenging because the lab may be laden with systems of labor and budgeting that simultaneously obscure and reify hierarchy and privileges that can limit experimentation, collaboration, and access.

Across the United States, higher education institutions have launched initiatives to bring together those already engaged or interested in digital humanities. Often called digital humanities initiatives (DHIs), they have gained traction across large swaths of higher education. Current universities with DHIs or DH centers read as a who's who of higher education: public research institutions including Indiana University, UCLA, and the University of North Carolina; private Ivies including Yale University, the University of Pennsylvania, and Columbia; and liberal arts schools including Bowdoin College and the Claremont colleges have all conducted institution-building exercises around digital humanities agendas. Most approaches have included talks by DH scholars within and beyond the institution to show the potential of DH, hands-on workshops for learning new methodologies, and meetings with key stakeholders to assess the kinds of DH the institution ought to pursue. Discussions of resources, procurement, and branding in the context of one's peers were key elements. Generally, these initiatives were followed by an effort to create long-term formal structures to assure investment and production. In some cases, this effort gave a name to a constellation of activities that fit under the recognized rubric of DH that were nascent on the particular campus. For example, the University of Wisconsin Madison DHI comprises several units including the College Library Media Studio, DesignLab, and Digital Humanities Research Network. Similarly, the Maryland Institute for Technology in the Humanities at the University of Maryland is jointly structured between the College of Arts and Humanities and the University Library. These hybrid or joint investment structures proliferate at large public universities, where their size and rapid growth over the last several decades has necessitated extensive growth in infrastructure resulting in centers, labs, and studios across different schools and libraries.

Other universities have focused on centralizing DH within a physical space administered by a singular entity. These spaces have seemingly interchangeable names: center, collaboratory, institute, studio, and lab. For example, the Princeton digital humanities initiative resulted in a center in the library; the Rutgers initiative led to a lab; and Hamilton College's Digital Humanities Initiative (DHi) is supported by a physical space on campus referred to as the *collaboratory*. At the University of Iowa, the digital humanities effort comprises a digital scholarship and a publishing component hosted at the library. Despite these different terms, the core values, labor systems, and administrative structures replicate a more traditional concept in higher education: the lab.

Efforts to develop lab spaces to pursue humanities scholarship have been led by those looking to institutionalize the digital humanities. Throughout the 1990s emerged some of today's most prominent DH labs as a focus on interdisciplinarity alongside the cultural turn that reshaped the humanities. George Mason University's Center for History and New Media (CHNM), University of Maryland's Maryland Institute for Technology in the Humanities (MITH), and the University of Virginia's Scholars' Lab are internationally recognized for their success in building community and developing innovative digital humanities scholarship over that last decade. Their achievements and the resulting recognition of digital humanities by the larger academy has elicited much excitement about the digital humanities' potential to change how we approach humanities scholarship. It is no longer possibly "the next big thing," but "the Thing," as Matt Gold wrote in the first *Debates in the Digital Humanities*.[2] Some people have gone as far as to declare digital humanities a potential salve for the current (or never ending, depending on one's position) crisis in the humanities.[3]

Funders have taken notice. Over the last decade, tens of millions of dollars of philanthropic support has flowed into universities and colleges to support the intersection of digital technologies and the humanities. Recipients include not only humanities programs, departments, and centers but also libraries, archives, and museums that intersect with the larger field. Most notably, the Andrew W. Mellon Foundation has been a key participant in the proliferation of institutional funding for the development of digital humanities. The Center for Digital Humanities at Vanderbilt University and the digital humanities initiative at Hamilton College each received $1.5 million in 2016 and over $1.6 million, respectively, since 2010. Peer small liberal arts and public research institutions have been quick to develop their own digital humanities initiatives with the hope of catching funders' attention. Significantly, several Ivy League institutions have recently made large investments in DH. For the Ivies, this has been facilitated by their great wealth and extraordinary access to private philanthropy. In 2015, Yale University received $3 million from the Goizueta Foundation to open their Digital Humanities Lab. A year later, the University of Pennsylvania received $7 million from a private donor and another $2 million from the Andrew W. Mellon Foundation to start the Price Lab for Digital Humanities. Such major investment in these labs brings opportunities as well as challenges.

We know that labs can be useful hubs for digital humanities; that is proven not only by their success at securing external funding but also by the extensive public recognition of their larger programs. At the same time, the way that labs are structured increases for some constituents but impedes for others lab access, collaboration, experimentation, and credit. While Urszula Pawlicka-Deger discusses multiple types of labs in this volume,[4] our chapter focuses on physical labs designed as community spaces and labs designed as research units with a narrower scholarly agenda. The former (i.e., labs centered on supporting the research and pedagogical goals of the community beyond faculty researchers) can be more inclusive and efficient because resources can be better shared and centralized, but they risk treating collaborators without faculty status as second-class citizens in the projects produced; the latter (i.e., labs organized around the scholarly agenda of a particular scholar or group of scholars sharing a similar approach) offer the ability to dive deeply into an object of study through collaborative scholarship. However, these labs often silo research and access to resources from the broader community. After delving further into the opportunities and challenges of these two models, we turn to how the labels we use—*center*, *collaboratory*, and *lab*—for digital humanities institutional formations signal who has access and funding. Each institution has particularities and therefore any effort to categorize and develop generalization will be partial. However, this does not mean that we can thus dismiss these challenges by citing our institutions' uniqueness or idiosyncrasies. We recognize that this chapter is not exhaustive. Rather, it is designed to contribute to the debates that occur within and across our institutions about why and how to develop digital humanities (DH) labs and the impact of such institutional structures on digital humanities and higher education writ large.

DH Labs as Open Community Spaces

A driving motivation for the creation of many DH labs is to support the research and pedagogical goals of the university and its attendant community. An open, community-oriented DH lab offers a clear central location, shared technical and personnel resources, and spaces for broader collaboration. When someone asks where to learn about and pursue DH, there is a clear answer; head to the DH lab! Ideally, its physical space and equipment serve as a hub in which community and collaboration are fostered. Drawing on the approach and promises of a science lab model, it is a place to experiment with new methods to answer questions, enduring or otherwise. The outcome might be an extensive multiyear interdisciplinary project involving a team across fields or an informal conversation where one shares the pros and cons of a method that they explored. All these components work together to facilitate a place that enacts three of DH's core tenets: collaboration, experimentation, and (open) access.[5]

Centering resources in a shared lab environment can come with fewer institutional or personal risks than funding equipment for a single scholar's agenda. Particularly for smaller institutions, the lab can be the place where users access equipment such as scanners that would otherwise be inaccessible. The lab can also centralize resources that previously were dispersed and difficult to identify. Equipment available to the entire campus such as digitization resources, 3D immersive systems, and computers with specialty software can be more easily justified through user metrics and the proliferation of project use cases when they are congregated under a single lab umbrella. The investment in staff and technical infrastructure can be easier when a lab can show that needs across the institution are being met. Equipment for a one-off research project or scholar is difficult to fund and more likely to be supported if there are more use cases. Full-time staff can then be sustained in lieu of contingent labor, which often takes the form of consultants, postdocs, or students.

Housed in the library, the University of Virginia Scholars' Lab is an early example of a lab primarily motivated by the need to engage with the university community and support a wide range of projects. It now houses administrative and managerial staff, design and visualization experts, GIS, 3D, augmented reality experts, and DH developers as well as large open lab space in the library accessible to all members of the university community. The lab functions as a central community hub for multiple constituencies and various projects across fields. The Praxis Program, for example, funds a cohort of graduate students to collaboratively develop a project or tool, and the LAMI program provides summer DH fellowships for undergraduates with the aim of supporting demographically underrepresented students who pursue graduate education. Smaller institutional labs may consist of only a single director, whereas larger labs consist of extensive teams with staff including area specialists, librarians, programmers, and outreach coordinators. It is also a place where members of the institution can access technologies such as 3D scanners, computers, scanners, and virtual reality equipment. Office hours with coffee, workshops, and lectures are programmed to foster experimentation and collaboration. The lab is intended to be a gathering place for the pursuit of DH scholarship by multiple stakeholders simultaneously.

Yale University's DH Lab, founded in 2015 while we were graduate students at Yale, is another good example of a community-focused lab. Housed in the library, the DH Lab has become the focal point for DH work on campus. If a member of the community is looking to support a project or learn a new method or is DH-curious, there is a clear physical location open daily during the week. The staff includes a director, programmers, an outreach coordinator, and a user experience designer. Their extensive expertise supports the entire pipeline of selected projects from conception to final output and publicity. The space includes equipment (mostly focused on digitization) to develop projects. Internal grants are awarded to support projects, initially led by faculty and students. Yale community members can attend drop-in hours, workshops, and talks. For three years, postdocs were hired to develop and share their research and expertise, but the program was halted. The lab is an accessible and open space where people can experiment with new methods, develop projects, collaborate with DH Lab staff, and meet others engaged in digital humanities. When buzzing with people, it is an exciting space that proactively builds connections across institutional boundaries.

Despite the enormous potential of DH labs to advance access, support collaboration, and nurture experimentation, structural and institutional constraints offer difficult challenges for achieving these lofty goals. Amy Earhart has outlined the great promise as a "space in which collaboration might occur" and where "equal participation" might be fostered.[6] Labs' orientation around developing and supporting projects can result in a series of nonrelated stakeholders seeking access and the bulk of staff labor used to build projects. Priority is often given to ladder faculty, who are employed by the institution to pursue new scholarship and depend on research output for tenure and promotion. At best, faculty-led projects are collaborative and acknowledge the labor of these critical experts. At worst, they are built entirely by the lab and this labor is rendered invisible; the project is presented as a single-author piece, effacing the affective, intellectual, and technological labor of colleagues. Many junior digital humanists who have worked in labs can recount colleagues talking about "their" and "my" projects.

The practice of effacing collaborative work is so acute that in a Mellon-funded survey of over forty institutions about how to support DH, a main concern was the exploitation of (often contingent) labor. As one respondent wrote, "[we] need to conceive of staff working on projects as coauthors and not merely as labor."[7] Survey participants suggested that care be taken to discourage the exploitation of contingent labor, and that the model be partnership not servitude. The sciences have long struggled to properly credit staff, who are key intellectual interlocutors; a practice those who work with DH Labs often replicate.[8] Continuing to efface the labor and resources required not only risks being unethical but can also harm long-term funding for the lab. This is particularly true when considering differing community norms regarding authorship and credit.

There are significant incentives for certain members of our communities to emphasize single or primary authorship. Momentum makes it easy to fall back into tendencies that a lab might otherwise challenge. Whereas organizations such as the

American Historical Association (AHA) and the Modern Language Association (MLA) are trying to change the landscape, guidelines for tenure and promotion in the humanities still often privilege single authorship. It is easier to borrow the label of the *lab* from the sciences than it is to adopt the norms of multiauthor scholarship that undergird the laboratory model. In practice, the disconnect between the collaborative space created by DH labs and practices within the humanities result in the presentation of such work as single-author scholarship. Such an approach often reaffirms the idea of scholarship as a finished product, a condition that is actually uncommon in the digital humanities and undermines efforts to build a DH inflected by intersectional feminism.[9] This issue is particularly acute because one of the most prominent currencies in the academy is not monetary compensation but credit through labor attribution, so it is equally important to be aware of the kinds of labor rewarded for each contributor and how credit is distributed and valued within and beyond an institution.[10]

Not only is collaboration often obscured, but the radical possibilities of fostering equal participation are often thwarted by the very structure of lab projects. DH projects have started to borrow the language of a primary investigator (PI). External funding agencies such as the NEH often require one or two people to be designated as a PI. This same language is applied to internal grants. For example, Yale's DH Lab offered two kinds of grants for the first three years with funds from an external grant. The largest and most prominent was the faculty-only project grants, which offered $20,000 for a project. Considerations that lead to these policies include the institutional status of faculty who are considered the prominent researchers on campus, concerns about how to hold people accountable if the funds are mismanaged, and allocating limited resources, which is among the most prominent challenges.

Experts in labs are often collectively labeled *staff*, a term that is premised on a meaningful distinction between service providers and service receivers. Faculty become the DH lab's client, which can cut against genuine collaboration. The lines are further blurred when institutions offer faculty status to members of the community such as librarians. Faculty status can be a major asset because it often allows the person to be a PI as well as be an instructor of record. This kind of institutional status can also signal that staff members are equal collaborators with valued expertise. Yet, their position as staff often works against the kind of collaboration intended by providing a status such as research faculty. As Alan Liu argues, DH must engage with cultural criticism in order not to be "merely servants" and "purely instrumental" to the humanities but also to consider how the ways that we organize DH labs are creating unequal partners within DH and within our institutions. If the DH lab is a service center for *humanities* professors, DH marginalizes its own labor and its own institutional position.[11] The labor of staff, students, and community members is at risk of being treated as second-class in the scholarly projects produced. Because of the problematic hierarchy produced by such kinds of labs, Muñoz argues that "digital humanities in the library isn't a service" because such a figuration "center[s] the focus of the discussion on faculty members or others outside the library . . . [and is] likely to stall rather than foster libraries engagement with digital humanities."[12]

Because resources are limited, labs must decide to what degree they will support a project, ranging from offering a few hours of expertise on database design to building and hosting a project. If *the* lab chooses not to support a project, it is difficult for projects to access resources and institutional legitimacy. The lab functions as a gatekeeper determining who and which projects are part of the lab. The result is that certain work is legitimized institutionally and beyond, a condition made more acute by the absence of a standard peer-review system for digital projects.[13] The emphasis on faculty-led projects further limits the opportunities for other members of the community. This approach to resource allocation often means that a member who develops a project must find a faculty member, usually either ladder or non-ladder with research status, to be the PI. Even within the sciences there have been many critiques of the two-tiered structure created by the PI designation, which is one more reason why DH should adopt the model critically and carefully.[14] For ideas about how to address these issues, see the chapters by Christina Boyles and Kelsey Corlett-Rivera et al. in this volume.[15]

DH Labs as Research Units

Another motivation for constructing a DH lab is to support a specific research agenda of one or two scholars. Undergraduate students, graduate students, or postdocs cohere as research teams under the faculty members' leadership. Activities may be supported by a few dedicated staff members. A lab may be oriented around a particular project or focused on methodological experimentation. This formation most closely mimics the lab models of the experimental sciences. Driven by a single faculty member's interests, a lab often becomes hyperspecialized. A lab with a defined scope allows for a deep dive into method and disciplinary questions, a level of specialization and experimentation that is difficult and often unsustainable for a central DH lab.

Stanford's Literary Lab (LitLab), which focuses on the computational analysis of literature, offers a nationally recognized model of the lab as research unit. Led by Department of English faculty member Mark Algee-Hewitt, LitLab works with a team of postdocs, graduate students, and undergraduate students. Importantly, however, anyone interested in literary text analysis cannot turn to the lab for support for a project unless the lab sees value in collaborating. What value is evaluated often remains murky to those outside the lab. In the case of LitLab, the lab is physically located in the Department of English, where it began and was initially funded. The lab continues to flourish because the prominence of the lab meant that Stanford was willing to support a new director after the founding director retired. The growing institutional commitment to digital humanities also resulted in the formation of the Center for Spatial and Text Analysis (CESTA), which recently began offering the LitLab financial and administrative support. The connection to CESTA has provided the LitLab further institutional stability.

LitLab applies computational criticism to study literature. The LitLab team is also able to support and train graduate students as well as build collaborations across institutional boundaries because of their specific and shared object of study. Although there are risks of exploitation labor, this model can be particularly fruitful for student collaboration and coauthorship. Often such labs borrow the multiauthor model from the sciences. However, the humanities' slow and cautious recognition of coauthorship often results in collaborative work either being attributed to the most prominent author (as is often the case in the sciences) or being characterized (incorrectly) as lesser work.[16] It can also be difficult for junior faculty members who run such labs because they have to explain how their scholarly production, often collaborative articles or digital projects, is equivalent to more traditional forms such as books that are better recognized by institutions.

At the same time, institutions can support as many parallel labs as they see fit. A major challenge then is that multiple labs can require extensive university resources, focus on (most often senior) faculty research agendas, and risk fracturing possible collaborative interdisciplinary work across campus. Multiple labs mean multiple spaces and technologies that can be redundant, underutilized, difficult to maintain, and siloed on campus. In contrast, one lab means sharing resources by aggregating expertise and infrastructure, increasing the possibility of supporting more projects, and developing a collaborative cross-disciplinary space. Because they are individual labs, it is nearly impossible to procure support for a lab for a community member other than a ladder faculty member, a practice borrowed from the sciences. Those interested in pursuing DH may find themselves locked out of institutional support if there is no central DH lab to turn to. If one is able to set up a lab, however, it comes with institutional cache that can help assure at least nominal support. Particularly for faculty at small or underresourced institutions, a lab could be a strategy for shoring up their research agenda, supporting their colleagues, and maintaining an institutional commitment to DH. As the rate of administrative turnover increases, labs can be a mechanism for weathering the (often rapid) shift in agendas implemented by upper-level administrators.[17]

Perhaps the biggest challenge of a lab built around a singular research agenda is the inherent lack of stability. Because of its narrow focus and singular leadership, much rests on the ability of the director to find support for the lab in the form of financial support and social capital. Funds often come in the form of grants or as a part of a prominent faculty member's research budget. The narrow focus of such lab's funding is often dependent on that person's employment by the university as well as linked to a specific academic department or positioned under a research division such as the Provost's Office. Colleagues, particularly faculty members, may then view them as fiefdoms that need either to be opened to all or disbanded, or may argue that they should have access to the resources to start their own. These conditions can cause instability and lend the lab a sense of precariousness, which often comes to a head when the director of a lab leaves or retires. With the person could go the lab, as is common in the sciences; either the lab is relocated to the new institution or closed. Alternatively, a lab can help maintain an investment in a particular research agenda and the people working on it having already invested significantly in it, as was the case with Stanford's LitLab. Upon the departure of the first director, Stanford did a national search and hired Mark Algee-Hewitt.

The Digital Scholar Lab (DSL) at the University of Richmond, where we are affiliated as research fellows, offers an example of the opportunities and challenges of a lab centered around a singular research agenda. The DSL sits at the intersection of several institutional challenges including labor, space, and management. The focus is on spatial analysis of nineteenth- and twentieth-century American history. The University of Richmond is a small, private liberal arts school. The School of Arts & Sciences is focused solely on undergraduates. Founded in 2007, the lab's research agenda is led by historians Ed Ayers and Rob Nelson. Fortunately, the university has made a commitment to the lab, supporting the three-person staff on hard money. However, housed at a small institution, the DSL often looks toward expertise beyond its grounds. The lab's projects, ambitious in scale, can require significant funding to support collaboration across institutions and paid undergraduate labor.

For example, *Mapping Inequality: Redlining in New Deal America* involved a partnership with University of Maryland, Johns Hopkins University, Virginia Tech, and Stamen Design, a data visualization and map studio in San Francisco. The public digital humanities project explained the history of housing discrimination in the 1930s through text and cutting-edge visualization techniques. Scholars at the institutions contributed area expertise, undergraduates and graduate students created data, and Stamen lent design and visualization expertise. The acknowledgment section of the "About *Mapping Inequality*" page lists every institution and person involved.[18] The exchange of expertise that made *Mapping Inequality* possible produced an award-winning project that pushes the field of digital history and the history of redlining in America; however, it comes with a significant investment of time and money that might not have been possible without significant support from the Andrew W. Mellon Foundation. For small and underfunded institutions, the significant investment is difficult to sustain. The DSL's focus on a particular subdiscipline (American history) and approach (spatial analysis) makes for a specific, well-focused research program that allows the lab to be a recognized national leader in digital history.

At the same time, such a specialized lab in the humanities (and in history specifically) is highly unusual. It is particularly unusual for a liberal arts school for which undergraduate education and research is a major driver. The lab has limited capacity to support classroom instruction and student research, which is done on an ad hoc basis. Classroom DH projects therefore are handled by the Center for Teaching, Learning and Technology; however, this unit does not support a project that expands beyond a course, which is a major issue for DH projects. Those seeking to start a project or programmatic offerings such as workshops or trainings find themselves stuck between institutional silos.

There is also no clear institutional home for this kind of lab, unlike its equivalent in the sciences. University of Richmond's American studies program and history department are not currently designed to support such a lab in the way that the biology department has the budget and physical space to open a new lab. As a result, the lab sits precariously within institutional structures, currently within the library that privileges a service model of which this lab was not set up to be a part. The University of Richmond DSL's position in the university's structure reveals how institutions of higher education need to grapple with how to support humanities or interdisciplinary research–oriented labs; a particularly acute issue as the humanities lab movement continues to gain traction.[19]

Questions for Future Practice

Institutions are proactively working to realize a more accessible, experimental, and collaborative model. For example, UVa's Scholars' Lab, is attempting to offer an alternative model. The Praxis Program supports a cohort of graduate students who work collaboratively to develop a DH project that is usually outside of their specific area of study. For example, the Scholars' Lab challenged the 2015–2016 cohort to develop a project about alternative ways to build timelines for representing time. The team developed ClockWork, a project that uses sound—what they call "sonifications"—to visualize time, applying this method to a particular case study. The next year's cohort was provided with the same prompt, to which they responded by developing a project of a very different sort called Dash Amerikan, which distant reads social media about one of America's cultural phenomena, the Kardashians. The emphasis on this kind of collaborative work is informed by the lab's broader approach to the job market. The lab is committed to training graduate students for academic jobs as well as positions in industry, for which former Scholars' Lab director Bethany Nowviskie coined the term *alternative academic positions* (alt-ac).[20] Not everyone wants to be a professor, she has noted, arguing that graduate training needs to acknowledge and destigmatize these alternative career paths. As a result, the Scholars' Lab is doing important work through their programs to offer a feminist-inflected model of labor, which emphasizes nonhierarchical experimentation and project development that challenges the logic of the single author or PI model from the sciences that DH labs have embraced.

Yale's Digital Humanities Lab continues to adapt as well. Previously tucked away in Sterling Memory Library, the lab has moved to a newly renovated space on the first floor that greatly increases visibility and access. The lab also recognizes the difficulty of being a one-stop shop and has thus identified four areas of experimentation: image analysis, network analysis, spatial analysis, and text analysis. With less funding for internal project grants since their external private philanthropy grant was completed, they have changed their grants process. Project grants, which were only available during the first three years of the lab, have been replaced with rapid prototyping grants and are now open to all students, faculty, librarians, and curators. The grants fund three one-week meetings with the lab to draft, design, and develop a project. Although such grants still result in lab staff prototyping (i.e., actually building the projects), the Yale DH Lab site now lists on individual project pages which DH Lab staff made the project. Because of the amount of work and intellectual labor that actually goes into building a project, it is critical that such collaborators be listed.

As DH labs continue to open and adjust, we share Earhart's optimism that a lab can "actively build, examine, and rebuild institutional environments" that foster a more equitable mode of collaboration and credit.[21] We also share James Malazita's call in this volume to "resolve the divide between critical inquiry and technical expertise" in order to create politically engaged interdisciplinary spaces that challenge rather than replicate "instrumentalist epistemic infrastructure."[22] In realizing this goal, institutions must think critically about the ways that communities form around the physical and imagined spaces constructed by the laboratory model. Being attuned and explicit about the potential and challenges of building and maintaining DH labs is a step to creating more equitable, inclusive structures. There is no one-size-fits-all approach to building DH, much less a DH lab, as Maria Cecire and Susan Merriam's chapter in this volume demonstrates.[23] Rather than prescriptive suggestions, we end with questions to consider:

- Should a lab be created?
- What kind of lab should be created?
- Who will have access to the lab, and how is this communicated?
- What is the structure of labor?
- How is work by members of the lab credited?
- How are resources allocated?
- If necessary, how will projects be sustained?
- What does success look like?

One final note. In the excitement to establish and maintain labs, an often-overlooked question is when might it be time to close a lab. Such questions are being asked increasingly about digital projects because few are in a position to be continually developed endlessly. Shuttering, merging, or shifting the mission of a lab can be difficult to consider, particularly when full-time staff are involved. Care should be taken to support all involved. At the same time, as with digital projects, it is helpful to acknowledge from the beginning that there may be a horizon. Modes of inquiry change, and a shift in course might mean rethinking, adjusting, and even closing a lab.

Notes

We would like to thank Catherine DeRose, Quinn Dombrowski, Jennifer Guilano, James Malazita, Robert Nelson, Anelise Shrout, Brandon Walsh, and the volume coeditors for their generous feedback on this chapter. We would also like to thank Mark Algee-Hewitt for speaking with us.

1. Joselow, "Labs."
2. Gold, "Digital Humanities Moment."
3. Gretman, "It's the End of the Humanities."
4. Pawlicka-Deger, "Laboratory."
5. McCarthy and Witmer, "Notes toward a Values-Driven Framework"; and Spiro, "This Is Why We Fight."
6. Earhart, "Digital Humanities as a Laboratory," 396.
7. DLAx, "Will This Make Us Famous?," 10.
8. Barley and Bechky, "In the Backrooms of Science."
9. Losh and Wernimont, *Bodies of Information.*
10. Nowviskie, "Two & a Half Cheers."
11. Liu, "Where Is Cultural Criticism?"
12. Muñoz, "Digital Humanities in the Library."
13. The landscape is changing with developments such as *Reviews in Digital Humanities,* edited by Dr. Jennifer Guiliano and Dr. Roopika Risam (https://reviewsindh.pubpub .org).
14. Hyman, "Biology Needs More Staff Scientists."
15. Boyles, "Intersectionality and Infrastructure"; and Corlett-Rivera et al., "In Service of Pedagogy."
16. Deegan and McCarty, *Collaborative Research;* and Koh, "Challenges."
17. Kiley, "Searching for an Answer"; and Mann, "Attrition."
18. Nelson et al., "About *Mapping Inequality.*"
19. Joselow, "Labs."
20. Nowviskie, "Two & a Half Cheers."
21. Earhart, "Digital Humanities as a Laboratory," 396.
22. Malazita, "Epistemic Infrastructure."
23. Cecire and Merriam, "Custom-Built DH."

Bibliography

Alvarado, Rafael. "Start Calling It Digital Liberal Arts." *The Transducer* (blog), February 19, 2013. https://transducer.ontoligent.com/?p=1013.

Barley, Stephen R., and Beth A. Bechky. "In the Backrooms of Science: The Work of Technicians in Science Labs." *Work and Occupations* 21, no. 1 (1994): 85–126.

Boyles, Christina. "Intersectionality and Infrastructure: Toward a Critical Digital Humanities." In *People, Practice, Power: Digital Humanities outside the Center,* edited by Anne B. McGrail, Angel David Nieves, and Siobhan Senier. Minneapolis: University of Minnesota Press, 2021.

Cecire, Maria Sachiko, and Susan Merriam. "Custom-Built DH and Institutional Culture: The Case of Experimental Humanities." In *People, Practice, Power: Digital Humanities outside the Center,* edited by Anne B. McGrail, Angel David Nieves, and Siobhan Senier. Minneapolis: University of Minnesota Press, 2021.

Corlett-Rivera, Kelsey, Nathan H. Dize, Abby R. Broughton, and Brittany de Gail. "In Service of Pedagogy: *A Colony in Crisis* and the Digital Humanities Center." In *People, Practice, Power: Digital Humanities outside the Center,* edited by Anne B. McGrail, Angel David Nieves, and Siobhan Senier. Minneapolis: University of Minnesota Press, 2021.

Deegan, Marilyn, and Williard McCarty. *Collaborative Research in the Digital Humanities.* London: Routledge, 2012.

DLAx. "Will This Make Us Famous? DLAx Report on Campus Focus Groups." Digital Liberal Artx Exchange (DLAx), September 2016. https://dlaexchange.files.wordpress.com/2017/01/dlax-report-on-campus-focus-groups1.pdf.

Earhart, Amy. "The Digital Humanities as a Laboratory." In *Between Humanities and the Digital,* edited by Patrik Svensson and David Theo Goldberg, 390–400. Cambridge, Mass.: MIT Press, 2015.

Flaherty, Colleen. "More Faculty Diversity, Not on Tenure Track." *Inside Higher Ed,* August 22, 2016. https://www.insidehighered.com/news/2016/08/22/study-finds-gains-faculty-diversity.

Gold, Matthew K. ed. *Debates in the Digital Humanities.* Minneapolis: University of Minnesota Press. 2012.

Goldenberg-Hart, Diane. "Report of a CNI-ARL Workshop Planning a Digital Scholarship Center 2016." *Coalition for Networked Information.* 2016. https://www.cni.org/wp-content/uploads/2016/08/report-DSCW16.pdf.

Gretman, Baline. "It's the End of the Humanities as We Know It: And I Feel Fine." *The New Republic,* June 13, 2014. https://newrepublic.com/article/118139/crisis-humanities-has-long-history.

Hyman, Steven. "Biology Needs More Staff Scientists." *Nature* 545, no. 7654 (May 16, 2017): 283–84.

Joselow, Maxine. "Labs Are for the Humanities, Too." *Inside Higher Education,* July 12, 2016. https://www.insidehighered.com/news/2016/07/12/conference-explores-humanities-labs.

Kezar, Adrianna, and Cecile Sam. "Special Issue: Understanding the New Majority of Non-Tenure-Track Faculty in Higher Education—Demographics, Experiences, and Plans of Action." *ASHE Higher Education Report* 36, no. 4 (2010): 1–133.

Kiley, Kevin. "Searching for an Answer." *Inside Higher Ed,* October 4, 2012. https://www
.insidehighered.com/news/2012/10/04/major-turnover-research-university-presi
dencies-could-lead-unconventional-picks.

Koh, Adeline. "The Challenges of Digital Scholarship." *Chronicle of Higher Education,*
January 24, 2012. https://www.chronicle.com/blogs/profhacker/the-challenges-of
-digital-scholarship/38103.

Liu, Alan. "Where Is Cultural Criticism in the Digital Humanities?" In *Debates in the
Digital Humanities,* edited by Matt Gold. Minneapolis: University of Minnesota
Press, 2012. https://dhdebates.gc.cuny.edu/read/untitled-88c11800-9446-469b-a3be
-3fdb36bfbd1e/section/896742e7-5218-42c5-89b0-0c3c75682a2f.

Losh, Elizabeth, and Jacque Wernimont, eds. *Bodies of Information: Intersectional
Feminism and Digital Humanities.* Minneapolis: University of Minnesota Press,
2018.

Malazita, James W. "Epistemic Infrastructure, the Instrumental Turn, and the Digital
Humanities." In *People, Practice, Power: Digital Humanities outside the Center,* edited
by Anne B. McGrail, Angel David Nieves, and Siobhan Senier. Minneapolis: University of Minnesota Press, 2021.

Mann, Tim. "Attrition Among Chief Academic Officers Threatens Strategic Plans."
Chronicle of Higher Education, June 27, 2010. https://www.chronicle.com/article
/Turnover-of-Chief-Academic/66064.

Maron, Nancy L., and Sarah Pickle. "Sustaining the Digital Humanities: Host Institution
Support beyond the Start-Up Period." Ithaka S+R, June 18, 2014. https://sr.ithaka.org
/publications/sustaining-the-digital-humanities/.

McCarthy, Seán, and Andrew Witmer. "Notes toward a Values-Driven Framework for
Digital Humanities Pedagogy." *Hybrid Pedagogy,* March 29, 2016. https://hybridped
agogy.org/values-driven-framework-digital-humanities-pedagogy/.

Muñoz, Trevor. "Digital Humanities in the Library Isn't a Service." *Trevor Muñoz: Writing* (blog), August 19, 2012. http://trevormunoz.com/notebook/2012/08/19/doing
-dh-in-the-library.html.

Nelson, Rob, et al. "About *Mapping Inequality*." *Mapping Inequality: Redlining in New
Deal America.* https://dsl.richmond.edu/panorama/redlining/#loc=5/39.1/-94.58
&text=about.

Nowviskie, Bethany. "Asking for It." *Bethany Nowviskie* (blog), February 8, 2014. http://
nowviskie.org/2014/asking-for-it/.

Nowviskie, Bethany. "Two & a Half Cheers for the Lunaticks." *Bethany Nowviskie* (blog),
January 8, 2012. http://nowviskie.org/2012/lunaticks/.

Pawlicka-Deger, Urszula. "Laboratory: A New Space in Digital Humanities." In *People,
Practice, Power: Digital Humanities outside the Center,* edited by Anne B. McGrail,
Angel David Nieves, and Siobhan Senier. Minneapolis: University of Minnesota
Press, 2021.

Schaffner, Jennifer, and Ricky Erway. *Does Every Research Library Need a Digital Humanities Center?* Dublin, Ohio: OCLC Research, 2014.

Spiro, Lisa. "'This Is Why We Fight': Defining the Values of the Digital Humanities." In *Debates in the Digital Humanities,* edited by Matthew K. Gold, 16–35. Minneapolis: University of Minnesota Press, 2012.

Wolski, Malcolm, and Joanna Richardson. "A Model for Institutional Infrastructure to Support Digital Scholarship." *Publications* 2, no. 4 (2014): 83–99.

Zorich, Diane. *A Survey of Digital Humanities Centers in the United States.* Washington D.C.: Council on Library and Information Resources, 2008.

Laboratory

A New Space in Digital Humanities

URSZULA PAWLICKA-DEGER

Over the past few years we have seen major infrastructure changes that indicate two directions in the development of digital humanities. The first change involves the reorganization of centers into departments and the institutionalization of the discipline; for instance, the Center for Computing in the Humanities was renamed the King's College Department of Digital Humanities in 2011. The second change is related to launching a laboratory within humanities departments and libraries, such as the Digital Humanities Lab at the Yale University library, which was founded in 2015. Some labs are already established as part of a digital humanities institute, as with the Digital Humanities Laboratory, established in 2012 in the Digital Humanities Institute at École Polytechnique Fédérale de Lausanne.

Thus, in addition to a center and department, a new unit, the laboratory, emerged in the field with a different structure and new conceptual models. The purpose of the infrastructure turn is to be an "agent of change," as Neil Fraistat rightly called it in the context of the digital humanities center.[1] The growing number of humanities laboratories raises questions about their role and impact. In contrast to place-based versions of digital humanities sites like centers and libraries, the laboratory model can function both as a physical working place (e.g., the Digital Humanities Lab located at the Yale University library) and a virtual space (e.g., the Kyoto Laboratory for Culture and Computing). This multifunctionality of laboratories affects digital humanities, which is seen both as a discipline located in a physical place and a practice used in various areas (virtual labs, lab-based courses, and collaboratories). A laboratory brings new practices to digital humanities and strengthens research methods developed by the model of the center. The laboratory should thus not be treated as the next place after the center but as a new space that offers different research practices (e.g., experiment, virtual research environment, and problem-based projects) and methods (e.g., data mining, 3D digitization, tinkering, coding, crafting, and prototyping). Hence, the purpose is to recognize the mission and characteristics of lab space rather than to draw a dividing line between a lab and a center. However, to a certain extent, the comparison is unavoidable in order to grasp the distinctive features of laboratory.

The goal of the chapter is to look at this new unit to comprehend its uniqueness, understand its function, and discern its influence on the transformation of digital humanities. The assumptions that underpin the paper are as follows: first, the infrastructure of digital humanities has changed from a discipline-based center to an interdisciplinary laboratory; second, the concept of the digital humanities field has been modified by providing digital tools and services with activities of solving problems and conducting critical theoretical research; third, digital humanities' research practices have shifted from situated practices occurring in physical locations like centers and labs to virtual practices and collaborations through various platforms like Slack and Humanities Commons; and fourth, digital humanities itself has been altered to be more a method and "dispersed practice" than a field, which is elaborated further in the last section of this chapter. These changes in digital humanities have emerged along with infrastructure transformations, including establishing laboratories. To investigate the function and the influence of labs on digital humanities, I begin with a short examination of centers and explain their major features and then analyze the laboratory unit established in the humanities.

Center: Institutionalizing Digital Humanities

Since the 1980s, the humanities has established many centers to propel and facilitate humanities research, support scholarship and teaching, stimulate cross-campus dialogue, and sponsor national workshops and conferences. At that time, the humanities computing center emerged, later becoming the digital humanities center, defined by Diane M. Zorich as "an entity where new media and technologies are used for humanities-based research, teaching, and intellectual engagement and experimentation."[2] The center played a crucial role in facilitating and reinforcing digital humanities research at the university by providing digital resources, services, and tools, supporting the teaching of new digital practices, and hosting symposia and lectures.

The next goal of the center was to gather researchers from a range of disciplines who were interested in applying and developing digital methods in one place because, as Fraistat claims, "centers, in short, can be invaluable community resources."[3] Establishing a digital humanities community was a key strategy to enhance the formation of a new field, bridge the gap between technology and humanities scholars, and build a solid foundation for the development of digital humanities.

Further, digital humanities centers have been housed in academic departments and libraries and organized around a particular area of knowledge, aiming to develop and strengthen the new research approach. Thus, the center as institutional unit contributed to formalizing digital humanities, which evolved into a discipline and transformed the center into a department.

Since 2010, however, centers have gradually been weakened in what was called the "death of the digital humanities center."[4] Above all, centers suffered from a lack of financial support, and they turned out to be fragile and unsustainable, existing on soft money and positioned somewhere between departments in discipline-dominated organizations. As Klein astutely observed, "The word 'center' is ironic, since many are not central to the mission of an institution. They are peripheral enclaves."[5] The issue of the isolation of centers was also addressed by Fraistat, who explained the consequences of centers operating as silos: "They rarely collaborate with other centers, with whom they compete for funding and prestige, and when working in isolation they are unable to address the larger problems of the field."[6] Ultimately, centers were found to be a contradictory idea that aimed to stimulate interdisciplinary and collaborative work but at the same time contributed to the separation of digital humanities from other disciplines.

The very function of centers has also decreased by entering a new stage of digital humanities that goes beyond baseline goals like introducing digital tools and providing services to advance innovative research and apply digital humanities methods in various disciplines. New functions of digital humanities have thus required new structure and new research practices to foster interdisciplinary collaboration, drive experiment, and enhance technology-based projects.

Weakening centers and redirecting digital humanities converged with the boom of laboratories in the humanities and social sciences, and also outside of the academy walls. Laboratories have been established to meet new requirements and develop a new vision of the humanities as mentioned in the report of the American Council of Learned Societies Commission on Cyberinfrastructure for the Humanities and Social Sciences.[7] Taken together, whereas a center and department foster digital humanities as a discipline, a laboratory propagates digital humanities as a method and practice that is by nature distributed and decentralized.

Laboratory: From Scientific Place to Social Space

A laboratory in the humanities grows out of a fusion of the scientific and social labs, distinguished by different features. By briefly juxtaposing these two models, we can trace the transformation of the laboratory concept from an experimental and instrumental physical place to a discursive and movable space arising around community and problems.

A scientific laboratory associated with chemistry, biology, and physics is a place that has instruments, devices, and equipment used to conduct experiments, investigate objects, manufacture knowledge, and explore innovative solutions.[8] The notion of laboratory, however, extends beyond a criterion of physical location to a "set of differentiated social and technical forms."[9] Drawing on Knorr Cetina's research, a laboratory is a space to reconfigure the natural and social orders. A laboratory is thus designed as a place for situated, experimental, and technology-based practices but also a space for social activities, symbolic practices, and collaborative systems. Therefore, it concerns both instrumental and material parts and symbolic and conceptual areas.

The vision of a laboratory as a placeless "conceptual vehicle" (the term used by the Critical Media Lab at the Academy of Art and Design FHNW in Basel) means that labs have made inroads into areas that had never been designed in such a way.[10] Therefore, a second model of a laboratory has arisen as a social and cultural institution fueled by social issues and challenges. This type of creative space, alternately called a citylab, labcraft, or makerspace, is established in a common space such as a library, museum, or urban place to gather the local community, enhance creativity, foster public engagement, and promote collaborative problem-solving.

One creative space is a social lab, described by Marlieke Kieboom as a "container for social experimentation."[11] Zaid Hassan says in *The Social Labs Revolution*, the first publication devoted to this issue, "We have scientific and technical labs for solving our most difficult scientific and technical challenges. We need social labs to solve our most pressing social challenges."[12] Therefore, as the editors of *Labcraft* explain, such labs seek to create new ways of seeing the world and construct an alternative world.[13]

By looking at the scientific and social model of laboratories, we can see that a lab is an environment defined by categories of place and space. These two concepts are used across various academic fields and investigated in different contexts, from a socially constructed physical place to virtual spaces involving geospatial technologies, platforms, and services. Significantly, the development of spatial technologies and digital research, which seems to detach work from a physical location, has led to a growing interest in the concepts of place and space, which are key elements in defining the culture of research. Based on essential studies on place and space by Edward Relph, Henri Lefebvre, Edward W. Soja, and Steve Harrison and Paul Dourish, we can identify place as a physical location that involves structure, materiality, connectedness, interaction, cultural representation, and social behavior. In contrast to place as the reality, space is seen in nonphysical categories including cyberspace, digital infrastructure, geographical space, and digital platforms. Space is associated with the idea of *placelessness,* which can be conceived as a "place without walls." As Robert E. Kohler explains, "Placelessness marks lab-made facts as true not just to their local makers but to everyone, anywhere. It marks the lab as a social form that travels and is easy to adopt, because it seems rooted in no particular cultural soil but, rather, in a universal modernity"; further, he stresses that "placeless means dispersible."[14]

Along with the growing popularity of mobile labs, virtual labs, and lab-as-platform, the concept of laboratory has gone beyond the category of place to a *placeless* and *mobile* idea created around people and issues rather than a specific location.

A laboratory is thus not determined by physical limitations, materials, and instruments, but it is defined by the experimental approach, concepts, and conditions for catalyzing innovative solutions, reinforcing collaborative actions, and translating ideas into practice. Therefore, the definition of laboratory extends beyond the very notion of physical location to an idea, action, and spirit that can be dispersed and activated "beyond the science" all over the world.

Laboratory beyond the Science

The 1980s and the early 1990s are associated with the emergence of the first laboratories "beyond the science" in media studies; for instance, MIT Media Lab was launched in 1985 and Media Lab Helsinki at Aalto University emerged in 1993. The 1980s and 1990s, as Kohler astutely observed, are recognized as a productive time for laboratory studies, and the laboratory itself was seen as a social institution.[15] The interest in laboratories was propelled by a series of key publications that presented new perspectives on science and the laboratory, such as *Laboratory Life* by Bruno Latour and Steve Woolgar (1979), *The Manufacture of Knowledge* by Karin Knorr Cetina (1981), *Art and Artifact in Laboratory Science* by Michael Lynch (1985), and *Science in Action* by Latour (1987).

After this period, the notion of the laboratory was neglected until its interest was revived in the twenty-first century, particularly after 2007–2008 when the idea of the laboratory started to enter other academic fields and areas beyond the university. Kohler's "Lab History" was published in a special issue of *Isis* focused on laboratory history in 2008. This article was significant, implying a surge of lab activity again after 2007–2008 and a need to track its history. Since that time, the laboratory landscape has grown with a new model of labs created in the humanities area, emerging from the intersection of technoscience labs, media labs, and social labs, and underpinning the development of a new field of digital humanities as well as the emergence of a new type of lab, the digital humanities lab, after 2010.

The last seven years has been called "a second wave of humanities lab" as numbers have increased sevenfold.[16] The proliferation and fragmentation of laboratories have caused landscape changes in the humanities and media labs that go beyond the academy walls (e.g., Maker Lab at Douglas College established in the River Market) and space limitations (e.g., LINHD Digital Humanities Innovation Lab is a virtual research environment). The array of humanities labs is immense and includes media labs, cultural labs, humanities labs, and digital humanities labs. Each focuses on different purposes, tasks, and challenges; however, all of them are linked by the humanities dimension.

The multiplication of this new architecture has occurred along with a new perspective on the humanities, distinguished by situated practices, technology, problem-based research, collaboration, community practice, and public engagement. The topic of new humanities shaped by a laboratory place has been explored by researchers in academic (Earhart, Svensson, Lane, and Pawlicka) and nonacademic publications (Hiatt, Joselow, and Breithaupt) and at particular conferences and workshops devoted to institutional transformations, such as "The Hum Lab: A Consortial Workshop," organized at Haverford College in 2014; "The Humanities Laboratory: Discussions of New Campus Model," organized by Arizona State University's Institute for Humanities Research at the National Endowment for the Humanities in 2016; and "Digital Humanities Forum: Places, Spaces, Sites: Mapping Critical Intersections in Digital Humanities" at the Institute for Digital Research in the Humanities at the University of Kansas in 2016. These activities show that the issues of lab, place, and space are becoming more significant in the face of institutional changes of the (digital) humanities that entail new forms of collaboration and new ways of constructing knowledge.

In particular, the notion of collaboration is at the forefront of discourse about humanities labs. The need to reinforce cooperation and interaction in this field was mentioned by Maxine Joselow in her convincing article, "Labs Are for the Humanities, Too," and by Gina Hiatt in her essay "We Need Humanities Labs." Hiatt exposed weak points in the humanities, including isolation of grad students; a lack of frequent interaction among students, peers, postdocs, and faculty; and a lack of one common place for learning, teaching, and discussion. The humanities suffers from time and logistical constraints of structural units: a classroom is for lecture, a seminar for conversation, a library for studying, and an office for consultation. Under these conditions of a "structural crisis," as Fritz Breithaupt says in "Designing a Lab in the Humanities," the humanities has taken action to revamp its architecture as a method to reorganize its teaching and research model.

Therefore, the laboratory works as a driving force to develop a new model of the humanities based on collaboration, partnership, interdisciplinarity, situated practices, technology-based research, and alternative empirical education. This new vision of the humanities drives the creation of laboratories whose missions and descriptions are strongly related to the idea of reconstructing the humanities. Two statements by two very different institutions sum up this vision: the Humanities Labs at Duke University seek to "redefine the role of the humanities," and Digital Humanities Lab Denmark aims to "rejuvenate fields of research within the humanities and social sciences."

The laboratory, with its features like cooperation, interdisciplinarity, hands-on practices, innovation, and experimental and technology-driven projects, significantly transforms the organization and operation of the humanities, including digital humanities.

The Landscape of Digital Humanities Labs

In "The Digital Humanities as a Laboratory," one of the first articles related to this issue, Amy E. Earhart rightly notes that digital humanities can especially benefit from adopting a laboratory model because this institutional structure by its nature fosters the aspects of digital humanities, including collaboration, interdisciplinarity, and team-based and technology-driven practices. The corollary of this is the growing number of digital humanities labs after 2010, which coincides with the proliferation of humanities labs in general.

Digital humanities labs have been launched in diverse locations and defined in various ways and perform different functions. They are located in centers and institutes of digital humanities (e.g., Digital Humanities Laboratory at the École Polytechnique Fédérale de Lausanne), in English departments (e.g., Digital Humanities Lab at Texas Tech University), in History departments (e.g., Digital History Lab at California State University, San Marcos), in libraries (e.g., Penn State Digital Humanities Lab), and in other institutions.

Along with the multiplication of humanities labs, their definition has significantly extended beyond the criterion of workplace toward categories that stress the role of practice, experience, and collaboration. A laboratory is thus called a hub (Electronic Textual Cultures Lab at the University of Victoria), a meeting place (Humlab at Umeå University), and a course (Global Humanities Lab at Northwestern University). The laboratory includes changes on how to conduct research and the perceptions of objects through collaborative, experimental, and tinkering practices.

The multiple meanings of laboratories illustrate their different functions and research objectives. The purposes of digital humanities labs range from facilitating and promoting innovative projects to designing knowledge and creating digital works.

The first purpose is thus associated with developing, supporting, and disseminating digital humanities research by providing training, consultancy, and technical facilities. The second goal is related to a workspace model, which means that the lab functions as a place that provides technical equipment, software, conference rooms, staff space, and more (e.g., Digital Scholarship Lab at the University of North Carolina at Charlotte). This type of lab is perceived instrumentally as a physical location that facilitates and supports technology-based research.

The third function of digital humanities labs results from the service model, providing help to digitize materials and preserve access to original collections (e.g., Stanford Media Preservation Lab) and to build websites and display data in new and dynamic ways (e.g., the UC Arts Digital Lab at the University of Canterbury). The next purpose refers to the platform and network model of the laboratory, which is focused on fostering global collaboration and building an international consortium and a research infrastructure (e.g., Digital Humanities Lab Denmark).

The last function of digital humanities labs is based on a research model that aims to investigate ideas, conduct research projects, and apply constructed knowledge and products. This type of lab is seen as an experimental space devoted to the exploration of cultural, social, media, and economic issues and the design of technologies, software, and applications, and then to their use in different research domains to solve particular problems, generate new ideas, and develop research areas. Digital humanities research is performed by a diverse and collaborative team built by scholars from various fields, including humanists, librarians, archivists, programmers, developers, managers, engineers, and others. Consequently, they jointly contribute to the creation of the following types of digital humanities products: software, tools, and applications (e.g., the text analysis tool Textometrica created in Humlab at Umeå University and open access tools provided by Humanities + Design at Stanford University); archives and collections (the Early Caribbean Digital Archive in the NULab for Texts, Maps, and Networks); digital platforms (the German Screen Studies Network in King's Digital Lab and a web-based platform, Photogrammar, which was supported by the Digital Humanities Lab at Yale University but preceded that lab's founding by several years); interactive maps (the Great Lakes mapping project in Nexus Laboratory for Digital Humanities and Transdisciplinary Informatics); games (video games produced in the ModLab at the University of California Davis); and more.

Digital humanities labs attract people with their equipment, their advanced technologies, and their statements, presenting labs as transdisciplinary communities and experimental and collaborative places with an innovative use of technology. These types of labs emphasize the laboratory itself, which is sometimes viewed only in the context of physical place, which consequently leads to the equation of laboratory with a workspace. The very notion of laboratory and technologies is, however, a starting point for creating an environment in which digital humanities can be perceived as useful research practice. Therefore, I present two significant impacts of the laboratory idea on digital humanities taken as a main research method that applies in interdisciplinary problem spaces.

Digital Humanities as Dispersed Practices in Problem Space

The assumptions that underpin laboratory nature are collaboration, interaction, interdisciplinarity, and experiment. Laboratories are established around problems and challenges rather than fields, so that labs are focused on solving particular issues through collaborative practices instead of on reinforcing a discipline. Therefore, labs related to digital humanities include units that are called digital humanities labs and also include places that apply digital humanities practices but whose names do not indicate the discipline itself; for instance, Knowledge Lab at the University of Chicago uses digital humanities methods to analyze the dynamics of knowledge creation, transformation, and dissemination. The proliferation of various labs in the humanities indicates that a division between digital humanities labs and nondigital humanities labs is hard to set.

Therefore, the concept of laboratory affects digital humanities, which has gradually become *dispersed practices* that can be used in various units in different departments and institutions. Further, digital humanities as dispersed practices means that it is perceived as a research method and concept that can be applied beyond space constraints, for instance, in virtual labs and global platforms.

Constructing a laboratory around urgent and crucial social issues brings us to the concept of laboratory as *problem space*, described by Lisa Osbeck et al. in the framework of "science as psychology."[17] According to this framework, the laboratory is not simply a physical location but also a problem space associated with the *cognitive partnerships* occurring between the technological artifacts and the researchers. Research laboratories address problems through situated and distributed practices, and the problem-solving process can occur among humans, technological instruments, materials, a place, and so on. Given the different scope of issues, laboratories vary in size, facilities, and operations. Each lab reveals itself as an individual environment in which construction depends on the research problem requiring different cognitive systems. Taken together, the laboratory is not a physical structure itself but an environment that seeks to take on specific and complex issues.

My perspective on the laboratory seen as problem space stems from a specific model of humanities lab represented by the Humanities Labs, founded by the Franklin Humanities Institute (FHI) at Duke University in 2010. This model functions as a "new architecture of multiple humanities laboratories," in which each lab is created around a central theme and involves faculty and students from across the humanities and other disciplines. Since 2010, the Humanities Labs have included ten laboratories; some are still supported, and others have been concluded. What distinguishes this structure is that each lab is set up for a fixed period and for a specific purpose. The first humanities laboratory at the FHI, the Haiti Lab, was established after the natural disaster in Haiti and driven by innovative thinking about the country's recovery, the expansion of Haitian studies in the United States and Haiti, and broadening knowledge about Haitian culture, history, and language. The laboratory is thus seen as the only structure entirely devoted to one specific research problem investigated in innovative, interdisciplinary, and collaborative ways. This model shows that the laboratory in the humanities is a unique and crucial architecture to develop the field into practices performed in a problem space constructed around challenges beyond disciplines.

The following labs, applying digital humanities practices, can be seen as the implementation of problem space, and the scope of their problem-based research is often indicated by the lab name itself. For instance, the Electronic Textual Cultures Lab (ETCL), established in a library at the University of Victoria in 2005, focuses on cross-disciplinary study of the past, present, and future of textual communication by using a digital humanities approach. Besides specific research areas, the unit focuses on strengthening the interdisciplinary research environment by establishing digital knowledge networks (like Iter Community and the Renaissance Knowledge Network) as the key way to solve complex issues. Therefore, the lab functions both as a physical place located in the McPherson Library and a space that models collaborative work, creates an international network, and applies interdisciplinary methods for problem-based research.

The second example is the Digital Humanities and Literary Cognition Lab, started in the Department of English at Michigan State University in 2012, which is a space dedicated to research on cognition, literary neuroscience, the history of cognition and media, and theories of knowledge production in the digital age. The lab is an open environment for scholars from different fields who want to explore the question of cognition in a collaborative and experimental way by using digital technologies. This space was thus launched to conduct national and international projects devoted to specific research problems using interdisciplinary methods, such as literary neuroscience, the history mind, and digital humanities.

The laboratory has arisen in the humanities as a physical place, transforming a field by becoming not simply a kind of knowledge but a form of activity that takes place in a concrete location and involving complex practices. The new structural unit also has a significant impact on digital humanities itself, which has developed in two directions: as an institutionalized field located in centers and departments and as dispersed practice applied in various humanities and media laboratories. A lab is an interesting environment in which digital humanities can be perceived as significant research methods and practices. The laboratory, however, due to its open structure, indeterminate function, placelessness, and temporariness, can be seen as an unsustainable unit that functions more as a project than a research place. Lauren Tilton and Taylor Arnold describe the benefits and drawbacks of pursuing a lab model in their chapter in this volume.[18]

There is a need for greater self-determination, a precise vision of development, and a specific function of digital humanities to enhance the role of the laboratory as an innovative problem space rather than treating the place as the only strategy to revive the humanities by involving collaborative and interdisciplinary technology-based projects.

Notes

1. Fraistat, "Function of Digital Humanities Centers."

2. Zorich, *Survey of Digital Humanities Centers*, 4.

3. Fraistat, "Function of Digital Humanities Centers."

4. Sample, "On the Death of the Digital Humanities Center."

5. Klein, *Humanities, Culture, and Interdisciplinarity*, 77.

6. Fraistat, "Function of Digital Humanities Centers."

7. ACLS, *Our Cultural Commonwealth*.

8. Hannaway, "Laboratory Design," 585.

9. Knorr Cetina, *Epistemic Cultures*, 26.

10. Institute of Experimental Design and Media Cultures, "Critical Media Lab."

11. Kieboom, *Lab Matters*, 9.

12. Hassan, *Social Labs Revolution,* 2.

13. Tiesinga and Berkhout, *Labcraft,* 34.

14. Kohler, "Lab History," 766.

15. Kohler, "Lab History," 761.

16. Duke University, "Franklin Humanities Institute Seeks Proposals."

17. Osbeck et al., *Science as Psychology.*

18. Tilton and Arnold, "What's in a Name?"

Bibliography

ACLS. *Our Cultural Commonwealth. The Report of the American Council of Learned Societies Commission on Cyberinfrastructure for the Humanities and Social Sciences.* New York: American Council of Learned Societies, 2006.

Breithaupt, Fritz. "Designing a Lab in the Humanities." *Chronicle of Higher Education,* February 6, 2017. http://www.chronicle.com/article/Designing-a-Lab-in-the/239132.

Digital Humanities and Literary Cognition Lab. Michigan State University. http://dhlc.cal.msu.edu/.

Digital Humanities Lab Denmark (DIGHUMLAB). Aarhus University. http://dighumlab.org/.

Duke University. "Franklin Humanities Institute Seeks Proposals for Humanities Lab Projects." January 20, 2017. https://sites.duke.edu/interdisciplinary/2016/11/18/franklin -humanities-institute-seeks-proposals-for-humanities-lab-projects/.

Earhart, Amy E. "The Digital Humanities as a Laboratory." In *Between Humanities and the Digital,* edited by Patrik Svensson and David Theo Goldberg, 391–400. Cambridge, Mass.: MIT Press, 2015.

Electronic Textual Cultures Lab. University of Victoria. http://etcl.uvic.ca/.

Fraistat, Neil. "The Function of Digital Humanities Centers at the Present Time." In *Debates in the Digital Humanities,* edited by Matthew K. Gold. Minneapolis: University of Minnesota Press, 2012. http://dhdebates.gc.cuny.edu/debates/text/23.

Hannaway, Owen. "Laboratory Design and the Aim of Science: Andreas Libavius versus Tycho Brahe." *Isis* 77, no. 4 (1986): 585–610.

Harrison, Steve, and Paul Dourish. "Re-Place-ing Space: The Roles of Space and Place in Collaborative Systems." In *Proceedings of the ACM Conference on Computer Supported Cooperative Work.* Boston: ACM Press, 1996.

Hassan, Zaid. *The Social Labs Revolution.* San Francisco: Berrett-Koehler, 2014.

Hiatt, Gina. "We Need Humanities Labs." *Inside Higher Ed,* October 26, 2005. https://www.insidehighered.com/views/2005/10/26/we-need-humanities-labs.

Humanities Labs. Duke University. https://fhi.duke.edu/labs.html.

Humlab. Umeå University. http://www.umu.se/en/humlab/.

Institute of Experimental Design and Media Cultures. "Critical Media Lab." https://www.ixdm.ch/critical-media-lab/.

Joselow, Maxine. "Labs Are for the Humanities, Too." *Inside Higher Ed,* July 12, 2016. https://www.insidehighered.com/news/2016/07/12/conference-explores-humanities-labs.

Kieboom, Marlieke. *Lab Matters: Challenging the Practice of Social Innovation Laboratories*. Amsterdam: Kennisland, 2014.

Klein, Julie Thompson. *Humanities, Culture, and Interdisciplinarity: The Changing American Academy*. Albany: State University of New York Press, 2005.

Knorr Cetina, Karin. *Epistemic Cultures. How the Sciences Make Knowledge*. Cambridge, Mass.: Harvard University Press, 1999.

Knorr Cetina, Karin. *The Manufacture of Knowledge*. Oxford: Pergamon Press, 1981.

Kohler, Robert E. "Lab History: Reflections." *Isis* 99 (2008): 761–68.

Kyoto Laboratory for Culture and Computing. Kyoto University. http://langrid.org/culture/en/.

Lane, Richard J. *The Big Humanities: Digital Humanities/Digital Laboratories*. New York: Routledge, 2017.

Latour, Bruno. *Science in Action: How to Follow Scientists and Engineers through Society*. Cambridge, Mass.: Harvard University Press, 1987.

Latour, Bruno, and Steve Woolgar. *Laboratory Life: The Construction of Scientific Facts*. Princeton, N.J.: Princeton University Press, 1979.

Lefebvre, Henri. *The Production of Space*. Malden, Mass.: Blackwell, 1991.

Lynch, Michael. *Art and Artifact in Laboratory Science*. London: Routledge & Kegan Paul, 1985.

Northwestern University. "Global Humanities Lab." https://www.humanities.northwestern.edu/undergraduate/global-humanities-lab/.

Osbeck, Lisa M., Nancy J. Nersessian, Kareen R. Malone, and Wendy C. Newstetter. *Science as Psychology: Sense-Making and Identity in Science Practice*. Cambridge: Cambridge University Press, 2011.

Pawlicka, Urszula. "Data, Collaboration, Laboratory: Bringing Concepts from Science into Humanities Practice." *English Studies* 98, no. 5 (2017): 526–41.

Relph, Edward. *Place and Placelessness*. London: Pion, 1976.

Sample, Mark. "On the Death of the Digital Humanities Center." *@samplereality* (blog), March 26, 2010. http://www.samplereality.com/2010/03/26/on-the-death-of-the-digital-humanities-center/.

Soja, Edward W. *Thirdspace: Journeys to Los Angeles and Other Real-and-imagined Places*. Malden, Mass.: Blackwell, 1996.

Svensson, Patrik. "The Humanistiscope—Exploring the Situatedness of Humanities Infrastructure." In *Between Humanities and the Digital*, edited by Patrik Svensson and David Theo Goldberg, 337–53. Cambridge, Mass.: MIT Press, 2015.

Tiesinga, Hendrik, and Remko Berkhout, eds. *Labcraft: How Social Labs Cultivate Change through Innovation and Collaboration*. London: Labcraft, 2014.

Tilton, Lauren, and Taylor Arnold. "What's in a Name?" In *People, Practice, Power: Digital Humanities outside the Center*, edited by Anne B. McGrail, Angel David Nieves, and Siobhan Senier. Minneapolis: University of Minnesota Press, 2021.

Zorich, Diane M. *A Survey of Digital Humanities Centers in the United States*. Washington, D.C.: Council on Library and Information Resources, 2008.

Zombies in the Library Stacks

LAURA R. BRAUNSTEIN AND MICHELLE R. WARREN

We begin in the library stacks—between the rows of shelves that keep books off the floor, out of piles, in order. In this narrow space, we are in the literal *interstices* of infrastructure: "standing between" (*inter* [between] + *sistere* [to stand]). From this vantage point, the library itself is a structure standing between its past as a shelter for books and its future as a digital network. Indeed, as libraries make space for the computers needed to access digital resources, some are directly displacing the stacks by sending printed books and their shelves to more distant buildings.

The digital humanities are entangled with these shifts. The expansion of library staff positions bearing titles that include the phrase *digital humanities* is just one aspect of DH's place within libraries' infrastructure. DH depends on the broader universe of things digital and digitized, from preservation to databases to social media. In this sense, DH is part of the digital infrastructure displacing the stacks. Yet even as physical stacks seem increasingly decentered in the library, *the stacks* have morphed into a metaphor that characterizes essential digital functions. In this essay, we browse through the metaphors in an effort to understand infrastructure as a nexus of material, conceptual, and social relations. We aim to calibrate some of the stress points between DH and libraries.

Our essay is not a case study of a DH project in a library (although we are very interested in those) but rather a conceptual exploration of how the vocabulary that we use to describe infrastructure is yet another element of infrastructure that shapes DH research.[1] Our reflections have grown out of a long-standing relationship in which we both worked in the library, but neither worked in DH. A decade later, DH has changed our work considerably even though we still have the same jobs— librarian (Laura) and faculty member (Michelle). This article fuses our respective trajectories into DH in order to engage with some of the fundamentals of institutions and infrastructures.

On Metaphor

The library stacks remind us that all infrastructure incorporates human social relations because their architectural forms are designed to enable people to move through their aisles to access books. Just as the term *computer* has denoted a person, a place, and a thing all at once, "the stacks" encompass domains otherwise considered separate and incommensurable.[2] Like computers, the stacks point to the enfolding of the social within the material. As Sheila Anderson has pointed out, even efforts to recognize social formations often end up focusing on material forms.[3] We take up this entanglement to align ourselves with Susan Leigh Star and Karen Ruhleder, who ask *when* is infrastructure: "we hold that infrastructure is a fundamentally relational concept. It becomes infrastructure in relation to organized practices. . . . Thus we ask, *when*—not *what*—is an infrastructure."[4] In this conception, *the stacks* can stand for different things at different times. They can also migrate in and out of the library, tracing malleable relations among things, technology, and people.

Even as we try to speak of the literal physical stacks, we are already in the realm of metaphor: "a pile of stuff" (*stakkr* meaning "haystack") has become a "structure for organizing a pile of stuff" (*stakkr* meaning "barn").[5] This transition happened without our conscious knowledge until just now, when we went digging into etymology as recorded in a finding tool, the dictionary, whose authority we have learned to trust. However, that finding tool is also a piece of knowledge infrastructure that calls for analysis.[6] And so, beginning in the stacks means beginning with metaphor as yet another mechanism that effaces the work of infrastructure.

As a rhetorical figure, metaphor shapes what can be thought. When it functions properly, we do not even notice the epistemic shifts that occur when one domain or scale substitutes for another. When infrastructure mobilizes metaphor, these slippages of self-effacement proliferate in ways both harmful and inspiring. As Michelle has written elsewhere: "Metaphors matter because they give subliminal structure to our knowledge systems. Sometimes they sharpen our perception of 'what is really happening.' At other times, they distract us from underlying forces. A new metaphor might reflect a new reality; truly successful metaphors generate reality itself."[7] Metaphor serves as software so subtle that it can be mistaken for hardware. Critical infrastructure studies aim to expose these processes.

A particular kind of metaphor known in sociology as a *zombie category* brings us to conceptualize *the stacks* as a complex social formation. The concept has been defined by Ulrich Beck and Elisabeth Beck-Gernsheim as "living-dead categories which blind [sociologists] to the realities and contradictions of globalizing and individualizing modernities."[8] They argue that the continued use of these categories that "have died yet live on" prevents researchers from truly understanding modern social life.[9] Beck elaborates on the example of "the family"—a category whose middle-class

European sense is still widely valued even though that sense does not correspond to most people's experience of family life.[10] For Beck and Beck-Gernsheim, the zombie category has a mostly negative force. For them, the task of scholarship is to dispense with outmoded categories in order to discover how society really works.

Yet the zombie category also has a positive capacity. For Nicholas Birns, categories that are no longer understood as originally meant and yet are still in use produce pluralities that can free us from the homogenizing march of time and ideas.[11] While Birns refers to Beck, he moves in the opposite direction. In this approach, zombie categories reveal how meanings can change even when the words do not. Their analysis can help uncover the work of vocabulary itself as part of our scholarly infrastructure. Zombies remind us that obsolescence does not mean the end (zombies may be dead, but they just keep coming). Persistence and resurgence can be advantageous. "Zombies in the stacks" thus means that we can value new and old meanings at the same time; they can coincide rather than compete. If we see the stacks as equal parts steel and discourse, we might be able to predict their movements. In this way, we further the understanding of infrastructure as something that does not just *exist* but *becomes*.

Our focus on the stacks derives from our focus on relationship between DH and the library. Just as the stacks are no longer just shelves, the library is no longer just a building. David Weinberger has made the influential suggestion that libraries should function less like portals and more like platforms: "A library as platform is more how than where, more hyperlinks than container, more hubbub than hub."[12] Shannon Mattern, however, has pointed to the limitations of the platform model by detailing the implications of the metaphor: "The platform doesn't have any implied depth, so we're not inclined to look underneath or behind it, or to question its structure." Mattern goes on to show how various metaphors for the library "obfuscate all the wires, pulleys, lights and scaffolding that you inevitably find underneath and above that stage—and the casting, staging and direction that determine what happens *on* the stage, and that allow it to function *as* a stage."[13] In lieu of this flattening, Mattern imagines multiple intersecting scales: "Thus we need to understand how our libraries function *as,* and as *part of,* infrastructural ecologies—as sites where spatial, technological, intellectual and social infrastructures shape and inform one another." Similarly, Emily Drabinski calls the library a "structuring machine" that not only organizes existing knowledge but determines what counts as knowledge and to whom.[14] DH lives in the interstices of this machine.

The stacks, like the library as a whole, are not just repositories. They are epistemological structures that order the questions we can ask of them. In the following sections, we browse through three of the stacks that sustain DH: first, the physical library stacks that are part of the information architecture that arranges scholarship; second, the technology stack of globalized computing that distributes scholarship; and finally, the social stack of human relationships that make everything possible. Each stack reveals something different about DH and the patterns of labor embedded within it.[15] Drawing on the sociological lessons of the zombie category, we aim to disaggregate *the stacks* as discursive assemblages, thereby exposing the mechanisms through which infrastructure effaces its own social labor while also rendering social labor a visible component of infrastructure.

Physical Stacks

Load-bearing bookshelves shape the library's architecture from the inside out. In a popular, well-illustrated book *The Book on the Bookshelf,* Henry Petroski provides an engaging history of Western shelf technologies, from ancient scrolls to medieval chained books to modern steel engineering to rolling compact shelves.[16] Petroski highlights the architectural arrangements that accompany changes in shelving technology. In a similar vein, Lydia Pyne describes how the cast-iron book stacks manufactured by Snead & Co. around the turn of the twentieth century transformed library architecture and services.[17] Standardized shelves enabled libraries to house more on-site collections, which in turn allowed open-stack browsing. Cast-iron stacks were the literal infrastructure that held up buildings, as the New York Public Library infamously discovered when it proposed to remove book stacks from its flagship Fifth Avenue research building.[18] In this case, the stacks could not be superseded by a futuristic renovation. The feat of engineering that made the stacks bear the weight of the building as well as the books illustrates how zombie categories maintain use-value through time.

When the stacks are not actually bearing weight, they become symbols of technological change. Compact shelving, where passage between the stacks is reduced to one opening at a time, are one mechanical solution to storage. But when space runs out, books and shelves move off site. In other cases, shelves move not to accommodate more books but more people, as square footage is dedicated to digital workspaces, administrative departments, coffee bars, and other social arrangements within the library. Furthermore, in all these pressures to maximize the dynamic uses of square footage, the availability of e-books through university press subscriptions and consortia collections enables libraries to increase their holdings while they shift from physical to digital shelf space.

These changes in the stacks' role provoke a range of emotional responses. Some express unbridled optimism for the positive impact of the "learning commons."[19] Others lament the loss of the "leisurely contemplation" of wandering through the stacks.[20] Both ends of this spectrum of feeling about the *stacks* occlude the inequities built into both past and future. Many traditionally built stacks, for example, are not wheelchair accessible; high and low shelves can be out of reach for a variety of reasons. The golden age of browsing that many look back to was also an era of stratification and exclusion.[21] And the discourse of serendipitous browsing, in which a scholar "discovers" material "hidden" in the stacks, effaces the labor of library workers who have organized material so that it can be discovered.[22] Meanwhile, the newly articulated spaces that have displaced some stacks cannot possibly deliver on all that their promoters have promised.[23] Amidst all these tensions, the stacks and the print materials that they house persist beyond the exaggerated reports of their death (i.e., that libraries are "throwing away all the books").

The stacks as bookshelves thus function as a zombie category in the sense that they are made to mean something in the present that they did not mean in the past. When they are identified with a nostalgia for a time before algorithms, they are made to obscure the ordering principles that they have always supported in one way or another. In this guise, they are part of the emotional infrastructure that enables digital technology. Even as they seem to be just standing there, they are compensating for the epistemic shifts wrought by the digital. These are zombie moves. And DH, as a scholarly practice that takes place partly in the library, relies on them—both conceptually and architecturally.

Technological Stacks

In today's library, the problem of shelf space for scholarship goes beyond the physical stacks to encompass the digital. Just like print scholarship, DH projects need physical homes. But it is not always obvious where in the university they should be "shelved." Platforms like Shared Shelf from JSTOR (which enables the storing and sharing of media files) make this issue apparent in the name itself (the platform's new name, JSTOR Forum, is another physical metaphor with a new set of technical and social implications). DH scholarship is thus embedded within the stacks of digital processing that are gathered within the library but are not centered there—or anywhere. As such, DH infrastructure includes a multitude of technological stacks. Each is already a metaphor built on a metaphor, alerting us to the highly probable presence of zombie categories.

In digital processing, the software *stack* is the layering of operations required to produce a result. It begins with the hardware that stores basic code, which enables an operating system to support more code in the form of programming languages, which organize more code as software, which enables interactions with inputs from various sources (keyboard, touch screen, microphone, etc.), which are processed back into the software for further distribution to other stacks. The operations need to take place in a fixed sequence in order for the applications to achieve their intended outcomes.

The ubiquity of technology has made the software stack a highly portable metaphor. John Herrman has recently reflected on how "stack logic" has spread far from software applications to characterize almost any organized function with multiple dependent parts.[24] Herrman begins and ends with John Daugman's influential "Brain Metaphor and Brain Theory," where Daugman shows how theories of brain function have tracked innovations in material infrastructure throughout history, from hydraulics to combustion engines to computers.[25] This observation shows both the limits and powers of metaphors, which slip from analogy to description only to become constraining blinders on our powers of observation. Daugman's historical view amounts to an illustration of how zombie categories keep eating the brain.

Similarly, the software stack seems to be taking over the world. The most elaborated conception of this process is Benjamin Bratton's *The Stack,* where computing structures become a global megastructure that transcends national boundaries and serves as a new form of sovereignty. The global stack is totalizing: it rises from raw materials mining at the bottom to hardware manufacture as the next layer, and thence upward to network infrastructure to web programming to user interface design to tech support. It has emerged as "an accidental megastructure, one that we are building both deliberately and unwittingly and is in turn building us in its own image."[26] This Stack is not just a new technology, but operates as "a scale of technology that comes to absorb functions of the state and the work of governance."[27] Bratton's stack-as-world has six layers: Earth, Cloud, City, Address, Interface, and User. Their layered interdependence defines a global infrastructure that orders every aspect of life.

The Stack as global megastructure reveals how the library itself functions as a zombie category whenever it is considered primarily as a repository. Library and information studies have long recognized that the library already includes interconnected technology stacks. Core functions like accessing books can take place via licensing with multinational corporations that provide password-protected digital resources. Browsing takes place via database rather than via shelf reading. Internal services, such as communication, record keeping, and financial management can be outsourced to cloud-based enterprise systems. In a Möbius strip of interlocking processes, the library both contains technology stacks and is subsumed by them. When it comes time to find a shelf for DH scholarship, we need to account for both dimensions. We need to continue to stack layers rather than displacing the old with the new—or treating the new (a digital project) like the old (a book to put on a library shelf). If we don't recognize the zombies here, we'll be lost in the stacks. But if we get rid of the zombies, we'll have nowhere to go. DH scholars need a stack-savvy approach to navigating the interstices that the library has become.

Social Stacks

Technology stacks and physical stacks rest on and are supported by social stacks— the people without whom there is no stacking. In the library, the social stack encompasses a whole range of activities often considered *services:* from the shelf reading that keeps the books in order to metadata curation that keeps the online catalogue functioning to database training for students and faculty. In response to DH, many libraries, even small ones, have created new services assigned to the "DH librarian." While appearing to reflect substantial changes in research methods, including a new collaborative ethos, the role is often haunted by the zombie category of the librarian as support staff. Many scholars are used to the invisibility of library services: they don't see shelves, just books. As a result, various kinds of social labor go unrecognized, which in turn compromises DH scholarship. Yet project development and preservation are social problems as much as technological ones.

The service model effaces all kinds of labor, none more perniciously than emotional labor. As Paige Morgan has written, this labor is not only invisible but generally viewed negatively—and yet the functions of managing expectations, calculating risk, and boosting confidence are essential to a successful DH project.[28] It is the DH librarian who most often has to handle any number of questions that begin "why can't you just..." ("... scan everything and put it online?" or "... maintain my website after I retire?"). Whether these questions are rhetorical or answer-seeking, they demand emotional labor that goes unrecognized as labor because it does not seem to lead to a tangible product. DH librarians must also manage their own emotions in the face of marginalization, as Alexis Logsdon, Amy Mars, and Heather Tompkins have elucidated. In order to maintain social relations, they invest labor in performing certain styles of collaboration regardless of personal feelings.[29] Emotional labor is in fact integral to all the stacks and thus to DH infrastructure: it is a form of expertise. By incorporating the social into our understandings of the stacks, it might become possible to redistribute emotional labor more equitably throughout the stacks.

The visibility of labor correlates to the attribution of credit, another dimension of the social stack that sustains DH. Martin Paul Eve has recently pointed out how authorship serves as "a proxy to credit many different labour systems that were necessary for the work."[30] The collaborative nature of DH scholarship, therefore, should entail authorial naming strategies similar to scientific papers, for which the list of contributors can stretch to double and even triple digits. Yet even the contributor roles taxonomy (CRediT) referenced by Eve does not include the social and emotional contributions often made by librarians.[31] What would have to change, culturally and socially, for scholarly discourse in the humanities to value and credit this labor? The DH community is in the midst of articulating—although we have not yet equitably implemented—a model for acknowledging and compensating those who labor in the DH stacks.[32] We remain too closely tied to the zombie category of the solo author, a model that has in fact never accurately reflected the social (and gendered) nature of scholarship.[33] Lauren Tilton and Taylor Arnold discuss in their essay for this volume how even in seemingly collaborative spaces like library DH labs, the force of the solo author as a legible category of scholarly credit tends to efface collaborative labor.[34] DH has yet to absorb models of collaborative creation that would routinely recognize the whole social stack as coauthor.

Finally, institutional arrangements for DH directly affect social relations and therefore the nature of scholarship. Where there are staff positions and administrative units that include the phrase *digital humanities*, the social stack is aligned with resource allocations. Conversely, the absence of such titles can create a negative emotional relationship to DH, producing a sense of scarcity or "center envy."[35] Yet successful DH programs, initiatives, and teams also arise organically out of social connections instead of being planned by a centralized hierarchy. Crucial roles are often filled by contingent laborers in the university's knowledge economy: graduate students, postdocs, and people in grant-funded term positions. Even as we recognize these inequities both within and across institutions, we can also recognize that there is no idealized arrangement for DH that would transcend all local circumstances. In the end, DH depends first and foremost on social relationships that are not wholly determined by org charts. The risk in this approach, as Elizabeth Rodrigues and Rachel Schnepper warn in their chapter in this volume, is that social relationships can lack institutional support and commitment: "Personality-dependent collaborations are not infrastructure; they are lucky happenstance."[36] The "lucky" nature of social relationships can help transcend institutional boundaries, however. Pinpointing the *when* of infrastructure is thus especially important for the social stack, so that relationships are dynamic rather than static, capable of change rather than fixed to familiar hierarchies.

Social relations remain shadowed by zombie categories whenever they rely on individualistic, monetized, or fixed models of value. Scholars need to engage with the library not as clients exploiting a service but as partners in an ecosystem of knowledge. If, as Sheila Anderson argues, infrastructure is conceptualized as itself a form of research, all participants' intellectual contributions become visible parts of a complex stack that integrates the spatial, technological, and social. Absent such mutually informing engagement, Anderson posits, digital humanists themselves will be "defined as servants and not as scholars."[37] The social stack works like a zombie when it animates old hierarchies that the ethos of DH was meant to end.

Stack is the tie-breaker in the old DH debate between *hack* and *yack*.[38] As Laura has observed elsewhere, the people who make things and the people who critique things all need to stack things.[39] The stacks are a useful metaphor for DH because they press together people, places, and things. Of course, unraveling metaphors is not a foolproof approach to exposing the realities of labor or the material challenges of preservation. However, it is a necessary step in the critical analysis of infrastructure. All the stacks—physical, technological, social—are fundamental to libraries' infrastructure. Assessing their work in the knowledge economy is the responsibility of everyone who works in the stacks: librarians, faculty, students, programmers, administrators, and so on. Librarians bear a special responsibility as the designated guardians of library infrastructure. Positioned at the hub of collaboration, where shelf space meets budgets, they have unique capacities to interpret the rapidly changing landscape of digital scholarship. Further, the library can directly restructure ethical collaboration as a defining feature of the digital humanities, as Roopika Risam, Justin Snow, and Susan Edwards have argued.[40] We can also borrow categories from critical pedagogy, such as the *progressive stack,* a technique for disrupting group habits by intentionally "stacking" participation in new ways.[41] On the way, however, let us be aware of zombies and the work that they do. Every metaphor will have its consequences.

Notes

1. Warren, ByrneSim, and Braunstein, "Remix the Medieval Manuscript."

2. Abbate, *Recoding Gender;* Shetterly, *Hidden Figures;* and Harris and Shetterly, "Human Computers at NASA."

3. Anderson, "What Are Research Infrastructures?"

4. Star and Ruhleder, "Steps toward an Ecology of Infrastructure," 113.

5. "stack, n.," *OED Online.*

6. Warren, "Post-Philology."

7. Warren, "Philology in Ruins."

8. Beck and Beck-Gernsheim, *Individualization,* xxiv. The term has spread kind of like an infectious outbreak whose origins are hard to trace. Many vectors do ultimately lead back to Beck, but unfootnoted appropriations abound. The most recent thought-provoking entry point is Lauro, *Zombie Theory.*

9. Beck and Beck-Gernsheim, *Individualization,* 27.

10. Beck and Beck-Gernsheim, *Individualization,* 204.

11. Birns, *Theory after Theory,* 65. For more details, see Warren, "Ar-ar-archive."

12. Weinberger, "Library as Platform."

13. Mattern, "Library as Infrastructure," From a media studies perspective, however, Anable has recently suggested that "platform studies" can open rather than foreclose deeper inquiry; see "Platform Studies."

14. See Drabinski, "Standard Practice."

15. Each of the following sections is adapted and expanded from Braunstein, "Open Stacks."

16. Petroski, *The Book on the Bookshelf.*

17. Pyne, *Bookshelf.*

18. Pogrebin, "Public Library Is Abandoning Disputed Plan."

19. For example, Holland, "21st-Century Libraries."

20. For example, "Banishing the Books." Most recently, see Zaretsky, "The Welcoming Labyrinth."

21. For example, Knott, *Not Free, Not for All;* and Beilin, "The Academic Research Library's White Past ."

22. Verhoeven, "As Luck Would Have It," especially 13–18; and Bowker and Star, *Sorting Things Out.*

23. Storey has described a "commons contagion" that has led some university administrators to transform spaces into learning commons without full engagement of library stakeholders: "Commons Consent."

24. Herrman, "New Technology Is Built on a 'Stack.'"

25. Daugman, "Brain Metaphor and Brain Theory."

26. Bratton, *The Stack*, 5.

27. Bratton, *The Stack*, 7.

28. In "Not Your DH Teddy-Bear," Morgan addresses how changes in research infrastructure can have emotional consequences.

29. Logsdon, Mars, and Tompkins, "Claiming Expertise from Betwixt and Between."

30. Eve, "On Being Open in Practice."

31. "CRediT."

32. Despite many attempts to draft a "Collaborators' Bill of Rights," few of these have been widely implemented. See "Collaborators' Bill of Rights" (https://archive.mith.umd .edu/offthetracks/recommendations/) Maryland Institute for Technology in the Humanities, and "A Student Collaborator's Bill of Rights," UCLA Center for Digital Humanities.

33. This was ably—and ironically—demonstrated by the *#thanksfortyping* Twitter thread, which itself was started by a male academic after historian Alexis Coe had written about her research into academic inequity in "Being Married Helps Professors Get Ahead."

34. Tilton and Arnold, "What's in a Name?"

35. Schaffner and Erway, "Does Every Research Library Need a Digital Humanities Center?"

36. Rodrigues and Schnepper, "After Autonomy."

37. Anderson, "What Are Research Infrastructures?" 6.

38. Nowviskie excavates (and puts to rest) this zombie metaphor in "On the Origins of 'Hack' and 'Yack.'"

39. Kim, "6 Questions for a Digital Humanities Librarian."

40. Risam, Snow, and Edwards, "Building an Ethical Digital Humanities Community."

41. For example, Gannon, "The Progressive Stack."

Bibliography

Abbate, Janet. *Recoding Gender: Women's Changing Participation in Computing.* Cambridge, Mass.: MIT Press, 2012.

Anable, Aubrey. "Platform Studies." *Feminist Media Histories* 4, no. 2 (2018): 135–40.

Anderson, Sheila. "What Are Research Infrastructures?" *International Journal of Humanities and Arts Computing* 7, no. 1–2 (2013): 4–23. https://doi.org/10.3366/ijhac.2013.0078.

"Banishing the Books." *New York Post,* January 31, 2012. https://nypost.com/2012/01/31 /banishing-the-books/.

Beck, Ulrich, and Elisabeth Beck-Gernsheim. *Individualization: Institutionalized Individualism and Its Social and Political Consequences.* Translated by Patrick Camiller. London: Sage, 2002.

Beilin, Ian. "The Academic Research Library's White Past and Present." In *Topographies of Whiteness: Mapping Whiteness in Library and Information Science,* edited by Gina Schlesselman-Tarango, 79–98. Sacramento, Calif.: Library Juice Press, 2017.

Birns, Nicholas. *Theory after Theory: An Intellectual History of Literary Theory from 1950 to the Early 21st Century.* Peterborough, Ont.: Broadview Press, 2010.

Bowker, Geoffrey C., and Susan Leigh Star. *Sorting Things Out: Classification and Its Consequences.* Cambridge, Mass.: MIT Press, 1999.

Bratton, Benjamin. *The Stack: On Software and Sovereignty.* Cambridge, Mass.: MIT Press, 2015.

Braunstein, Laura. "Open Stacks: Making DH Labor Visible." *dh+lib,* June 7, 2017. http://acrl.ala.org/dh/2017/06/07/open-stacks-making-dh-labor-visible/.

Coe, Alexis. "Being Married Helps Professors Get Ahead, But Only If They're Male." *The Atlantic,* January 17, 2013. https://www.theatlantic.com/sexes/archive/2013/01/being-married-helps-professors-get-ahead-but-only-if-theyre-male/267289/.

Daugman, John. "Brain Metaphor and Brain Theory." In *Computational Neuroscience,* edited by Eric Schwartz, 9–18. Cambridge, Mass.: MIT Press, 1993.

Drabinski, Emily. "Standard Practice: Libraries as Structuring Machines." *Parameters* (blog), July 5, 2017. http://parameters.ssrc.org/2017/07/standard-practice-libraries-as-structuring-machines/.

Eve, Martin Paul. "On Being Open in Practice: Giving Credit Where It Is Due." *Open Research at Reading* (blog), April 3, 2017. http://blogs.reading.ac.uk/open-research/2017/04/03/on-being-open-in-practice-giving-credit-where-it-is-due/.

Gannon, Kevin. "The Progressive Stack and Standing for Inclusive Teaching." *The Tattooed Prof* (blog), October 20, 2017. http://www.thetattooedprof.com/2017/10/20/the-progressive-stack-and-standing-for-inclusive-teaching/.

Harris, Duchess, and Margot Lee Shetterly. "Human Computers at NASA." Macalester College. http://omeka.macalester.edu/humancomputerproject/about, accessed February 6, 2020.

Herrman, John. "New Technology Is Built on a 'Stack': Is That the Best Way to Understand Everything Else, Too?" *New York Times Magazine,* April 11, 2017. https://nyti.ms/2omklRV.

Holland, Beth. "21st-Century Libraries: The Learning Commons." *Edutopia* (blog), January 14, 2015. https://www.edutopia.org/blog/21st-century-libraries-learning-commons-beth-holland.

Kim, Joshua. "6 Questions for a Digital Humanities Librarian." *Inside Higher Ed* (blog), August 17, 2016. https://www.insidehighered.com/blogs/technology-and-learning/6-questions-digital-humanities-librarian.

Knott, Cheryl. *Not Free, Not for All: Public Libraries in the Age of Jim Crow.* Amherst: University of Massachusetts Press, 2015.

Lauro, Sarah Juliet, ed. *Zombie Theory: A Reader.* Minneapolis: University of Minnesota Press, 2017.

Logsdon, Alexis, Amy Mars, and Heather Tompkins. "Claiming Expertise from Betwixt and Between: Digital Humanities Librarians, Emotional Labor, and Genre Theory." *College & Undergraduate Libraries* 24, nos. 2–4 (2017): 155–70.

Mattern, Shannon. "Library as Infrastructure." *Places Journal* (June 2014). https://places journal.org/article/library-as-infrastructure/.

Morgan, Paige. "Not Your DH Teddy-Bear: Or, Emotional Labor Is Not Going Away." *dh+lib,* July 29, 2016. http://acrl.ala.org/dh/2016/07/29/not-your-dh-teddy-bear/.

Nowviskie, Bethany. "On the Origins of 'Hack' and 'Yack.'" In *Debates in the Digital Humanities: Histories and Futures of the Digital Humanities,* edited by Lauren Klein and Matthew Gold. Minneapolis: University of Minnesota Press, 2016. http://dhde bates.gc.cuny.edu/debates/text/58.

Petroski, Henry. *The Book on the Bookshelf.* New York: Knopf, 1999.

Pogrebin, Robin. "Public Library Is Abandoning Disputed Plan for Landmark." *New York Times,* May 8, 2014, A1. https://nyti.ms/2oA7FJD.

Pyne, Lydia. *Bookshelf.* New York: Bloomsbury, 2016.

Risam, Roopika, Justin Snow, and Susan Edwards. "Building an Ethical Digital Humanities Community: Librarian, Faculty, and Student Collaboration." *College & Undergraduate Libraries* 24, nos. 2–4 (2017): 337–49.

Rodrigues, Elizabeth, and Rachel Schnepper. "After Autonomy: Digital Humanities Practices in Small Liberal Arts Colleges & Higher Education as Collaboration." In *People, Practice, Power: Digital Humanities outside the Center,* edited by Anne McGrail, Angel David Nieves, and Siobhan Senier. Minneapolis: University of Minnesota Press, 2021.

Schaffner, Jennifer, and Ricky Erway. "Does Every Research Library Need a Digital Humanities Center?" Dublin, Ohio: OCLC Research, 2014. https://www.oclc.org /content/dam/research/publications/library/2014/oclcresearch-digital-humanities -center-2014.pdf.

Shetterly, Margot Lee. *Hidden Figures: The American Dream and the Untold Story of the Black Women Mathematicians Who Helped Win the Space Race.* New York: HarperCollins, 2016.

Star, Susan Leigh, and Karen Ruhleder. "Steps toward an Ecology of Infrastructure: Design and Access for Large Information Spaces." *Information Systems Research* 7, no. 1 (1996): 111–34.

Storey, Colin. "Commons Consent: Librarians, Architects, and Community Culture in Co-Creating Library Learning Spaces." *Library Management* 36, no. 8–9 (2015): 570–83.

Tilton, Lauren, and Taylor Arnold. "What's in a Name?" In *People, Practice, Power: Digital Humanities outside the Center,* edited by Anne McGrail, Angel David Nieves, and Siobhan Senier. Minneapolis: University of Minnesota Press, 2021.

Verhoeven, Deb. "As Luck Would Have It: Serendipity and Solace in Digital Research Infrastructure." *Feminist Media Histories* 2, no. 1 (2016): 7–28.

Warren, Michelle R. "Ar-ar-archive." Paper presented at the conference Surface, Symptom, and the State of Critique, University of Texas, Austin, February 9–12, 2012. http:// dx.doi.org/10.17613/M6KC7V.

Warren, Michelle R. "Philology in Ruins." *Florilegium* 32 (2015): 59–76. http://dx.doi .org/10.3138/flor.32.003.

Warren, Michelle R. "Post-Philology." In *Postcolonial Moves: Medieval through Modern,* edited by Patricia Clare Ingham and Michelle R. Warren, 19–45. New York: Palgrave Macmillan, 2003.

Warren, Michelle R., Bay Lauris ByrneSim, and Laura Braunstein. "Remix the Medieval Manuscript: Experiments in Digital Infrastructure." *Archive Journal* (May 2018). http://www.archivejournal.net/essays/remix-the-medieval-manuscript-experiments-with-digital-infrastructure/.

Weinberger, David. "Library as Platform." *Library Journal* (September 4, 2012). http://lj.libraryjournal.com/2012/09/future-of-libraries/by-david-weinberger/#.

Zaretsky, Robert. "The Welcoming Labyrinth: What We Gain and Lose as Libraries Change." *Chronicle of Higher Education,* May 8, 2018. https://www.chronicle.com/article/The-Welcoming-Labyrinth-What/243364.

The Directory Paradox

QUINN DOMBROWSKI

"Getting started with digital humanities" is a well-populated genre in the academic literature connected with the field. These books and articles fill a continuing gap in the formal training of most humanities scholars: a practical orientation to the tools, methods, and community norms of the digital humanities. In addition to formal publications, there are countless blog posts, mailing list threads, and web pages (many contextualizing the "getting started" process within an individual institution[1]) that aim to help individual scholars find entry points for engaging with the digital humanities, even in contexts where there is little or no institutional support for doing so. Within this body of literature, a subset is written for an audience of librarians who are interested in how their library can support, or partner with, scholars in their digital humanities work.[2] Relatedly, there is a segment of library studies literature that familiarizes librarians with individual tools and websites (including directories) that may be relevant to the scholars with whom they engage.[3] Less common but still represented are pieces written for an IT- and administration-oriented audience.[4] Across these pieces written for divergent audiences, directories are frequently referred to as an important component of digital humanities infrastructure, though the term "infrastructure" itself is rarely used. Some articles include a categorized list of specific resources.[5] Others make more general reference to "online portals."[6]

For all the attention and praise given to directories, sustainability remains a major weakness. The low technical barrier to entry makes it easy to create a directory: a simple HTML web page, using authoring tools provided by any number of free services that also offer no-cost hosting, suffices for getting started. Crowdsourcing is often employed to distribute the maintenance burden, rather than leaving it the long-term responsibility of the directory's creator. Directories typically come into existence to address a specific information-seeking need within a particular community; as time passes and the needs and interests of those communities evolve, some of those directories fall out of use, fail to be updated, and are abandoned or cease to exist. While directories are typically created with high hopes of serving as a valuable resource for years to come, a life cycle that concludes with the demise of the project is neither unexpected nor inherently problematic.[7] There is, however, cause for concern in cases in which significant time and financial resources have gone toward developing a directory that successfully attracts a large user base and develops a reputation as a valuable resource, but the directory is unable to maintain the resources necessary for ongoing curation and updates. This unfortunate situation has been the rule more than the exception.

This paper takes the digital resource tools (DiRT) directory, formerly known as Bamboo DiRT, and as DiRT (Digital Research Tools) prior to that, as the primary exemplar from which to argue for the inherent long-term instability of directories, even given favorable conditions of widespread attention, generous funding, integration with other projects, a steering committee, and an editorial board. DiRT's evolution highlights numerous tensions within the field of digital humanities, including the status and autonomy of alt-ac roles, funding models for common-good resources, the limits of voluntarism, and the collision between shadow work and familial responsibilities. The DH Toychest and TAPoR provide points of contrast as long-running directory projects led by individual, tenured faculty members that have attained a greater level of stability as a consequence of their directors' positions but face similar challenges over a longer time frame.

Origins of DiRT

In spring 2008, Lisa Spiro, then the director of the Digital Media Center at Rice University, launched *Digital Research Tools* (DiRT) with an initial editorial team consisting of five library colleagues at Rice and at Sam Houston State University. She described it in a blog post announcing the soft launch of the directory:

> Not everyone has the time or inclination to read blogs, software reviews, and listserv announcements obsessively, but now researchers can quickly identify relevant tools by checking out the newly-launched Digital Research Tools (DiRT) wiki. DiRT lists dozens of useful tools for discovering, organizing, analyzing, visualizing, sharing and disseminating information, such as tools for compiling bibliographies, taking notes, analyzing texts, and visualizing data.[8]

From a technical perspective, DiRT was minimalist but functional, serving the project's goals of information dissemination in the absence of technical resources or a mandate to implement the project. It used the free tier of the PBWiki service and consisted of 30 initial categories corresponding to some kind of activity (e.g., Build and Share Collections, and Communicate with Colleagues). Each category was represented by a single wiki page, which contained a definition of the category and an alphabetical list of relevant tools, with a link to and brief description of each. Some listings included annotations about platform (e.g., web based, Mac, Windows), cost, and licensing (e.g., open source versus proprietary). An RSS feed was available for monitoring site updates.

The public launch of DiRT in June was briefly covered in the *Chronicle of Higher Education,* and the site quickly gained traction.[9] In August 2008, Spiro reflected positively on the project's reception and expansion, including offers from Dan Cohen (Tools Center Wiki) and Alan Liu (Digital Toolchest) to share their data with the developing DiRT. But the conclusion of the blog post spoke directly to the fact that directories require ongoing upkeep, and it is unrealistic for an individual— particularly in an alternative academic career track—to do that work indefinitely: "I'll end with an invitation: Please contribute to DiRT. You can sign up to be an editor or reviewer, recommend tools to be added, or provide feedback via our survey."[10]

The development of directories in the late 2000s spoke to the challenges faced by digital humanists at the time. Although more people were doing digital humanities, many individual practitioners felt isolated. Directories provided an easy way to find out what tools others were using and what projects were under development, even in the absence of digital humanities colleagues within one's own institution. When presented with the opportunity through the Mellon-funded Project Bamboo initiative to shape the development of technical cyberinfrastructure to scale the deployment of digital humanities tools and services, scholars resoundingly advocated for more directories instead.[11]

From DiRT to Bamboo DiRT

Between 2008 and 2009, DiRT's content and audience expanded, and it became a familiar referent in discussions of digital humanities tools in general and how to get started with digital humanities, specifically.[12] A 2009 Rice University news article notes that "DiRT is already generating a positive buzz," noting praise for the site from the *Chronicle of Higher Education*'s *Wired Campus* blog, the National Endowment for the Humanities' Office of Digital Humanities, and the Humanities, Arts, Science and Technology Advanced Collaboratory.[13] Nonetheless, the public enthusiasm for DiRT failed to translate into the hoped-for groundswell of edits. Spiro remained primarily responsible for maintaining DiRT, while being drawn into other projects. The tools and projects listed in DiRT and other directories were themselves emerging, changing, and falling into disuse. As a result, links would quickly become deprecated, and keeping up with these changes was challenging. As time passed, the increasingly stale content became more evident. A 2010 review of DiRT on the American Historical Society blog notes "While some of DiRT's pages have not been recently updated, the site still offers a wealth of information we found worthy of being highlighted."[14]

In 2011, Spiro took a new position with the National Institute for Technology in Liberal Education (NITLE) as Director of NITLE Labs.[15] At the time, maintaining

DiRT was not seen as a priority for NITLE, and Spiro was encouraged to transition responsibility for its upkeep. Major shifts in job responsibilities are a common aspect of alt-ac career paths, jeopardizing the stability of "passion projects," such as directories, that emerged in a different workplace context. Luckily for DiRT, Project Bamboo—more than a year into its technical implementation phase—saw an opportunity to refocus a technical deliverable, the tool and services registry (TSR), as a scholar-oriented community resource that would generate positive publicity for a cyberinfrastructure initiative that was perceived as opaque at best.[16]

Following extensive internal analysis, discussion, and debate, Bamboo project staff decided in July 2011 to eliminate the TSR as a component of Bamboo's technical infrastructure in favor of developing a scholar-facing TSR based on DiRT.[17] Official discussions with Lisa Spiro about a merger commenced in August 2011, and within a week, I (at the time the scholarly technology manager at the University of Chicago, a partner institution on the Project Bamboo grant) developed an initial prototype of Bamboo DiRT, a Drupal-based reformulation of the directory in which each tool would have its own page and unique URL, with metadata standardized across the entries. I intended this re-architecture to facilitate commenting, reviews, more precise and shareable links, and data exchange with other directories.

The previous iteration of DiRT had failed to sufficiently incentivize ongoing crowdsourced contributions. I hoped to more effectively leverage the reputation economy by automatically tracking who created or edited each tool profile, with revisions publicly viewable and attributable to users, as on Wikipedia. A list of a user's contributions, with clickable links back to the tool profile in question, automatically appeared as part of each user's profile, with the goal of making visible the unseen labor that goes into directory maintenance and conferring some sort of credit that contributors could point to as part of a digital CV. In practice this was ineffective, because although DiRT was perceived as generally valuable, there were many competing and more visible opportunities for engaging with the digital humanities community that did more for building one's reputation (e.g., weighing in on the latest debate or outrage on Twitter) than adding or editing tool listings.

Project Bamboo saw the creation of a large-scale consortium as an essential component of its own long-term financial sustainability but deferred consortial development until an anticipated second phase. As a whole, Bamboo staff felt that a similar model was necessary for Bamboo DiRT before it officially launched, albeit with the focus more on defraying the time involved in sustaining the site rather than the modest financial resources (hosting costs) it required. In May 2012, we put out a call for a curatorial/steering committee with the responsibility of updating and expanding DiRT, engaging in outreach, and attending monthly steering committee meetings. The response was modest but sufficient: three people applied directly in response to the call, I was already in touch with a user who had become a frequent contributor, and Lisa Spiro and two Project Bamboo staff members (project manager Seth Denbo and myself) formed the initial committee which began to meet monthly to discuss topics including metadata standardization, adding new tools, and potential partnerships.[18] After a very active first month that included a site redesign, metadata cleanup, and the addition of hundreds of new tools, Bamboo DiRT had its official launch in July 2012, just in time to send promotional pens (analog tools) to the DH 2012 conference.[19] Providing tangible "swag" at the international conference for this project associated with Project Bamboo was meant to signal that the amorphous cyberinfrastructure project still existed and was producing something valuable that merited exploration and consideration by the community. A branded pen, moreover, could remind its user of Bamboo DiRT and potentially spur a visit, supporting the directory's relevance through its continued use.

DiRT Directory and Mellon Funding

During discussions with the Mellon Foundation about Project Bamboo's ultimately unsuccessful second-phase proposal, program officers indicated an interest in supporting DiRT as a project separate from the defunct Bamboo. Having relocated to UC Berkeley shortly before the demise of Bamboo, I began work on a proposal to the Mellon Foundation that would fund a technical integration with DHCommons (a project directory I had cofounded with Ryan Cordell) and Commons in a Box (CBOX), a new scholarly networking platform that had been adopted as the basis for the Mellon-funded MLA Commons, as well as numerous regional DH initiatives. In addition, the grant would support the process of identifying an organizational home for DiRT. Without being part of a larger Project Bamboo development effort, DiRT fit awkwardly into the portfolio of UC Berkeley's central Research IT department, just as there was no groundswell of support to continue DiRT at Rice University after Lisa Spiro's move to NITLE. As a general community resource, it made more sense for DiRT to ally itself with a larger-scale organization with a mission that DiRT directly supported. The Mellon Foundation funded this proposal, beginning in September 2013.

Technical development constituted the majority of the work laid out in the grant. Centering the grant around technical deliverables aligned it to well-established funding models and programs, making it a relatively straightforward funding request. Each of these new technical components was intended to set the site up for success as a valued digital humanities resource for at least the following five years. However, technical development for DiRT without a realistic, sustainable model for ensuring the currency and expansion of its content was akin to directing a ship's crew to optimize the rigging while steadfastly ignoring the leaking hull.

The technical developments implemented for the DiRT site held potential for supporting DiRT's ongoing relevance, if the core issue of basic upkeep were addressed somehow. A *tool list* feature enabled any registered user to generate and export a list of that user's favorite tools, and was used by the ADHO Geohumanities Special Interest Group to power the GeoDiRT listing of geospatial tools on their website. I hoped other groups would replicate this model, drawing upon discipline-specific subsets of DiRT's data and improving those listings on DiRT itself rather than creating a separate directory whose ongoing care and attention would compete with, rather than contribute to, DiRT. Another related effort was the development of the TaDiRAH taxonomy, a partnership between DiRT and DARIAH-DE to create a shared digital humanities taxonomy that could apply to the full range of digital humanities activities and scholarly products for meaningful exchange of linked open data.[20] I used this newly created taxonomy, whose development was informed by the use case of DiRT, to replace the ad hoc tool taxonomies characteristic of many directory projects, and I also added a SPARQL query interface to DiRT.[21]

For the integrations with CBOX and DHCommons, developing the DiRT API was a trivial task, requiring minimal configuration of the services module created and supported by the international open source Drupal developer community. This was sufficient for Matthew Gold and Boone Gorges from the CUNY Graduate Center to develop an integration between DiRT and CBOX that would bring "DiRT's tool listings directly to people in an environment where they can discuss digital tools and share their expertise and suggestions within trusted communities."[22] When central IT staff at UC Berkeley became unavailable to do the integration between DiRT and DHCommons, a serendipitous encounter with Dean Irvine from Dalhousie University led to an alternative staffing model, as the integration between DiRT and DHCommons became one of the first projects of Irvine's new Agile Humanities Agency.[23] I adapted this DiRT/DHCommons integration code to additionally support integration between DiRT and Methodi.ca, a sister project to TAPoR under development in early 2015, with the intention of publishing "recipes," that is, information about how tools could be used together.[24]

One technical development was aimed squarely at addressing the feedback that adding a tool to DiRT required too much work for people to create entries for new tools as they discovered them.[25] Leveraging the ubiquitous use of Twitter among digital humanists, tweets that followed the syntax *@dirtdirectory Tool Name http://tool-url.org/ #dhtool* would trigger the creation of a DiRT stub page for the tool that would appear only on a Twitter submissions page (similar to a list of Wikipedia stub pages) until the listing was expanded by volunteer editors. Despite early enthusiasm from the community and assurances that this approach would make the contribution process so easy that submissions would flood in, there were only six submissions ever, with five of them appearing within a month of launching the feature. This suggests that overcoming the inertia that impedes *any* contribution is by far the most fundamental challenge of crowdsourced directory maintenance and that simplifying the contribution process should be treated as a secondary concern rather than a solution of any sort.

Rebranding Bamboo DiRT to distance it from the failed cyberinfrastructure initiative and finding an organizational home aligned with DiRT's mission were the two aspects of the grant most directly connected to the long-term sustainability of the project. The former removed a source of some embarrassment, and the latter was meant to ensure that DiRT would not fall victim to local budget cuts and changes in IT organizational priorities at UC Berkeley. After putting out a call to a wide range of well-established DH, library, and higher ed IT organizations, the only responses came from ADHO member centerNet and DARIAH. centerNet's international scope, timeline for obtaining the nonprofit status necessary to receive future grant funding, and straightforward access to the ADHO web hosting infrastructure tipped the scales in its favor. ADHO hosting, now available at no cost to DiRT, nullified one of the most common threats to web-based directories and projects: the cessation of web hosting, be it through the collapse of a free service or the end of funding to cover hosting costs. But DiRT's new status as a centerNet initiative did not address either of the directory's biggest obstacles: the difficulty of maintaining a steady stream of crowdsourced additions and edits and the directory's dependence on me personally for overall coordination. Even if the directory itself were no longer under the auspices of UC Berkeley's IT organization, UC Berkeley still determined the priorities for my job. centerNet lacked paid staff who could take on those responsibilities, without the burden essentially shifting from one volunteer to another.

Content Curation and Maintenance

While developing a strategy for content curation was not within the funded scope of the Mellon grant, I pursued a number of approaches contemporaneously with the grant to ameliorate this fundamental problem. Over the course of 2013, the steering/curatorial board had served more as a consultative and project development body than an active group of curators. This trajectory was unsurprising: actively maintaining the directory is much more time-consuming and tedious than periodically weighing in on the site's development, in addition to sounding less prestigious when one is trying to justify work time spent on it. An email exchange with Christopher Erdmann (then at the Harvard-Smithsonian Center for Astrophysics) led to the conceptualization of a new editorial board for DiRT whose charge would explicitly be to address the curation and contribution gap on the site.[26] The tremendous response to this call—fifty applications in total—was a testament to the work the original steering/curatorial board and I did to develop the new DiRT and raise its profile in the DH community. The steering/curatorial board and I reviewed applications and ultimately selected thirty members for the first editorial board, aiming to capture a geographically and linguistically diverse group of participants.[27] The geographic diversity, in particular, came at a price: attempting to arrange a call for the editorial board across so many time zones proved daunting. Although the group's large size reduced the amount of work any individual was tasked to do, it required a tremendous amount of coordination overhead on my part. After the initial orientation call, I assigned each of the new editors a set of existing tool profiles in DiRT to check over, and update with the new TaDiRAH terms. The results were mixed, as not all editors were able to complete the task. The significant effort needed to organize, assign tasks to, and follow up with the editorial board made it easy to postpone that work in the face of the project's other demands, and the first call for editorial board engagement was also the last. Selecting a smaller and less geographically dispersed group for this role would have addressed some of the factors contributing to the quick demise of the editorial board, but a group of any size demands nontrivial coordination work to be effective, and with the grant's resources directed toward technical development, I simply did not have the time necessary to maintain engagement with a group of any size. The two-year commitment DiRT asked of its editorial board also would have doomed it in the long term, as most of the participants held alt-ac positions subject to the same fluctuations in funding and availability that I had experienced.

One of the most substantive outcomes of the largely failed editorial board was the opportunity to connect with colleagues outside the United States and Canada. Elena Gonzalez-Blanco, a member of DiRT's editorial board and the director of the Digital Humanities Innovation Laboratory (LINHD) at the National Distance Education University (UNED) in Madrid, initiated a Spanish translation project for DiRT, which was subsequently led by Gimena del Rio Riande, from the Argentine Center of Scientific and Technological Information of the National Scientific and Technical Research Council (CAICYT-CONICET). Even though making DiRT's content more accessible to Spanish speakers seemed like a positive development, it introduced another sustainability challenge: now both the content and its translation had to be consistently monitored and updated.

Collaborating with discipline- or methodology-focused groups seemed like a potentially more promising approach. Instead of managing a team of volunteers, DiRT could instead engage with organizations that could manage their own members as volunteers. Piloting this approach with the ADHO Geohumanities SIG led to a set of geohumanities volunteers undertaking a one-time editing pass over geospatial tools on DiRT. However, Geohumanities was no more successful than DiRT in transforming one-time volunteers into a source of ongoing curatorial support.

The Next Transition

Following the conclusion of the Mellon grant, a mix of local and other grant funding sources fundamentally reshaped the nature of my job in UC Berkeley's central research IT organization. As such, it became increasingly difficult to justify spending time on a directory of tools that were mostly not supported in any way at Berkeley itself. The website remained functional if increasingly spam-littered, requiring little technical maintenance beyond Drupal module updates, which the

ADHO sysadmin began to provide in 2016. Without my setting up monthly meetings, the DiRT board became inactive. By the summer of 2016, I acknowledged to the DiRT board that I needed to move on from the project and received their blessing in doing so. The act of leaving a project responsibly requires a significant amount of work by itself, however, and it took until early 2017 for me to formulate a specific succession plan for the project.

I engaged with Geoffrey Rockwell, the founder and long-standing director of TAPoR and the Methodi.ca Commons, about a potential merger of DiRT with TAPoR. While TAPoR had historically focused exclusively on text analysis tools, its notion of tool profiles generally aligned with DiRT's. TAPoR had stable, reliable hosting and technical support at the University of Alberta (Rockwell's home institution), and Rockwell had a long track record of ensuring the upkeep of TAPoR's content through a mix of grant funding and graduate student assistant positions. The completion of the migration of DiRT's content to TAPoR, coordinated by University of Alberta graduate student Kaitlyn Grant, was announced to the Humanist listhost in May 2018.[28] DiRT lingered online, with limited functionality after an ADHO server crash, until its domain name, unrenewed by centerNet, expired in late 2019.

Sustainability and the Directory Paradox

The sustainability challenges illustrated by DiRT's development and decline are broadly shared by digital humanities projects. The grant funding models in place for one-time technical development, digitization, or archive-building work assume that ongoing maintenance costs will be covered by the project's home institution, even when the project provides something that could be deemed infrastructure.[29] Technical maintenance costs (e.g., hosting and routine upgrades of open source platforms) are relatively straightforward to estimate, but directories are inherently more demanding than archives or finished digital humanities projects, insofar as they demand constant human intervention to maintain their currency.

Crowdsourcing is a philosophically appealing model for maintaining a directory, particularly because directories that provide information not inherently linked to time or space (e.g., tools or projects, as opposed to events or jobs) are a common good in which all members of the community can benefit from the fruits of volunteers' maintenance efforts. However, there is strong evidence from multiple projects that a volunteer-coordination role is essential for successful crowdsourcing. For the *Transcribe Bentham* project, "[f]eedback and a level of moderation were, therefore, important not only to maintain the pace and quality of transcription, but were a vital part of the general user experience, as we discovered when most regular transcribers ceased participating at the end of the fully-staffed testing period."[30] Similarly, the *Civil War Diaries Transcription* project and *Papers of Abraham Lincoln* both found crowdsourced transcription to be more expensive than hiring skilled professionals for the job, after factoring in the time spent on quality control and user engagement.[31] Arts-humanities.net had a research assistant position funded by the Arts and Humanities Research Council in the UK to work with grant recipients on filling out information for their funded projects, but the grant recipients were largely uncooperative. Once there was no longer a dedicated position to support the curatorial work, arts-humanities.net proved impossible to maintain.[32]

The two longest-running digital humanities tool directories that predate DiRT and continue to be maintained as of 2020, Geoffrey Rockwell's TAPoR and Alan Liu's DH Toychest, do not rely on crowdsourcing for content maintenance. TAPoR allows registered users to comment on and rate tools, but principal upkeep is done by paid graduate student assistants. Alan Liu maintains the DH Toychest himself. The scope of both sites is much narrower than DiRT's aspiration of gathering all tools relevant to digital humanities: TAPoR has, at least until the merger with DiRT, focused exclusively on text analysis. The DH Toychest is a highly curated list of tools Liu selects himself, meaning there is no sense of obligation for him to spend time entering and updating listings for tools in which he is not personally interested. As professors with tenure at the point when they started their respective directories, Rockwell and Liu had much more control and flexibility over their work schedule and responsibilities than either Spiro or myself in our alt-ac roles. In addition, both Lisa Spiro and I became further constrained in our ability to volunteer nonwork hours on DiRT as a consequence of intensive, daily caregiver responsibilities for young children.

The Rockwell/Liu model of tenured professors having primary or sole responsibility for the creation and upkeep of digital humanities directories is hardly ideal. These directories are inherently shaped by the interests of a privileged subset of the digital humanities community rather than the interests of alt-acs, students, or adjuncts who are not in a position to lead a directory over the course of multiple years. Furthermore, while having a professor at the helm of a directory may provide a better guarantee of institutional support for multiple decades, retirement and mortality are inescapable threats to sustainability. Stéfan Sinclair's death in summer 2020 was a stark and painful reminder of the risks that come with DH infrastructure, in this case *Voyant Tools,* being tied too closely to a single faculty member.

The structure and arrangement of digital humanities directories may evolve as the field itself becomes more complex; NeMO (the NeDiMAH Methods Ontology, 2014–2015), for instance, offered a more nuanced way to categorize resources, and anticipated that adoption of linked open data will continue apace.[33] Whether they take the form of a simple HTML page, a PHP/MySQL database, a minimal computing website,[34] or a web of data, directories are, and are likely to remain, an integral part of digital humanities infrastructure, given their value for new practitioners exploring the terrain and for experienced scholars looking for specific resources. It is unrealistic to expect to contain the impulse for creating new directories, although anyone undertaking such an endeavor should temper their enthusiasm with an understanding of the inescapable maintenance burden required for a directory to sustain itself and anticipate upfront that the directory will be relevant for a short time only. Luckily, sustainability is not a prerequisite for success: a directory of work within a particular field or subfield may serve a valuable role in catalyzing conversations between colleagues, even if it is abandoned as relationships solidify between individuals and people move on to new projects.

To reduce, or at least postpone, the high likelihood that a directory will be ephemeral after all the funding and effort feeding its development, the larger digital humanities community needs to explore and adopt new support models that can be run centrally. One approach could be to treat key directories as common-good infrastructure and ensure their upkeep by institutionalizing them as part of the Alliance of Digital Humanities Organizations (ADHO), perhaps through the creation of an annual position compensated through a mix of prestige (that can be leveraged in a student or alt-ac context) and pay, similar to the ADHO Communications Fellow. While such an approach would be at odds with current trends toward decentralization toward ADHO's constituent organizations (COs), it would be difficult to make a compelling case for one particular CO to be more responsible than others for funding upkeep of shared directories, and the relatively frequent turnover in CO executive boards would put directory maintenance at risk, even if a given CO were to take responsibility for it. The DARIAH European research infrastructure consortium, which has begun to advocate for its relevance beyond Europe, may serve as another venue for a centralized directory.[35] Since 2018, Geoffrey Rockwell and I have been meeting with Frank Fischer and Laure Barbot from DARIAH's SSH Open Marketplace project to inform the development of that initiative by sharing lessons learned from DiRT and TAPoR. These discussions will additionally serve as the basis for a presentation at the ACH 2021 conference (postponed from DH 2020) entitled "Who Needs Tool Directories? A Forum on Sustaining Discovery Portals Large and Small."

The past, present, and future of digital humanities directories such as DiRT provide vivid illustrations of tensions within the discipline as a whole, including grant funding models, individual initiative versus institutionalization, the mixed landscape of paid and volunteer labor, and how to meaningfully support and recognize work across a highly diverse group of individuals and institutional roles. After nearly a decade of being a frequently mentioned guide for digital humanities practitioners, DiRT died quietly the night its domain name expired, but this ending is only the beginning of DiRT's impact on discussions and decisions about whether and how the broad digital humanities community should take action to sustain the directories that people claim to value.

Notes

1. As one example, *The Digital Humanities Literacy Guidebook* includes both "global" and "local" resources.

2. See, for example, Vandegrift and Varner, "Evolving in Common"; Kijas, "An Introduction to Getting Started"; Rockenbach, "Digital Humanities in Libraries"; and Sula, "Digital Humanities and Libraries."

3. For example, Carr, "Review of the Darwin Manuscripts."

4. See Anne et al., "Building Capacity for Digital Humanities."

5. See, for example, Burdick et al., *Digital Humanities.*

6. For example, Anne, "Building Capacity for Digital Humanities."

7. See parallels, for instance, in the technology life cycle "whale" chart in Beck, "Technology Development Life Cycle Processes."

8. Spiro, "Digging in the DiRT."

9. Young, "New Wiki Helps Humanities Researchers."

10. Spiro, "Doing Digital Scholarship."

11. Dombrowski, "Outreach about What Is Possible."

12. For example, Finley, "DiRT."

13. Spiro, "Fondren Library Develops Research Aid."

14. Grant, "Get the DiRT on Research."

15. NITLE (2001–2018) was a community-based nonprofit initiative to help liberal arts colleges adopt emerging technologies in innovative, effective, and sustainable ways, including offering academic technology services to liberal arts colleges. Project Bamboo regularly presented at the annual NITLE Summit during the project's early years as a way to connect with liberal arts colleges, which it saw as a key constituency.

16. Dombrowski, "What Ever Happened to Project Bamboo?"

17. Project Bamboo, "TSR Decision Meeting Notes 7-22-11."

18. DiRT, "Bamboo DiRT Seeks Curatorial/Steering Committee."

19. DiRT, "Bamboo DiRT Now Out of Beta."

20. Borek et al., "TaDiRAH."

21. DiRT, "New Categories for DiRT"; and "DiRT Adopts TaDiRAH Terms."

22. DiRT, "DiRT Plugin Available for Commons in a Box."

23. Irvine, "From Angel to Agile."

24. DiRT, "DiRT Partners with TAPoR."

25. DiRT, "Add Tools to DiRT by Tweeting."

26. DiRT, "DiRT Seeks Editorial Board."

27. DiRT, "Editorial Board."

28. Grant, "Absorbing DiRT."

29. Rockwell, "As Transparent as Infrastructure."

30. Causer, Tonra, and Wallace, "Transcription Maximized; Expense Minimized?"

31. Zou, "Civil War Project"; and Cohen, "Scholars Recruit Public for Project."

32. Personal communication with Lorna Hughes, July 28, 2017.

33. Hughes, Constantopoulos, Dallas, and "Digital Methods in the Humanities."

34. Gil et al., "A Directory of Caribbean Digital Scholarship."

35. DARIAH, "DARIAH beyond Europe."

Bibliography

Anne, Kirk, Tara Carlisle, Quinn Dombrowski, Erin Glass, Tassie Gniady, Jason Jones, Joan Lippincott, John MacDermott, Megan Meredith-Lobay, Barbara Rockenbach, Annelie Rugg, Ashley Sanders, John Simpson, Bryan Sinclair, and Justin Sipher. "Building Capacity for Digital Humanities: A Framework for Institutional Planning." EDUCAUSE Center for Analysis and Research (ECAR) Working Group Paper, May 30, 2017. https://library.educause.edu/resources/2017/5/building-capacity-for -digital-humanities-a-framework-for-institutional-planning.

Beck, David F. "Technology Development Life Cycle Processes." Albuquerque: Sandia National Laboratories, 2013. http://prod.sandia.gov/techlib/access-control.cgi/2013 /133933.pdf.

Borek, Luise, Quinn Dombrowski, Jody Perkins, and Christof Schöch. "TaDiRAH: A Case Study in Pragmatic Classification." *DHQ: Digital Humanities Quarterly* 10, no. 1 (2016). http://www.digitalhumanities.org/dhq/vol/10/1/000235/000235.html.

Burdick, Anne, Johanna Drucker, Peter Lunenfeld, Todd Presner, and Jeffrey Schnapp. *Digital Humanities.* Cambridge, Mass.: MIT Press, 2012.

Carr, Gregory L. "Review of the Darwin Manuscripts from the Cambridge Digital Library." *Choice: Current Reviews for Academic Libraries*, 52, no. 12: 58. http://dx.doi .org/10.5860/CHOICE.189651.

Causer, Tim, Justin Tonra, and Valerie Wallace. "Transcription Maximized; Expense Minimized? Crowdsourcing and Editing the Collected Works of Jeremy Bentham." *Literary and Linguistic Computing* 27, no. 2 (2012). https://doi.org/10.1093/llc/fqs004.

Cohen, Patricia. "Scholars Recruit Public for Project." *New York Times*, December 27, 2010. http://www.nytimes.com/2010/12/28/books/28transcribe.html?pagewanted=all.

DARIAH. "DARIAH beyond Europe: About." 2018. https://dbe.hypotheses.org/about.

DiRT Directory. "Add Tools to DiRT by Tweeting." March 22, 2015. https://web.archive. org/web/20150419032425/http://dirtdirectory.org/add-tools-dirt-tweeting.

DiRT Directory. "Assignment-in-a-Box." https://web.archive.org/web/20161202102920 /http://dirtdirectory.org:80/assignment.

DiRT Directory. "Bamboo DiRT Now Out of Beta." July 15, 2012. https://web.archive.org /web/20150414170454/http://dirtdirectory.org/bamboo-dirt-now-out-beta.

DiRT Directory. "Bamboo DiRT Seeks Curatorial/Steering Committee." May 7, 2012. https://web.archive.org/web/20150414181913/http://dirtdirectory.org/bamboo-dirt -seeks-curatorialsteering-committee.

DiRT Directory. "DiRT Adopts TaDiRAH Terms, Provides RDF Data." March 25, 2015. https://web.archive.org/web/20170301044623/http://dirtdirectory.org/dirt-adopts -tadirah-terms-provides-rdf-data.

DiRT Directory. "DiRT Partners with TAPoR to Provide 'Recipes.'" March 27, 2015. https://web.archive.org/web/20161023063028/http://dirtdirectory.org/dirt-partners -tapor-provide-recipes.

DiRT Directory. "DiRT Plugin Available for Commons in a Box (CBOX) Scholarly Network." March 27, 2015. https://web.archive.org/web/20170612080818/http://dirtdirectory.org/dirt-plugin-available-commons-box-cbox-scholarly-network.

DiRT Directory. "DiRT Seeks Editorial Board." May 7, 2014. http://web.archive.org/web/20170801155253/http://dirtdirectory.org/dirt-seeks-editorial-board.

DiRT Directory. "Editorial Board." https://web.archive.org/web/20160301121754/http://dirtdirectory.org/editorial-board.

DiRT Directory. "New Categories for DiRT." September 12, 2013. https://web.archive.org/web/20150414073025/http://dirtdirectory.org/new-categories-dirt.

Dombrowski, Quinn. "Outreach about What Is Possible." 2012. http://quinndombrowski.com/projects/project-bamboo/data/outreach-about-what-possible#.

Dombrowski, Quinn. "What Ever Happened to Project Bamboo?" *Literary and Linguistic Computing* 29, no. 3 (2014): 326–39. https://doi.org/10.1093/llc/fqu026.

Finley, Priscilla. "DiRT: Digital Research Tools Wiki." *Choice* 47, no. 2: 1. http://digitalscholarship.unlv.edu/lib_articles/272.

Gil, Alex et al. "A Directory of Caribbean Digital Scholarship." 2020. https://caribbeandigitalnyc.net/caridischo/.

Grant, Elisabeth. "Get the DiRT on Research." *AHA Today* (blog), July 28, 2010. http://blog.historians.org/2010/07/get-the-dirt-on-research/.

Grant, K., Q. Dombrowski, K. Ranaweera, O. Rodriguez-Arenas, S. Sinclair, and G. Rockwell. "Absorbing DiRT: Tool Directories in the Digital Age." *Digital Studies/Le champ numérique* 10, no. 1 (2020). https://www.digitalstudies.org/articles/10.16995/dscn.325/.

Hartsell-Gundy, Arianne, Laura Braunstein, and Liorah Golomb, eds. *Digital Humanities in the Library: Challenges and Opportunities for Subject Specialists*. Chicago: Association of College & Research Libraries, 2015. http://www.ala.org/acrl/sites/ala.org.acrl/files/content/publications/booksanddigitalresources/digital/9780838987681_humanities_OA.pdf.

Hughes, Lorna, Panos Constantopoulos, and Costis Dallas. "Digital Methods in the Humanities: Understanding and Describing Their Use across the Disciplines." In *The New Companion to Digital Humanities*, edited by Susan Schreibman, Ray Siemens, and John Unsworth. Wiley Online Library, 2015. http://onlinelibrary.wiley.com/doi/10.1002/9781118680605.ch11/summary.

Irvine, Dean. "From Angel to Agile: The Business of the Digital Humanities." *Scholarly and Research Communication* 6, no. 4 (2015). http://src-online.ca/index.php/src/article/view/208.

Kijas, Anna E. "An Introduction to Getting Started in the Digital Humanities for Library Professionals." *Music Reference Services Quarterly* 20, no. 1 (2017). http://dx.doi.org/10.1080/10588167.2017.1274595.

Perkins, Jody, Luise Borek, Quinn Dombrowski, and Christof Schöch. "Building Bridges to the Future of a Distributed Network: From DiRT Categories to TaDiRAH, a Methods

Taxonomy for Digital Humanities." Scholarly Commons @ MU. n.d. http://hdl.han dle.net/2374.MIA/6152.

Project Bamboo. "Terroir—Related References." August 25, 2008. https://web.archive.org /web/20170621195154/https://wikihub.berkeley.edu/pages/viewpage.action?pageId =68620261&navigatingVersions=true.

Project Bamboo. "Terroir—Related References." November 6, 2008. https://web.archive. org/web/20170621200429/https://wikihub.berkeley.edu/pages/viewpage.action?pag eId=68625870&navigatingVersions=true.

Project Bamboo. "Terroir—Related References." February 20, 2009. https://web.archive. org/web/20170621201741/https://wikihub.berkeley.edu/pages/viewpage.action ?pageId=68622701.

Project Bamboo. "TSR Decision Meeting Notes 7-22-11." https://web.archive.org /web/20170801154616/https://wikihub.berkeley.edu/pages/viewpage.action?pageId =74058307.

Rockenbach, Barbara A. "Digital Humanities in Libraries: New Models for Scholarly Engagement." *Journal of Library Administration* 53, nos. 1–4 (2013). https://doi.org /10.1080/01930826.2013.756676.

Rockwell, Geoffrey. "As Transparent as Infrastructure: On the Research of Cyberin-frastructure in the Humanities." In *Online Humanities Scholarship: The Shape of Things to Come,* 1–20. Houston: Rice University, 2010. https://cnx.org/contents /PVdH0-lD@1.3:_USvuzFn@2/As-Transparent-as-Infrastructure-On-the-research -of-cyberinfrastructure-in-the-humanities.

Spiro, Lisa. "Digging in the DiRT: Sneak Preview of the Digital Research Tools (DiRT) wiki." 2008. https://digitalscholarship.wordpress.com/2008/05/27/digging-up-dirt -sneak-preview-of-the-digital-research-tools-dirt-wiki/.

Spiro, Lisa. "Doing Digital Scholarship: Presentation at Digital Humanities 2008." https:// digitalscholarship.wordpress.com/2008/08/11/doing-digital-scholarship-presenta tion-at-digital-humanities-2008/.

Spiro, Lisa. "Fondren Library Develops Research Aid for Tools of the Trade." *Rice University News,* May 21, 2005. http://news.rice.edu/2009/05/21/fondren-library-develops -research-aid-for-tools-of-the-trade/.

Sula, Chris Alen. "Digital Humanities and Libraries: A Conceptual Model." *Journal of Library Administration* 53, no. 1 (2013). http://dx.doi.org/10.1080/01930826.2013. 756680.

Vandegrift, Micah, and Stewart Varner. "Evolving in Common: Creating Mutually Sup-portive Relationships between Libraries and the Digital Humanities." *Journal of Library Administration* 53, no. 1 (2013). http://doi.org/10.1080/01930826.2013.7 56699.

Weingart, Scott B., Susan Grunewald, Matthew Lincoln et al., eds. *The Digital Humani-ties Literacy Guidebook.* Pittsburgh: Carnegie Mellon University, updated February 26, 2021. https://cmu-lib.github.io/dhlg/.

Young, Jeffrey R. "New Wiki Helps Humanities Researchers Find Online Tools." *Chronicle of Higher Education, Wired Campus* (blog), June 6, 2008. http://www.chronicle.com /blogs/wiredcampus/new-wiki-helps-humanities-researchers-find-online-tools/3998.

Zou, Jie Jenny. "Civil War Project Shows Pros and Cons of Crowdsourcing." *Chronicle of Higher Education, Wired Campus* (blog), June 14, 2011. http://www.chronicle.com/ blogs/wiredcampus/civil-war-project-shows-pros-and-cons-of-crowdsourcing/31749.

Custom-Built DH and Institutional Culture
The Case of Experimental Humanities

MARIA SACHIKO CECIRE AND SUSAN MERRIAM

Imagine yourself as a bird flying over all that makes up your college or university, however wide its geographical reach. If you could map not only the buildings, parking lots, facilities, grounds, physical hubs for virtual activity, and places where your community lives and works but also all of the invisible strategies, pressures, hopes, and expectations that shape your institution's culture, how would such a map look? How might your digital humanities or DH-friendly initiative fit into this kind of visualization? In *The Practice of Everyday Life,* French theorist Michel de Certeau used the metaphor of walking in the city to describe how individuals chart their own desired courses around monolithic structures that otherwise may seem impossible to influence. Although the city's physical attributes may be pre-existing and relatively fixed, the walker can determine how to move through and around these spaces in ways that the walker finds useful and pleasurable, effectively making them their own. De Certeau wrote,

> The long poem of walking manipulates spatial organizations, no matter how panoptic they may be: it is neither foreign to them (it can only take place within them) nor in conformity with them (it does not receive its identity from them). It creates shadows and ambiguities within them. It inserts its multitudinous references and citations into them (social models, cultural mores, personal factors).[1]

James Malazita opens the first section of *People, Practice, Power* by using de Certeau's description of city walking as a frame for conceptualizing a "tactical digital humanities." Such a frame might equip STEM students to "grapple with, and ideally subvert, the very real political and normative entanglements of computing infrastructure."[2] And Urszula Pawlicka-Deger demonstrates in this volume that spatial thinking can helpfully metaphorize the social and intellectual resonances of DH infrastructure.[3]

We also build on de Certeau's notion of tactical negotiations "from below" but do so to suggest that the fluid negotiations of de Certeau's walker in the city can offer inspiration for how faculty and staff might develop sustainable, institution-specific approaches to the digital humanities from within the pre-existing context of their college or university.[4] While DH is often seen as new, different, and even cutting-edge in relation to other humanities disciplines, we argue that developing a DH initiative that grows up around, rather than ignoring or departing from, a college or university's unique character and mission can make it easier to put down roots, get buy-in from colleagues and students, and build meaningful projects. Paradoxically, this process not only anchors your initiative in the particularities of your institution but can also be an opportunity to rethink and reshape aspects of institutional culture as part of a grassroots movement.

Given the capacious definition of digital humanities (the *big tent* that some celebrate and others decry), it is nearly impossible to offer all aspects of DH at any one institution anyway, and this is especially true for small and/or underresourced colleges and universities. Designing a DH or DH-friendly initiative therefore necessarily requires determining what your team wants DH to mean at your institution. We propose using this process as an opportunity to revisit your institution's priorities, consider how you approach the humanities, and create a bespoke program in line with your unique institutional culture. Rather than asking, "How do we 'do' DH?" and attempting to re-create an existing model, we suggest asking, "How can digital humanities help us rethink the humanities at our institution?" and building from there. This is not only a practical approach that can make a program more likely to take hold and thrive in the conditions of a specific college or university but is also an exciting opportunity to reconsider how and why we study humanities subjects and is a way to access what may be otherwise untapped potential within a given institution. In many cases, as in ours, this means moving beyond the digital humanities center (DHC) model that has become the presumed infrastructural default for DH to develop an alternative structure that serves a collectively determined mission.

In this piece, we draw upon our experience launching the Experimental Humanities (EH) initiative at Bard College, a small liberal arts college (SLAC) in New York's Hudson Valley.[5] Our decision to use the term *experimental* rather than *digital* signals EH's commitment to the process of asking humanities questions and pushing boundaries around the methods we use to pursue them, over a commitment to particular tools or media. Originally a curricular initiative, we soon expanded EH to include a wide array of extracurricular elements and formally launched the Center for Experimental Humanities as well in 2017. In this chapter, we emphasize the importance of identifying institutional culture, grassroots leadership practices, and the central role of community in laying the foundations for our Bard-appropriate program. We draw upon our personal experiences as faculty members of different ranks and backgrounds when we started this process; Cecire, the founding director of Experimental Humanities, was a visiting assistant professor when she began laying the groundwork for EH. After two years of conversations and planning, she was converted to a tenure-track position just before Experimental Humanities launched as part of the curriculum in 2012. Merriam, a tenured associate professor and part of the initial discussions that helped to shape Experimental Humanities, became associate dean of academic affairs in 2013. It is important to note that we were lucky to work with the blessing of our administration: although we did not have significant funds dedicated to our project at first (initially up to $2,500 per year), we were encouraged to meet and move forward, and in 2014 we received a generous grant from the Andrew W. Mellon Foundation. This chapter includes projects and events that we funded through the grant, but the early stages of establishing EH that we describe took place before securing these very welcome financial resources. We conclude the chapter with a three-part list of suggestions for developing tailored DH programs organized around (1) building community, (2) (re)assessing your college or university's approach to the humanities, and (3) taking advantage of existing infrastructure.

Identifying Institutional Culture

By institutional culture, we mean what Williams et al. define as "the entrenched behaviors of individuals working within organizations as well as the common 'values, assumptions, beliefs or ideologies that members have about their organization or its work.'"[6] Our suggestion to take advantage of institutional culture in starting a new initiative is not itself radical, but we have found that this approach can have surprisingly revolutionary outcomes when creatively used as a guiding principle for structuring a DH-style program from the ground up. In her useful piece "Here and There: Creating DH Community," Miriam Posner emphasizes the importance of working with an institution's existing culture when attempting to "spark DH activity." She offers practical examples of how one might do this, such as taking advantage of standing meetings to present material or working with course development grant opportunities to incentivize DH pedagogy.[7] We suggest stepping back even further to consider an institution's fundamental self-identity before forging ahead with designing and implementing a DH initiative. What is your institution proud of? Whom does it serve? Is it focused more on pedagogy or research? What are its unique commitments? (To the arts? To its sports teams? To first-generation college students? To a regional area?) What does it identify as key elements in an ethical and well-informed study of the humanities? Although not always stated explicitly, these factors are as much a part of institutional culture as when meetings are held and how departments are structured.

In our case, Bard has a reputation for progressivism, fierce advocacy for the arts and humanities, and a faculty devoted to teaching. Even though Bard has long run on a restricted budget, it allots more to student financial aid than many wealthier institutions, and spends liberally to bring its vision of social justice, liberal education for all, and the arts to life in the world. Bard supports credit-bearing liberal arts programs in inner-city public high schools, state prisons, underserved communities across the United States, and maintains an enduring commitment to international undergraduate education in countries including Belarus, Kyrgyzstan, and Palestine, and is a key part of the Open Society University Network.[8] It also runs a conservatory, a world-class summer festival of music, opera, theater, dance, film, and cabaret, several major exhibition spaces, and competitive graduate programs in curatorial studies, the fine arts, and decorative arts / design history / material culture. Faculty in all of Bard's educational programs are encouraged to think boldly and creatively about classroom pedagogy and are offered an array of opportunities to develop their skills. So, although Bard undergraduates are as likely as anyone else to feel anxious about practical concerns such as postgraduation job prospects, they have chosen to attend an institution that privileges the arts and humanities and that sees access to a rigorous liberal arts education as a social justice issue.

Given this climate, it would have been impossible to shape a successful DH-style initiative at Bard that did not begin with pedagogy, meaningfully include artistic experimentation, and engage with the history and theory of technological change. And in keeping with our community's emphasis on social justice, the projects that have grown out of Experimental Humanities have tended toward civic engagement and advocacy. Roopika Risam has written about framing different approaches to DH in terms of a *DH accent,* drawing on postcolonial theory to decentralize what we consider to be "good" DH and to recontextualize this in terms of a DH center or initiative's local circumstances.[9] To borrow this concept for the intensely local circumstances of Bard College, our DH accent ended up taking the shape of Experimental Humanities, a curricular initiative and hub for faculty research that is as interested in the experimentation of the artist's studio as in the experiments of a scientific lab and that places as much value on pedagogical experiments as on research projects. When we use and think about technologies, we necessarily build critical analysis and creative reimaginings of tech's uses into what we do; as our mission states, "We are committed to the notion that embracing experimental approaches is essential to fostering practices that are inclusive for all learners and transformative for the societies in which we live."

In their essay about whether or how small liberal arts colleges might "do" DH, Bryan Alexander and Rebecca Frost Davis outline several challenges to establishing DH programs and centers at institutions like Bard.[10] They note a lack of infrastructure to support major research projects, the difficulty of pulling together the human resources to do work that requires a wide range of skills, our limited access to graduate students that can sustain long-term research, and the pedagogical focus at SLACs. However, they argue that models that include curricular elements and partner with existing campus resources like library/IT can still be successful, developing proficiency in select project areas and sending students on to DH graduate programs. Experimental Humanities does work closely with library/IT and encourages faculty projects through training opportunities, the guidance of a digital projects coordinator with a PhD in the humanities, and the support of a student media corps. However, while several successful DH initiatives at other small liberal arts colleges have grown out of the library, such as Occidental's Center for Digital Liberal Arts, or out of faculty research, as with Hamilton's Digital Humanities Initiative, EH was from its first imaginings a primarily curricular initiative, built on the three pillars of history, theory, and practice.[11]

At an administrative level, EH is a concentration (it functions like an interdisciplinary minor), which means that our students pair their course work with a foundation in a major program of study, and that EH faculty also belong to a home program. All EH students take the core courses Introduction to Media and History of Experiment, which were created for our concentration and which faculty in different fields rotate teaching. They cover media theory and the history of different kinds of experimental methods and approaches from the classical period through today, and both aim to integrate hands-on projects into the syllabus. To graduate with an Experimental Humanities concentration, students must also take at least one practice-based course beyond the college arts requirement—this may be computer science or an electronic arts course, but may also be another visual, written, or performing art—and at least two courses from the wide offering of EH-listed courses. These are typically designed by faculty according to their research interests, include a number of interdisciplinary team-taught courses, and are available in a wide range of fields. The following is a sample listing of elective courses:

A Selection of Experimental Humanities Courses at Bard College

Predigital to Digital
ANTH: Surveillance: Human to Digital (Laura Kunreuther)
ARTH: Multi-Media Gothic (Katherine Boivin)
HIST: From Analog to Digital: Photography and Visual History (Drew Thompson)
HIST: Gutenberg 2.0: Making Books for Everyday Life and Ordinary People (Tabetha Ewing)
LIT: The Book before Print (Marisa Libbon)

Computational/Digital Methods
FILM/ANTH: Ethnography in Image, Sound, and Text (Laura Kunreuther and Jacqueline Goss)
FILM/CS: Games at Work: Participation, Procedure, and Play (Ben Coonley and Keith O'Hara)
LIT/CS: Technologies of Reading: Human and Machine Approaches to Literature (Collin Jennings and Sven Anderson)

Topic-Based Faculty Research Clusters (example: Sound cluster)
ARTH: Geographies of Sound (Maria Sonevytsky and Olga Touloumi)
LIT: Sound in American Literature (Alex Benson)
SCI: A Comparative Approach to Music Cognition (Sven Anderson and five other faculty)

Individual Student and Faculty Interests
LIT: Woman as Cyborg (Maria Sachiko Cecire)
SPAN: Archive Fever: Lit and Film (Patricia Lopez-Gay)
THTR: Going Viral: Performance, Media, Memes (Miriam Felton-Dansky)

All EH faculty are encouraged to include experimental projects and opportunities for student-driven inquiry in their courses, and students present their work to one another at collective Share Events each semester. These vibrant and sometimes raucous events look like a cross between a scientific poster session, a media fair, and an arts exhibition, with lightning presentations to explain the work being done in different courses. Our curricular goals are for students to think about the complex relationships between form and content, to get a sense of the long and varied history of how people have sought to make and share knowledge, and to develop the hands-on skills to test out their own questions in the media of their choice.

The energy for creating Experimental Humanities at Bard came from faculty and staff who put their heads together to imagine how a humanities approach to digital studies and technology could usefully fit into the culture at Bard, amplifying what's best about our institution and taking advantage of the resources that we have. Kezar, Gallant, and Lester have demonstrated how the concept of grassroots leadership, more commonly studied in the context of social movements, can also be applied to bottom-up approaches to change in academia. In the case of the academy, this means initiatives and cultural shifts driven by faculty and staff rather than passed down from the administration. The findings of their study emphasize the importance of taking institutional culture into account but do so at the level of higher education in general as a profession and environment with its own norms and rules. They have written:

> The tactics used by faculty and staff are distinctly shaped by and aligned with the culture and character of the academy. For example, the collegial and shared governance culture of the academy shaped a more tempered approach to community organizing, through tactics such as working with and mentoring students, hiring like-minded social activists, and utilizing existing networks.

The authors go on to note that different kinds of institutions respond better to different grassroots tactics toward change. For instance, they note that "obtaining grants and using data were more effective and pervasive at research universities, curricular changes at the teaching institutions, working with external (alumni and community) groups at the community college and liberal arts campuses."[12] Being embedded in your own college or university, with access to its histories and hopes for the future, positions you to identify the best approaches to creating a DH initiative for your institution.

Beyond identifying institutional category (R1, SLAC, regional comprehensive, community college, etc.), we recommend addressing your local interests, concerns, and points of pride. With Bard's teaching focus, taking a curricular approach was essential to laying a firm foundation for Experimental Humanities, ensuring that a regular (and rotating) core of faculty could be engaged in developing and continuing the concentration each semester through their courses. This ongoing activity made it easier to encourage and maintain extracurricular elements of the initiative, from lectures and workshops to faculty projects. While a similar curricular model could work for other colleges and universities with a strong teaching mission, not all such institutions would necessarily welcome an initiative like EH. Cecire recalls being asked by a colleague from another institution how she managed to get a program with a name like Experimental Humanities accepted by her Bard peers and administration; "At Bard," she replied, "it's a lot easier to get through 'Experimental Humanities' than 'Digital Humanities'!" Bard's vigorous commitment to the arts and liberal arts meant that there was some significant initial suspicion of any program that could be seen as seeking to displace traditional practices of humanistic inquiry or automate the work of human minds and hands. By framing our engagement with the digital in terms of a much longer tradition of technological change and shifting approaches to knowledge creation and artistic expression, Experimental Humanities was able to take colleagues' legitimate concerns on board and indeed make them part of what students are required to consider as part of their studies.

Building a Community to Build a Program

In fundamental ways, many of which will be familiar to folks who work at other small liberal arts colleges, Bard is an unlikely candidate for a DH program. When Cecire began thinking about the possibility of developing something DH-related at Bard, we lacked the infrastructure and financial wherewithal to support many, or perhaps even most aspects of a traditional DH initiative. Our colleagues in IT were already consumed with the day-to-day work of the college, so that asking them to take on additional responsibility for a program would be difficult. We would moreover not be given much space on the college server and would not have access to new computing technology unless we could obtain it ourselves. Like many other institutions, Bard experiences constraints on office and classroom space, so we could not plan on having a dedicated place for faculty or students to convene or store equipment. Finally, while Bard does have graduate students, the graduate schools are for the most part not located on the main campus, so any student work would be done by undergraduates.

We also faced more Bard-specific barriers to a DH program. Bard has a reputation for being cutting edge, but that reputation is driven primarily by Bard's strong arts programs and belief in risk taking and creativity. Bard's curriculum is in most ways very traditional—it has a strong set of core requirements, for example, including extensive general education requirements and a set of rigorous distribution requirements—and the faculty and administration are in general careful about adopting new programs, particularly those that seem of the moment. The attitude "new is not necessarily better" is pervasive. Additionally, faculty commonly associate DH with big data, and many had the presumption that working with a DH program would mean somehow diminishing one of the most important aspects of the liberal arts college classroom: work in small groups with a teacher. Our faculty were also initially disinclined to use or explore the use of technology in the classroom beyond learning management systems or PowerPoint. Massive open online courses (MOOCs), which were widely discussed in higher education at the time of EH's founding, or anything similar ran directly counter to Bard's pedagogical ethos and brand. Finally, while a small percentage of the Bard student body was deeply interested in technology, a much larger percentage were not particularly technologically adept or poised to think rigorously about the way technology shapes their experience.

More positively, Bard faculty were and are close knit and have an entrepreneurial spirit. Because the administration encourages faculty (at every level and type of contract) and students to explore ways that they can contribute to the college, it is not unusual for junior faculty or visitors to take initiative and pilot something new. Characteristic of Bard's culture, for instance, is that an undergraduate founded the Bard Prison Initiative, one of the largest degree-granting college in prison programs in the country. The faculty are also given a great deal of power in shaping the curriculum, and as professors we take pride in our focus on undergraduate teaching and advising. Teaching is often interdisciplinary, so faculty welcome and are comfortable working outside their fields. Finally, we have resources—the graduate and international schools, a vibrant Center for Civic Engagement, a distinguished arts faculty, knowledgeable and flexible staff—that might prove valuable in developing a program.

Given Bard's profile, it was clear that a typical DH program would not be financially feasible or desirable to the faculty. Cecire and other members of the early EH planning team reasoned that Bard's strengths, particularly the faculty investment in the curriculum and teaching, as well as Bard's focus on liberal inquiry pointed toward developing a curricular-driven program. We imagined that Experimental Humanities would initially be framed as a liberal arts–driven answer to the digital humanities: it could use a network of courses and faculty-identified research clusters to variously interrogate how technology mediates what it means to be human. While DH scholarship at its most visible typically creates and employs digital tools to pursue project-based humanities research, EH emphasizes reconsidering the methods and subjects of humanistic study in the light of changing material conditions. This often means coming up with projects and pedagogies that engage the digital, but it can also result in totally analog work that pushes at the boundaries of disciplinary norms. The EH frame also created room for studying and experimenting with the kind of multimodal work that artists, scholars, and students—especially those from minoritized communities—were doing both in and outside the academy. These were often not being treated as "DH" at the time, but we found them to be compelling and important to integrate into our approach.[13]

In the course of thinking about starting a DH program, and as a new visiting professor, Cecire was advised by a senior mentor to simply talk to as many people as possible. At a college where the entire faculty can fit into one multipurpose room for faculty meetings, talking to colleagues from a wide range of backgrounds (faculty from different disciplines, librarians, and staff who work in areas from student life to civic engagement) was eminently possible. She ate lunch in the faculty dining room, set up coffee dates, joined committees that were open to visitors, and over her first year embarked on the kind of "listening tour" that Posner suggests.

Cecire's listening tour helped shape some of her initial ideas about the program. Next, she held a one-day faculty and staff retreat in the early fall of her second year, to which she invited people that had expressed interest and/or had an important perspective to contribute. In keeping with the offbeat, countercultural ethos that she had identified as a source of pride for Bardians, she found a cost-effective but productive environment for the retreat: a quirky local inn on the Hudson River. Its eclectic indoor and outdoor spaces helped the group maintain energy and encouraged thinking "outside the box" of usual campus procedure as they ate, discussed, and outlined throughout the day. Cecire presented a sketch of curricular and extracurricular activities for the proposed initiative based on the conversations she had been having over the previous year, and together the group rearranged and fleshed out this plan into the foundations of the Experimental Humanities concentration and initiative. This day-long workshop advanced the program because it helped faculty identify like-minded colleagues and concretize some of their own ideas about EH, and its emphasis on listening and collaboration underlined the humanistic nature of the initiative. Building on this consensus, we outlined the core courses and put together teams to develop and teach them, identified existing courses that were already appropriate to cross-list under EH, and established recommendations for retooling existing courses for EH.

The concentration launched in 2012, offering ten to twelve EH-listed courses per semester and providing faculty with new opportunities for teaching and research. Next, armed with a clear mission, Cecire created a steering committee of core faculty and staff to help guide the new program and take part in drafting an application for the Mellon grant. Upon receiving the grant in spring of 2014, EH expanded its reach through several new hires (the digital projects coordinator, a web developer for the arts and humanities, two postdoctoral fellows, and a team of student media corps workers), and gained significant funding to support faculty development and research and pedagogical projects.

While we were thrilled to grow with the grant support, it is important to recognize that many of our key initiatives were already in place and would have moved forward in some form even without Mellon. In its very early stages, EH operated under severe financial constraints, and we had no choice but to develop the program on a shoestring. Instead of being flummoxed or deterred by challenges, we (perhaps somewhat optimistically) developed a series of workarounds. We lacked a designated space, the typical marker of shared programmatic relationship or identity on a campus, so worked doubly hard to establish a sense of cohort to anchor the program instead. We lacked IT infrastructure, so we committed to using expertise and equipment that colleagues on campus were willing to share. We began developing a map of where equipment could be found, for instance, and created a list of people with some expertise who would be willing to run workshops or train individual faculty. We researched and used free software whenever possible. We collaborated with staff such as the educational technologist and the curator of visual resources to find classroom tech solutions that enabled them to pilot programs and platforms that they could eventually roll out college-wide (including Omeka, WordPress, and Amazon server space).

We also created initiatives that could be free or low cost to run. Virtually free and incredibly successful, our topic-based research clusters draw faculty and staff from disciplines as disparate as physics, anthropology, theater, and human rights around subjects like *sound* and *food*. Many faculty reported feeling invigorated by their monthly discussions with colleagues, including one associate professor who reported that the experience was like being "in grad school again—in the best way!" because it allowed her to think about her research area from new perspectives with smart, creative people. Thus, at the same time that the clusters are cost effective, they also support Bard faculty in their research and enable their willingness to work interdisciplinarily. With the support of the grant, the clusters have yielded new courses, public symposia involving students and faculty, works of art, and faculty publications. The symposia, in turn, have ignited productive new relationships with other institutions and entities.

Humanities labs, another EH initiative, respond to Bard's financial and structural limitations in a different way. We left the definition of such humanities labs open to faculty and staff, in order to encourage faculty to work experimentally—to think of new ways that research in the humanities might be undertaken, and new outcomes found and narratives constructed. Our two main labs, the Immersive Media Arts Lab and the Digital History Lab, each take very different approaches to experimenting in arts and humanities, but both engage with undergraduates as meaningful partners in their work.[14] Students in these humanities labs are introduced to research by working alongside a faculty member, just as they would be in a biology or chemistry lab. In response to this initiative, Merriam created a Mobile History van (actually whichever faculty member's car is free) as part of the Digital History lab. Outfitted with technology that includes scanners, a digital camera, and sound equipment, these "vans" go out to record local history in an area that Merriam has researched for many years. Consistent with Bard's social justice mission, Merriam and students work with underserved or marginalized communities, taking a ground-up approach to developing projects that yield original research and create new college–community relationships. The van's ethos is fundamentally shaped by a traditional understanding of the humanities, which encourages a spirit of inquiry, experimentation, and openness. Although the van uses equipment purchased with Mellon funds, we could have cobbled together much of the technology by creating a borrowing system, working with programs that were willing to share what they had, and we could have pursued paid student internships through our Center for Civic Engagement. If designed right, the labs can be low-cost to run and at the same time spark new ways of undertaking research, which is always a struggle at liberal arts colleges that place a premium on teaching.

In retrospect, our approach to developing the EH concentration at Bard might be viewed as exploring the productive tension between freedom and constraint. We believe that it is valuable to think about how constraints—financial, infrastructural, and cultural—can enable creative, resourceful thinking. In other words, it is sometimes possible to think of institutional constraints not as limitations or hindrances but as spurs to create alternative, new, or radical solutions to problems.

To-Do List

In the spirit of Posner's piece on building DH community, we offer this bulleted to-do list for faculty and staff looking to create or rethink a digital humanities–style initiative at their institution on the basis of our experiences at Bard. Specific conditions will shape how each of these points play out, and we found that flexibility, imagination, and a sense of humor are crucial tools for creating and maintaining momentum.

BUILD COMMUNITY

As several other contributors in this volume suggest, community is central to DH projects, centers, and even the digital humanities' idea itself. We posit that building a meaningful, inclusive community is perhaps *the most* important aspect of starting an initiative. Even without funding, designated space, advanced tech, or administrative backing, a group of passionate and like-minded individuals can create intellectual space for new research and pedagogical approaches and begin to brainstorm how to secure those other important elements together.

TALK TO EVERYONE

In order to create an initiative in line with your institution's culture, it is important to try to understand that culture by speaking with a broad cross-section of people from the community. Make a point of meeting and listening to both natural allies and potential skeptics. Sound out what colleagues and students care about, what these different stakeholders find unique about your institution, what kinds of initiatives have been attempted in the past (successfully and unsuccessfully), and how each person reacts to the notion of a new initiative that addresses the intersection of technology and the humanities. It is important to acknowledge that this, too, is work: such grassroots ground-laying can be tiring and whenever possible should be recognized as labor. However, it can also be a genuine pleasure, and it puts the listener in a good position to not only recruit fellow organizers and understand the challenges and opportunities of a given institution but also to fulfill the next point.

BE A HUB

Do instructors in dance and computer science share a fascination with motion and recursion? Is a librarian digitizing a collection of papers by an author that an English professor is teaching in an upcoming course? Being able to connect people who have similar interests and needs, and helping them to see your nascent initiative as an institutional space for working together, is invaluable to laying the groundwork for a meaningful enterprise. At the same time, it allows you, the organizer(s), to keep track of the kinds of projects and avenues that people actually want to pursue and to shape your initiative accordingly. We recommend, when possible, creating a steering committee that includes invested members who represent many parts of your institution and who can not only help manage the day-to-day development of your initiative but also dramatically extend your knowledge and capacity to connect people across campus.

GET TOGETHER

Once you have identified collaborators and allies, bring them into the same room to articulate what the humanities mean to you and to hammer out how you want your initiative to work, as discussed in the next section. This step is key not only for concretizing your plans and creating a sense of shared ownership but also for advertising what you are doing to people from across campus. Humility and generosity are essential at this stage: junior members and newcomers to the institution should draw on colleagues' institutional and disciplinary knowledge, while senior faculty can keep an open mind to unusual suggestions and bring an encouraging, can-do attitude. Working with staff as partners, rather than as service-providers, is crucial. This moment of coming together is also a great opportunity for people to take on leadership positions within your initiative—perhaps to join the steering committee, to develop new courses, or to be point people for specific work that needs doing, from liaising with administration and other entities on campus to fundraising.

KEEP GETTING TOGETHER—AND GROWING!

Following the process of crystallizing the practical shape of your initiative, it is important to keep up momentum even in the midst of busy semesters. For us, this meant deepening the interpersonal bonds between the people at the heart of organizing, inviting more people to be involved at various levels of intensity, and being able to offer intellectually fulfilling and/or fun opportunities to gather and share ideas (we cannot overstate the usefulness of regular happy hours and other events, including family-friendly ones, even if you cannot afford to pay for refreshments!). Given how overcommitted most people are on teaching-intensive campuses, you want being part of your initiative to be a return to the kind of activities that made people want to work in the academy in the first place. Kezar, Gallant, and Lester have reported that

> Faculty and staff are drawn to campus employment because they believe that the academy provides opportunities to debate interesting ideas. So, consistent with the intellectual climate of college and university campuses, a prominent grassroots leadership tactic used by both faculty and staff is the creation and organization of intellectual opportunities, where issues of interest can be intelligently discussed and debated.[15]

Even when you do not have the funds to compensate people as much as you would like for their time, you can strive to offer such scholarly camaraderie. Sustained opportunities seem to be the most effective in this regard, and we would add that creating a truly collegial environment of intellectual engagement is also important: generous, egalitarian, and motivated by the spirit of experimentation and a shared joy in learning. Extending personal invitations and working as a *hub* is especially important here.

Assessing Your Approach to the Humanities to Imagine a DH for Your Institution

Assessing your approach may take place gradually or at an intensive retreat, but however you choose to structure this process, we have found that bringing in voices from across the community and *building consensus* is key to deciding whether and how to create a digital humanities or DH-friendly initiative at your institution.

IDENTIFY YOUR INSTITUTION'S APPROACH TO THE HUMANITIES

This process is an opportunity to reconsider the first principles of humanities research and pedagogy at your institution. This step is essential: every college and university approaches the humanities differently, and it is important to identify and discuss how this works at your institution in order to design a sustainable initiative. Leaving the digital aside for a moment, consider as a group the following:

- What questions do we most urgently ask about human culture and experience?
- What methods do we use to ask, answer, and share our responses to these questions, as both educators and scholars?
- What are our institution's particular areas of humanistic interest, based, for instance, on geography, demographics, traditional strengths, library holdings, institutional mission, community relationships, or other aspects?
- How are our approaches to the humanities part of a larger "vibe" that reflects our institution's identity and priorities?

You should be realistic in your responses, but it is also alright to be aspirational as long as you can begin to chart a viable path from how things are in the present to how you would like them to work in the future.

(HOW) CAN THE DIGITAL ENRICH THIS VISION?

The first question to ask is whether or not digital methods and culture are actually central, or even necessary, to what you want to achieve in rethinking the humanities at your institution. If not, what is it that you really wish to do? If your answer is yes, this is a chance to reflect on the technologies that you would be introducing: what's interesting about them? In what ways can they help you better conduct or express the outcomes of humanistic inquiry? If you can clearly articulate how digital scholarship will extend or enable the existing priorities of humanities teaching and research at your institution, this will make it much easier to explain the need for your initiative to peers and draw in otherwise reluctant faculty, staff, and student participants. Be sure to consider what digital resources you have at your disposal when answering this question, as this will affect what your initiative can realistically plan to deliver.

DETERMINE THE MOST PRACTICAL PATH OF EXECUTION

Looking at both the culture and priorities of your institution and the affiliations of your core organizing team, decide how to anchor your new initiative. Will it fit best as part of the curriculum? As a center based in the library? As a hub for faculty and graduate or undergraduate research? Is there some other organizational structure, perhaps one unique to your institution, that makes more sense given your strengths and goals? While your initiative may ultimately grow to do all of these kinds of work, begin with a shape that will enable your initiative to maintain momentum and provide a home for interested people on campus to connect with it at their convenience.

ONCE DECIDED, BE CONFIDENT IN YOUR APPROACH

The planned shape of your initiative may be a modest modification of structures that you have seen elsewhere, or it may be a wholly novel arrangement. Either way, it will best be designed in a way that fits the practicalities and the ethos of your institution. Do not worry if this does not look the same as the DH centers you admire at big research institutions; as this volume demonstrates, small, undergraduate-focused, regional, and other kinds of colleges and universities have much to contribute to the DH landscape. Indeed, there is plenty of pushback against the rhetoric of "bigger is better"—whether we are talking about bigger institutions, big data, or expensive tech. DH work increasingly takes a wide range of forms and originates at a number of institutional settings: from the Minimal Computing Group to FemTechNet's Distributed Open Collaborative Courses to the Digital Liberal Arts Exchange to various regional DH collectives.[16] There has even been a recent surge of interest in the notion of experimental versus digital humanities—a conversation in which we have been proud to become a leading example through our efforts at a small liberal arts college.

Taking Advantage of Existing Infrastructure

Starting a new initiative takes both human and financial resources, but many of our institutions do not have much of either to spare. Therefore, a creative mind and the ability to work with people from other parts of your college or university to find mutually beneficial solutions can really come in handy in this regard. You will likely want to sit down with your administration, meet with your institution's development office, and at some point start brainstorming possible sources of outside funding because having your own lines of funding, space, and hires dedicated to your initiative can bring crucial freedom and flexibility. Until then, however, it may still be possible to start something new with limited funds, space, and people power.

GO WITH THE FLOW

Whenever possible, structure your initiative to work in ways that people on your campus have seen before. This provides a comprehensible skeleton that others can quickly recognize and may provide natural entry points for students, faculty, and staff to connect with the initiative. Whether it is an existing curricular model, a service-providing center, or a faculty reading group, starting with something known and then modifying it to meet your needs can help you get off the ground quickly and balance stability and innovation.

JUMP ON BOARD

Identify the pockets of resources available at your institution, and consider how your initiative can benefit those who offer them. If there are internal grants being disbursed for course or faculty development, student work-study quotas that need filling, or underused collections, spaces, or technologies on campus, these can all be opportunities to help support your initiative while furthering the aims of other partners on campus (administration, students, librarians, office for civic engagement, IT professionals, and more).

ADVERTISE!

Try to broadcast what you are doing on campus, and to do it in a tone that reflects your institution's culture and connect it to the ideals that your college or university holds most dear. Beyond emails, word of mouth, and posters, what other tools do you have at your disposal? How can you grab the interest of people on campus who will be able to benefit from and contribute to your initiative? For instance, Experimental Humanities' Share Events ensure that at least once a term we take over a public space on campus with installations, projected work, tables covered in projects, and enthusiastic faculty and students from EH courses.

Our experiences starting Experimental Humanities have been largely positive, but we have also had our share of failures. Indeed, an important part of developing an initiative is recognizing where (and why) missteps have occurred. For example, in the Mellon grant proposal we asked for funding to support what we called "student-driven courses." Given Bard's emphasis on teaching and history of initiatives coming from passionate student leaders, we believed that allowing students to work in tandem with faculty to develop EH courses was a natural winning combination. In implementing the courses, however, we soon realized that even bright, creative, and well-intending students can lack the full information and experience required to create an undergraduate course, and in some cases their swift progression through college, often punctuated by study abroad and other obligations, made it difficult for even the most committed students to pair reliably with faculty members. Student applications to create new courses were limited, and of those that we did receive and approve, several students dropped out of the planning process. In retrospect, spending more time interviewing students about how best to include them in shaping the curriculum would have likely yielded a more successful structure. While disappointing, such failures can be instructive as long as your team is committed to the idea that engaging with institutional culture is an ongoing and ever-evolving process that involves trial and error.

Michel de Certeau's refiguring of the power relations between walkers and the city that they traverse shifts attention away from the immobility of urban structures to the creative ways in which individuals and groups might navigate their environment. Their unique relationships to the spaces of the city allow them to work with what is there to draw out new paths that reshape or reassign meaning to the landscape. Similarly, our experience designing and implementing a novel, bespoke DH-friendly program at our SLAC has left us with the belief that it is fundamentally important to be responsive to your institution. This means not just thinking on the level of your institutional category but on the much more individualized level of your college or university's distinctive culture. This can mean taking advantage of the particular benefits of your institution but also provides the opportunity to be conscious of the positive role that apparent constraints can play. Certainly, there are serious and legitimate needs that must be met to successfully launch a sustainable DH initiative. But taking stock of what is and is not available or desirable at your institution can enable you to design an initiative that best reflects your needs and interests and even to begin to spark change in your institution's culture. For example, Experimental Humanities took advantage of the collegial relationships across Bard's small campus and the multidisciplinary structure of concentrations to encourage even greater collaboration across fields, and in the process it enabled faculty to see these relationships in more creative ways. This fresh spirit of collaboration, which includes alternative modes of partnering with the community, released a wave of interdisciplinary, civically engaged projects that have reshaped how faculty and staff work with undergraduates and one another.

Finally, it is worth noting that in the face of both cynical and legitimate critiques of colleges and universities, it is particularly important that institutions of higher education engage in the process of reflecting on their core mission and that those of us who work in the humanities have a strong sense of what we do and why. The grassroots approach to developing a DH or DH-friendly initiative that we have outlined here places such self-interrogation and shared articulation at the heart of its practice. We believe that by building diverse communities that together can map out the structures that shape our institutions, we can begin to imagine new paths for digital humanities work and, more broadly, for higher education. Working locally, it is possible to develop novel initiatives with the potential to make a difference at our own institutions, to contribute to broader scholarly discourse, and to affect the world beyond academia.

Notes

1. de Certeau, *The Practice of Everyday Life*, 101.
2. Malazita, "Epistemic Infrastructure."

3. Pawlicka-Deger, "Laboratory."

4. De Certeau's metaphor is founded on his recognition of an overt power differential between the structures of the city, created by the strategies of institutional bodies, and the tactics of the walkers who must negotiate these structures and carve out their own paths. A full discussion of the power relations between institutions of higher education and the faculty, students, and staff who make up these institutions is beyond the scope of this essay, and we recognize they often look or function differently from one place to another. Nevertheless, the grassroots approach we discuss here acknowledges that such power differentials do exist and that it may still be possible to work from a position of relative weakness to develop a meaningful and useful initiative for your institution.

5. http://eh.bard.edu.

6. Williams et al., "The Power of Social Networks," 51. They here quote Peterson and Spencer.

7. Posner, "Here and There."

8. See Bard Early College, http://www.bard.edu/earlycollege/; Bard Prison Initiative, http://bpi.bard.edu/; Clemente Course in the Humanities, http://clemente.bard.edu/; Bard International Network, http://www.bard.edu/internationalnetwork/; and, as of 2020, the Open Society University Network, https://osun.bard.edu/.

9. Risam, "Other Worlds, Other DHs."

10. Alexander and Davis, "Should Liberal Arts Campuses Do Digital Humanities?"

11. Occidental, https://www.oxy.edu/center-digital-liberal-arts; and Hamilton, http://www.dhinitiative.org/.

12. Kezar, Gallant, and Lester, "Everyday People Making a Difference," 137, 149.

13. See Bailey, "All the Digital Humanists Are White"; and Lothian and Phillips, "Can Digital Humanities Mean Transformative Critique?"

14. https://eh.bard.edu/projects/immersive-media-art-lab-imal/; https://eh.bard.edu/projects/digital-history-lab-dhl/.

15. Kezar, Gallant, and Lester, "Everyday People," 139.

16. http://go-dh.github.io/mincomp/about/; https://femtechnet.org/docc/; and https://dlaexchange.wordpress.com/.

Bibliography

Alexander, Bryan, and Rebecca Frost Davis. "Should Liberal Arts Campuses Do Digital Humanities? Process and Products in the Small College World." In *Debates in the Digital Humanities,* edited by Matthew K. Gold. Minneapolis: University of Minnesota Press, 2012. http://dhdebates.gc.cuny.edu/debates/text/25.

Bailey, Moya Z. "All the Digital Humanists Are White, All the Nerds Are Men, but Some of Us Are Brave." *Journal of Digital Humanities* 1, no. 1 (Winter 2011). http://journalofdigitalhumanities.org/1-1/all-the-digital-humanists-are-white-all-the-nerds-are-men-but-some-of-us-are-brave-by-moya-z-bailey/.

de Certeau, Michel. *The Practice of Everyday Life*. Translated by Steven Rendall. Berkeley: University of California Press, 1988.

Kezar, A., T. B. Gallant, and J. Lester. "Everyday People Making a Difference on College Campuses: The Tempered Grassroots Leadership Tactics of Faculty and Staff." *Studies in Higher Education* 36, no. 2 (2011): 129–51.

Lothian, Alexis, and Amanda Philips. "Can Digital Humanities Mean Transformative Critique?" *e-Media Studies* 3, no. 1 (2013). https://journals.dartmouth.edu/cgi-bin/WebObjects/Journals.woa/xmlpage/4/article/425.

Malazita, James. "Epistemic Infrastructure, the Instrumental Turn, and the Digital Humanities." In *People, Practice, Power: Digital Humanities outside the Center*, edited by Anne McGrail, Angel David Nieves, and Siobhan Senier. Minneapolis: University of Minnesota Press, 2021.

Pawlicka-Deger, Urszula. "Laboratory: A New Space in Digital Humanities." In *People, Practice, Power: Digital Humanities outside the Center*, edited by Anne McGrail, Angel David Nieves, and Siobhan Senier. Minneapolis: University of Minnesota Press, 2021.

Peterson, M., and M. Spencer. "Understanding Academic Culture and Climate." In *ASHE Reader on Organization and Governance*, edited by M. Peterson, 140–55. Needham Heights, Mass.: Simon and Schuster, 1991.

Posner, Miriam. "Here and There: Creating DH Community." In *Debates in the Digital Humanities*, edited by Matthew K. Gold and Lauren Klein. Minneapolis: University of Minnesota Press, 2016. http://dhdebates.gc.cuny.edu/debates/text/73.

Risam, Roopika. "Other Worlds, Other DHs: Notes towards a DH Accent." *Digital Scholarship in the Humanities* 32, no. 2 (June 1, 2017): 377–84. https://academic.oup.com/dsh/article-abstract/32/2/377/2669630.

Williams, Andrea L., Roselynn Verwoord, Theresa A. Beery, Helen Dalton, James McKinnon, Karen Strickland, Jessica Pace, and Gary Poole. "The Power of Social Networks: A Model for Weaving the Scholarship of Teaching and Learning into Institutional Culture." *Teaching & Learning Inquiry* 1, no. 2 (2013): 49–62.

Intersectionality and Infrastructure
Toward a Critical Digital Humanities

CHRISTINA BOYLES

Since Alan Liu's clarion call in 2011, digital humanities has undergone a cultural turn that has reshaped many of the ways that we think about the relationship between technologies, oppression, and social justice. Texts like Elizabeth Losh and Jacqueline Wernimont's edited collection *Bodies of Information: Intersectional Feminism and the Digital Humanities* and Roopika Risam's "Beyond the Margins: Intersectionality and the Digital Humanities" consider how the theories and practices within digital humanities tend to reinforce hegemonic notions of power and offer strategies for intervention and resistance. Their work begins to dismantle the divide between *hack* and *yack,* or theory and practice, which historically has structured and influenced many conversations about the future of digital humanities work. Martha Nell Smith has argued that these divisions were intentional, noting, "It was as if these matters of objective and hard science provided an oasis for folks who did not want to clutter sharp, disciplined, methodical philosophy with considerations of the gender-, race-, and class-determined facts of life. . . . Humanities computing seemed to offer a space free from all this messiness and a return to objective questions of representation."[1]

The goal of critical digital humanities, then, is to weave considerations of race, gender, and sexuality into our theory and praxis. One powerful framework for doing so is intersectionality. Kimberlé Crenshaw coined the term in 1989 to express how "the experiences of women of color are frequently the product of intersecting patterns of racism and sexism."[2] Developed specifically to address the multiple layers of oppression experienced by black women, the term is often used to describe the intersecting forms of discrimination an individual may face based on that person's ethnicity, race, gender, sexuality, or socioeconomic status. Risam has described the application of intersectionality to the digital humanities as follows: "intersectional Digital Humanities asks us to begin with the specificities of a data set, identify the layers of difference that intersect within it, and use that knowledge as a basis for project design."[3] This article expands on and adds to Risam's model by offering methods for applying intersectionality to digital humanities infrastructure, including our history, our campuses, and our communities.

Many of my colleagues represented in this section of the book have outlined their desire to develop more inclusive digital humanities infrastructure on their campuses, and others have offered new ways of theorizing our relationship to our materials and tools. Each narrative intervenes in traditional notions of digital humanities by advocating for more inclusive practices within the field and/or by denoting potential pitfalls embedded in our current practices. Intersectionality contributes to these arguments by providing a framework that helps us understand how to implement these practices in ethical and inclusive ways.

Intersectionality and the DH Origin Story

The history of higher education is embroiled in racial capitalism. Risam has noted, "Stolen labor on stolen land generated capital for the university, wealth produced through the oppression of Indigenous and Black people, the essence of racial capitalism. . . . All the while, white scholars in the university produced knowledge to ossify the backbone of white supremacy that undergirds the nation."[4] Departments and fields without a clear commitment to dismantling these injustices only reinscribe them into their theories and methodologies, and digital humanities is no exception. Our origin story upholds the values of racial capitalism by emphasizing the tenets of Western logics as implemented by white male elites. This narrative also elides the harms wrought by these same processes. As Susan Hockey has noted,

> Unlike many other interdisciplinary experiments, humanities computing has a very well-known beginning. In 1949, an Italian Jesuit priest, Father Robert Busa, began what even to this day is a monumental task: to make an *index verborum* of all the words in the works of St. Thomas Aquinas and related authors, totaling some 11 million words of medieval Latin. Father Busa imagined that a machine might be able to help him, and, having heard of computers, went to visit Thomas J. Watson at IBM in the United States in search of support."[5]

While Father Busa's concordance certainly offers an early and prominent example of humanities computing, citing it as the only source of the digital humanities is both exclusionary and reductive. Notably, the field's resistance to cultural criticism meant that the problematic aspects of Busa's work remained invisible for a whole generation of digital humanists. After sorting through photos in Busa's archive, Melissa Terras shared that Busa employed a number of women to develop the punch cards for his concordance. She notes, "it shouldn't be that surprising to us that women were so important in Father Busa's pioneering computing project: in the early 1960s computer programmers were commonly women."[6] Their invisibility—and our understandings of these women as nameless, voiceless, and static—will forever impede us from gaining a full understanding of their contributions to the project.

Moreover, this history elides the harms wrought by Busa's project, particularly its use of classification technologies that advanced the aims of racial capitalism and the complicity of the men and women who worked on the project. Using technology developed by IBM, Busa's concordance served as an endorsement of a tool used to perpetuate racism during apartheid. Michael Kwet has observed that "During apartheid, with Thomas Watson, Jr. now president, IBM New York leased its IBM South Africa subsidiary with specialized technology tailored for the apartheid state. In 1952, the apartheid regime ordered its first electronic tabulator to IBM South Africa. There is ample evidence their technology was used to categorize, segregate and denationalize blacks."[7]

While these classification systems were implemented just after Busa launched his project, IBM had a long history of profiting from genocide. Kwet goes on to say that "Beginning in the 1930s, IBM New York, under the direction of its president, Thomas Watson, Sr., supplied Hollerith punch card systems to their IBM Germany subsidiary for use by the Third Reich. IBM machines were customized for the Nazis to efficiently track and sort groups targeted for persecution and genocide. Numbers tattooed on Auschwitz inmates began as IBM punch card system identification numbers."[8]

It is crucial that we acknowledge the links between our field and the colonial capitalistic enterprise. It is only by unpacking these histories that we can develop new structures and processes that resist and refuse to cause harm to marginalized communities. Tuck and Yang offer us the framework of refusal, which "provide[s] ways to negotiate how we as [. . .] researchers can learn from experiences of dispossessed peoples—often painful, but also wise, full of desire and dissent—without serving up pain stories on a silver platter for the settler colonial academy, which hungers so ravenously for them."[9] Refusing can take many forms: focusing on structural inequalities rather than individual experiences, emphasizing failures to respond to injustices rather than the injustices themselves, and refusing to blindly reproduce the inequalities of the past.

We also can reconcile our problematic history by acknowledging its flaws and by recognizing the myriad other influences that shaped the foundation of the field. The speakers on the "Alternate Histories of the Digital Humanities" panel at the 2017 Alliance of Digital Humanities Organizations Conference outlined a handful of alternate histories that shaped digital humanities scholarship, including presentations on early digital scholarship in India, activist strains in early digital work, feminist media histories, and Busa's female labor force. Each of these presentations demonstrated the ways in which digital scholarship is far more nuanced, diverse, and global than is depicted by the stories surrounding Busa's project.[10] They also were an invitation to the field, asking us to reconsider our relationship to both our origin story and its adherence to the values of racial capitalism.

Virginia Eubanks has noted that "we can create technologies that protect socially just values or we can build technologies that permit those values to disappear. We must actively choose the kind of technosocial worlds we want to inhabit."[11] The same is true for our histories.

Intersectionality and Our Campuses

If we fail to acknowledge the problems with our field's history, we will only reinforce the errors of the past—benefiting from the labor of women and black and indigenous people of color (BIPOC) while barring their entry into the upper echelons of digital humanities. According to a 2017 report released by the American Council on Education, "The data show that women are not ascending to leadership roles, given that they hold a greater share of the entry-level, service, and teaching-only positions than their male counterparts. This is true for all women when looking across degree-granting postsecondary institutions; the trend is exacerbated for women of color." Things are no different within the Digital Humanities. With the proliferation of alt-ac positions in the field and academic writ large, many of our colleagues are precarious. Boyles et al. have observed that

> Despite the money and prestige that seems to come with the label, Digital Humanities is a field that relies on grants and temporary positions to establish credibility on campuses. As a result, DH laborers are frequently precarious across institutions. They occupy a startling range of positions: administrators, adjuncts, postdocs, graduate and undergraduate students, tenure-track and contingent faculty, librarians, archivists, programmers, IT and edtech specialists, consultants, museum curators, artists, authors, editors, and more.[12]

This precarity coincides with "an underrepresentation of women, of people of color, of folks who don't identify with a heteronormative category in the Digital Humanities as it is recognized by the academy."[13] Both factors exacerbate the marginalization of scholars of color within the field. Collaborations with precariously positioned scholars and communities are some of the most innovative work in the field—like the Mapathon for Puerto Rico, the Torn Apart/Separados Project, and BlackWomenToo; the development of innovative teaching materials and curriculum through online forums including Humanities Commons and the HASTAC blog; and the organization of collaborative networks, such as HASTAC, FemTechNet, and SurvDH. Global Outlook::Digital Humanities highlights these interventions on a global scale by "break[ing] down barriers that hinder communication and collaboration among researchers and students of the Digital Arts, Humanities, and Cultural Heritage sectors in high, mid, and low income economies."[14]

In spite of their tremendous contributions to the field, precariously positioned scholars are rarely credited appropriately for their work. As Laura Braunstein observes, "Scholars who are used to the invisibility of traditional library services . . . find that digital projects expose hierarchies and bureaucracies that they don't want to negotiate or even think about."[15] One of the most significant hurdles is the emphasis on single authorship in the humanities, which is an act that asks scholars to either erase the contributions of others or devalue the significance of their work. University hierarchies that emphasize the scholarship of faculty over that of librarians, alt-ac scholars, and community partners are equally damaging to collaborative digital work. Although upending conventional models may be challenging, doing so is necessary to prevent abuses of power and to ensure that the contributions of graduate students, librarians, and precarious scholars and community members are properly recognized.

If digital humanities is to live up to its identity as a big tent, it needs to embrace broader definitions of collaboration or embrace another metaphor altogether. Debates about whom to include in the big tent often reinforce old notions about the fields, methods, and people suited to digital scholarship and fail to decenter those in positions of relative power—white, typically male, faculty members with technical skills. Now is the time not only to discuss more options for inclusion but also to enact them through transformative change. Doing so will require a unanimous effort from all parties involved, including administration, faculty, staff, and students. One way may be to leverage the digital humanities cluster hires that have become increasingly popular in institutions of higher education. These groups often work closely with digital humanities labs, specialists, librarians, and administrators, and as such may be able to unify behind ethical notions of collaboration and authorship.

Another way to promote a healthy ethic of collaboration is to outline ownership expectations at the onset of a project. By using a memorandum of understanding, contributors can discuss their desired ownership of a project prior to its development. Doing so ensures that all involved parties are on the same page before investing significant time and resources in a project. Building equitable ownership into this agreement can prevent or alleviate future discussions about who has the right to promote or publish the project. It also encourages participants to be invested in a project through a clear acknowledgment of their labor. The Modern Language Association and American Historical Association have taken steps to promote these types of collaboration by releasing guidelines for the evaluation of digital work; however, these statements do not explicitly address issues pertaining to collaboration. This, then, is a site where our infrastructure needs to be amended.

Issues of equality and collaboration are not limited to digital humanities, but they are a common feature of large-scale digital work. As such, digital humanities is primed to address these issues through thoughtful critique and experimentation. Jessica DeSpain notes that while "these rules may not seem revolutionary, they do go against the grain of current DH research practices that emphasize a lead scholar with a team of graduate students working on the most adaptable digital platforms and designing tools as needed."[16] Jacqueline Wernimont reinforces this call, stating that "[p]art of what is at stake for students is their own sense of agency—it is not always clear how they might intervene in an academic context where traditional hierarchies still largely dictate what counts as good or useful scholarship."[17] In other words, advancing an equitable model of digital humanities requires a deconstructing of traditional hierarchies, which requires utmost collaboration and a shared creative vision.

Intersectionality and Our Communities

The need for ethical practices extends beyond academia to include the communities with which we interact. While many digital humanities projects examine the behaviors of a particular community, very little digital humanities scholarship discusses how to best interact with community partners. As a result, digital humanists often have little to no knowledge of how to best engage with communities. Moya Bailey, in her talk "#robinhoodfail: The Ethics of Public Scholarship and the Digital Liberal Arts" at Grinnell College, outlined the ways in which academic infrastructure runs counter to community engagement. She noted that many projects require travel and long-term commitments with little to no up-front compensation. As a result, each collaborator must make a significant commitment to the project in terms of both labor and finances. Reimbursement processes may provide a modicum of relief from these financial burdens, but they are often long and unwieldy, particularly for entities without a clear connection to an academic institution. Most community members cannot afford to forgo their liquid assets for the duration of the reimbursement, so many of them simply do not participate in academic collaborations, even though their input is highly beneficial to scholarly projects.[18]

To address this issue, grant agencies need to be more flexible in their funding and reimbursement policies. In his inaugural report, Earl Lewis, the former president of the Andrew W. Mellon Foundation, emphasized the role of increasingly diverse digital scholarship, stating, "We do foresee significant modifications to our grant making priorities. Perhaps the biggest change, especially for a foundation that has prided itself on being quiet, will be the production of an annual report that synthesizes the very best scholarship on the value of diversity to social and civil life in democratic societies."[19] On the basis of the organization's recent funding habits, it seems that this new mission will include support for community-engaged research, teaching, and programming. According to the Mellon Foundation's grant database, the organization has funded the following projects since December 2016: public humanities initiatives at the University of Wisconsin-Madison, Rhodes College, Davidson College, Carleton College, and the University of California-Santa Barbara; community-engaged tool development such as the LLILAS Archives at the University of Texas-Austin; community-based projects such as the crowd-sourced photographic archive at New Mexico Highlands University; my own project, the Archivo de Respuestas Emergencias de Puerto Rico; and services for the public such as the development of the Mukurtu content management system at Washington State University.[20]

Individuals also need to adopt intersectional methods into their work with community partners. One option is to implement postcustodial approaches to data collection into our digital humanities projects. The Society of American Archivists defines postcustodial archiving as "the idea that archivists will no longer physically acquire and maintain records, but that they will provide management oversight for records that will remain in the custody of the record creators."[21] In other words, community groups retain the rights to their own data, thus upending traditional scholarly models in which community data is colonized and commodified. Michelle Caswell et al. view postcustodial archiving as a way "to conceive of and build a world in which communities that have historically been and are currently being marginalized due to white supremacy, patriarchy, capitalism, gender binaries, colonialism and ableism are fully empowered to represent their past, construct their present and envision their futures."[22] Postcustodial practice can extend beyond archiving work to include any project dependent upon the data of others. By establishing collaborative, horizontal relationships between participants and archivists; keeping records locally accessible to invested communities; and focusing on human rights, community development, and social justice, postcustodial praxis provides numerous strategies for implementing intersectionality into our methodologies.

Moreover, scholars and practitioners need to listen to their communities' acts of refusal. One of the best ways that we can ensure that the work we are doing is transformative, ethical, and inclusive is by listening to the needs of our community collaborators. Eve Tuck and K. Wayne Yang's "Unbecoming Claims: Pedagogies of Refusal in Qualitative Research," offers powerful models on how to work with communities and establish healthy and professional boundaries.[23] We must remember that our community work is valuable only if it is driven by community needs and if it is beneficial to the groups with which we interact.

The Iroquois Great Law of Peace outlines the concept of seventh-generation stewardship, in which individuals and communities consider the implications of their decision-making for seven generations into the future. Applying this notion to the digital humanities in its present state is alarming. We are capable of sustaining the field for future generations, but we must make it more accessible, inclusive, and meaningful for those who have been kept on the margins. We need to ask ourselves, "How can we develop an ethical framework that is focused on our relationships to people rather than data?" and "How would this transform our work with our communities and institutions?" The answer lies in our pursuit of ethical practices, and intersectionality offers us one such model. By taking intersectional approaches to digital humanities, particularly our history, our campuses, and our communities, we can transform the field into something that is not only valuable today but will benefit and sustain future generations of scholars.

Notes

1. Smith, "Human Touch Software," 4.
2. Crenshaw, "Mapping the Margins," 1243.
3. Risam, "Beyond the Margins."
4. Risam, "Ethnic Studies Now."
5. Hockey. "History of Humanities Computing," 4.
6. Terras, "For Ada Lovelace Day."
7. Kwet, "Apartheid in the Shadows."
8. Kwet, "Apartheid in the Shadows."
9. Tuck and Yang, "Unbecoming Claims," 812.
10. Earhart et al., "Alternate Histories of the Digital Humanities."
11. Eubanks, *Digital Dead End*, 85.
12. Boyles et al., "Precarious Labor and the Digital Humanities." 693.
13. Johnson, "Digital in the Humanities."
14. Global Outlook::Digital Humanities, "About."
15. Braunstein, "Open Stacks."
16. DeSpain, "Feminist Digital Humanities Pedagogy," 65–73.
17. Wernimont, "Whence Feminism?"
18. Bailey, "#robinhoodfail."
19. Boyles, "Counting the Costs."
20. Andrew W. Mellon Foundation, *Report of the Andrew W. Mellon Foundation 2013*.
21. SAA, "Postcustodial Theory of Archives."
22. Caswell et al., " 'To Suddenly Discover Yourself Existing,' " 56–81.
23. Tuck and Yang, "Unbecoming Claims."

Bibliography

Andrew W. Mellon Foundation. *Report of the Andrew W. Mellon Foundation 2013*. December 31, 2013. New York: Andrew W. Mellon Foundation, 8, 11. https://mellon.org/media /filer_public/a6/51/a6515255-46f3-4b6f-9b4a-b1f1d0ef1205/awmf-ar-2013.pdf.

Bailey, Moya. "#robinhoodfail: The Ethics of Public Scholarship and the Digital Liberal Arts." Lecture, Grinnell College, Grinnell, Iowa, April 20, 2017. https://www.grinnell .edu/news/robinhoodfail-ethics-public-scholarship-and-digital-liberal-arts.

Boyles, Christina. "Counting the Costs: Funding Feminism in the Digital Humanities." In *Bodies of Information: Feminist Debates in Digital Humanities*. Minneapolis: University of Minnesota Press, 2018.

Boyles, Christina, Anne Cong-Huyen, Carrie Johnston, Jim McGrath, and Amanda Phillips. "Precarious Labor and the Digital Humanities." *American Quarterly* 70, no. 3 (2018): 693–700. https://doi.org/10.1353/aq.2018.0054.

Braunstein, Laura. "Open Stacks: Making DH Labor Visible." *dh+lib*, June 7, 2017. http:// acrl.ala.org/dh/2017/06/07/open-stacks-making-dh-labor-visible/.

Caswell, Michelle, Alda Allina Migoni, Noah Geraci, and Marika Cifor. "'To Suddenly Discover Yourself Existing': Uncovering the Impact of Community Archives." *The American Archivist* 79, no. 1 (2016): 56–81.

Crenshaw, Kimberlé. "Mapping the Margins: Intersectionality, Identity Politics, and Violence against Women of Color." *Stanford Law Review* 43 (1991): 1241–99.

DeSpain, Jessica. "A Feminist Digital Humanities Pedagogy beyond the Classroom." *Transformations: The Journal of Inclusive Scholarship and Pedagogy* 26, no. 1 (2016).

Earhart, Amy, Steven Jones, Tara McPherson, Padmini Ray Murray, and Roger Whitson. "Alternate Histories of the Digital Humanities." Panel, Annual Alliance of Digital Humanities Organizations Conference, Montreal, Quebec, August 8–11, 2017.

Eubanks, Virginia. *Digital Dead End.* Cambridge, Mass.: MIT Press, 2011.

Global Outlook:: Digital Humanities. "About." Last modified August 22, 2017. http://www.globaloutlookdh.org/.

Hockey, Susan. "The History of Humanities Computing." In *A Companion to Digital Humanities,* edited by Susan Shreibman, Ray Siemens, and John Unsworth. Malden, Mass.: Blackwell, 2004.

Johnson, Jessica Marie. "The Digital in the Humanities: An Interview with Jessica Marie Johnson." *Los Angeles Review of Books,* July 23, 2016. https://lareviewofbooks.org/article/digital-humanities-interview-jessica-marie-johnson/.

Kwet, Michael. "Apartheid in the Shadows: the USA, IBM and South Africa's Digital Police State." *CounterPunch,* May 3, 2017. https://www.counterpunch.org/2017/05/03/apartheid-in-the-shadows-the-usa-ibm-and-south-africas-digital-police-state/.

Losh, Elizabeth, and Jacqueline Wernimont, eds. *Bodies of Information: Intersectional Feminism and the Digital Humanities.* Minneapolis: University of Minnesota Press, 2018.

Risam, Roopika. "Beyond the Margins: Intersectionality and the Digital Humanities." *Digital Humanities Quarterly* 9, no. 2 (2015). http://www.digitalhumanities.org/dhq/vol/9/2/000208/000208.html.

Risam, Roopika. "Ethnic Studies Now." *Ethnic Studies Rise,* December 19, 2019. https://ethnicrise.github.io/roundtable/ethnic-studies-now/.

SAA. "Postcustodial Theory of Archives." *SAA: Society of American Archivists.* https://dictionary.archivists.org/entry/postcustodial.html.

Smith, Martha Nell. "The Human Touch Software of the Highest Order: Revisiting Editing as Interpretation." *Textual Cultures: Texts, Contexts, Interpretation* 2, no. 1 (2007): 1–15.

Terras, Melissa. "For Ada Lovelace Day—Father Busa's Female Punch Card Operatives." *Melissa Terras* (blog), October 15, 2013. https://melissaterras.org/2013/10/15/for-ada-lovelace-day-father-busas-female-punch-card-operatives/.

Tuck, Eve, and K. Wayne Yang. "Unbecoming Claims: Pedagogies of Refusal in Qualitative Research." *Qualitative Inquiry* 20 (2014): 812.

Wernimont, Jacqueline. "Whence Feminism? Assessing Feminist Interventions in Digital Literacy Archives." *Digital Humanities Quarterly* 7, no. 1 (2013). http://digitalhumanities.org:8081/dhq/vol/7/1/000156/000156.html.

PART II

HUMAN INFRASTRUCTURES

Labor Considerations and
Communities of Practice

In Service of Pedagogy
A Colony in Crisis *and the Digital Humanities Center*

KELSEY CORLETT-RIVERA, NATHAN H. DIZE,
ABBY R. BROUGHTON, AND BRITTANY DE GAIL

And fortunately too, a digital humanities *center* is not the digital humanities. The digital humanities—or I should say, digital humanists—are much more diverse, much more dispersed, and stunningly resourceful to boot.

So if you're interested in the transformative power of technology upon your teaching and research, don't sit around waiting for a digital humanities center to pop up on your campus or make you a primary investigator on a grant.

Act as if there's no such thing as a digital humanities center.

Instead, create your own network of possible collaborators. Don't hope for or rely upon institutional support or recognition. To survive and thrive, digital humanists must be agile, mobile, insurgent. Decentralized and nonhierarchical.

Stop forming committees and begin creating coalitions. Seek affinities over affiliations, networks over institutes.[1]

Mark Sample shared these insights in 2010, when he was writing "On the Death of the Digital Humanities Center." In 2020 we found that his advice still held true. In creating and building our small digital humanities (DH) project *A Colony in Crisis* (CIC), we focused on pedagogical goals, primarily undergraduate classroom use of digitized primary sources. While groundwork was laid through the 2013 DH Incubator, our project was not selected for a fellowship and so we did not rely heavily on the University of Maryland's MITH-centered DH infrastructure, which primarily supports large-scale, research-driven initiatives.[2] The Maryland Institute for Technology in the Humanities (MITH) and similar centers have avoided providing support as a service and instead have focused on inclusion in grants as equal participants, which has significantly raised their standing as research centers over time.[3] Rather than participating primarily in "Big DH" instead of smaller projects (to avoid being pigeonholed as a service center), we find that large DH centers should *both* lead large-scale, grant-funded projects *and* support small, low-tech iterative projects. On the other hand, DH practitioners should *both* apply for large grants in collaboration with centers *and* try out new ideas with low-budget efforts requiring minimal computing resources and staffing. In this way, big research-focused DH centers can support small-scale, pedagogy-focused DH projects, and vice versa, in a model similar to that of Broadway/off-Broadway productions.[4]

In 2014, French studies librarian Kelsey Corlett-Rivera and French studies graduate students Nathan H. Dize and Abby R. Broughton began work on *A Colony in Crisis: The Saint-Domingue Grain Crisis of 1789,* a translated online primary source reader of colonial Saint-Domingue (Haiti). *A Colony in Crisis* was developed as a pedagogical tool, facilitating classroom use of historical documents written in French by translating and curating excerpts.[5] The project team never aspired to create a comprehensive online archive but rather a manageable pedagogical tool for historians, teachers, and students. The first issue of translations focused on the grain crisis of 1789, presenting official documents detailing correspondence between deputies living in Saint-Domingue and the mainland officials in France. The project's Board of Advisors, a group of scholars specializing in Haitian and colonial French history, Haitian anthropology, and French literary studies, reviewed all translations before the site launched on September 17, 2014, about five months after initial planning conversations.

Since that time, the site has been viewed over 50,000 times, and we have added two more sets of translations, including issue 3.0, which highlights documents pertaining to the lives of the enslaved and the conditions that they faced during this prerevolutionary period. French undergraduate students contributed background notes for the site, and most recently, students at Montclair State University added Haitian Creole translations of key pamphlets and corresponding audio recordings, a feature that opens up our content to a whole new audience and really returns it to its rightful owners.

As with many Big DH projects, our Little DH project resulted in several traditional publications (peer-reviewed journal articles, conference presentations, and book chapters), which helped us identify our primary audience: the broader Caribbean studies and DH communities.[6]

Many factors have contributed to the success achieved by *A Colony in Crisis,* most of which derive from the project's small scale as well as its institutional and financial independence. There are, of course, disadvantages to this approach, and we further explore both the positives and negatives in this chapter.

On Broadway: Big DH

In his 2012 state-of-the-field survey, "The Function of Digital Humanities Centers at the Present Time," Neil Fraistat highlighted the importance of DH centers as "crosswalks between cyberinfrastructure and users" where both the professoriate and graduate students are able to pass from traditional research avenues to digital boulevards paved with computational methods, encoding practices, and tools to transform their traditional research methods into digital.[7] Fraistat's vision privileges the DH center as the hub for digital research methods on university campuses around the globe. Yet, some uncertainty surrounds these centers: are they service centers? research centers? Is the DH center capable of functioning as a crosswalk, or is it a turnpike requiring entrants to buy into their specific research practices and workflows in order to participate? Do these centers create environments wherein nonfaculty members of the university community, such as students, information technologists, librarians, and contingent workers, can get credit for interacting, teaching, contributing, and producing knowledge?

Back in 2012, the institution of MITH could seem impervious, especially to graduate and undergraduate students in departments not affiliated with MITH. In general, its scope appeared clearly defined and thus somewhat inaccessible for projects outside of its current research agenda. Prior to the creation of the Digital Studies in the Arts and Humanities Certificate (DSAH) and the Mellon-funded African American History, Culture and Digital Humanities initiative (AADHum), it was difficult for graduate students not affiliated with either the libraries or the English department to receive training in digital research methods and practice.[8] This, coupled with fixed degree requirements for graduate students, made pursuing DH training opportunities or projects seem unimaginable. The DH Incubator did aim to support librarians who were not directly involved in Center research, but in 2014 the DH infrastructure provided by MITH and the libraries allowed for only limited synergy and coworking across the university and the numerous colleges therein.[9] From the outside looking in, projects without tenured faculty members, nationally competitive research grants, and elaborate web interfaces constituted a minority in the broad scope of MITH's institutional history.

As less DH attention has been directed to marginalized groups, scholars have found that support for projects focusing on underserved regions is less readily available.[10] When the project team began working on *A Colony in Crisis,* MITH had sponsored or supported numerous digital archives, text mining projects, databases, and large-scale projects like the *Shelley-Godwin Archive* and *Walt Whitman's Annotations.*[11] At that time, small-scale projects rarely figured into MITH's research agenda, and even by 2014 very few projects, with notable exceptions, featured content from noncanonical literary or historical corpora.[12] More and more, DH tools and praxes are moving away from a solely institutional or hierarchical approach, as seen with the Black Code studies movement, which focuses on black culture and thought in digital spaces and "rejects formulations of Black Studies that tie intellectual production only to institutional structures or the digital humanities only to grant-seeking projects with university affiliations."[13]

Off Broadway: Little DH

A Colony in Crisis was created without relying heavily on the MITH-centered DH infrastructure at the University of Maryland.[14] This afforded a degree of flexibility that allowed the project team to conduct its own research, structure the project, and determine its own set of goals independent of expectations set forth by large sponsors. Benefits included the following:

LOW COST BUT NOT LOW VALUE

While our project has always been run on a small budget, it has not been done cheaply. Corlett-Rivera has a project management background and benefited greatly from the project development training offered in 2013 at the Digital Humanities Winter Institute (now Humanities Intensive Learning and Teaching [HILT]). Her experience ensured that we took a highly professional approach to the project. We documented in-kind and paid working hours, implemented a level of separation between the graduate student translators and the board of advisors to allow for nearly blind review, sent monthly reports to stakeholders, and developed a communication plan, among other approaches that are common to larger-scale projects. The site was also rigorously tested through guerilla usability trials, as instructed in HILT's Crowdsourcing Cultural Heritage training course in 2014.

The project team also prioritized recognizing the contributions of all collaborators. The four authors have dedicated many hours of their lives to *A Colony in Crisis;* in the case of Dize and Broughton, the majority of those hours unpaid. That said, their names, biographies, and photos have been featured on the *Colony in Crisis* site since the moment it went live, and they have worked on all related publications as coauthors.[15] The site also features acknowledgments for the many others who contributed to the project, and a special section that recognizes the service contributions of our Board of Advisors.[16] Apart from the Board, which has grown to fifteen total scholars over the six-year lifespan of the project, *A Colony in Crisis* currently has only four project team members.[17] Brittany de Gail, a former UMD libraries staff member, joined the team in 2016, and our low-tech, iterative approach has reduced the need for a large staff. After the first issue of translations, the graduate-student authors began working on the site without compensation, viewing their contributions as integral parts of their professional scholarship and thereby further reducing funding requirements.[18]

Recognizing contributions to the project has especially benefited the authors. The project parlays into meaningful professional experience for Broughton and Dize, who are both instructors of French seeking tenure-track appointments. The publishing experience and the pedagogical focus of the project have already significantly impacted their work and will serve them well on the competitive job market. Dize, a scholar of Haitian literature and history, was introduced to his professional community when the project provided access by way of DH rather than through more traditional connections (such as a dissertation advisor). For Corlett-Rivera and de Gail, *A Colony in Crisis* has led to diverse publication and project management experience that has strengthened Corlett-Rivera's successful application for tenure and will continue to serve de Gail's professional portfolio in her postbac career pursuits.

SHORTER TIMELINE

MITH is firmly ensconced in the big-R research enterprise at the University of Maryland and typically participates in large, grant-funded projects, in which an idea is generated, a grant is awarded twelve to eighteen months later, and work commences. Although the large-scale DH projects that feature prominently in MITH's research agenda could not succeed following our low-tech, iterative approach, we argue that this approach, is, in fact, better for Little DH projects like ours, which allow for a fast prototype that can later be scaled up. In the same amount of time that it would have taken a faculty member collaborating with MITH to even submit an application for funding, *A Colony in Crisis* had already gone live. As most National Endowment for the Humanities (NEH) grants typically notify applicants six to twelve months after submission, project work on a traditionally run DH project likely would have started as we were preparing our second issue of translations for the *Colony in Crisis* site.[19] By moving quickly, we were able to spend time identifying our primary audience and marketing the site, but we did not miss opportunities like the founding of the *caribbean digital* conference and the journal *sx archipelago* as well as the opportunity to counter the early-2018 surge in Haiti-focused press brought about by President Donald Trump's racist remarks about Haitian immigrants.[20]

While uptake was not immediate, within a year our translated pamphlets were being used in the French-language classroom, by which point in time a larger project likely would not have even been notified about grant funding.[21] Both during initial project stages and as the project expanded we have prioritized project work, and more recently scholarship documenting our experiences, over identifying and applying for large grants.[22] The time required to apply for such grants is significant and is more difficult to justify when the majority of the project team is working on an unpaid basis. More and more projects like ours have received funding in recent rounds of grant awards.[23] Had we begun the project in 2017, we might have started with a grant application given these awards and MITH's expansion into UMD's curriculum and the AADHum project. That said, the success rates for NEH grant applications remain very low, averaging 16 percent.[24] Also, as Miriam Posner notes, an NEH grant does not necessarily provide more long-term project security than we have through our Little DH approach.[25]

Rather than restricting project growth, the iterative approach focusing on pedagogy allowed the team to enhance the project in stages, honing the scope of the content and affording other scholars ways to get involved with the pedagogical goals of the site.

MINIMAL COMPUTING

Major developments in digital scholarship such as the Minimal Computing movement argue for "architectures of necessity" that reduce the technological learning curve and encourage the participation of new users.[26] Principles such as "ease of use, ease of creation, increased access and reductions in computing—and by extension, electricity" can guide a project's selection of technology.[27] We asked, "What do we need?" and concluded that the answer was something inexpensive, without intensive development requirements, that was flexible and could be updated quickly, that allowed for some level of linked subject categorization, and that could be used on a mobile device with low bandwidth to facilitate use in Haiti, where these documents originated.[28] A WordPress blog, which was then supported by UMD's central division of IT, could fulfill those needs to an acceptable level. Drupal would have been more appropriate had we needed to involve more content authors or include more advanced code. A full-fledged Omeka site, while very attractive and certainly in vogue when we were developing the project, would not have provided sufficient return on investment. We would have either spent significant time learning the software or significant money on developers, and it would have likely been difficult to access on a mobile device.

The flexibility inherent in a self-managed, low-tech site also facilitated the rapid content growth. While we had always imagined ways to add translations to the site, when we were ready to go live with Issue 2.0, a number of adjustments had to be made to the original structure to allow for the new content. No change requests were submitted and no developers contacted; instead, the site designer identified several hours when traffic was expected to be low and made the necessary changes during those hours. While *low-tech* may also signify a lack of robust archiving and data management, we mitigated that risk by participating in the UMD Libraries' nascent digital publishing program. We signed an agreement, without relinquishing any of our author rights, that states that the UMD Libraries will, among other things,

    i)   make the contents of the e-publication available free of charge via the Internet or any subsequent technology . . .

    v)   strive, in the absence of unforeseen technical difficulties and routine maintenance, to provide 24/7 access . . .

    vii)   digitally archive all e-publication content produced under this agreement . . .[29]

This agreement provides peace of mind that our project will be preserved as technology advances and the team moves forward with their careers at separate institutions.

PEDAGOGY, OR ANOTHER WAY TO DO DH

While some scholars may indeed find *A Colony in Crisis* independently, one crucial step toward establishing our user base relies on pedagogical interventions in the undergraduate classroom. Working directly with instructors and students presents teaching opportunities that have the potential to be personalized and intimately monitored.

A Colony in Crisis's first teaching intervention came together in the fall of 2015.[30] Dr. Sarah Benharrech, then an assistant professor of French at the University of Maryland and a member of the *Colony in Crisis* Board of Advisors, was slated to teach an upper-level French course titled Rebellions, Riots and Revolutions. Since Corlett-Rivera and Dize were both on campus, they were available to help students navigate the site and understand the documents. The students' advanced reading level in French allowed them not only to use the translated documents but also to explore the digitized originals. Students were tasked with creating background notes on figures that they found in the documents, such as individual colonial deputies, groups of people, or significant geographic locations. The students were aware that the notes would be used on the site, highlighted in the main navigation bar as an equal component of the project. Using both the French original documents and the team's translations and references, the students paired up to submit notes of approximately two hundred words, written in both French and English. Dr. Benharrech graded their work and transmitted student submissions to the *Colony in Crisis* team, with the French grammar edited for clarity. However, adding the notes to the site was not as streamlined as the team originally anticipated. Independent of the students, the team was tasked with reworking the notes into content appropriate for the site and pursuing citations of questionable scholarship in order to maintain the site's level of quality meant for students and professional scholars alike.

Independent study is an alternative model to classroom instruction in a traditional course. In January 2016, Dr. Laurence Jay-Rayon Ibrahim Aibo, then director of Montclair State University's Center for Translation and Interpreting, and A. J. Kelton, director of the university's Center for the Digital Humanities, proposed a joint translation project with *A Colony in Crisis*. Remarking that the site centered on colonial Saint-Domingue yet did not speak directly to Haitian people, Dr. Jay-Rayon sought to initiate the translation of the documents into Haitian Creole by her translation students. Two MSU students, Daphney Vastey and Pierre Malbranche, worked on translating documents from issue 1.0 into Creole, receiving university credit for their work as part of an independent study with Dr. Jay-Rayon. In April 2017, with the CIC team virtually present over video conference, the students presented their work on the translations in the MSU Center for the Digital Humanities, speaking to both the work's impact on their scholarship and its link to their personal relationship with Haitian Creole. CIC's reach is unquestionably bolstered by their contributions, through six Creole translations available on the site, three of which are accompanied by audio versions. Dr. Jay-Rayon Ibrahim Aibo has tirelessly pursued further grant funding to compensate additional translation and recording work. Corlett-Rivera, Dize, Jay-Rayon Ibrahim Aibo, and Vastey shared their experiences at the 2018 AADHum conference through a panel presentation titled "Decolonizing Colonial Documents: Translating a Colony in Crisis into Kreyòl."

CHALLENGES

Naturally, Little DH does have its disadvantages. While our small team means we can move quickly without obtaining sponsor approval or submitting lengthy reports, there are fewer hands to do the work. Project work ceases if a team member spends a year abroad or takes family leave. We do not have backups. Our short timeline has also impacted our ability to plan work far into the future, as in the case of the student-generated background notes. We did not incorporate a feedback loop to students, as many had left the university by the time the project team began reviewing the completed notes.

While our basic WordPress site helps us follow minimal computing tenets, its limited options for customization impacts site design and functionality. Since *A Colony in Crisis* functions as a hosted Wordpress.com website rather than as a locally hosted Wordpress.org website, we have not been able to implement ideas that would require the use of JavaScript or plugins developed for Wordpress.org, such as a visual timeline marking relevant historical events. Additionally, by loading the digitized source documents into Wikisource, we made it possible to crowdsource correction of the OCRed text but have not had the bandwidth to market that part of the project or to consider the type of research that TEI-encoded full text transcriptions would allow.

Collaborations such as the MSU partnership and our focus on pedagogy reinforce the multiplicity of *A Colony in Crisis*'s goals and buttress dialogues for various avenues for compensation, whether financial, academic, or personal. Our team works without funding in order to promote productive scholarship that we see as integral to the field of Caribbean studies and to our professional portfolios. *A Colony in Crisis* is no simple "labor of love," but rather a conscientious addition of scholarship to the academic community. Digital humanities projects as pedagogy, rather than as exclusively research-oriented projects, allow the DH center to confront institutional productivity mandates. By creating a space for pedagogy to grow, the DH center will be better able to adapt to a dynamic digital research agenda while training faculty and graduate students.

By starting our project off Broadway (or perhaps even off off Broadway), we had the flexibility and independence to move quickly and focus on a little-known episode from an underserved region. In his explanation of the Broadway structure, Robert Viagas explains, "Off-off-Broadway theatres also can be located anywhere in the city. Because of their tiny size, most charge little for tickets and pay actors and others very little, as well. However, because so little is invested, off off Broadway tends to be a hothouse of experimentation. Because so much of the work is specialized and has a limited audience, the small size of off-off-Broadway theaters is perfect."[31] The metaphor of the off-off-Broadway theater is perhaps the best way to describe the genesis of *A Colony in Crisis.*

MITH, in its position "on Broadway," inspired our experimentation on the *Colony in Crisis* project. Our next steps may lead us up to Broadway and MITH, or we may cease to be "profitable" and consequently close.[32] Unbeholden to any one DH center or funder, we are able to keep our project an evolving work in progress, with the Digital Publishing Agreement in place to ensure access and preservation should progress stop. Regardless of the final outcome, we should still be working to expand our networks, following Mark Sample's advice to "act as if there's no such thing as a digital humanities center."[33]

Notes

1. Examples of Digital Humanities networks that transcend institutional boundaries are abundant. Participants at the Caribbean Digital conferences as well as the Colored Conventions Project have been crucial for the development of *A Colony in Crisis* as a community network and for the coauthors as scholars. Communities have not only hosted conferences but have created forums and venues to showcase new DH scholarship such as *Sx Archipelagos* (http://smallaxe.net/sxarchipelagos/); the fall 2017 issue (47, no. 3) of *The Black Scholar* on Black Code studies ("Introduction: Wild Seed in the Machine," edited by Jessica Marie Johnson and Mark Anthony Neal); and even community-generated lists such as Black Digital Humanities Projects & Resources, https://docs.google.com/document/d/1rZwucjyAAR7QiEZl238_hhRPXo5-UKXt2_KCrwPZkiQ/edit?usp=sharing, which originated at the Digital Humanities 2017 Conference in Montreal, Canada. Additionally, within the field of Caribbean DH, the Digital Library of the Caribbean has served as a veritable buoy for extra-university DH networks, fostering linkages between scholars, community members, and institutions.

2. Muñoz, "Digital Humanities in the Library."

3. Muñoz, "Digital Humanities in the Library."

4. Our experience doing Little DH on a campus with Big DH infrastructure likely differs from DH initiatives at smaller institutions, such as those described by Marisa Parham at the 2018 MLA Conference in New York City (https://mla.confex.com/mla/2018/meetingapp.cgi/Session/1635) and by Risam, Snow, and Edwards at Salem State University ("Building an Ethical Digital Humanities Community"). Affordances such as MITH's DH Incubator and the University of Maryland (UMD) Libraries' Digital Publishing Program provided Broadway-like underpinnings to our off-Broadway operation.

5. Dize et al., "Intervening in French."

6. Examples of Big DH projects include Aljoe et al., "Obeah and the Early Caribbean Digital Archive." Roopika Risam and Susan Edwards presented on Micro DH at Digital

Humanities 2017 ("Micro DH: Digital Humanities"), sharing their work to meaningfully (and ethically) involve undergraduates in Digital Humanities projects at Salem State University. Other DH projects focusing on colonial Caribbean history include the Early Caribbean Digital Archive (ECDA), which began working to create a radical digital archive of early Caribbean history in 2011 (ECDA, "About"). Although focusing on a similar time period and region as *A Colony in Crisis,* ECDA is an example of a larger-scale DH project that requires more institutional and financial support; Northeastern University's NULab for Texts, Maps, and Networks houses the project, and partners include the Digital Library of the Caribbean (DLoC). The ECDA project has received numerous distinctions for their work and project vision (Wooldridge et al., "DLoC Awards," 12) from institutions such as DLoC and the Association for Caribbean University, Research and Institutional Libraries (ACURIL) (ECDA, "News"). For more on best practices, labor, and digital publishing in the Caribbean realm, see Josephs, "Handling with Care," and Agostinho, "Archival Encounters."

7. Fraistat, "Function of Digital Humanities Centers," 281.

8. The centrality of English departments in DH infrastructure is a foundational matter that continues to be unraveled (Kirschenbaum, "What Is Digital Humanities?"). It is also worth noting that since 2006, the MITH Digital Dialogues series has supported 241 individual DH presentations by scholars from various fields of inquiry, with and without PhD credentials.

9. Muñoz, "Digital Humanities in the Library."

10. Boyles, "Counting the Costs"; McPherson, "Why Are the Digital Humanities So White?"; and Martin and Runyon, "Digital Humanities, Digital Hegemony."

11. Maryland Institute for Technology in the Humanities, "Research."

12. Two excellent exceptions are the *Our Americas Partnership* and the *Soweto '76 A Living Digital Archive.* Both of these projects focus on non-European (or coded white) geographical locations, literary corpora, and histories.

13. Johnson and Neal, "Introduction," 1–2. Along with Johnson and Neal's Introduction, for more on digital tools and praxis as it relates to the study of slavery, blackness, the archive, and feminist practice, see Melissa Dinsman and Jessica Marie Johnson, "The Digital in the Humanities: An Interview with Jessica Marie Johnson," *Los Angeles Review of Books,* July 23, 2016, https://lareviewofbooks.org/article/digital-humanities-interview-jessica-marie-johnson/.

14. For further details regarding the development of *Colony in Crisis,* see Kelsey Corlett-Rivera, "Subject Librarian as Coauthor: A Case Study with Recommendations," *College & Undergraduate Libraries* 24, nos. 2–4 (2017): 189–202, https://doi.org/10.1080/10691316.2017.1326191

15. Authors, *Colony in Crisis.*

16. Project, *Colony in Crisis*; and Board of Advisors, *Colony in Crisis.*

17. Authors, *Colony in Crisis.*

18. Huet et al., "Roundtable"; Broughton, Corlett-Rivera, and Dize, "Lessons from *A Colony in Crisis.*"

19. National Endowment for the Humanities, "Grants."

20. Campaigns by Haitian digital communities such as H-Net Haiti (https://
networks.h-net.org/node/116721/discussions/1252301/official-statement-hsa-board
-us-based-haitian-studies-association) began aggregating related news stories, placing
Trump's comments in broader historical context vis-à-vis anti-Haitian U.S. imperialism
and immigration policies.

21. Broughton, Corlett-Rivera, and Dize, "Lessons from *A Colony in Crisis.*"

22. Byrd and Dize, "Black Lives in a Colony in Crisis."

23. National Endowment for the Humanities, "National Endowment for the Humanities Grant Awards and Offers"; and British Library, "EAP1024: Beyond the Revolution."

24. National Endowment for the Humanities, "NEH's Application Review Process."

25. Posner, "Money and Time."

26. Gil, "The User."

27. Gil, "The User."

28. Gil, "The User."

29. University of Maryland Libraries, *Digital Publishing Agreement.*

30. Broughton, Corlett-Rivera, and Dize, "(De)Constructing Boundaries."

31. Viagas, "How to Tell."

32. Viagas, "How to Tell."

33. Sample, "On the Death of the Digital Humanities Center."

Bibliography

Agostinho, Daniela. "Archival Encounters: Rethinking Access and Care in Digital Colonial Archives." *Archival Science* 19, no. 2 (2019): 141–65. https://doi.org/10.1007
/s10502-019-09312-0.

Aljoe, Nicole N., Elizabeth Maddock Dillon, Benjamin J. Doyle, and Elizabeth Hopwood.
"Obeah and the Early Caribbean Digital Archive." *Atlantic Studies* 1, no. 2 (2015):
258–66. https://doi.org/10.1080/14788810.2015.1025217.

Authors. *A Colony in Crisis: The Saint-Domingue Grain Shortage of 1789.* August 31, 2016.
https://colonyincrisis.lib.umd.edu/the-team/authors/.

Board of Advisors. *A Colony in Crisis: The Saint-Domingue Grain Shortage of 1789.* July 10,
2014. https://colonyincrisis.lib.umd.edu/the-team/board-of-advisors/.

Boyles, Christina. "Counting the Costs: Funding Feminism in the Digital Humanities." In
Bodies of Information: Intersectional Feminism and the Digital Humanities, edited by
Elizabeth Losh and Jacqueline Wernimont. Feminist Debates in the Digital Humani-
ties. Minneapolis: University of Minnesota Press, 2019.

British Library. "EAP1024: Beyond the Revolution: Bibliothèque Haïtienne Des Frères de
l'Instruction Chrétienne Collections, Bringing Nineteenth-Century Haitian History
to the World." 2017. *Endangered Archives Programme: Project Overview.* https://eap
.bl.uk/project/EAP1024.

Broughton, Abby, Kelsey Corlett-Rivera, and Nathan H. Dize. "(De)Constructing Boundaries through the Digital Humanities: Collaborative Pedagogy and a Colony in Crisis."

Conference Presentation at the Caribbean Digital III, Maison Française, Columbia University, December 2, 2016. http://caribbeandigitalnyc.net/2016/.

Broughton, Abby, Kelsey Corlett-Rivera, and Nathan H. Dize. "Lessons from *A Colony in Crisis:* Collaborative Pedagogy and the Digital Humanities." *Age of Revolutions,* July 15, 2016. https://ageofrevolutions.com/2016/07/15/lessons-from-a-colony-in-crisis -collaborative-pedagogy-and-the-digital-humanities/.

Byrd, Brandon R., and Nathan H. Dize. "Black Lives in a Colony in Crisis: An Interview with Nathan H. Dize—AAIHS." *Black Perspectives,* November 13, 2016. http://www .aaihs.org/black-lives-in-a-colony-in-crisis-an-interview-with-nathan-h-dize/.

Corlett-Rivera, Kelsey. "Subject Librarian as Coauthor: A Case Study with Recommenda-tions." *College & Undergraduate Libraries* 24, nos. 2–4 (2017): 189–202. https://doi .org/10.1080/10691316.2017.1326191.

Daut, Marlene L. "Haiti @ the Digital Crossroads: Archiving Black Sovereignty." *Sx Archi-pelagos,* no. 3 (July 2019). https://doi.org/10.7916/archipelagos-53xt-3v66.

Dinsman, Melissa, and Jessica Marie Johnson. "The Digital in the Humanities: An Inter-view with Jessica Marie Johnson." *Los Angeles Review of Books,* July 23, 2016. https:// lareviewofbooks.org/article/digital-humanities-interview-jessica-marie-johnson/

Dize, Nathan H., Kelsey Corlett-Rivera, Abby R. Broughton, and Brittany M. de Gail. "Intervening in French: *A Colony in Crisis,* the Digital Humanities, and the French Classroom." *Sx Archipelagos,* no. 2 (July 2017). https://doi.org/10.7916/D88K7NG5.

ECDA. "About." *Early Caribbean Digital Archive.* Accessed August 7, 2017. https://ecda .northeastern.edu/home/about/.

ECDA. "News." *Early Caribbean Digital Archive.* Accessed August 7, 2017. https://ecda .northeastern.edu/.

Fraistat, Neil. "The Function of Digital Humanities Centers at the Present Time." In *Debates in the Digital Humanities,* NED-New edition, 281–91. University of Min-nesota Press, 2012.

Gil, Alex. "The User, the Learner and the Machines We Make." *Minimal Computing: A Working Group of GO::DH,* May 21, 2015. http://go-dh.github.io/mincomp/thoughts /2015/05/21/user-vs-learner/.

Huet, Hélène, Melanie Conroy, Nathan H. Dize, and Sophie Marcotte. "Roundtable: Digital Humanities in French and Francophone Studies." Paper presented at the Society for French Historical Studies 63rd Annual Conference, Washington, D.C., April 22, 2017.

Johnson, Jessica Marie, and Mark Anthony Neal. "Introduction: Wild Seed in the Machine." *The Black Scholar* 47, no. 3 (2017): 1–2. https://doi.org/10.1080/00064246.2017.1329608.

Josephs, Kelly Baker. "Handling with Care: On Editing, Invisibility, and Affective Labor." *Small Axe* 20, no. 2 (50) (2016): 98–105. https://doi.org/10.1215/07990537-3626824.

Kirschenbaum, Matthew. "What Is Digital Humanities and What's It Doing in English Departments?" *ADE Bulletin* 150 (2010): 55–61. https://doi.org/10.1632/ade.150.55.

Martin, John D., III, and Carolyn Runyon. "Digital Humanities, Digital Hegemony: Exploring Funding Practices and Unequal Access in the Digital Humanities." *Com-puters and Society* 46, no. 1 (2016): 20–26. https://doi.org/10.1145/2908216.2908219.

Maryland Institute for Technology in the Humanities. "Hester Baer Named MITH Fellow." *Maryland Institute for Technology in the Humanities,* September 25, 2014. http://mith.umd.edu/hester-baer-named-mith-fellow/.

Maryland Institute for Technology in the Humanities. "Research." *Maryland Institute for Technology in the Humanities.* 2017. http://mith.umd.edu/research/.

McPherson, Tara. "Why Are the Digital Humanities So White? Or Thinking the Histories of Race and Computation." In *Debates in the Digital Humanities,* NED-New edition, 139–60. Minneapolis: University of Minnesota Press, 2012.

Muñoz, Trevor. "Digital Humanities in the Library Isn't a Service." *Trevor Muñoz: Writing,* August 19, 2012. http://trevormunoz.com/notebook/2012/08/19/doing-dh-in-the-library.html.

National Endowment for the Humanities. "Grants." *National Endowment for the Humanities.* Accessed August 7, 2017. https://www.neh.gov/grants.

National Endowment for the Humanities. "National Endowment for the Humanities Grant Awards and Offers, August 2017." *National Endowment for the Humanities.* https://www.neh.gov/sites/default/files/inline-files/neh_grants_august_2017_final_.pdf.

National Endowment for the Humanities. "NEH's Application Review Process." *National Endowment for the Humanities,* October 1, 2014. https://www.neh.gov/grants/application-process.

Posner, Miriam. "Money and Time." *Miriam Posner's Blog,* March 14, 2016. http://miriamposner.com/blog/money-and-time/.

Project. *A Colony in Crisis: The Saint-Domingue Grain Shortage of 1789.* n.d. https://colonyincrisis.lib.umd.edu/about/.

Risam, Roopika. *New Digital Worlds: Postcolonial Digital Humanities in Theory, Praxis, and Pedagogy.* Evanston, Ill.: Northwestern University Press, 2018.

Risam, Roopika, and Susan Edwards. "Micro DH: Digital Humanities at the Small Scale." Paper presented at Digital Humanities 2017, Montreal, Quebec. https://dh2017.adho.org/abstracts/196/196.pdf.

Risam, Roopika, Justin Snow, and Susan Edwards. "Building an Ethical Digital Humanities Community: Librarian, Faculty, and Student Collaboration." *College & Undergraduate Libraries* 24, nos. 2–4 (2017): 337–49. https://doi.org/10.1080/10691316.2017.1337530.

Sample, Mark. "On the Death of the Digital Humanities Center." *@samplereality* (blog), March 26. http://www.samplereality.com/2010/03/26/on-the-death-of-the-digital-humanities-center/.

University of Maryland Libraries. *Digital Publishing Agreement.* 2014.

Viagas, Robert. "How to Tell Broadway from Off-Broadway from . . ." *Playbill,* January 4, 1998. http://www.playbill.com/article/how-to-tell-broadway-from-off-broadway-from-com-110450.

Wooldridge, Brooke, Laurie Taylor, Mark Sullivan, Lourdes Santamaría-Wheeler, and Rose Nicholson, eds. "DLoC Awards." *Digital Library of the Caribbean (DLOC) Newsletter* 4 (2012): 12–13.

A "No Tent" / No Center Model for Digital Work in the Humanities

BRENNAN COLLINS AND DYLAN RUEDIGER

Georgia State University (GSU) is a large, urban, public institution and one of the most diverse universities in the country, with a high percentage of first generation and Pell-eligible students. We are an R1 university, but in terms of endowment, funding, and a focus on undergraduate education we share more with comprehensive teaching universities than with flagship public schools or elite private institutions. As is the case in many similar institutions, the humanities have been a low institutional priority. However, GSU does have a strong commitment to undergraduate education and the sum total of resources spread across the university is considerable. The Student Innovation Fellowship (SIF) takes advantage of these dispersed resources, gathering bits and pieces of resources from many university units to collaborate with faculty and staff on research and pedagogy projects, particularly those that involve emerging technologies, creative media, and humanistic inquiry. By accessing this network of human, technological, location, and funding resources and connecting our work to undergraduate education at every turn, we have managed to create something that looks like a DH center at an institution that otherwise is unlikely to fund one.

Although it took four years to fully realize it, SIF is a node rather than a tent. We connect people and spaces rather than claim them. Our projects arise through an opportunistic willingness to find interesting work being done anywhere in the university and connect ourselves to it. Though this decision arose out of contingency rather than intention, it has helped us avoid the territorialism and silos that often prevent transdisciplinary, interinstitutional, and public-facing work. This has given SIF a distinctive shape. Our direction has often been set by proximity and chance rather through foresight and strategic planning. At times, the resulting amorphousness has caused substantial problems of identity and made it difficult to produce high-quality work. Yet, as we have developed a labor model designed to engage with diffuse and surprising collaborators, we have recognized that our interstitial institutional location and readiness to redefine our work is perhaps our greatest strength.

After four years of developing the program, SIF became consciously situated as a student labor node intaking and working on projects across disciplines and centers. Funded by student tech fee dollars and managed by faculty and staff from the Center for Excellence in Teaching and Learning (CETL) and the University Library, the SIF program hires around twenty students (roughly half grad and half undergrad) to work on digital projects. Graduate fellows work twenty hours per week and undergrads work between eight and twenty hours. These students come to the program with a mix of developed skills including coding, web development, 3D modeling, teaching, writing, video production, marketing, database design, and archival research. They are asked to develop new skills as they work on projects. SIF students come from many different disciplines, although proportionally we have moved toward hiring a large number of computer science undergrads and humanities grad students. Faculty and staff leadership of the SIF program has been voluntary, and although based in CETL and the library, for the most part they have humanities backgrounds.

We have done some literary DH work, but our projects have also included the creation of open educational resources, promotional materials for university centers, and active learning modules for courses. The sprawling range of projects, the selection of which for our first couple of years was based on interest and circumstance, suggests our initial lack of a clear mission beyond putting student tech fee funds toward student work. As the program has developed, we are increasingly looking to take advantage of our location in a major metropolitan area, using our physical location to drive our project selection and mission. This has helped us develop a coherent identity while we retain our ability to engage with projects from many fields and connect with individuals, offices, and centers around the university. It also means that we are now increasingly engaged with projects that are difficult to label as digital humanities, in part because our work is less interdisciplinary than transdisciplinary. Rather than forming research questions from English or history, for example, we are clustering our efforts around using technology to understand the spatial experience of urban life in Atlanta. This is humanistic work, but it is also connected to the methodologies and subject knowledge of disciplines outside of the humanities, sometimes making the DH label an uncomfortable fit.

The SIF program is not a digital humanities center operating under another name. We own no real estate and we have no dedicated leadership staff beyond volunteers. Most of our student fellows, particularly the undergraduates, are not humanities majors. We do relatively little traditional DH work, particularly in the sense of disciplinary projects. However, if as Patrik Svensson has suggested in "Beyond the Big Tent," the "[DH] community may benefit from a 'no tent' approach," the SIF program may be a useful model for seeing how large digital projects, often guided by humanities questions and methods, can be developed outside of humanities departments or digital humanities centers (36). At the end of his essay, Svensson posited that "it could be argued that the digital humanities is not a discipline and that the intermediary role of the digital is useful to the digital humanities in multiple ways" (47). By opening this possibility, he has avoided debates over the definition of DH or whether DH should be situated within or across humanities disciplines and instead focuses on three useful roles for a decidedly uncapitalized digital humanities:

1. "It allows connections to all of humanities disciplines as well as to the large parts of the academy and the world outside";
2. "The digital can be used as a way of canalizing interest in rethinking the humanities and the academy"; and
3. As "a site for innovation, dialogue, and engagement with the future" in institutions that need "intersectional meeting places" (47).

Although Svensson only briefly mentioned infrastructure in his essay, issues of management, organization, location, and funding for digital work at a particular institution would seem to dictate the likelihood that these goals are met. Theoretically, at least, a center for digital work in one humanities department is less likely to fill these roles than a DH center. The *no tent* model that Svensson has advocated, however, does not lend itself to a similarly easy comparison, which would necessarily depend on where and how digital work in the humanities was taking place. In our case, Svensson's list fairly accurately describes the roles that the SIF program has played across our large, sprawling institution. This has not been an intentional journey. Had we read Svensson's article earlier, we may have gotten here sooner but may not have learned as much along the way.

That SIF has been able to play these roles is likely connected to the infrastructure of the program being located outside of humanities departments. One of the defining factors of SIF is that senior leadership and administrative support has come out of CETL and the University Library. The people who run SIF are located outside of disciplinary departments and thus outside of standard tenure-track professional concerns. Upper-level administrators of these units, including deans and directors, are highly supportive of the program and allow a great deal of autonomy, not only because of the quality of our work but also because we support their missions yet use little or none of their funding. Both CETL and the library are disconnected from disciplinary silos and so are natural places for interdisciplinary work across the university. This interdisciplinary focus is more than just an ideal. In practice, our spaces and programs connect us to hundreds of faculty members, giving us direct and deep connections to the work going on across the university.

Projects and Accomplishments

As we have come to understand our strengths and weaknesses, we have narrowed the scope of projects we take on. In particular, we have moved away from instructional design and promotional media for campus centers and toward mapping, virtual reality, and curation projects focused on Atlanta. These changes have come from shifts in leadership, the skills and interests of our students, and a better understanding of our strengths and weaknesses. The following list of projects and accomplishments are all from the 2016–17 academic year. This is not a complete list but gives a sense of how our work is connected to the humanities, the type of work we do, and what is possible with our particular model.

ATLMaps: ATLMaps.org is a mapping platform that connects archival collections at Georgia State and Emory University libraries to allow users to explore and mash up archival maps, geospatial data visualization, and user-contributed multimedia geolocation pinpoints. The project has received Knight funding and was exhibited at the UN Habitat III conference, where it was shortlisted for a CityVis Award. SIF students have played a role in content creation, project management, community outreach, and metadata creation.

Unpacking Manuel's Tavern: UnpackingManuels.com is another joint project between GSU and Emory. The project was created in light of the forthcoming renovation of the building in order to preserve, via 3D scans and gigapan photography, the original appearance of the interior of the historic Atlanta restaurant and bar. It also provides an opportunity for future classroom and community research into the stunning collection of artifacts housed in the building and into the role Manuel's Tavern has played in Atlanta history. The project has been featured in the *New York Times* and GSU's magazine. SIF students have stitched together the gigapan photos, developed the 3D environment, collected data on the wall artifacts, and written stories for the online exhibit.

Open World Atlanta: Open World Atlanta, a third project with Emory, is re-creating downtown Atlanta circa 1928 in virtual reality using archival photographs and maps and other resources to build a historically accurate, properly scaled simulation that will serve as a platform for educational gaming. SIF students have been researchers for the project, built many of the 3D models in Blender, and created the Unity build.

NEH Next Generation PhD Planning Grant and White Paper: The SIF program was the centerpiece of GSU's successful NEH planning grant, aimed at broadening career preparation for humanities PhDs by integrating SIF projects into departmental training. SIF students played a major role in writing the proposal and white paper for the grant.

VR for the Visually Impaired: This project focuses on establishing virtual reality environments for the visually impaired community. SIF fellows are developing an environment for the Oculus Rift that utilizes audible cues and gaming scripts, allowing users to experience virtual worlds without relying on sight.

Hoccleve Archive: A true digital humanities project, the Hoccleve Archive is working toward a crowdsourced, digital variorum edition of the works of the Middle English poet Thomas Hoccleve. SIF students worked as coders and project managers for the project.

Executive Approval Database: The EAD automates data collection practices for an application that conglomerates polling data on Latin American politics. SIF fellows built the algorithm and managed this portion of the project.

DALN: The Digital Archives of Literacy Narratives (DALN) is a publicly available archive of personal literacy narratives in a variety of formats (text, video, and audio) that together provide a historical record of the literacy practices and values of contributors as those practices and values change. Working with faculty and staff at GSU and Ohio State University, SIF fellows redesigned the site to improve administrative functions, user experience, and mobility.

Building Capacity with Care: Graduate Students and DH Work in the Library: The SIF program was connected to a day-long workshop at the International Digital Humanities conference in Krakow in summer 2016. The workshop (including GSU, Emory, Brown, Columbia, UCLA, and Penn State) focused on best practices for programs that have graduate students work on digital scholarship projects.

Library and CETL Connections

That SIF is run out of Georgia State's university library and Center for Excellence in Teaching and Learning places our program in a unique yet central position within larger DH discussions about infrastructure. Much attention, from Diane Zorich's *A Survey of Digital Humanities Centers in the United States* to Melissa Dinsman's "Digital in the Humanities" interview series in the *Los Angeles Review of Books*, has focused on the physical location of DH infrastructure. The standard models are department-based labs, independent DH centers, or library centers. Our connection to the library places us within a fairly standard model, but our close relationship with CETL has meant that our projects and work consistently attend to pedagogy. Although, as Lauren Klein and Matthew Gold pointed out in "Digital Humanities: The Expanded Field," "pedagogy has become a central point of concern and investment" in the DH community, our origins as a pedagogical program give us deeper ties to classrooms than DH centers with teaching components or Centers for Teaching and Learning with DH components (xiii). Certainly, in our case and many others, institutional location is less a deliberate choice than a matter of circumstance. Nonetheless, location has both practical consequences and ideological implications.

In her interviews, Dinsman has situated the library as the obvious alternative to departments through her question, "does the future of digital work lie in individual departments or libraries?" At the heart of this question is whether resources for DH work should be located in traditional disciplinary structures or in a center that serves the humanities or the entire university, the former model promoting a focus on more traditional discipline-based scholarship but with digital components, and the latter disrupting departmental silos and encouraging, or at least facilitating, digital work across or beyond disciplines. Most institutions do not have the funds for an all-of-the-above approach, so the answer to this question of location has consequences. In the Dinsman interview, David Golumbia argued against the interdisciplinarity that a library-housed DH center would entail—"I would really like to see DH move away from the idea that it covers all of the humanities—which I think is false—and parcel itself out into disciplinary studies." Golumbia's answer here was a strongly stated defense of traditional disciplinary boundaries. The *humanities* is made up of multiple disciplines, and so, he argued, digital work and the resources to make this work possible should be situated within departments. For Golumbia, this is not just a practical choice of where to locate DH infrastructure. In both the Dinsman interview and the much discussed "Neoliberal Tools (and Archives): A Political History of Digital Humanities," cowritten with Daniel Allington and Sarah Brouillette, Golumbia has connected digital work in the library to neoliberal trends in universities. In contrast, departments are presumably less exposed to the influence of capital in higher education.

Bethany Nowviskie, in her interview with Dinsman, has offered a far less ominous take on DH and the role of libraries in doing digital work in the humanities. She has argued that "we've moved into an era in which *the library itself*—which has always been a kind of laboratory for the liberal arts—takes on [humanities interdisciplinary work] in new ways and at a vastly greater, networked scale." Nowviskie insisted that there is a long history of the library encouraging humanities work between and across disciplines. She then laid out the new ways the work of the library furthers this project:

> work in digitization, data curation and digital stewardship, metadata and description, search and discovery interfaces, visualization and analysis, embodied interaction like augmented reality and physical computing, leveraging linked open data so as to help scholars make meaning across a variety of disparate datasets—all the things that libraries are and do today—plus the ways they interact with and serve the communities (and not just academic research communities, but also larger publics) that they're embedded in.

Nothing in Nowviskie's explanation of the potential for library-based DHCs supports Golumbia's concerns. Libraries have long served units across universities without suggesting that disciplines do not exist or are not important. Situating digital centers outside of departments, however, does require researchers' coming out of disciplinary silos. Library centers do not prevent discipline-specific work whereas departmental centers are far less likely to be able to do interdisciplinary work. Nor is it clear how disciplinary boundaries provide insulation against neoliberalism. SIF has always had one foot in the library, giving the program a direct connection to archival collections and the expertise that Nowviskie has catalogued. GSU's library collections have certainly shaped what projects the SIF program takes on, but it is the expertise that the library offers that has made much of our work possible, whether disciplinary, interdisciplinary, or transdisciplinary. Most of our projects raise questions about metadata, rights, and storage. For those of us without a background in library sciences, we quickly realized that ignoring these issues immediately limits the possibility, success, and longevity of a project. Most humanities faculty do not have a background in solving these problems. The library offers both the neutral space for disciplinary, interdisciplinary, and transdisciplinary projects and much of the expertise needed for tackling digital projects.

If SIF's connections to the library place the program in a fairly standard DH model, our links to CETL make the program fairly distinct. Lauren Klein and Matthew Gold argued in *Debates in the Digital Humanities* (2016) that essays like Luke Waltzer's and Stephen Brier's in the 2012 edition of the book had "intervened in the discourse of the field" and that "in the ensuing years, pedagogy has become a central point of concern and investment" (xiii). Certainly, DH conferences and journals increasingly include discussions of pedagogy. Klein and Gold pointed to several examples, and many of the contributors to this volume suggest that the pedagogical resources and networks devoted to teaching undergraduate students are a core component of a sustainable infrastructure for the digital humanities, especially at teaching-focused institutions. At such institutions, internal funding and institutional support for DH work depends on building connections to undergraduate instruction. Centers for Teaching and Learning (CTLs) often serve as nodal points for innovative pedagogical practices, particularly those involving technology, and many offer DH and digital pedagogy workshops or have faculty learning communities on these issues. CUNY's (not surprisingly, where both Brier and Waltzer are located) CTL is deeply immersed in DH and digital pedagogy, but we are unaware of other centers producing large digital projects in the humanities with roots in a CTL. One lesson of the SIF program has been to consider the CTL as an essential bridge between DH and the classroom.

Brier's and Waltzer's essays in *Debates in the Digital Humanities* (2012) did not only ask that pedagogy have a seat at the DH table but argued that an increased focus on teaching and learning would be potentially transformative to DH, the humanities, and institutions of higher learning. In his essay "Digital Humanities and the 'Ugly Stepchildren' of American Higher Education," Waltzer maintained that "Even though many digital humanists think and speak of themselves and their work as rising in opposition to the traditional structures of the academy, much current work in the digital humanities also values research and scholarship far more than teaching, learning, and curriculum development. In this sense, the digital humanities are hard to distinguish significantly from other academic disciplines" (338). This lack of distinction, Waltzer argues, directly ties the DH community to the *traditional structures of the academy* and thus to the failure to prepare students for the digital and online worlds in which they live, the lack of vigorous arguments for the relevancy of the humanities, and the rise of #alt-ac positions and contingent labor. He and Brier have insisted that a focus on pedagogy, particularly digital pedagogy, is part of the solution. In his essay, "Where's the Pedagogy? The Role of Teaching and Learning in the Digital Humanities," Brier suggested that

> If we are willing to broaden our definition of digital humanities beyond academic research and related issues of academic publication, peer review, and tenure and promotion to encompass critical questions about ways to improve teaching and learning, then CUNY's various digital pedagogy projects and strategies offer an alternative pathway to broaden the impact of the digital humanities movement and make it more relevant to the ongoing and increasingly beleaguered educational mission of contemporary colleges and universities. (398)

Since 2012, the definition of DH has widened to increasingly include work in teaching and learning. This shift brings to the fore how pedagogy should be a part of the infrastructure of DHCs.

Thanks to our ties to CETL, the SIF model has a pedagogical mission at its core. This was as much circumstance as intention in the first year of the program. Many of our early projects were connected to instructional design simply because we had instructional design projects lined up and because key early personnel had a background in the Writing Across the Curriculum (WAC) program and Atlanta's Digital Pedagogy Group. From the beginning our project intake, even for more research-focused projects, included questions about how a project would connect with classrooms. Over the past few years, the pedagogical roots of the program have led us to more fully consider the needs of SIF students and our role in the educational purpose of the university. Our pedagogical goals include the following:

- Training graduate and undergraduate students to understand, create, and interact with DH work;
- Training students to successfully participate in an increasingly online and digital world;
- Training humanities students, particularly PhD candidates in English and history, to manage complex projects, supervise teams, and communicate ideas to stakeholders with different perspectives;
- Making library resources usable and available to the public;
- Developing student skills by giving them meaningful work in building public-facing projects; and
- Connecting digital research projects to classes and the Scholarship of Teaching and Learning to DH projects.

We have not fully met these goals, and we do not intend to suggest that other DHCs do not have similar goals. Our CETL roots, however, do place pedagogy as a definitional part of the program and connect us to pedagogical resources including CETL faculty and staff, training workshops, and our most innovative teachers at the university.

Student Funds Driving a Student-Centered Program

Our initial mission was directly tied to our source of funding. Students at GSU pay a technology fee in addition to tuition and other fees. SIF was created in response to the perception that the university spent too much of it on technology and not enough on the people who could use that technology to create meaningful projects, platforms, and experiences. In spring 2014, George Pullman, the head of the Center for Instructional Innovation at the time, piloted the Tech Fee Fellows program. The guiding principle was to create a program that would put student tech fee funds in student hands. Using a small amount of excess funds from our Writing Across the Curriculum program, we hired six grad students from English, Communications, and Computer Science to work ten hours per week on faculty- and staff-led projects at the university. The pilot project proved successful enough to receive a second year of significantly expanded funding. In the fall of 2015, the Tech Fee Fellows, now dubbed the Student Innovation Fellows, became a joint venture of the University Library, the Center for Instructional Effectiveness, and the Center for Instructional Innovation (the last two soon afterward combined to become CETL). Using student tech fee funds, the SIF program hired twenty-six student fellows, eighteen graduate students working twenty hours per week, and eight undergraduates working varying hours per week (after the first year, funding decreased and we had around twenty students). This dramatic expansion of labor was not accompanied by any well-conceived plan for managing what had become a large workforce of students, ranging from first-year undergraduates to advanced PhD candidates from eleven university departments. We quickly learned that we needed to develop a leadership structure capable of ensuring that work was getting done. Our decision to use humanities graduate student fellows as project managers grew from these challenges and is an essential component of our subsequent success.

Student tech fee dollars made up the vast majority of our funds with smaller additional amounts from CETL and the office of the provost. Each year, we made a funding request to a tech fee committee of faculty, students, and staff who vote on our proposal along with others. This process made our funding and thus our existence unstable from year to year. We were told by leaders of the tech fee committee that funding was unlikely to continue; however, for six years we continued to receive support. On principle, we would like to continue receiving tech fee funds for the program on the basis of our achievements and the belief that some student fees should go directly back to students. Practically, we would be happy to receive stable internal funding from any university budget.

As we struggle to secure stable internal funding, we are finding ways to cobble together extra resources to hire more students. The goal is to have a stable pot of funds to work from every year that can expand or contract as we receive grants or additional internal funding for projects or students. We have received funding from the Knight Foundation for the ATLMaps project and an NEH Next Generation PhD Planning grant. Around half of those funds went into the SIF program, allowing us to put a team of students on those projects and then hire more students. SIF students have created several prototype projects with GSU faculty interested in applying for outside funding. The program has also connected to already-funded projects. Instead of using those funds to hire one student who likely does not have the skills to complete a project on their own, we can put an interdisciplinary team of students on a project and the funds can be added back to the pool of labor so we can hire more students. PhD students in English with a funded package have the option of increasing their stipend in exchange for one hundred hours of professionalization each year. This professionalization has traditionally included serving as GRAs for professors, working in administrative roles, or helping run one of the several journals connected to the department. In the summer of 2017, the SIF program became one of the choices that students could take for their professionalization hours. The funds will not become a part of our budget and these students will not be official fellows because their work will be limited. The hope is that these students can choose a SIF project to work on over the year that will allow them to develop a skill and to connect their name to a large, public-facing digital project. The SIF program gains more student work hours. We are discussing similar funding mechanisms in other departments. GSU is currently considering developing a DH graduate certificate. Part of the program could include practicum hours with SIF projects as an option.

CREATING A HUMAN INFRASTRUCTURE (FACULTY, STUDENT, AND STAFF)

SIF's success has depended on the development of a network of collaborators spanning multiple core constituencies and areas of expertise across the university: tenure-track and non-tenure-track faculty, academic administrative staff, librarians, and undergraduate and graduate students. After the pilot program, none of the overall leadership for the SIF program has been tenure-track. While tenure-track faculty remain involved and are essential to many SIF projects, overall program management comes from staff and faculty from CETL and the library, with reasonably secure positions that could be described as #alt-ac and/or administrative. Brennan Collins, associate director of CETL for digital pedagogy and Atlanta studies, has helped manage the program from the pilot onward. Justin Lonsbury, assistant director of CETL in charge of instructional design, and Joe Hurley, GSU's data services and GIS librarian, were a part of the management team for the first and second years. Spencer Roberts, the GSU digital scholarship librarian, comanaged the program for years four and five. Their work is completely voluntary and uncompensated. No official title is connected to these positions.

This lack of official existence has its disadvantages. As with our funding for students, these leadership roles, while encouraged by higher administrators, are not stable. With full-time work in other areas, taking on a SIF leadership role can often mean overwork, and eventual burnout is to be expected. The negatives of this leadership model are very real and will need to be addressed if the program is to continue.

There have, however, been advantages to developing a funded student labor program with little official existence run by non-tenure-track faculty and staff outside of academic departments. It is important to note again that those in SIF leadership are in stable positions, and we are not arguing for the advantages of more contingent #alt-ac labor. Our positions give us skills, experience, and exposure outside of what most tenure-track faculty know or even want to know. We are more likely to understand budgets and the funding mechanisms at our institution. We regularly work with faculty, staff, and administrators across the university. Our research interests are not governed by the tenure hoops and disciplinary expectations that tend to undervalue digital, interdisciplinary, teaching-focused, collaborative, and public-facing work. All of these factors, combined with little program oversight, have allowed us to experiment, fail, and learn.

DH discussions of #alt-ac labor rightly criticize the often contingent, ambiguous, overworked nature of these positions. At the same time, critics like Waltzer ("Digital Humanities and the 'Ugly Stepchildren'") acknowledge that their typically "support oriented" labor is critical to the research and educational roles of the university:

> The very presence and growing prominence of #alt-ac work is evidence that cracks have opened in the academy that are being filled by talented people, many of whom would prefer to be on the tenure track. If folks in the digital humanities had their way, those positions would not be space fillers but rather secure jobs that come with allowances for some of the generative autonomy that faculty enjoy ("Alternative Academic Careers"). Yet there is little indication that the labor structure of the academy will adjust to accommodate the inglorious work that so many #alt-ac academics are actually doing. (340)

In calling much of #alt-ac work "support oriented" and "inglorious," Waltzer seems ambivalent about the service labor often associated with these positions. This work includes "building curricula; organizing faculty development initiatives; and planting, congealing, and connecting communities of practice," work that Waltzer clearly champions in his essay (340). However, service also suggests a lack of "generative autonomy" and is often connected to short-term and overburdened positions. Sharon Leon, in her interview with Dinsman, explicitly argued against a service model, at least in the context of a DHC: "One of the things that has been really freeing for us at the Center for History and New Media is that we don't service the university.

We don't answer people's technology questions. We don't have faculty who come and say 'help me do this project.' Because we are mostly funded by grants, we don't have somebody who is salaried to be on call to answer those questions." It would be difficult to argue against the success of George Mason's center, although its long history and endowment do not necessarily make it a replicable model for most schools.

Instead, we have tried to make a virtue out of service, looking for collaborative, connective, and interstitial advantages to offset the well-known costs of being branded as "service workers" at a research university. The SIF program is decidedly service oriented, and the managers of the program all have service-oriented jobs. This orientation certainly comes with the "inglorious" work of answering questions and helping faculty, both in the work of the SIF program and the roles connected to the library and CETL. This work can, at times, be overwhelming, thankless, and frustrating. However, our service focus has also allowed us to do much of the work we do. Hundreds of GSU faculty have gone through our intensive two-day WAC training, attended the many workshops that CETL and the library offer, and contact our offices for help with questions and on projects. We know faculty and staff from most departments and units across the university and have talked with them about their research and teaching. The SIF program does offer project assistance for faculty, but far more often we partner with or ask faculty for assistance on projects that originate partially or fully in the SIF program.

Despite our leadership's service and administrative experience, we had little preparation for managing the SIF program. This has been a problem we are still attempting to address. SIF grad students have played a major role in figuring this out. In its first year, graduate students played no unique role in SIF projects—they were simply team members among an egalitarian team. However, it soon became apparent that in addition to the deeper disciplinary perspective they brought to SIF work, they brought something perhaps even more valuable to the table: leadership and organizational skills and a willingness to mentor undergraduates. This was an unexpected but welcome discovery, and it quickly emerged as a potential solution to one of the earliest flaws in the SIF model, the shortage of staff time available to provide logistical support to a dozen or more projects. By the beginning of the second year of the program, we began experimenting with making the most experienced graduate students responsible for managing one or more projects.

The initial impulse was essentially self-interested, insofar as a number of graduate students in the program were proving interested in taking on increasing responsibility for organizing and regularizing workflows and supervising the progress of several SIF projects. Before long, an early cohort of humanities grad students, including English PhD candidates Thomas Briedeband and Ashley Cheyemi McNeil and history PhD candidate Dylan Ruediger, became instrumental to the daily running of SIF projects and began to push for a more formalized and coherent identity for the program as a whole, engaging in conversations with each other and in consultation on an increasingly equitable standing with SIF staff leads on discussions relating to strategic planning, branding, and organizational structure. The fruits of this are still in development. Rocky starts as project managers for several projects made it clear, for instance, that we needed to develop opportunities for graduate students to receive feedback and advice from professional project managers. We continue to struggle with lines of authority, as graduate students are asked to lead teams of faculty and undergraduates, none of whom are under their direct authority. Nevertheless, the decision to hand the daily administration of many SIF projects to graduate students was a key step in creating an organization that began making substantial and consistent progress.

More importantly, grad students began making the case, in a series of blog posts, conversations, and conference papers, that the SIF program had real implications for the training of graduate students in a rapidly shifting marketplace for intellectual labor. Recent work being done by the American Historical Association and the Modern Language Association suggests that PhD programs in the humanities need to do considerably better at teaching students digital skills, flexible communication skills, and managerial and administrative skills and at providing meaningful exposure to collaborative work. Although not explicitly designed to do so, the SIF labor model provided for all of these.

This was a new angle for the program, and rapidly began pulling it in new directions. The origins of the SIF were based on the idea that collaborative teams could help realize the promises of technology to transform undergraduate educational experiences. What would happen if the SIF was also treated as an intervention in graduate pedagogy? This possibility was already emerging as an important part of the future of the SIF by the summer of 2016, but when the NEH announced funding for its Next Generation Humanities PhD program, grants designed to foster innovative ways of thinking about how graduate students in the humanities are trained, we saw an opportunity to more fully articulate how the SIF could contribute to graduate education in the humanities.

This vision was predicated on the idea of integrating SIF work into the curriculum of humanities departments at GSU via an institutional commitment to digital humanities projects as ways of training humanists. At its core was the idea of turning the SIF into a funding platform for humanities graduate students and an institutional home for student-led, outward-facing digital humanities projects, combined with curricular changes designed to help students develop digital skills. The SIF could serve as a kind of hub, collaborating with academic departments, research institutes at GSU (notably the recently opened Humanities Center and the Creative Media Industries Institute), and a panel of representatives from Atlanta's media and technology industries to design and support new long-term DH projects designed to combine meaningful humanities research with specific technical and soft skills necessary to succeed in 21st-century careers inside and outside the professoriate.

Faculty are under increasing pressure to incorporate digital scholarship into their research and teaching. But they often lack the technical expertise to do so. At

GSU, even those who do are unlikely to have ready access to the staff support necessary to tackle even modestly scaled projects. Working with the SIF program offers faculty access to students with technology skills and graduate student supervisors who can take on much of the logistical burden. In exchange, faculty agree to help train and participate as team members in the work.

Faculty often "own" SIF projects but are not actually supervising them, and generally do not fully understand the technical challenges of the work. Grad student and SIF faculty supervisors often have this limitation as well and sometimes—no matter how well trained—do not see what is and what is not possible. Reaching out to staff in CETL, the library, and other centers has improved our hiring practices, project intake, project management, workflow implementation, training options, and development capacity. For the first couple of years of the SIF program, one of our primary struggles was with managing our computer science students. None of the managers were coders and the program could not offer the training or leadership that they needed. These computer science students either had the technical, collaboration, and organizational skills needed for a project or they did not, and this was a major failing of the program. Eventually, we connected with Jaro Klc from GSU Instructional Innovation and Technology on a couple of projects. His interest in the SIF program was to help develop a pipeline of talented computer science students to eventually work under him on university projects. He has helped interview student candidates, making us less reliant on student reporting of their skills, and met with faculty proposing new ideas to help us determine if we had the necessary resources to complete the project. Jaro also introduced us to a project manager who worked with us on a project and provided some training for some of our graduate student managers. Other staff members in CETL and the library have also joined SIF projects because of proximity and interest. Taylor Burch, an instructional designer in CETL, works next to SIF's two high-powered computers and started conversations with our main student working on our 3D and VR projects. Taylor has a background in 3D modeling and graphic design and has offered assistance on coherent organization, standards, and workflow for these projects. Eric Willoughby, a lead programmer at our library, set up GSU's GeoServer to host our geospatial material for the ATLMaps project and started working on the development team for the project with SIF students and a lead developer at Emory's library.

PHYSICAL SPACES

The SIF program does not own real estate. We have been fortunate to have privileged access to technology and meeting spaces connected to the library and CETL, as well as some access to IT meeting rooms and departmental spaces connected to project work. Not having a space of our own has its disadvantages. While we have fairly stable access to space, we are not certain from year to year that this will continue. Shared space can occasionally cause conflict over reservations and noise levels (particularly considering that we are working with around twenty students, half of them undergrads). We are gradually understanding, however, that there are advantages to not having our own location. We have space that is managed by others and is likely better than our own space would be. Our students have a sense of multiple resources spread out over campus and regularly come in contact with the faculty and staff connected to those spaces. Also, as more technology spaces open on our very large and expanding campus, we are being encouraged to use those spaces because our students and projects are what these spaces want to highlight. With the building of these spaces, most of the initial effort is put into buildout and technology and not the content and labor that will need to activate these spaces. Using space opportunistically has allowed us to focus on mission rather than expend energy managing our own spaces.

The SIF program had around ten computers located in CETL's offices along with some equipment in the space's storage closet. CETL also has several meeting and workshop spaces that students and faculty can reserve. Most of our meetings and much of the individual and group work on our projects took place here. The CETL space opened in 2016 with two rows of tables set aside for SIF students. Beyond work and meeting spaces, the office also has a small green room, two audio recording rooms, and a 3D printing area. The open nature of the office has led to some tension as we figured out the appropriate etiquette for clusters of sometimes unsupervised undergrads working in close proximity to faculty and staff, but the close proximity has also had the unintended benefit of putting SIFs in close proximity to an experienced multimedia team and instructional design staff. Through some direct communication but also through inevitably overheard work discussions, CETL staff began to advise and work on SIF projects.

Before the new CETL space opened, most of our work was done in the library's Collaborative University Research & Visualization Environment (CURVE). CURVE's centerpiece is a 24-foot touch-controlled visualization wall. The center also has an 84-inch 4K display, 3D scanners, and six collaborative workstations with large displays, high-powered computers, and movable whiteboards. The space is open and large and is able to accommodate multiple groups of different sizes. For the first couple of years of the SIF program, most of our meetings and much project work was done here. The large touch displays have been game changers for many of our projects involving maps, photography, and 3D visualization that benefit from the ability to see clearly at multiple scales and angles. CURVE also provided a dramatic space for events showcasing the SIF program and SIF projects. Unlike CETL, CURVE is open to any faculty or students who reserve the space. Opened in 2014, the space has gradually become more filled as classes, faculty, and students understand the potential of the space. Although this has caused some problems when our group meetings are taking place at the same time as a presentation, our group often comes into contact with students, faculty, and staff who are working on interesting projects and who sometimes become resources or advocates for our work.

The open-access nature of the space also requires the regular erasing of files from their computers. With strong processing and display power, these computers are perfect for meetings, research, testing, and showcasing but are not ideal for much of our project work.

After several years of figuring out location we landed in an ideal, if somewhat unstable, situation. We had dedicated work and storage space with easy access to meeting, showcase, and workshop space. We were in regular physical contact with students, faculty, and staff doing innovative work across the campus. As more technology spaces opened on our campus, SIF students were invited to help activate these locations by working on and showcasing our projects. SIF students and projects are ideal for helping demonstrate the potential of these spaces as they open, and we hope to form immediate, mutually beneficial relationships.

Beginning in the fall of 2019, SIF lost access to the student tech fee, our main source of funding for the program. Although loss of this funding dealt a major blow to the SIF program and is a clear example of the precarity of our model, the experience of developing and running a highly adaptable student labor lab largely rooted in humanities projects has directly led to the development of, and leadership in, a much larger project-based learning initiative at GSU. Many of our students from the previous year graduated, and we have been able to fund most students who wanted to continue on our projects. Seven of the SIF students continue to work on our projects, which are now part of the new Project Labs initiative at GSU. Project Labs are based on the Vertically Integrated Projects (VIP) program at Georgia Tech that is now practiced at over thirty universities around the world. The VIP approach allows students to earn course credit over multiple semesters while working on faculty-led, public-facing, interdisciplinary projects. One of our Project Labs is currently based in mapping projects started in SIF, and two labs that are planned to start in fall 2020 are partially based in projects connected to the program. We were recently awarded three years of funding from the Teagle Foundation, which will allow us to continue creating Project Labs in the humanities and social sciences as well as connect these labs to a liberal arts core curriculum. We are currently securing internal funds from colleges and centers at GSU for student support of these initiatives. The hope is to use the SIF paid labor model to place experienced student workers on new Project Labs teams, training students earning course credit to take on skilled leadership roles within their lab. Paid students would gradually be placed in developing labs as they became no longer needed in stable labs.

The humanities at GSU, as in many other universities, are underresourced. Had we asked for a digital humanities center, the odds of receiving it would have been low. However, GSU's commitment to the quality of its undergraduate education gave us a backdoor into the digital humanities via digital pedagogy, albeit one gained by squatting on resources that were allocated for other purposes. In ways that we did not always intend and certainly could not always foresee, this has profoundly shaped us. Our squatting has, perhaps surprisingly, generally been welcomed. We have been able to build alliances with many branches of the university because in addition to ideas and expertise, we bring a source of labor and a collaborative ethos to the table. Our early decision to focus on projects with a strong pedagogical focus has connected us with classrooms and teachers from across the university that would not likely have engaged with a digital humanities center. If our trajectory has necessarily given us a certain amorphousness and a sometimes precariously interstitial institutional location, it has also been central to our successes. Without our roots in pedagogy and opportunistic willingness to take on worthwhile projects from any discipline, we could never have arrived where we are.

Bibliography

Allington, Daniel, Sarah Brouillette, and David Golumbia. "Neoliberal Tools (and Archives): A Political History of Digital Humanities." *Los Angeles Review of Books,* May 1, 2016. https://lareviewofbooks.org/article/neoliberal-tools-archives-political -history-digital-humanities/.

Brier, Stephen. "Where's the Pedagogy? The Role of Teaching and Learning in the Digital Humanities." In *Debates in the Digital Humanities,* edited by Matthew K. Gold. Minneapolis: University of Minnesota Press, 2012. http://dhdebates.gc.cuny.edu/debates /text/8.

Dinsman, Melissa. "The Digital in the Humanities: An Interview with Bethany Nowviskie." *Los Angeles Review of Books,* May 9, 2016. https://lareviewofbooks.org/article/digital -humanities-interview-bethany-nowviskie/.

Dinsman, Melissa. "The Digital in the Humanities: An Interview with David Golumbia." *Los Angeles Review of Books,* June 30, 2016. https://lareviewofbooks.org/article /digital-humanities-interview-david-golumbia/.

Dinsman, Melissa. "The Digital in the Humanities: An Interview with Sharon M. Leon." *Los Angeles Review of Books,* July 10, 2016. https://lareviewofbooks.org/article/the -digital-in-the-humanities-an-interview-with-sharon-m-leon/.

Klein, Lauren and Matthew Gold. "Digital Humanities: The Expanded Field." In *Debates in the Digital Humanities,* edited by Lauren Klein and Matthew Gold. Minneapolis: University of Minnesota Press, 2016. http://dhdebates.gc.cuny.edu/debates/text/51.

Svensson, Patrik. "Beyond the Big Tent." In *Debates in the Digital Humanities,* edited by Matthew K. Gold. Minneapolis: University of Minnesota Press, 2012. http://dhdebates .gc.cuny.edu/debates/text/22.

Waltzer, Luke. "Digital Humanities and the 'Ugly Stepchildren' of American Higher Education." In *Debates in the Digital Humanities,* edited by Matthew K. Gold. Minneapolis: University of Minnesota Press, 2012. http://dhdebates.gc.cuny.edu/debates/text/33.

Zorich, Diane W. *A Survey of Digital Humanities Centers in the United States.* Washington, D.C.: CLIR, 2008.

After Autonomy
*Digital Humanities Practices in Small Liberal Arts Colleges
and Higher Education as Collaboration*

ELIZABETH RODRIGUES AND RACHEL SCHNEPPER

Once the province of elite research universities, institutions from regional comprehensive universities to small liberal arts colleges (SLACs) are investing in the people, spaces, and tools necessary to foster the digital humanities. While William Pannapacker's 2013 essay in *The Chronicle of Higher Education,* "Stop Calling It 'Digital Humanities' and Nine Other Strategies to Help Liberal Arts Colleges Join the Movement," may have been the opening salvo in the public campaign to promote the involvement of liberal arts colleges in digital humanities, he was quickly joined by others such as Rafael Alvarado, who noted how digital humanities in a liberal arts context such as a SLAC looks different and functions differently than it does at larger universities.[1] Digital humanities as digital liberal arts "involves more than a cluster of disciplines can encompass; it involves rethinking the curriculum as a whole, the spaces within which education happens, and the careers of students who pass through them both."[2] Digital humanities at a SLAC performs a mutually transformational reorientation: the SLAC's focus on undergraduate education has the potential to reorient the digital humanities to cross-disciplinary contexts, pedagogical questions, and face-to-face dialogic encounter, whereas the practice of digital humanities, at least potentially, reorients many of the SLAC's traditional divisions of labor—divisions by department (both disciplinary and administrative) and divisions by status (faculty, staff, and student). This reorientation toward broader recognition of labor is the result of both the inherently collaborative nature of digital projects and a robust critique of academic labor practices emerging from critical digital humanities, exemplified by the #transformdh community. To realize the potential of the digital liberal arts as a cornerstone of critical pedagogy, empowered undergraduate research, and expanded networks of dialogue and discovery, we must grapple with the social infrastructure that makes our labor legible and possible.

As evidence for this argument, we first offer a cautionary tale. In the fall of 2015, a small group of Grinnell College faculty, staff, and students set out to digitize a thematically focused subset of the College libraries' archives and special collections. Supported by an internal grant, this was a pedagogy-driven project, intended to create research opportunities for the undergraduates working on the project as well as resources for future undergraduates working with newly accessible digital primary sources. By design, the majority of the work was to be done by undergraduates after receiving training from the librarians. In addition to the undergraduates, the team working on the project included staff from the Digital Liberal Arts Collaborative (DLAC, Grinnell's digital humanities center) and librarians, but the project lead was a professor who also served as the project manager and student supervisor. The grant money, as well as all project management, was dependent on that professor. Although an expert in the relevant subject area, the project lead was, unfortunately yet understandably, unfamiliar with the processes and workflows of digitizing an archive. Furthermore, the students employed on the project were also all enrolled in the project lead's class, creating an unexpected power dynamic for a pretenure professor who would be called to account for student course evaluations.

What happened over the next fifteen months will probably not surprise most digital humanities practitioners, already familiar with other projects that share commonalities such as dependence on undergraduate labor, coordination of many collaborators from across the institution, and power concentrated in the hands of a faculty primary investigator (PI). Indeed, we encountered pretty much every single one of the disadvantages of doing Little DH listed by Kelsey Corlett-Rivera et al. in their essay in this volume.[3] For, despite the cast of many, the institutional infrastructure for the project forced it to hinge on one person alone—the faculty member. This not only created an undue burden on that person but also created a situation in which the expertise of the librarians and staff were unrecognized, underutilized, and uncompensated. Without the leadership of the professionals best positioned to help, the project proceeded in fits and starts and extended periods of dormancy. Workflows were slow to be created, subject matter expertise was not provided at crucial junctures, and tasks assigned to students went uncompleted. The project lead readily admitted that the professor needed help, but did not follow through on any of the help or advice that was offered or address student job performance issues. Finally, just as it appeared that the project was finally gaining some momentum, the project lead announced that the professor was leaving Grinnell to take up a new position at the end of the semester. Without the faculty project lead, it was entirely possible that the internal grant supporting the project would be withdrawn, thereby effectively ending the project.

Luckily this did not happen. Upon notification of the faculty member's imminent departure, the librarians and staff working on the project quickly submitted a revised project proposal to the internal grant's committee chair that was accepted, and they then assumed management and supervision of the students. Now, with the ability to make decisions rather than suggestions, they were able to evaluate the scope of the remaining work and set strategic priorities, agree on and implement best practices for digitization and metadata creation, and draw on their experience supervising students.[4] Choosing to focus exclusively on three specific subcollections allowed them to fully complete the digitization process for about half of the selected materials, which also tied up loose ends generated from the previous months. It also produced enough content discoverable through Grinnell's institutional repository to be useful to future students, which was one of the intended goals of the project.

While this project has a relatively happy ending, this history typifies the infrastructural challenges to effective and ethical collaboration on digital projects at a SLAC. The infrastructure of such institutions rarely enables autonomous development of digital humanities projects by digital humanities practitioners outside of tenured/tenure-track faculty roles. Rather, unexamined hierarchies in funding, compensation, and recognition make these efforts practically dependent upon traditional faculty members.[5] Typically, only tenured/tenure-track faculty are incentivized and compensated for original research; therefore the financial support for projects often is available only through faculty leadership. Only when a faculty-led project emerges are DH staff members and librarians given the go-ahead to spring into action and then only in a supporting role, with the faculty member alone empowered to make scholarly, technical, and timeline decisions. DH staff members are often in more contingent positions in centers that are relatively new with uneven funding histories and are not seen as a sound investment for grant funding. Alternately, librarians, although often in more stable positions, are often perceived to be so entrenched in a service role that their original project proposals generate more head scratching and consternation over time away from duties than curiosity. Student labor is either contingent on course credit, which only teaching faculty can give, or money, which again often depends on funding restricted to faculty.

Underlying these dynamics is the differing recognition and reward structures for these groups of practitioners. Faculty gain status when awarded a grant and often receive additional compensation during the course of the grant but face uncertain returns on even a successfully completed digital humanities project. Projects may or may not count as publications for tenure and they may or may not generate more typical publications. Put another way, there are often fewer penalties for an abandoned digital humanities project than there are rewards for a completed one.

Although the emphasis on process over product is not inherently wrong and may even be desirable in the digital liberal arts, lost opportunities for student research and growth in institutional capacity for such projects are costly over time. DH staff members and librarians, conversely, are often evaluated primarily as service providers.[6] In some cases, this means that it is seen as more important for staff and librarians to retain cordial working relationships than to push for project completion or fulfillment of stated goals.[7] This dynamic is only one of the frequent demands for emotional labor that digital projects tend to entail for those in non-PI roles. As Alexis Logsdon, Amy Mars, and Heather Tompkins have elaborated in the context of digital humanities librarianship, these demands can include "appearing enthusiastic about projects that you suspect will be too unwieldy to succeed given the time and human resources available and knowing how to manage the proposer's expectations without damaging their enthusiasm for the digital project" as well as "maintaining a professional demeanor even when your expertise is marginalized in a given project."[8] In other cases, we are indeed being evaluated on project success and will be seen as ineffective if our tenured/tenurable faculty leaders choose to abandon a project on which we have spent time.

When faculty involvement is the only route to material support and visibility, what can digital humanities practitioners such as librarians and staff members at liberal arts colleges faced with an infrastructurally produced lack of agency, autonomy, and sustained monetary support actually do? How can a digital humanities program with a contingent budget, whose mission is to support pedagogy that it does not teach and to create opportunities for undergraduate research it does not supervise, develop and maintain its own projects while building a program that endeavors not to replicate the most inequitable practices of academia? How can the promise of critical digital humanities approaches for student learning be realized?

Our point here is not to add another lament for circumstances and dynamics that have already been identified in critical DH discussions, to impugn those in faculty positions as a class, or to claim that our institutions are exceptionally inept. There are happy exceptions—faculty members who practice genuine collaboration and are deeply respectful of others' expertise; library and DH center directors who encourage librarian/staff research and development time and support self-initiated projects; and labor that is fairly compensated. Nor is our point to demand that the types of autonomy and agency built into faculty status be extended to some of us on the basis of a specific credential or institutional position. Rather, by engaging in these issues as infrastructural rather than personal, we aim to reflect on common circumstances that perpetuate poor collaborative practices, abandoned projects, and most importantly a lack of student research opportunities in DH.[9] The human infrastructure around digital humanities projects is not just a set of complementary skills but is often a sedimented history of higher education's hierarchies, reward structures, and expectations. Our reflection on this infrastructural situation seeks to emphasize that reimagining the power structures inherent in our institutions will not be a matter of personal education or enlightenment; it will require rethinking how our institutions recognize labor, design incentives and rewards for that labor, and conceptualize all forms of labor in service to undergraduate learning. From this reflection, we seek to identify a set of affordances for movement within this infrastructure that denaturalize systemic, inequitable labor hierarchies within academe and create learning-centered collaborations. Over time, we hope these may allow the digital liberal arts to foster not only innovative teaching and scholarship but also new campus cultures of collaboration and respect for labor.

Equally Unequal: Uncertain Footing as Common Ground

We begin our reflection on the human infrastructure of DH projects at a SLAC with an examination of how the roles we occupied were designed and positioned to foster the digital liberal arts at Grinnell. As associate director of academic technology and manager of the Digital Liberal Arts Collaborative (Schnepper) and as humanities and digital scholarship librarian (Rodrigues), both of us and our roles were new to Grinnell. The Digital Liberal Arts Collaborative (DLAC) was created in 2015, and the digital scholarship librarian was a newly reimagined version of a reference and instruction position. In addition to being tasked with performing roughly the same mission in different institutional contexts, we also share a common professional background: Liz has a PhD in English and Rachel a PhD in history.

Despite the overlap of our professional lives before and at Grinnell, our positions are not *equal* in the College. As a librarian, Liz has faculty status, albeit in a modified form, whereas Rachel was a staff member. This difference brought with it a disparity of power. As a faculty member, Liz can teach and advise students, apply more widely for grants internal and external to the College, and, perhaps most importantly at an institution with a very strong tradition of faculty governance, participate in the governance of the College. These real and tangible avenues to power at the College were not available to Rachel as a staff member. Moreover, the DLAC is institutionally housed in the Center for Teaching, Learning, and Assessment, not in IT or the libraries. The Center for Teaching, Learning, and Assessment is also a new unit within the College, formed only one year prior to Rachel's arrival. Its mission was and is still evolving. This organizational isolation from traditional power structures on campus and the lack of a clear hook into the College's mission further undermined Rachel's ability to foster a culture of critical digital liberal arts that functioned outside of disciplinary and departmental silos to connect students to educational and research opportunities.

It is important to note that in using the word *undermined* we do not mean to imply that the institution or individuals within it were actively undermining the work of this role. Far from it. The creation of this role reflected real financial investment and a genuine desire to bring new modes of learning to campus. The passive yet real undermining of structural equality, however, predetermined that this role would be responsive rather than generative and depend on its occupant's emotional labor as much as her expertise. It predetermined, in other words, that as Amy Collier has lamented, the "essential work of taking critical lenses to our technologies, to our classrooms, to our institution," of creating a digital scholarship center "that is not neutral, that is activist and critical" would take its leader "down a path of heartache and loss."[10]

Although a faculty member, as a librarian Liz also occupied a liminal role within the larger faculty body. Librarians at Grinnell are not eligible for tenure; they are expected to work in their campus office for regular hours, twelve months a year, tracking hours and vacation days; and they are barred from receiving any of the compensatory stipends offered to faculty for taking on additional duties like leading a grant-funded project or teaching a course outside of their job description. There are also differences of culture between library and other faculty that work against a genuine peer relationship—librarians usually have a different terminal degree (although not in this case), publish more practice-oriented scholarship (although not always), and usually teach sessions for others' classes rather than leading their own semester-long courses. These disciplinary differences, combined with the status signals sent by infrastructural inequities, create an unequal footing for collaborative digital project work.

In spite of the real and practical differences between our positions, we consciously adopted a collaborative approach from the outset of Liz's arrival. We also very quickly realized that we shared a common approach to digital humanities, an approach that was very strongly influenced by the emphasis on ethical collaboration forwarded by the #transformdh movement and that embraced a critical digital humanities approach in theory and method. Perhaps because of this intellectual framework, we also were both very cognizant of the institutional precarity of our respective positions, of how we were both tasked with building a digital humanities program and yet all too often lacked access to the usual avenues of program building, and of the affective results of one's professional identity being subject to the approval, supervision, and priorities of others. In the face of these challenges, we chose to see each other as allies and to proceed collaboratively.

As a librarian and a staff member, both of us were expected to successfully build and implement a digital humanities program at Grinnell but neither of us was in a position that facilitated autonomous action toward that goal. As we have described in our project account, Grinnell is far from unique in that its infrastructure does not enable autonomous development of digital humanities projects by all digital humanities professionals. Almost exclusively, the sine qua non of digital humanities projects at a small liberal arts college, from small classroom assignments to large, multiunit collaborations, is traditional faculty involvement, preferably as a principal investigator. The emphasis on the involvement of teaching faculty is integral to digital humanities in a liberal arts context. We do not have graduate students to train or long-term, large-scale projects. The designation of a traditional faculty line to digital humanities is difficult to prioritize in small departments that must cover a critical breadth of their discipline in teaching, and it may not be feasible to recruit a dedicated digital humanities researcher to a teaching-oriented position. Instead, digital humanities professionals are typically hired to support less digitally oriented humanities professionals to do digital humanities work, with the end goal of enhancing student learning in courses now taught by faculty who are more versed in digital methods, more aware of the need to teach digital literacies, and more equipped to integrate digital projects into coursework. Larger projects, including those that are originated in the classroom, are all funded through soft money that is available only for traditional, tenured/tenure-track faculty, in such forms as extra compensation or course releases.

Our recognition that we were equally unequal at Grinnell, albeit not in the same ways, allowed us to build our collaboration to take advantage of our different points of access to power. We were incredibly fortunate, however, in how much we shared in common: our mandates meshed, and our stakes meshed. Moreover, we had the intangible but important resources of time and space to build our collaboration and to learn about each other, our positions and their respective affordances, our strengths, and our methods, which ultimately allowed us to envision and strategize the different ways of approaching our shared mission.[11] The equality of our collaboration was built on the inequities and the productive ambiguities of our formal status. When we thought about it, we realized that such a collaboration would not have been possible if one of us had had traditional faculty status. This would have had nothing to do with us as individuals but everything about the College's infrastructure and the ways in which our expectations were articulated and structured. Huculak and Goddard are among the recent observers to note that the collaborative realities of digital project work challenge norms of legible scholarship: "scholars— especially assistant professors on the tenure track—are encouraged to produce work that fits this individual-focused, competitive evaluation mold."[12] We might have delayed integrating digital pedagogies into our courses because we surmised that the safest route to tenure was to teach in the way most legible to senior colleagues. We would have been focused on establishing our disciplinary and subject area bona fides rather than being able to entertain coteaching an interdisciplinary course. In an alternate universe where one of us had a traditional tenure-track teaching job and the motivation to embark on a digital project, the other would have struggled to contribute her expertise in a genuine manner, being structurally delegated to a subordinate, service role. With our heads down in our own career trajectories, we might have never met. As digital humanities practitioners not in traditional faculty positions, however, we could not rely on our own institutional power to accomplish our goals. We had to become attuned to recognizing openings within the spaces we occupied. We had to seek alternate models of autonomy and agency.

Exposing Labor Exposes Hierarchies

As digital humanists on a liberal arts campus, we are academic resources often seen as support for faculty but would be more effective if positioned as intellectual partners in the cocreation of critical digital projects and the pedagogy that grows from them. The infrastructural positions of DH practitioners outside of faculty roles are in many ways analogous to that of the library. The work of librarians is often seen as cut-and-dried custodianship, whereas librarians understand it to be critical and creative. Librarians work to build a dynamic information ecology that takes into account the needs of current and future researchers, to catalyze discovery of the human record, to expand and defend access to information, and to teach students how to navigate traditional and emerging information sources. None of these objectives, however, can actually be met autonomously. Instructional librarians, for example, are trained for and tasked with teaching information literacy, a set of concepts and practices that is complex and contextual, but they do not have courses of their own in which to teach. Instead, they must cultivate the trust and interest of faculty who can then choose to invite them into their classes. This is a process with highs and lows, fruitful collaborations and dispiriting misrecognition. Doing this work successfully requires librarians' constant relationship building and strategizing new connections between what librarians do and what others do without expecting the others to immediately understand it, value it, or make time for it.

Defining libraries' and librarians' relationships to digital humanities on campus can either recapitulate this dynamic or prompt a new visibility for librarians' labor. DH projects bring librarians' traditional strengths of deep collection knowledge and long-range preservation planning together with their more recently built capacity for digitization, metadata creation, and web publication and the project management skills necessary for the successful conclusion of digital projects. These areas of expert practice are essential complementary skills for the DH project proposed by a faculty member, recently returned from her first digital humanities boot camp, who is not yet as aware as librarians are that the sustainability and maintenance of her project depends on strategic planning, and that lack of planning guarantees a future of obsolete file formats and dead links. Librarians are prepared to perform types of labor that are not readily duplicated by faculty scholars. They expose, again, that "every hour of faculty work is brought into being by hundreds of hours of time spent maintaining the physical and administrative space within which that work is conducted: libraries, network, payroll, buildings, and all the rest of it."[13] Because they expose the necessity of nonfaculty labor, digital humanities projects necessarily blur the boundary between service, which is being asked to do specific tasks in isolation from larger projects carried out primarily by others, and collaboration, which is being invited to help define the project and determine the methods as well as carry out specific tasks and being invited to do so iteratively as part of an ongoing conversation about what is possible, what is necessary, and what is desired.

Yet the association of *librarian* with *service* rather than *scholarship* can easily persist even as digital humanities work flourishes. Dot Porter trenchantly notes of the 2014 OCLC report, "Does Every Library Need a Digital Humanities Center?," that multiple terms are used to refer to "faculty who do (or who wish to do) Digital Humanities" including "DH scholars," "DH researchers," and "DH academics." Porter continues, "Although all these terms remain undefined, it's pretty clear from context that these scholars, researchers, and academics are not librarians—they are something else, another class of people who exist to be served by libraries and, by extension, by librarians."[14] Researcher on one side, and librarian on the other; research on one side, and service on the other.

With the emergence of digital humanities as a library-connected endeavor has come a series of calls for libraries and librarians to decouple themselves from a service mentality.[15] Trevor Muñoz, for example, has argued "Digital humanities in libraries isn't a service and libraries will be more successful at generating engagement with digital humanities if they focus on helping librarians lead their own DH initiatives and projects." Bethany Nowviskie pushes further, asking "What if . . . part of the *operational service* libraries provided to the digital humanities world—were: to experiment; to iterate; to assert our *own* intellectual agendas as part of the DH research landscape; to be just as "bad" at service (conventionally conceived) as some of our scholarly partners are at being served?"[16]

There is a great deal of liberatory fresh air in these declarations: an affirmation that digital projects can occasion a new recognition of librarians' technical expertise as well as scholarly creativity, and a permission, even an exhortation to stop the self-deprecatory downplaying of knowledge in order to reproduce a comfortable and familiar academic hierarchy.[17] Some of us could indeed empower ourselves to do these things within the realm of the library. But would this be the best outcome for digital humanities on our campuses? Would this be the best outcome for libraries? We do not want to mischaracterize or write off Muñoz's and others' reflections on this issue. We agree that librarians should take advantage of their own institutional affordances to pursue digital humanities projects connected to the library's goals. However, we also want to underscore what Roxanne Shirazi has observed: "when we call for librarians to approach collaborative digital work as partners and not service providers, I would like to see some acknowledgement of the fact that there are different power relations at play in these collaborative relationships." These power relations have affective consequences but they are not the product of our personalities. They "are embedded in the hierarchies that make up academia, in both the social stratification of varying job ranks and the hierarchical classification of service and scholarship."[18] The perception of our labor and our potential is determined by our status. A service role is a byproduct of lack of autonomy. Lack of autonomy is a byproduct of lack of security, lack of incentive, lack of reward, and lack of resources.

Yet, the solution to this lack of autonomy is not, we have found, simply more autonomy granted to different people. On a practical level, no one can pursue DH alone, and on a philosophical level, the field is in many ways an ongoing critique of autonomy. Transformation is not accomplished by fiat. It is not service that is the problem; it's what goals are being served and, more deeply, the process through which those goals are determined and how recognition, compensation, and agency are incorporated into the process. A critical approach to scholarship and pedagogy perhaps even requires incorporating selected elements of a service orientation in that it requires deep relationality—listening, communal goal setting, and a fairer distribution of recognition and reward. Therefore, it is not the simple rejection of service or bolstering of autonomy that is going to move us forward. It is a reclaiming of shared goals and an active scouting for openings in which collaboration is required to meet those goals. Digital project work on our liberal arts campus has made visible a set of openings into which we can move in order to reclaim and recast service as learner-centering collaboration.

Digital Liberal Arts as New Culture of Collaboration

The liberal arts college is essentially student centered in mission, although not always in practice. Although its faculty are valued scholars in their fields whose research is vital to their growth as teachers, it is not primarily measuring itself by its research output. Its mission, however it might be specifically articulated at each institution, is to provide its students with a strong grounding in critical thinking and communication via exposure to multiple disciplines and (usually) intensive work in one or two, often accompanied by close faculty–student relationships, small classrooms, and the opportunity to pursue mentored research projects. To this basic mission each institution brings its own history and values. Grinnell in particular among its peer institutions is recognized for its commitment to social justice and social responsibility. These missions provide a rubric for goal setting and a common vocabulary for defining value. What our effort to build a critical digital humanities program evidenced was that our institution lacked a space for putting this vocabulary into practice, a space for conversation across departments, and roles for setting these shared goals.

As we surveyed the infrastructural landscape before us, we began to recognize that the practice of the digital liberal arts at Grinnell could provide us with an occasion to begin building such a space by modeling a culture of digital humanities at Grinnell in which labor and innovation were equally valued and rewarded, whether they originated from faculty, staff, or student. We merged the libraries' academic status with the DLAC's entrepreneurial mandate. We deployed Liz's quasi-faculty status with Rachel's hustle to form strategic alliances with units, programs, and centers that enabled us to open pots of funding and doors to opportunities. Despite not being traditional teaching faculty, we found affordances within our relative positions of power to advance a critical digital humanities program by centering the needs of students.[19] Like the Student Innovation Fellowships that Brennan Collins and Dylan Ruediger describe at Georgia State, our positions in the library and the DLAC allowed us to keep the pedagogical mission at the core.[20]

By strategically focusing on creating opportunities for the students, we were able to explicitly align critical digital humanities with the mission of the College and create space for practice and conversation. This is not to say that the opportunities that we, Rachel and Liz, were particularly involved in creating were the only digital liberal arts projects taking place on campus, nor that any of the opportunities we detail here could have been created without material support from people and units beyond ourselves. The *we* here is less a reference to ourselves as individuals and more a recognition that it took conscious and strategic alliance to create the spaces into which DLA could grow. It is also a *we* of shifting boundaries, as each endeavor required outreach, collaboration, and participation of other individuals and/or units on campus. Specifically, we sought opportunities to connect digital humanities with a campus mandate that every department provide the opportunity for a significant mentored student research experience. Creating research opportunities for students in digital humanities is unique for undergraduates focused in the humanities and/or humanistic social sciences, where collaborative research opportunities are less frequent than they are for their peers in STEM fields. These digital humanities research opportunities are valuable and exciting for undergraduates, for they also create a space in which failure is expected, play is part of practice, and collaboration is more than a matter of dividing up paper sections. Focusing on student research created a space for us to lay the foundations for a digital humanities program that would allow faculty and students, researchers and collaborators, to pursue transformative work that had the potential to challenge the status quo. We were able to augment this work by focusing on providing opportunities for students to engage with critical digital humanities intellectual frameworks and methods by drawing attention to Grinnell's commitment to social justice.

Our focus on the students has yielded three sites of opportunity: a program for faculty–student collaborations, a digital humanities class, and an undergraduate fellowship program.

DH-focused faculty–student summer collaborations built on the successes of a program that pre-dated the creation of the DLAC. In 2014, the College received an alumnus donation to support faculty's infusing technology into their courses. Over the course of the summer, faculty received a stipend for summer course development, and each faculty recruited a student assistant who worked forty hours a week for eight weeks over the summer. This program ran in the summers of 2014 and 2015. Upon reflection, it was clear that this model pinpointed a sweet spot between faculty need and student opportunity. The following year, the Mellon-funded Digital Bridges for Humanistic Inquiry created a faculty–student summer grant explicitly based on this model and funded DLA projects during the summers of 2016 and 2017. Through this program, students have had the opportunity to work on a range of digital humanities projects, from analyzing "big data" to track trends in the public discourse surrounding bullying since the Columbine Massacre, to using GIS in the scholarship of the American Civil War and Reconstruction, to using Omeka to create online scholarly exhibits or research databases. It was particularly successful because it encouraged realistic goal-setting and allowed a greater immersion into the work for students due to the short summer time frame. In addition, these projects are fully supported by the staff of the DLAC and the librarians, who have worked very closely with the faculty and students in developing and implementing these projects. Particularly in the later iteration of these collaborations, these relationships are encouraged from the outset, as Rachel and the Digital Bridges co-PI meet with faculty–student pairs before they begin their summer work, consulting not only on goals and methods but also on identifying potential collaborators at the College. Accordingly, the faculty and students have come to recognize these digital humanities practitioners as necessary and valued intellectual partners and collaborators, without whom these projects would not exist.

The second site of opportunity has been the development of a digital humanities short course. Originally created as a vehicle for visiting scholars and alumni to be able to teach for credit while on campus, it is also the only type of course that we, outside of teaching departments, were eligible to run. It was important to us that while the class provides students with a foundation in digital humanities tools and methods such as digital mapping, data visualizations, and digital archives, it also would teach students how to approach these emerging digital practices with a critical awareness of race, gender, class, power, and marginalization. Accordingly, the class focused on how the digital environments and tools of digital humanists could be used to promote a social justice agenda. For example, in exploring libraries and archives, students read Angel David Nieves and Siobhan Senier's essay on creating subaltern archives. We paid close attention to the ways in which the digital humanities can perpetuate systems of inequality through labor practices, creation of metadata, and accessibility and what they as practitioners can do to challenge these systems. For their final projects, students were asked to craft an original digital narrative that interrogated Grinnell's past and present as a site of social justice movements. We scaffolded this project by introducing the students to the College's Special Collections and Archives very early in the class. In a session led by the College's archivist, Christopher Jones, students were presented with archival materials selected for their connection to social justice movements at the College and asked to create metadata for three of them. Final projects included mapping harassment at Grinnell, a timeline of early divestment movements at the College, a video archive of Vietnam War protests, and an archive for the Concerned Black Students student group. This last group is currently working with the Office of Student Affairs to secure funding to more fully realize their vision for their project, which could serve as a digital resource/archive of the Black student experience at Grinnell.

Finally, the third and perhaps most fully realized site of opportunity has been the creation and implementation of an undergraduate fellowship program. The Vivero Digital Scholarship Fellows program is a two-year training and mentorship program. The idea for this program emerged after Mirzam Perez, a faculty member of color on our campus attended a nationally known digital scholarship conference and realized she was one of two persons of color in the room (the other being the Grinnell undergrad who accompanied her). What could we do at Grinnell, we asked, to address this? Pooling our time and statuses, Rachel, Liz, and Mirzam submitted a grant proposal for a three-year pilot to create Vivero. In the fall of 2017, our first cohort of students from underrepresented groups and/or with a demonstrated interest in diversifying scholarship, would be partnered with faculty and staff at the College to work on digital humanities projects.

Each of these programs shares a common set of values and opportunities to address compelling needs on campus. Their goals are student focused with explicit reference to core missions of enabling significant mentored undergraduate research and working toward the common good, and this helps them find common ground with faculty agendas. On a professional level, they are born collaborative: conversation, shared planning, listening, and implementing suggestions undertaken from the outset. Moreover, like Pamela Lach and Jessica Pressman from SDSU, "we aspire . . . to build a campus-based, people-focused infrastructure that promotes social justice via DH."[21] We developed a map of experts on campus outside of faculty roles and actively sought their input in course planning and instruction. We developed our short course project, for example, in close consultation with the archivist of the College. We developed Vivero in consultation with the associate dean focusing on diversity and the office of Careers, Life, and Service. This commitment to collaboration extends to students, albeit imperfectly.[22] We work with faculty on project conceptualization to ensure that students are positioned as genuine contributors. Initial project recruitment includes discussion of the principles in the Student Collaborator's Bill of Rights.[23] Regular paid training and check-ins support the students to become, relative to their faculty leads, experts in particular domains of the project, such as specific softwares, workflows, and scoping decisions.

From Affordances to Infrastructure: Can We Get There from Here?

These accomplishments are imperfect but real. Our concern, though, is that they are temporary at best. What will happen when external funding for summer collaborations is over, when the two-time limit on running a particular short course is reached, and when we face faculty turnover in project leadership for Vivero? The space we found to move could close on us at any point, which is why the affordances found within these positions can hardly be called advantages. For a SLAC that wants to develop a culture of digital liberal arts, traditional models of funding and recognition place too much emphasis on the role of the faculty member in the project, creating unsustainable demands upon them. Many of the central, important questions of creating a digital humanities project—sustainability, development, even certain forms of content creation—are not necessarily in a faculty's wheelhouse but rather are why digital humanities projects are necessarily collaborative. Further, the work of conceiving, organizing, and supervising all elements of a project is highly demanding, especially for a project that is most likely conceived of as an addition to other scholarly commitments.

The question of how to make the spaces that our collaboration has opened accessible to future students, staff, and faculty became particularly salient when, in the spring of 2017, Rachel accepted a new position. Our drafting of this essay overlapped with Liz's preparation for her departure and our reflection made it clear to us that without conscious cultivation, this all could have been otherwise, and worse. Liz could have been seen as a peripheral service provider. Rachel could have seen library involvement as encroachment on already precarious turf. These alternate pasts seem especially salient given that we are now in the midst of recruiting Rachel's replacement, which without supportive infrastructures in place, offers no guarantee that the collaboration between the libraries and the DLAC will continue. Personality-dependent collaborations are not infrastructure; they are lucky happenstance.

At the same time, we believe it would be a mistake to replicate faculty autonomy in nonfaculty positions and rigidly codify who gets to do digital humanities. One of the transformative potentials of DH work is that it can unsettle our assumptions of expertise and who has it. As Sarah Catherine Stanley has suggested, "DH is a response to an environment where the hierarchical structures of the academy don't always map onto the actual expertise held by various members of the community."[24] There is a moment for the people in their institutional environments to become visible and to redefine the processes, values, and infrastructure, before they naturalize older hierarchies. We miss this potential when we do not pay attention to the ways in which this moment fails to last or, put another way, the ways in which we are forced to abandon it when we leave the heady space of conversation and experiment and return to our offices, cubicles, or service points; our hourly, twelve-month, or tenured contracts; our statuses as faculty, librarian, staff, and/or student. Attention to labor, like methodological metacognition, is constitutive and not incidental to digital humanities.

While we certainly empathize with Collier's description of the affective and moral consequences of the institutional precarity that digital scholarship centers face with regards to lack of agency, autonomy, and sustained monetary support, we remain hopeful that the future is not destined to be one of heartache. We believe this, in part, because of our experience reconstituting conceptions of leadership. Labor issues, the tension between service and collaboration, and reward and recognition structures in digital humanities centers at liberal arts colleges have the potential to catalyze a paradigmatic realignment of hierarchical approaches to student learning. Returning to Alvarado's characterization of the digital liberal arts as "rethinking the curriculum as a whole, the spaces within which education happens, and the careers of students who pass through them both," we can see that this rethinking is all connected to how labor is divided, leadership is conceptualized, and expertise is recognized. A critical digital humanities approach to scholarship and pedagogy that prioritizes a blending of service orientation with a recognition that strict autonomy is not desired nor even ideal can create a new culture of collaboration in which faculty, staff, and student are all colearners.

Notes

1. Pannapacker, "Stop Calling It 'Digital Humanities.'"
2. Alvarado, "Start Calling It Digital Liberal Arts."

3. Corlett-Rivera et al., "In Service of Pedagogy."

4. As Paige Morgan notes, the distinction between these two actions is a fundamental distinction in labor positionality: "While [a DH librarian] can make strong recommendations, the scholars I work with are the ultimate decision makers; and this is why my work *is* emotional labor, as opposed to pure technical advice." Morgan, "Not Your DH Teddy-Bear."

5. *Traditional* is, admittedly, a stand-in term for the idea of a faculty member enshrined in the broad outlines of tenure requirements, incentivizing single- or first-author research publications, professor-led courses, and service on committees with some degree of governance power. As Trevor Muñoz has observed of librarianship, "There is no such thing as 'traditional library service'" (Muñoz, "In Service?"). There is, we recognize, no such thing as a traditional faculty member across our various institutions.

6. As Alexander and Davis note in "Should Liberal Arts Campuses Do Digital Humanities?," "This process-over-product focus distinguishes the digital humanities as practiced at small liberal arts colleges from the production focus in much of the digital humanities community."

7. We do not intend to fetishize completion as a clear or permanent achievement. We do, however, hold that there is a difference between meeting a set of goals, no matter how revised or provisional, and unintentional, indefinite hiatus.

8. Logsdon, Mars, and Tompkins, "Claiming Expertise from Betwixt and Between."

9. Star, "The Ethnography of Infrastructure." Citing Star, Matthew K. Gold has also recently suggested in respect to scholarly communication, "foregrounding the embeddedness of human relations around infrastructure . . . can ultimately help us mobilize a critically informed resistance to capital and set of building practices that move the scholarly communications infrastructure of the academy away from corporations and towards the faculty, staff, and students who can build, care for, maintain, and use them" (Gold, "Response to Critical Infrastructure Panel"). Our reflection seeks to call attention to the fact that even as such new infrastructures are created, the work of building, caring, maintaining, and using will not be evenly distributed, recognized, or rewarded if the historical roles of faculty, staff, and student remain unexamined.

10. Collier, "Chapter 3 WMTRBW #HortonFreire #OpenEd16."

11. Concretely, what we had was the ability to schedule a weekly two-hour meeting in an office with a door. The literal time and space of conversation is crucial, as Logsdon, Mars, and Tompkins reflect, to "the ability to have frank and nuanced conversations about common successes and struggles is not only crucial for creating capacity and building expertise. . . . By discussing our personal frustrations and successes . . . we were able to puzzle out some of the core issues at stake in our own DH collaborations, including power dynamics and institutional politics, as well as our own individual positionality within these structures and in society more broadly" (Logsdon, Mars, and Tompkins, "Claiming Expertise from Betwixt and Between").

12. Huculak and Goddard, "Is Promotion and Tenure Inhibiting DH/Library Collaboration?"

13. Flanders, "Time, Labor, and 'Alternate Careers.'"

14. Porter, "What if We Do, in Fact, Know Best?"

15. Muñoz, "In Service?"

16. Nowviskie, "A Skunk in the Library."

17. As Julia Flanders has observed, the downplaying of one's own knowledge is a natural outcome of the hierarchical nature of faculty-staff collaboration, no matter what the two individuals' actual abilities are: "Precisely because of its potential value (if I were being considered as a colleague), it must be explicitly devalued here to show that I am not so considered: it creates a necessity for gestures of demarcation by which the boundaries of my role can be drawn, with technical knowledge on the inside and subject knowledge on the outside." Flanders, "Time, Labor, and 'Alternate Careers.'"

18. Shirazi, "Reproducing the Academy."

19. Relative positions of power as holders of professional positions with PhDs, as well as being white, cis women in a predominantly white institution.

20. Collins and Ruediger, "A 'No Tent' / No Center Model."

21. Lach and Pressman, "Digital Infrastructures."

22. As Anderson et al. incisively point out in "Student Labour and Training," the rhetoric of openness and collaboration and a shift to digital modes does not magically transform the hierarchized labor of academia. Our training was structured to incorporate their suggested best practices around making the work of organization transparent and valued and formalizing expectations while leaving room for individual initiative. Still, there is an understandable experience gap that we must find new ways to overcome in order for students to make full use of these opportunities.

23. Di Pressi et al., "A Student Collaborator's Bill of Rights."

24. Stanley, "Why Is Digital Humanities?"

Bibliography

Alexander, Byran, and Rebecca Frost Davis. "Should Liberal Arts Campuses Do Digital Humanities? Process and Products in the Small College World." In *Debates in Digital Humanities,* edited by Matthew Gold. Minneapolis: University of Minnesota Press, 2012. http://dhdebates.gc.cuny.edu/debates/text/25.

Alvarado, Rafael. "Start Calling It Digital Liberal Arts." *The Transducer* (blog), February 19, 2013. https://transducer.ontoligent.com/?p=1013.

Anderson, Katrina, Lindsey Bannister, Janey Dodd, Deanna Fong, Michelle Levy, and Lindsey Seatter. "Student Labour and Training in Digital Humanities." *Digital Humanities Quarterly* 10, no. 1 (2016). http://www.digitalhumanities.org/dhq/vol/10/1/000233/000233.html.

Collier, Amy. "Chapter 3 WMTRBW #HortonFreire #OpenEd16. See also: The Immorality of Service Organizations." *the red pincushion* (blog), December 6, 2016. http://redpincushion.us/blog/i-cant-categorize-this/chapter3-wmtrbw/.

Collins, Brennan, and Dylan Ruediger. "A 'No Tent' / No Center Model for Digital Work in the Humanities." In *People, Practice, Power: Digital Humanities outside the Center,* edited by Anne B. McGrail, Angel David Nieves, and Siobhan Senier. Minneapolis: University of Minnesota Press, 2021.

Corlett-Rivera, Kelsey, Nathan H. Dize, Abby R. Broughton, and Brittany M. de Gail. "In Service of Pedagogy: *A Colony in Crisis* and the Digital Humanities Center." In *People, Practice, Power: Digital Humanities outside the Center,* edited by Anne B. McGrail, Angel David Nieves, and Siobhan Senier. Minneapolis: University of Minnesota Press, 2021.

Di Pressi, Haley, Stephanie Gorman, Miriam Posner, Raphael Sasayama, and Tori Schmitt, with contributions from Roderic Crooks, Megan Driscoll, Amy Earhart, Spencer Keralis, Tiffany Naiman, and Todd Presner. "A Student Collaborator's Bill of Rights." Humanities Technology, UCLA, June 8, 2015. https://humtech.ucla.edu /news/a-student-collaborators-bill-of-rights/.

Flanders, Julia. "Time, Labor, and 'Alternate Careers' in Digital Humanities Knowledge Work." In *Debates in Digital Humanities,* edited by Matthew Gold. Minneapolis: University of Minnesota Press, 2012. https://dhdebates.gc.cuny.edu/read/untitled-88c11800-9446 -469b-a3be-3fdb36bfbd1e/section/769e1bc9-25c1-49c0-89ed-8580290b7695#ch17.

Gold, Matthew K. "Response to Critical Infrastructure Panel." January 6, 2018. http:// dx.doi.org/10.17613/M6FZ7G.

Huculak, J. Matthew, and Lisa Goddard. "Is Promotion and Tenure Inhibiting DH/Library Collaboration? A Case for Care and Repair." *dh+lib,* July 29, 2016. https://acrl.ala.org /dh/2016/07/29/a-case-for-care-and-repair/.

Lach, Pamella R., and Jessica Pressman. "Digital Infrastructures: People, Place, and Passion—a Case Study of San Diego State University." In *People, Practice, Power: Digital Humanities outside the Center,* edited by Anne B. McGrail, Angel David Nieves, and Siobhan Senier. Minneapolis: University of Minnesota Press, 2021.

Logsdon, Alexis, Amy Mars, and Heather Tompkins. "Claiming Expertise from Betwixt and Between: Digital Humanities Librarians, Emotional Labor, and Genre Theory." *College & Undergraduate Libraries* 24, nos. 2–4 (2017): 155–70. https://doi.org/10.1 080/10691316.2017.1326862.

Morgan, Paige. "Not Your DH Teddy-Bear; or, Emotional Labor Is Not Going Away." *dh+lib,* July 29, 2016. https://acrl.ala.org/dh/2016/07/29/not-your-dh-teddy-bear/.

Muñoz, Trevor. "In Service? A Further Provocation on Digital Humanities Research in Libraries." *dh+lib,* June 19, 2013. https://acrl.ala.org/dh/2013/06/19/in-service-a-fur ther-provocation-on-digital-humanities-research-in-libraries/.

Nowviskie, Bethany. "A Skunk in the Library." *Bethany Nowviskie* (blog), June 28, 2011. http://nowviskie.org/2011/a-skunk-in-the-library/.

Pannapacker, William. "Stop Calling It 'Digital Humanities' and Nine Other Strategies to Help Liberal Arts Colleges Join the Movement." *Chronicle of Higher Education,* February 18, 2013. https://www.chronicle.com/article/Stop-Calling-It-Digital/137325.

Porter, Dot. "What if We Do, in Fact, Know Best? A Response to the OCLC Report on DH and Research Libraries." *dh+lib,* February 12, 2014. http://acrl.ala.org/dh/2014/02/12/what-if-we-do-in-fact-know-best-a-response-to-the-oclc-report-on-dh-and-research-libraries/.

Shirazi, Roxanne. "Reproducing the Academy: Librarians and the Question of Service in the Digital Humanities." In *Making Things and Drawing Boundaries: Experiments in the Digital Humanities,* edited by Jentery Sayers. Minneapolis: University of Minnesota Press, 2017. https://dhdebates.gc.cuny.edu/read/untitled-aa1769f2-6c55-485a-81af-ea82cce86966/section/544313f1-eec6-4c2b-8988-62ed898ec288.

Stanley, Sarah. "Why Is Digital Humanities?" *Sarah Catherine Stanley* (blog), June 21, 2017. http://scatherinestanley.us/2017/06/why-is-dh.

Star, Susan Leigh. "The Ethnography of Infrastructure." *American Behavioral Scientist* 43 (1999): 377–91.

Epistemological Inclusion in the Digital Humanities
Expanded Infrastructure in Service-Oriented Universities and Community Organizations

EDUARD ARRIAGA

In the last few years we have witnessed the expansion of the digital humanities in both geographical and epistemological terms, which has added more complex and contextual perspectives that make it difficult to propose a single definition of what its work entails.[1] Moreover, due to the diversity of global communities and infrastructural ecologies, it is increasingly necessary to examine how the digital humanities operate in different parts of the world.[2] In order to do this, it is important to understand how infrastructures permit or hinder digital humanities work in different contexts. This, I argue, entails reassessing the conception of infrastructure itself so as to include a broader and more inclusive framework that incorporates how practitioners and communities from diverse epistemological and sociocultural perspectives interact with the digital realm. In other words, we must consider not only infrastructure's *what* or *when,* as proposed by Jennifer Edmond, who quotes Susan Leigh Star and Karen Ruhleder, but more importantly its *where.*[3]

Throughout this article I therefore suggest that in the digital humanities we need to think about infrastructure in terms of what I call an *expanded infrastructure.* This is not an entirely new idea, because some scholars recognize that "the original knowledge infrastructures (libraries, archives and museums) have been pushed towards change" due to the impact of digital technologies that are allegedly centered around the user and promote values such as access and openness.[4] However, discussions about knowledge, cyber, or research infrastructures tend to concentrate on "the material systems whereby we exchange the objects of our intellectual labor."[5] In contrast, the conception of expanded infrastructure that I am proposing also considers how human beings, their cultural assets and knowledge, and their existing social and cultural structures connect with digital tools and digital networks that might already be in place. In that sense, an expanded infrastructure may be understood as set of processes and cultural interconnections in which existing structures (physical, symbolic, etc.), people, values, and knowledge all play a fundamental role.

To analyze how expanded infrastructures work, I examine and discuss the following three examples that highlight how digital tools are used in particular contexts that determine resources and conditions: (1) Patrik Svensson's article on the HUMLab, the digital humanities research center he directs in the University of Uppsala in Sweden; (2) digital humanities initiatives carried out at the University of Indianapolis, a small institution of higher education focused on service learning as an educational model; and (3) two Afro–Latin American communities/organizations that carry out digital projects as a strategy to showcase, advance, and articulate their social justice goals: Proyecto Afrolatin@ and C.N.O.A. It is important to note that some of these actors do not aim to study the impact of digital culture or preserve cultural heritage as a practice that extends an exclusive world order. Instead, they use digital tools to pursue actions related to human rights, territory, and racial representations in diverse national contexts. This becomes more apparent as my argument proceeds from the more usual institutional setting of the digital humanities toward sites far removed from the halls of academia. What all these initiatives have in common, however, is that each in its own way pursues an agenda that questions conceptions of humanity, development, and inclusion.

Expanded Infrastructure: Processes and Interconnections

In the digital humanities, one of the most interesting analyses of infrastructure as a concept is a three-tiered model suggested by Patrik Svensson that consists of a *conceptual cyberinfrastructure,* which is understood as the use of ideas to develop certain material infrastructure; *design principles,* which are used to organize and connect those ideas to produce the expected outcomes; and the *actual cyberinfrastructure,* which refers to what is actually produced.[6] Svensson formulated his model based on his own experience in the HUMLab, "a digital humanities laboratory in the North of Sweden . . . , situated in a comprehensive research university, Umeå University."[7] At HUMLab, the aim of the conceptual cyberinfrastructure is to facilitate cross-sectional meetings between researchers. To achieve this, the design principles stress attributes such as *translucence* (the possibility to see and be seen), *flexibility* (in terms of use and movement), and *nonlinearity* (of space). Finally, the implementation of these ideas is contingent on the actual possibilities of the space to be rearranged and customized according to the first two levels of more abstract needs and wants. In short, Svensson has recognized that, although the discourse of research infrastructure is sometimes too abstract or, conversely, too grounded in pure materiality, "most infrastructures are highly situated in . . . particular context(s)," and so are conditioned by a variety of concrete and material factors that can exceed the initial plans.[8] Such a model serves as inspiration and point of departure from which I propose the concept of expanded infrastructure throughout this essay.

The articulation of an expanded conception of infrastructure is important for analyzing, understanding, and indeed challenging how infrastructure and digital/ cyberinfrastructure, associated with the industrial and the knowledge economies, respectively, are defined and debated with regard to the production and dissemination of knowledge. Moreover, many such definitions and debates have tended to stress the material foundations of infrastructure, so that in the early 2000s, for example, cyberinfrastructure was understood to consist of "large-scale facilities for the storage, sharing and algorithmic analysis of massive digital datasets."[9] However, in the humanities in particular we need not only to develop the facilities and tools but also to translate traditional humanistic content into digital formats capable of being analyzed via algorithmic methodologies. This is of particular importance in an environment in which the digital can take on the role of a *regulatory technology* through which researchers, policy makers, and funding bodies renegotiate their position in the knowledge production circuit.[10] Therefore, I propose the notion of an expanded infrastructure so that we in the digital humanities question not only the idea of infrastructure as mere materiality but also the *we,* the *what,* and the *when* that are implied in the exchanges of knowledge and goods. Finally, an expanded conception of infrastructure allows the growing digital humanities communities, as well as the communities that produce, store, and research digital knowledge with social and humanistic goals in mind, to reimagine and reconsider diverse forms of knowledge, funding formulas, and models as centered on complex human interactions that sustain digital projects along with other sociocultural initiatives.

Digital Humanities Resources in Small Colleges and Service-Oriented Universities

As Bryan Alexander and Rebecca Frost Davis have noted, small colleges, universities, and service-oriented institutions "take advantage of existing structures and networks to implement digital humanities initiatives more concerned with teaching/learning."[11] In the larger field of the digital humanities, smaller institutions have modest resources, and yet they have been able to develop initiatives in which the "humane digital," understood by Burke as "the human element and . . . the intersubjective judgement," continues to be central.[12] This recycling and reuse of existing institutional resources and human interconnections, with concrete beneficiary communities in mind, is a good example of what I call an expanded infrastructure. This is also very much in line with what scholars such as Johanna Drucker have suggested when they have posited that the digital humanities needs to consider more closely its humanistic aspect and, more radically, human connections.[13] In the case of service-oriented universities, the connections with communities and constituencies they serve and from whom they learn, in a type of reciprocal ethnographic model of knowledge construction, become assets that help us rethink the way digital humanities can or should be understood.

Morever, small service-oriented institutions operate in the current environment in which research (usually associated with expensive tools and labs) is overvalued at the expense of teaching. Critics such as Wendy Hui Kyong Chun, Richard Grusin, Patrick Jagoda, and Rita Raley, among others, have clearly underscored the sinking of the academic ship centered around neoliberal logics that decenter the human component from the humanities in favor of digital utopianisms that leave ethnic communities and small educational institutions alike at the margin of how digital technologies are created and theorized.[14] On the other hand, initiatives at small and community colleges such as La Guardia, Central College, and Lane Community College, among others, or in virtual spaces such as hybrid pedagogy and critical digital pedagogy are examples showing that creative digital humanities practices are already established in many places.[15] As a concrete example, I present in summary the initial steps that are being taken to advance the digital humanities at the University of Indianapolis. In essence, these steps are an exercise in assessing what the infrastructural needs of the university are, which shows that an expanded notion of infrastructure is at the core of the institution's mandate.

The University of Indianapolis is a service-oriented institution of higher education whose motto, "Education for service," is in effect a succinct summary of the pedagogical practices, educational philosophies, and academic actions and projects at the institution. The university develops a large part of its academic endeavors and activities through service-learning programs at the local, national, and international levels, which allow students to experience at first hand what they learn in the classroom. Additionally, the institution relies on a general-education curriculum that prepares students for logical and critical thinking through writing, reading, speaking, and listening. By serving the communities, students build knowledge not only *about* or *from* but also *with* the communities they serve. These connections in turn become, through a process of adaptation and interconnection, parts of an expanded infrastructure in which material objects and digital tools are only part of the equation.

Although the university does not have a program that is institutionally named *digital humanities* or is particularly devoted to this field, it is possible to identify what the ECAR working group has termed an "early stage" implementation of digital humanities.[16] In that sense, elements already in place such as the Faculty Design Studio, a space created to "organize learning communities and support the daily practice of faculty at all ranks to excel as teachers, scholars and mentors,"[17] and the groups that have resulted from such endeavor, Faculty Learning Communities, have played a central role in doing digital humanities.

The Faculty Design Studio and the groups that consequently formed did not focus on the study of a particular topic; however, one group devoted its efforts to the exploration of digital humanities and their implementation in a service-oriented institution. Formed by members with a diverse range of knowledge about the field, this particular group started to reflect on what infrastructure would be needed and what infrastructural elements were already accessible to them and to other members of the institution.

The group understood what Gregory Crane, Brent Seals, and Melissa Terras pointed out in 2009: "the center of gravity for intellectual life in every society is now digital," meaning that digital tools and sophisticated repositories already in existence are central to the development of any cultural and intellectual action.[18] Furthermore, the group came to the conclusion that human beings and their complex interactions are the core of such cultural and intellectual actions, consequently changing the perspective from which infrastructure might be seen.

With this idea that infrastructure encompasses material structures, people, expertise, and methodologies, the Faculty Learning Community reached out to librarians already working with digital collections and to faculty members from departments such as computer sciences, arts, English, modern languages, and history who were pursuing small projects that involved digital analysis, criticism, or some other approach to the digital world. The group began singling out existing projects within the university that could be used to leverage productive connections between digital scholarship and service learning. One of the most important examples of this is the mayoral archives project, which was initiated in 2011 under the direction of Professor Edward Frantz from the department of history and political science.[19] Another is a project to document and register oral histories and traditions of the Indianapolis Latino community by reusing and adapting existing social connections and interactions with the surrounding community.[20] These and other projects will be fundamental for the implementation of digital humanities and particularly for understanding that infrastructure involves a constant process of interconnection to what already exists in a community in a particular time and place. Respecting community ties is therefore as important for a robust infrastructure as acquiring gadgets and objects that can endure and remain useful only with the support of these communities. This way of thinking is important, and even critical, in places where access to technology and educational institutions is scarce or nonexistent, as made clear in the two case studies that follow.

Proyecto Afrolatin@ and C.N.O.A.

In 2013 the University of Guelph organized a conference devoted to the study of Afro-Hispanic culture. Although the topic of the conference was not related to the debates about digital culture or digital humanities, the way that the conference was conceived and carried out was completely in line with them: it was a virtual conference that gathered people from the Americas, Africa, and Europe. During the synchronous and asynchronous sessions, the attendees discussed diverse topics, most of them related to the way African and Afro-descendant cultures were being represented by art, literature, and other means. In one of the sessions, however, the discussion ended up focusing on the possible uses of existing digital tools and platforms to foster development in African and African-descendant cultures. One of the participants took a radical stand by questioning the benefits of the digital age with respect to the images of Africa and the dissemination of its cultures. This person argued that the problem with such tools was that they were no different from the tractor or other technologies from the industrial era, in that Africa and its descendants have always been presented with tools that promise to solve their issues and put them in a better position. The real issues faced by countries in Africa and other locations around the world were, the speaker continued, basic infrastructure fundamental to the adoption of digital or any other technologies: electrical power, water, education, and land, among others. Although the conference was completely virtual and based on the power of digital tools, his argument was valid and anchored in a tradition of resistance and decolonial thought that challenges a hierarchy of values based on epistemic presuppositions originating in the West.

What could be termed colonial narratives, or narratives of victimization, have been used to represent Africa and its descendants worldwide as humans playing catch-up with other continents, peoples, and social organizations. However, such narratives of dependency have been challenged by ethnic and social communities on how they interact with technologies and, in the process, reevaluate conceptions of infrastructure. For example, Anna Everett and Alondra Nelson have shown how African, African-descendant, and other racialized communities have produced, transformed, appropriated, and consumed technologies, particularly digital tools.[21] This is evident in the adoption of technologies by Afro-descendant musical communities to produce rhythms such as hip-hop and house music, which establish new forms of communication action by using readily available digital objects. The same is true for other activist endeavors, such as the virtual barrio or the Chicano internet, as well as the indigenous Zapatista revolution, which showed the power of social, cultural, and activist infrastructures when combined with those that use digital tools.[22]

An interesting case in which racial and ethnic communities created alternative practices and expanded digital infrastructures is that of Proyecto Afrolatin@ (here called Proyecto), which emerged as an initiative interested in exploring and recovering Afro-descendant experiences in the Americas. Although initially created as a traditional social sciences and humanities venture to explore and uncover hidden relations between African Americans and Afro-Latinos, in 2012 it was relaunched with the idea of "using web-based and mobile technologies to facilitate development of digital citizenship for Afro-descendant communities and social movements."[23] The project, formerly affiliated with universities and institutions of higher education, became an independent initiative with limited access to funding and material resources, which made it difficult for Proyecto to achieve their cultural preservation and social action objectives. However, like the Zapatistas, Proyecto solved that gap by taking advantage of existing structures, networks, and technologies already being used by the communities with which they were working. This led Proyecto's directors to rethink the infrastructure for their digital endeavors strategically by conceiving of it not only in terms of expensive systems and computers (which were out of their reach) but also in terms of existing social connections developed through basic analog media (such as personal narratives and treating traditional narratives as artifacts) and electronic devices such as smartphones. Infrastructure, in this case, was used in helping reconnect Afro-Latinos throughout the Americas as diverse complex communities with political power in the region. Likewise, through interacting with censuses and other tools for civic engagement, these communities became aware of their roles and possibilities as citizens at a time when they can combine the power of the digital with their traditional analog systems of representation, communication, and political and cultural engagement. In this case, the infrastructure for digital projects among Afro-Latin American populations in the Americas was the result of a productive connection between a particular community's assets (their local knowledge) and existing digital platforms.

What Proyecto demonstrated is that when combined with digital tools, the complex connection between Afro-descendant people, cultural objects (such as narratives, rites, traditions, and writings), histories, and forms of expression became a productive and expanded way to understand infrastructure. Proyecto collaborators realized that social and cultural connections and strategies have been in existence for generations and have been in continuous use by communities to create, store, transmit, and disseminate, through networks of diasporic communication, their *lived experiences* as Afro-Latinos.[24] The incorporation of digital tools based on open-source platforms and easily accessible electronic devices (e.g., Google platform, Facebook, basic blogs, and voice recording tools) was made possible because of the existence of these other interconnections (historic, symbolic, and cultural infrastructures to transmit information from member to member) that conditioned the way that digital tools were adopted. In other words, Proyecto took advantage of the historical connections between people and the dynamics of cultural information and how it was disseminated to create its own conception of infrastructure. For instance, although Proyecto created an open-source digital voice recorder that community members could use as both a desktop and a mobile application, such a digital tool would be useless without preexisting connections (family, racial, ethnic, etc.) with subjects who were bearers of knowledge (usually elders). Community members would in turn need a connector (a person helping to connect knowledge and collect it via digital gadgets) who would become a fundamental part of the expanded infrastructure created by Proyecto.

Moreover, with this expanded infrastructure in place, Proyecto gathered information, histories, and accounts from Afro-Latin American communities in Colombia, Panama, the United States, Puerto Rico, the Dominican Republic, Peru, Ecuador, Mexico, and other places. The gathering process involved a decentralized network of participants, each of whom used her or his own device to record that participant's own account and those of others, and the curation and archiving was centralized and managed by the Proyecto's staff, who were part-time collaborators and volunteers.

Like Proyecto, C.N.O.A. (abbreviation of Conferencia Nacional de Organizaciones Afrocolombianas, the Spanish title of the National Assembly of Afro-descendant Organizations), a Colombian network of regional social movements devoted to working with Afro-Colombian communities, uses previously existing human and epistemological objects and interactions to create digital projects focused on social justice. C.N.O.A.'s main goals are connected to safeguarding the human rights and the interests of Afro-descendant communities, and the organization has turned to the use of digital tools as a way to store memories, educate, and reach wider communities. C.N.O.A. does most of its work in rural areas, where access to digital tools and the expertise to use them are low. To overcome the challenges that this situation poses, the organization has adopted a methodology based on extensive collaboration and sharing of knowledge. In practice, when C.N.O.A. approaches a given community in which the elders and other members do not know how to use or access the digital tools necessary to record information, the organization relies on the more experienced users in the community who do have the access and know-how.

Facing the limitations of access and expertise, C.N.O.A. created material analog devices such as a *caja de herramientas* (toolbox) to educate Afro-Colombians about their rights and on how to defend them. The toolbox consists of a cardboard box with materials inside, including a CD with information regarding rights of Afro-Colombian communities, as well as possibilities of connection and interconnection through the use of digital tools. The toolbox is very useful in rural contexts where there is no internet coverage but where the communities have access to electricity and a computer. Even in regions without electricity or computers, the toolbox is another way to create connections and share knowledge thanks to the written and graphical information it contains. This toolbox is also a useful aid on how to participate in the digital realm in order to educate, showcase knowledge and culture, achieve concrete goals related to human rights and to issues of discrimination, and enhance the visibility of Afro-descendants as political actors at both the national and international levels. In short, like Proyecto, C.N.O.A. used existing digital tools (in this case the Google and WordPress platforms, Twitter, phones, and mobile applications), preexisting community connections, knowledge transmitted from generation to generation, and the support of diverse people to create a complex but effective expanded infrastructure to carry out digital projects and initiatives.

The important implication of both these projects is that they have created practices and methodologies that challenge and make us rethink how infrastructure has been conceptualized in the digital humanities and other related fields that use digital technologies. One of the most interesting features of both projects is the use of existing elements such as networks and community protocols to achieve their goals. On the one hand, the advantage of digital tools is that they have provided powerful means to increase the visibility of Afro-descendant peoples in many social and national settings in which the invisibility of African heritage has been the norm. Some of these people can even claim their status as citizens—something that is not granted in some parts of the world, including developed nations. On the other hand, it is important to keep in mind that many of these Afro-descendant communities and networks in the Americas have existed for more than five hundred years. In that sense, the expanded vision of infrastructure constructed by Proyecto and C.N.O.A. taps into preexisting processes and relations, and so it is, itself, most usefully understood as a process that uses and reuses existing sociocultural and technological structures in order to construct more open and diverse conceptions of humanity.

It is also interesting to note that these projects were funded by agencies that are not usually connected to the field of digital humanities: The Ford Foundation (Proyecto) and USAID (C.N.O.A.). Although these are big foundations that generally fund large projects, that was not the case for the examples studied here. The projects emerged from grants dedicated to programs of economic development in general, particularly those tied to ethnic and racial groups seen as poor and therefore underdeveloped. It was the communities, however, who decided to add a digital component as a way for them to achieve their goals and reach wider communities, making visible part of the "unseen labor behind our digital infrastructures."[25] In that sense, an expanded infrastructure also shows how agencies and practitioners who are not so predominant in the field can contribute to a global economic development in which the digital humanities is both a contributor and a beneficiary.

As I have stated at the beginning of this work, it is undeniable that the digital humanities have been expanding globally and coming into contact with diverse and very different contextual realities. In that landscape, as evidenced by the University of Indianapolis, Proyecto, and C.N.O.A., there is a need for an expanded notion of infrastructure, especially if we do not want the human of the digital humanities to be displaced by material, technocratic visions that leave human beings (complex, diverse, and different) at the margins of existence. Moreover, an expanded notion of infrastructure that includes processes and cultural interconnections in which existing structures (physical, symbolic, etc.), people, values, and knowledge play a fundamental role will also allow us to pursue a form of digital humanities that can contribute to social and human justice.

Notes

1. Klein and Gold, in the introductory piece to *Debates in the Digital Humanities 2016,* resort to the concept of "Expanded field" in order to better explain the relational, interconnected, contextual, and malleable nature of the field. See Klein and Gold, "Digital Humanities."

2. Mattern, "Library as Infrastructure."

3. Edmond, "Collaboration and Infrastructure"; Star and Ruhleder, "Steps."

4. Edmond, "Collaboration and Infrastructure," 59.

5. Crane, Seales, and Terras, "Cyberinfrastructure."

6. Svensson, "Cyberinfrastructure," 74.

7. Svensson, "Cyberinfrastructure," 45.

8. Svensson, "Cyberinfrastructure," 44.

9. Kaltenbrunner, "Digital Infrastructure," 275.

10. Kaltenbrunner, "Digital Infrastructure," 276.

11. Alexander and Davis, "Should Liberal Arts?," 375.

12. Burke, "The Humane Digital."

13. Drucker, "Humanistic Theory," 96.

14. Chun et al., "The Dark Side."

15. McGrail et al., "Community College."

16. ECAR, *Building Capacity.*

17. University of Indianapolis, "Faculty Development."

18. Crane, Seales, and Terras, "Cyberinfrastructure," 27.

19. Institute for Civic Leadership, *Digital Mayoral Archives.*

20. Mattern, "Library as Infrastructure."

21. Everett, *Digital Diasporas;* and Nelson and Tu, *Technicolor.*

22. Cleaver, "The Zapatista Effect."

23. Proyecto Afrolatin@, "About Us."

24. Wade, "Rethinking Mestizaje."

25. Eghbal, *Roads and Bridges.*

Bibliography

Alexander, Bryan, and Rebecca Frost Davis. "Should Liberal Arts Campuses Do Digital Humanities?" In *Debates in the Digital Humanities,* edited by Matthew K. Gold, 368–89. Minneapolis: University of Minnesota Press, 2012.

Burke, Timothy. "The Humane Digital." In *Debates in the Digital Humanities,* edited by Lauren F. Klein and Matthew K. Gold. Minneapolis: University of Minnesota Press, 2016. http://dhdebates.gc.cuny.edu/debates/text/91.

Chun, Wendy Hui Kyong, Richard Grusin, Patrick Jagoda, and Rita Raley. "The Dark Side of the Digital Humanities." In *Debates in the Digital Humanities,* edited by Lauren F. Klein and Matthew K. Gold. Minneapolis: University of Minnesota Press, 2016. http://dhdebates.gc.cuny.edu/debates/text/89.

Cleaver, Harry. "The Zapatista Effect: The Internet and the Rise of an Alternative Political Fabric." *Journal of International Affairs* 51, no. 2 (Spring 1998): 621–40.

Conferencia Nacional de Organizaciones Afrocolombianas (C.N.O.A.). "¿Quiénes somos?" Accessed June 10, 2017. http://convergenciacnoa.org/quienes-somos/.

Crane, Gregory, Brent Seales, and Melissa Terras. "Cyberinfrastructure for Classical Philology." *DHQ: Digital Humanities Quarterly* 3, no. 1 (Winter 2009). http://digitalhumanities.org/dhq/vol/3/1/000023/000023.html.

Drucker, Johanna. "Humanistic Theory and Digital Scholarship." In *Debates in the Digital Humanities,* edited by Matthew K. Gold, 85–95. Minneapolis: University of Minnesota Press, 2012.

Dyson, Michael Eric. *Know What I Mean? Reflections on Hip Hop.* New York: Basic Civitas Books, 2007.

ECAR Working Group. *Building Capacity for Digital Humanities: A Framework for Institutional Planning.* Boulder, Colo.: EDUCAUSE Center for Analysis and Research, 2017. https://er.educause.edu/~/media/files/library/2017/5/ewg1702.pdf?la=en.

Edmond, Jennifer. "Collaboration and Infrastructure." In *New Companion to Digital Humanities,* edited by Susan Schreibman, Ray Simens, and John Unsword, 54–66. Chichester, U.K.: Wiley Blackwell, 2016.

Eghbal, Nadia. *Roads and Bridges: The Unseen Labor behind Our Digital Infrastructure.* Ford Foundation Reports. Accessed March 13, 2018. https://www.fordfoundation.org/library/reports-and-studies/roads-and-bridges-the-unseen-labor-behind-our-digital-infrastructure.

Everett, Anna. *Digital Diasporas: A Race for Cyberspace.* Albany: State University of New York Press, 2009.

Halliwell, Martin, and Andrew Mousley. *Critical Humanisms: Humanist/Anti-Humanist Dialogues.* Edinburgh: Edinburgh University Press, 2003.

Heidegger, Martin. *Basic Writings.* New York: HarperCollins, 2008.

Institute for Civic Leadership. *Digital Mayoral Archives.* Indianapolis: University of Indianapolis. Accessed June 16, 2017. http://uindy.historyit.com/.

Kaltenbrunner, Wolfgang. "Digital Infrastructure for the Humanities in Europe and the US: Governing Scholarship through Coordinated Tool Development." *Computer Supported Cooperative Work* 26 (2017): 275–308. https://doi.org/10.1007/s10606-017-9272-2.

Klein, Lauren F., and Matthew K. Gold. "Digital Humanities: The Expanded Field." In *Debates in the Digital Humanities 2016,* edited by Matthew K. Gold and Lauren F. Klein, ix–xv. Minneapolis: University of Minnesota Press, 2016. http://dhdebates.gc.cuny.edu/debates/text/51.

Mattern, Shannon. "Library as Infrastructure." *Places Journal* (June 2014). https://doi.org/10.22269/140609.

McGrail, Anne B., Dominique Zino, Jaime Cardenas, and Bethany Holmstrom. "Community College." In *MLA Commons.* Accessed February 20, 2018. https://digitalpedagogy.mla.hcommons.org/keywords/community-college/.

Nelson, Alondra, and Thuy Lihn N. Tu, eds. *Technicolor: Race, Technology and Everyday Life.* New York: New York University Press, 2001.

Prescott, Andrew. "Why Infrastructure?" July 8, 2016. https://medium.com/digital-riffs/why-infrastructure-ccc8f79a3ba8.

Proyecto Afrolatin@. "About Us." Accessed June 15, 2017. http://afrolatinoproject.org/about-us/.

Star, Susan L., and Karen Ruhleder. "Steps towards an Ecology of Infrastructure: Design and Access for Large Information Spaces." *Information Systems Research* 7, no. 1 (March 1996): 111–34. https://pdfs.semanticscholar.org/9cfc/d2dfe7927451f2c39617 e6ac0aa499fd2edb.pdf.

Svensson, Patrik. "Cyberinfrastructure for the Digital Humanities." *Digital Humanities Quarterly* 5, no. 1 (2011). http://digitalhumanities.org:8081/dhq/vol/5/1/000090/000090 .html.

University of Indianapolis. "Faculty Development." Accessed June 19, 2017. https://uindy .edu/faculty-development/index.

Wade, Peter. "Rethinking Mestizaje: Ideology and Live Experience." *Journal of Latin American Studies* 37, no. 2 (Spring 2005): 239–57.

Digital Infrastructures

People, Place, and Passion—a Case Study of
San Diego State University

PAMELLA R. LACH AND JESSICA PRESSMAN

NOTE: This essay was written in 2018 and typeset before the COVID-19 global pandemic.

At San Diego State University (SDSU) we are building a digital humanities initiative from the ground up, a grassroots and faculty-based movement intentionally organized around recognition of the importance of people, their labor and their passions. Digital humanities (DH) supports, examines, and is built upon infrastructures, the networked system of cables, servers, middleware, interfaces that undergird knowledge production in digital contexts, and so forth—but the human aspects of collaboration, care, and extra work are also essential. Bethany Nowviskie has described a "feminist ethic of care," a praxis that "seeks . . . to illuminate the relationships of small components, one to another, within great systems."[1] We are building our program in alignment with the idea that social networks, bureaucratic practices, and political policies are not just about technologies and budgets but also about reputations, feelings, and friendships. Pursuing a DH program based on people means taking seriously the people part of this infrastructure, often described in derogatory and sexist ways as *soft skills*, and making it not only visible but valuable. Decades of feminist and postcolonial theory have taught us to recognize the role of humans—actual humans and not just "the human" as concept—as part of technological, spatial, social, capitalistic, and ideological infrastructures and also to be attentive to the "imbrication of infrastructure and human organization."[2] Yet, putting this into practice is hard. There are inspiring models of feminist-focused social action work in DH, FemTechNet in particular, and we aspire to work in a similar vein to build a campus-based, people-focused infrastructure that promotes social justice via DH.[3]

SDSU is a large and diverse public university, a Hispanic-Serving Institution (HSI), and DH serves a special role here. DH offers opportunities for teachers to experiment and for students, particularly humanities majors, to enter STEM fields, but those opportunities come with costs: training for faculty and students as well as resources to support project-based and community-focused collaboration. Such implementation is harder at some schools than others, resulting in unequal access to DH. This is especially felt on our campus, a state school rebounding from years of severe budget cuts wherein overburdened faculty continue to grapple with impacted class sizes and have little time or enthusiasm for extra work even if that (DH-related) work is positive and passion-filled; our students are from divergent backgrounds working full-time and feeling the effects of increasing debt responsibilities and family pressure to focus on "practical" job skills; our administrative leaders face uncertain financial futures and cannot commit budgets for long-term planning. These real humans and their real needs, capabilities, fears, and desires shape DH@SDSU, as we call it. We believe that SDSU is not unique in its focus on people as a means of changing the way the university operates. We use DH@SDSU in this essay as a case study for sharing our theory-based practice for developing a DH initiative and for presenting a larger claim about the importance of local and situated practices and feminist perspectives as a form of DH infrastructure.

Digital + Humanities

The term *digital humanities*, with its competing definitions, can be a stumbling block or roadblock for many, and this was the case for us. Ours is not a liberal arts campus wherein the value of the humanities is evident and promoted. For us, DH is less a distinct field or discipline than a strategic maneuver. As our newly printed and brightly colored promotional bookmarks state, SDSU's digital humanities initiative is about "advocating for the humanities in a digital age." We understand and often explain the term as *digital plus humanities* or digital in the service of enhancing, expanding, and extending the humanities. We ground our initiative in the strengths of the humanities. Investigations of power structures—historical, social, and political—are the domain of the humanities, as are articulations of imaginaries and the critical examinations of them. It is incumbent upon DH practitioners to consider the ways in which we develop DH through historically informed perspectives focused not just on projects and tools but on the social structures that undergird them, which are not just physical and disciplinary but also ideological and dependent on orientation.[4] DH is an opportunity not only to encounter new orientations (tools, technologies, data, visualizations, and people from other disciplines) but also to consider why we have not had such encounters before, that is, to recognize that encounters are possible. Such consideration is important so that we avoid unintentionally replicating power structures from older models. "A real risk," Patrik Svensson warns, is "that new humanities infrastructures will be based on existing infrastructures, often filtered through the technological side of the humanities or through the predominant models from science and engineering, rather than being based on the core and central needs of the humanities."[5] For this reason, we rely on traditional humanistic thinking, particularly media studies, to help us understand digital infrastructure as we work slowly, collaboratively, and in a transdisciplinary manner.

Because media theory and history is by nature interdisciplinary and challenges ownership by a single research area, approach, or department, its study supports community-building around the discussion of ideas. That is where DH@SDSU started: as a community of colearners who meet monthly to read scholarship in media history and culture. Our ongoing faculty research group remains the cornerstone of our DH initiative. This is where we gather and learn together and from each other while situating our initiative within scholarship that dispels cultural myths about computing, particularly the idea that the digital is inherently democratizing. We have studied the work of such humanists as David Golumbia, who reminds us, "There is little more to understanding computation than comprehending this simple principle: mathematical calculation can be made to stand for propositions that are themselves not mathematical, but must conform to mathematical rules"; Alexander Galloway, who focuses on the internet to show that "protocol is how technological control exists after decentralization"; and Wendy Chun, who addresses ideologies of software to argue, "Code is executable because it embodied the power of the executive, the power of enforcement that has traditionally—even within classic neoliberal logic—been the provenance of government."[6] We are learning to become attentive to the biases built into the "algorithms of oppression" that drive the digital.[7] We also use as a guiding star the work of Lisa Parks, who "emphasizes materiality and physicality and as such challenges us to consider the specific locations, installations, hardware, and processes" of media infrastructure as well as "foreground processes of distribution that have taken a back seat in much humanities research."[8] Such scholarship teaches us that DH should not only be technologically enhanced humanities work but should pursue a humanities-informed mode of thinking reflexively. We can and should be considering what Parks calls *infrastructural imaginaries*: "ways of thinking about what infrastructures are, where they are located, who controls them, and what they do."[9] Infrastructures are, in part, imagined; so too is our ability to study them or build them from an objective stance or unbiased orientation. We (digital) humanists use our monthly reading group to examine the operations of the digital and its impacts on the daily so that we can make changes. It is the province of DH to explain and explore these situations and realities, and at SDSU we proceed from this perspective.

We claim this cause because of the larger institutional context and infrastructure in which we work. SDSU is part of the California State University (CSU) system, which spans the length of the state, from Humboldt in the northernmost region, to SDSU in the south. One of the central tenets of the CSU is to support and advance diversity and inclusion on campus and in the broader community; twenty-one of its twenty-three campuses have HSI status. SDSU is an incredibly diverse HSI with a strong tradition of social justice. We claim the first Women's Studies program in the nation (established in 1970), enroll a racially and ethnically diverse undergraduate student population with no discernible majority group, and have been celebrated as a top LGBT friendly campus, to name a few distinctive characteristics.[10] Yet, our campus is not without its contradictions and limitations. Our architecture is modeled after the Spanish colonial Mission style, and our mascot is an (often angry-looking) Aztec, an ire-invoking fact that has stimulated many protests and spurred the formation of a task force in 2017–18 to consider the elimination of the Aztec moniker, though ultimately very little changed. The land that our campus occupies once belonged to the local Kumeyaay peoples, and these contexts and contradictions are woven into our institution's fabric in visible and invisible ways.[11] San Diego is likewise a contradictory place, a military town and diverse border city with a history of accepting refugees from around the world, even as prototypes of a new border wall have been installed in the region. SDSU is located nearly twenty miles from the border with Mexico, and many of our students and staff cross that border daily. Our work in digital humanities traverses different types of borders, between disciplines and departments, but it has the potential to unite. Although we could have followed any number of institutional models for building a DH program, we have chosen to use DH as a modality through which to work for social change—even as we must work within the confines of limited budgets, heavy instruction and service loads, and disciplinary turf wars—and to do so by centering our efforts around the unique needs of our local community.

DH @ SDSU

Our digital humanities initiative began several years ago as a home-grown, grass-roots, faculty-driven project. We had no institute or center, special tools, or substantial funding. What we had was a smart, savvy professor who was looking to reignite faculty enthusiasm for research and collaboration. Dr. Joanna Brooks, then chair of the Department of English and Comparative Literature, had steered her department through economic crisis and faculty furloughs. In 2013, she ventured across town to the University of California, San Diego (UCSD) to hear N. Katherine Hayles Jessica Pressman discuss their 2013 edited collection *Comparative Textual Media: Transforming the Humanities in the Postprint Era,* a book that argues that text is media and that recognition of this fact can help humanities departments, especially literature departments, claim an important role in training today's students for the digital media ecology. Joanna saw an opportunity and asked Jessica, who had just moved back to San Diego, to help apply this paradigm to SDSU. Together they sought to use digital humanities to stimulate faculty interest in new research questions or practices, build community around these issues, and experiment in ways of translating this new knowledge into lessons for the classroom.

We pursued a two-pronged approach to bringing people together around and through digital humanities, but both approaches focused on facilitating human-to-human interaction and the sharing of knowledge. First, we initiated a monthly lunchtime reading group to discuss recent scholarship in media studies. We watched as a group of isolated professors who each individually expressed lack of knowledge about DH became a community of DH scholars. We also started a separate working group devoted to DH pedagogy. This group met weekly for a year and supported each other on developing and revamping lesson plans. The second part of our strategy was a more intense investment in collaborative digital humanities learning. In May 2014 and again in May 2015, we held Reboot Camp, a daylong opportunity for humanities faculty to come together at the end of the term to learn about major trends and tools in DH. We discussed recent scholarship, experimented with new tools in camp-like fashion, and brainstormed desires for a DH program at SDSU. More importantly, we forged personal relationships around the possibility of making something together. It was clear to us then, as it is now, that whatever DH@ SDSU becomes is determined by whoever shows up to the table.

We began to formalize our efforts when we set our sights on a prestigious new initiative at SDSU aimed at strategically advancing research on campus, a funding measure called Area of Excellence (AoE). AoE allotted a cluster of tenure-track faculty hires in a research area, and we determined that ours would cohere around the intersectional topic Digital Humanities and Global Diversity. Our earliest faculty leaders, who always showed up to the proverbial but also very real table, included scholars interested in diversity and global DH by way of very different entry points: a professor of Italian and European Studies (Clarissa Clò) interested in global migration, a literature professor (William Nericcio) exploring stereotypes of Mexican-Americans in popular culture, a linguist (Doug Bingham) experimenting with artificial languages, to name a few. In this context, *diversity* meant many things, but it mostly allowed a way of connecting people who cared about exploring the intertwined relationship between digital, human, humanities, diversity, and global. We centered our proposal around the profound need for humanities scholarship to explain why and how digital tools for creation, distribution, and consumption are not diffused evenly across human societies.[12] We were awarded the prestigious AoE designation and funding support to produce research that, on the one hand, demonstrates how a focus on the digital informs and even transforms the humanities, and on the other hand how focusing on the human shapes our understanding of the digital. Our AoE seeks to build on the recognition that technological innovation levies profound human consequences that must be understood through the methodologies of humanities research, including historiographical study of the past, critical theorization of the present, and creative vision for the future. This perspective is, of course, built upon decades of humanities scholarship and theory: Marxist examinations of materialist contexts, Foucauldian illuminations of discursive and disciplinary power structures, the insistence of critical race theory that gaps matter and hold meaning, and historical scholarship providing archival examples upon which to draw comparisons. Winning the AoE was a coup, not only for our nascent DH group but also for humanities in general because SDSU had never before granted AoE designation to a humanities area. In addition to the cluster hire and small start-up funds, the AoE award brought on-campus recognition that DH was legitimate.

With this foundation, we determined to hire faculty in three departments from the DH table (linguistics, journalism and media studies, and the library). Realizing that DH research transgresses departmental and disciplinary boundaries, we decided not to specify a department for the fourth faculty hire and instead make it an open call wherein the candidate could choose a departmental home from across four of our partnering departments (history, Chicana and Chicano studies, Africana studies, and European studies). The process of forming the search committee, crafting the position (Digital Humanist focused on Technology and Diversity in Historical Context), and screening the candidates embodied the sort of diversity of perspectives that we hoped the new AoE would advance. More than anything else, the job search got faculty together from different departments who never before talked about DH to hire an innovative new scholar who could continue to bring us together. Although it was quite challenging to balance the needs and wants of disparate departments, the hire that everyone agreed was of vital importance to our AoE was the position of DH librarian. This was in part because the library had been at the table and also because we needed a leader. We hired Pamella Lach as our DH librarian, specifically chosen because of her humanities training (PhD in history) and her experience in DH infrastructure development. With this hire, the library solidified its role as cornerstone in DH@SDSU, and Pam led the library in its commitment to advance DH with a dedicated space, the DH Center.

Located at the geographic center of campus, the library's new DH Center (which officially opened January 2018) is a meeting space molded to support human interaction while fostering flexibility, reconfigurability, openness, community growth, and collaboration. Unlike library spaces at other institutions that were built to support digital scholarship services (data services, scholarly communications and copyright, data visualization, etc.), our DH Center was designed on a model of partnership, having already earned the buy-in of the faculty community. The Center, in its design and function, is not a place for faculty to ask the library to do things *for* them, but rather to do things *with* them. Our focus is on fostering human connection rather than hosting specific technologies. To that end, our design process has been iterative and user-centered, creating the space bit by bit, slowly, through conversations and feedback that have allowed us to be flexible and attentive to the actual, local needs of our constituents (faculty, staff, students, and administrators). That means asking questions, finding out what people need and want, and building in time to reflect upon their responses as much as our processes. We have therefore kept the space open and clean, even somewhat unfinished, a blank canvas upon which to create. What we have in the space is purposeful—a small amount of comfortable, reconfigurable furniture with writable surfaces to support human connection and minimize the appearance of a conventional computer lab. With a small budget and large desire to encourage human interactions, we purchased a minimal amount of technology: ten large screens on movable stands and a laptop cart (we have since purchased ten additional screens and some podcasting equipment). While we do not deny the importance of technology to doing digital work, we wanted to make the most of our financial constraints and encourage our community to contemplate the value of the nondigital—real spaces and interactions with real people in them. It came as no surprise to hear a professor who does interdisciplinary work in Education comment that it was in the DH Center that she finally "found my people."

Now that we have opened, we are observing how community members use the space, and we are asking them what they need to do what they envision. This shaped the next round of design and purchasing of more sophisticated technology. Currently, we are using the space to bring people together with scholarly talks and panel discussions and informal meetings and social gatherings. Faculty members are starting to hold their weekly office hours in the Center to encourage student engagement, and our recognized student organization, the Digital Humanities Collaborative, plans to host meetings and peer-to-peer workshops in the space. To introduce the space to campus, we invited departments and student groups to use the space in creative ways, as long as their events addressed global diversity in the digital age. Between the end of the fall 2017 semester and the conclusion of the spring 2018 semester, we hosted eighty-one events organized by twenty-two departments/schools/units/organizations, including public lectures, tool-based workshops, showcases, symposia, and class-related activities. Hundreds of faculty, staff, students, and community members came through our doors for these events, not to mention the countless individuals who used the space for individual or collaborative work. Indeed, we were quickly becoming victims of our own success, so we developed a narrower usage policy to reduce the number of activities for future semesters. We feel the need to protect what we have created. We must regularly remind library administration that this space is different from other library spaces. It is not a general study space or a traditional service point, and as such has more limited hours of operation. We are working to determine best practices for ensuring that the Center supports the strategic, cross-campus initiative and does not become just another space for events. Having a space supports our theoretical practice for DH development because we use it as infrastructure to showcase and support humanities work, making visible and public the labor that usually happens in discrete, individual classrooms and hidden practices of humanities research.[13]

Sharing our work with each other and the broader campus community is an essential element for the AoE's work, in part because it embodies the ethos of collaboration and openness that is foundational to the digital humanities. More broadly, creating opportunities to share digitally centered class assignments, rigorous digital scholarship, creative digital works, and works-in-progress expands capacity for DH@SDSU. In May 2017 we hosted our first formal DH showcase in what would soon become the DH Center. The event was structured like a digital poster session with faculty, staff, and students standing next to their projects and engaged in one-on-one conversations about their processes. Screens adorned the room, displaying student works of electronic literature submitted for an annual competition, collaboratively produced historical maps, and digital assignments carefully designed by faculty and executed by students. Participants discussed the payoffs of lesson plans; book sculptures made by students for final projects in a literature class intrigued viewers; and a graduate student demonstrated his master's thesis about visual rhetoric within virtual reality;[14] audio played from podcasts produced for journalism assignments; and more. It was a huge success. The conversations that occurred at our showcase encouraged individuals to talk about their processes, design decisions, and the lessons they learned, making digital work seem more accessible to those contemplating a digital turn. The community gathered, learned, and left inspired. The source of this inspiration was recognition that we have what we need here at SDSU—the talent and willingness to grow and share together. Equally importantly, the showcase and the Center that housed it proved to be generative. We saw an uptick in the number and variety of projects at our second showcase, held April 2018 in conjunction with the formal DH Center grand opening. We had more projects (from twenty-six to thirty-eight entries, some of which were actually clusters of student projects) and an increased number of entries in the annual electronic literature competition, more departments (from thirteen to fifteen), and more campus units (from four to six) in just one year. The 2018 showcase engendered even more cross-disciplinary conversation and has led to new, interdisciplinary grant pursuits. The showcases, which continue to grow in scale, are now a centerpiece of our DH Initiative, embodying our intention to use DH as a means of building social networks and communities.

Showcasing DH research also advances the main pedagogical thrust of our initiative: using DH to teach critical digital literacy. Many of our students are English language learners, Dreamers, housing or food insecure, or first-generation college students. Many are so-called digital natives based on birthdate but not on access or affinity to the digital. And most are wholly comfortable using technology but do not understand how that technology shapes and constrains their lives. We want our students to learn not just how to use tools but how to think reflexively about their use. We do this, and plan to do more, in classes devoted to critical digital literacy and DH while also encouraging our faculty network to incorporate such lessons into existing classes creatively and efficiently. For example, as a faculty-led DH initiative, we will help organize guest lectures by faculty willing to guest lecture for each other; we will offer tools workshops and scholarly lectures framed around critical digital literacy; and we intend to develop digital literacy modules that can be quickly deployed in courses across the disciplines (and, we hope, in local K–12 classrooms). Exemplary of the work we hope to support is the partnership between Pamella Lach and Elizabeth Pollard (associate professor of history) to scaffold and scale digital tools into an upper-level history class.[15]

SD|DH

DH has served community-building beyond the boundaries of SDSU. The SD|DH Regional Network began informally in 2014 with a few faculty members from different institutions in San Diego: SDSU; University of San Diego (USD); the University of California, San Diego (UCSD); and California State University San Marcos (CSUSM). What started as informal connections based on personal relationships gradually grew as we recognized the importance of working together for something larger than our own individual projects and institutional responsibilities. Here it is important to recognize the feminist component of our history and infrastructure. All of the individuals working on SD|DH (with one exception) were women; all were working outside of our "real" jobs, doing extra work, in order to build something collective and innovative. Moreover, all of us were aware of our collaboration as feminist practice: based on situatedness, committed to social equity, and operating through personal relationships and attachments. Throughout our collaboration, we recognized that what is good for an individual and her institution is good for the whole group. Thus, rather than compete for scarce resources, we work cooperatively to strengthen DH across the region. Some campuses have significant financial resources but lack administrative support, other campuses have administrative support but limited resources, and still others are trying to build enough grassroots interest to be able to advocate for formal support. Taken together, we form a network of growing expertise and experience. We can also be a source of comfort and care for each other in the process.

SDSU is just a few miles from UCSD and USD, but our faculty and students rarely come into contact let alone meet in organized ways. Yet, if DH is truly about interdisciplinarity and creative-critical practices, then it is incumbent upon faculty to traverse the web of California freeways in order to collaborate with colleagues at other, local institutions. As humanities scholars, we are used to sharing knowledge (in the form of books, articles, and talks), but not about the practices of knowledge production. Building DH capacity, best practices, ways of speaking to administrators, and so forth is knowledge worth sharing that is hard to come by. To address this challenge, in 2015 we met in the dean's office at CSU San Marcos (organized by Katherine Hijar, then assistant professor of history at CSU San Marcos) to discuss the possibility of a more formal local regional DH group. From this table, we organized a large-scale conference, "THATCamp: Diving into Digital Humanities" (October 24–25, 2014), held at SDSU but organized by a cross-institutional team: Jessica Pressman (SDSU), Maura Giles-Watson (USD), Sarah McCullough and Stefan Tanaka (UCSD), and Katherine Hijar (CSUSM). The collaboration between the four regional institutions drew over one hundred people from across Southern California. The event promoted and modeled working together across disciplinary, departmental, and institutional divides. It worked. We felt productive, connected, seen, and supported. So, we kept going.

We applied for and received a start-up grant from the National Endowment for the Humanities Office of Digital Humanities for Building and Strengthening Digital Humanities through a Regional Network. This year-long project (2015–16) was directed at faculty in San Diego with limited time and access to minimal technical resources who nonetheless were interested in incorporating digital pedagogy into their classrooms.[16] We drew twenty-nine participants across a range of institutions: a public research university (UCSD), a hybrid research and intensive-teaching public university (SDSU), a teaching-intensive four-year comprehensive public university (CSUSM), a private liberal arts college (USD), and several community colleges (City College, Mesa College, Palomar College). The imprimatur of the NEH helped us make the case to our respective administrations that DH matters and is worth the investment of time, resources, and support.

When the grant was complete, we continued building momentum for cross-campus collaborative learning by sharing its results. We held a public event at USD in October 2016, SD|DH—Learning *Through* Digital Humanities: A Showcase, which brought faculty and their students together to reflect on the impact of the digital pedagogy experiments enacted in individual classes during the year of the grant-funded experiment. Students presented with their professors in ways that expanded our DH community across learning levels as well as institutional boundaries. We were able to hold the event in USD's new Humanities Center, which, due in large part to the collaborative work of our group (and USD's DH leader, Maura Giles-Watson, then assistant professor of English), includes a DH Studio. As USD's story testifies, our SD|DH is not just a community of researchers, teachers, and organizers but also a community of advocates. The regional network supports faculty in teaching DH where such programs and resources are not available. The network advocates for each other's DH work by showing up for DH events and writing letters of support to local administrators; we share visiting speakers and expert advice and have plans to do much more to provide collaborative capabilities beyond the confines of a particular campus. We have seen a quick uptick. Local faculty job postings have begun touting digital humanities and the regional working group. USD hired a postdoctoral fellow who teaches in their DH Studio; SDSU has now completed five tenure-track faculty cluster hires, launched the DH Center, and acquired a postdoctoral fellowship in classics and digital humanities; the community colleges are developing a cross-campus internship for DH skill-acquisition; the CSUSM history department is building out their Digital History Lab and supported a SDSU MA student advocating for a born-digital thesis; and UCSD's beta implementation of a regional, cross-border, public-facing digital commons, spearheaded by then-digital scholarship librarian Erin Glass, has begun to develop a regional digital infrastructure. We take all these successes as good signs that our work is paying off and that our campuses and administrations see value in what we are doing. Our work is also garnering broader attention: we have been contacted by DH groups in Florida, Georgia, and Northern California to provide guidance in building regional collectives.

Members of our network have spoken about SD|DH at various conferences: UCLA's Digital Infrastructure conference (2016 and 2017), DH 2017 in Montreal, and more.

The SD|DH network depends upon personal relationships. It is not a paid project or service fulfillment to a department or college. It is, we agree, also the motivation to continue doing DH work. Reconfiguring the role, power, and pitfalls of a collective means grappling with which kind of labor is valued and paid, what labor goes invisible and uncompensated, and our varying underlying motivations for doing such work. Such labor is part of the digital economy, and critical examination of it is the role of the humanities.[17] As humanists, we see our actual location—at the United States–Mexico border in the age of border walls and travel bans—as an opportunity to use digital networks and infrastructures to build bridges between departmental and campus borders and, we hope, to build out from there. Just as the internet was developed to avoid attacks to centralized locations and the web conceived in a utopian spirit along the lines of Vannevar Bush's Memex or Ted Nelson's *docuverse* as making open and interconnected the best ideas of humanity, so too do we imagine using DH infrastructure, including our regional network, to build defenses that can sustain local crisis by thinking across institutional boundaries through humanities traditions.[18]

Digital Humanities for the Humanities

The last few years have been a hard time for the humanities and also for humans working within it. Threats of defunding the NEH, as well as the broader devaluation of the humanities, institutions of higher learning, and public education, coupled with resurgences of hate speech and the implementation of policy grounded in racist and xenophobic exclusion of certain peoples, have shaken the core of humanistic, let alone humane, principles. These are threats to the lives of many of our students and community members. The prevalence of neoliberalism in institutions of higher learning propels quickness, completion, upgrade, and disruption, thus challenging the slow, critical, ethical thinking that undergirds the humanities. Increasingly we hear university administrators ask departments to justify their return on investments and look to predictive analytics and algorithms to improve retention and graduation rates. These approaches reduce people to numbers and obscure the individual stories that make up our campus's unique diversity.

As humanists in the age of the digital and big data, we advocate for the opposite. We reject a one-size-fits-all approach to teaching and learning, just as we reject a technology-driven approach to a DH program. We are trying to slow down and to identify, consider, and meet the particular needs and circumstances of our local community. This takes time, and it also engenders reflection, which can run counter to a digital culture based on habits of constant crisis.[19] We believe that DH, understood as digital *plus* humanities, can serve this effort. There has perhaps never been such an important time for humanists and certainly digital humanists to reflect, act up, and insist on the value of the human and the humanities. We hope our efforts help support, inspire, and provide space for such work at SDSU and beyond.

Notes

1. Nowviskie, "Capacity through Care."

2. Star, "Ethnography of Infrastructure," 379.

3. On FemTechNet, see https://femtechnet.org/about/.

4. Sara Ahmed has written, "To be orientated is to be turned toward certain objects, those that help us to find our way." The humanities teach us to consider not only the recognizable objects before but also the reasons why those objects and not others are visible and near. Ahmed noted how "exclusions—the constitution of a field of unreachable objects—are the indirect consequence of following lines that are before us." Ahmed, *Queer Phenomenology*, 1, 15.

5. Svensson, "Humanistiscope," 337.

6. Golumbia, *Cultural Logic of Computation,* 14; Galloway, *Protocol,* 8; and Chun, *Programmed Visions,* 27.

7. Noble, *Algorithms of Oppression.*

8. Parks, "'Stuff You Can Kick,'" 356.

9. Parks, "'Stuff You Can Kick,'" 355.

10. Regarding women's studies, see https://womensstudies.sdsu.edu/history.htm. SDSU enrollment data is available at SDSU Analytic Studies & Institutional Research Dashboard, https://asir.sdsu.edu/enrollment-ethnicity-data-table/. See also Sklar, "SDSU Named Top College for LGBTQ Students."

11. SDSU Land Acknowledgment is available at https://sacd.sdsu.edu/diversity-resources/land-acknowledgment.

12. Digital Humanities and Global Diversity proposal for Area of Excellence is available at https://dh.sdsu.edu/docs/Area_of_Excellence%20.pdf.

13. For more on the DH Center, see Lach, "Launching a Library Digital Humanities Center."

14. Salvo, "Rhetorical Forms and Perceptual Realities."

15. See their website, which includes assignments, tutorials, and sample projects: https://sites.google.com/sdsu.edu/hist503/.

16. See http://regional-dh.sdsu.edu/.

17. See Scholz, *Digital Labor.*

18. Bush, "As We May Think"; and Nelson, *Literary Machines.*

19. See Chun, *Updating to Remain the Same.*

Bibliography

Ahmed, Sara. *Queer Phenomenology: Orientations, Objects, Others.* Durham, N.C.: Duke University Press, 2006.

Bush, Vannevar. "As We May Think." *The Atlantic,* July 1945. https://www.theatlantic.com
    /magazine/archive/1945/07/as-we-may-think/303881/.

Chun, Wendy Huy Kyong. *Programmed Visions: Software and Memory.* Cambridge,
    Mass.: MIT Press, 2011.

Chun, Wendy Huy Kyong. *Updating to Remain the Same: Habitual New Media.* Cam-
    bridge, Mass.: MIT Press, 2016.

Galloway, Alexander R. *Protocol: How Control Exists After Decentralization.* Cambridge,
    Mass.: MIT Press, 2004.

Golumbia, David. *The Cultural Logic of Computation.* Cambridge, Mass.: Harvard Uni-
    versity Press, 2009.

Hayles, N. Katherine, and Jessica Pressman, eds. *Comparative Textual Media: Transform-
    ing the Humanities in the Postprint Era.* Minneapolis: University of Minnesota Press,
    2013.

Lach, Pamella R. "Launching a Library Digital Humanities Center: Reflections and Les-
    sons Learned." *Library Connect,* October 28, 2019. https://www.elsevier.com/con
    nect/library-connect/launching-a-library-digital-humanities-center-reflections
    -and-lessons-learned.

Nelson, Theodor Holm. *Literary Machines.* 87.1 ed. Sausalito, Calif.: Mindful Press, 1987.
    First published 1980.

Noble, Safiya Umoja. *Algorithms of Oppression: How Search Engines Reinforce Racism.*
    New York: New York University Press, 2018.

Nowviskie, Bethany. "Capacity through Care." *Bethany Nowviskie* (blog), February 20,
    2016. http://nowviskie.org/2016/capacity-through-care/.

Parks, Lisa. " 'Stuff You Can Kick': Toward a Theory of Media Infrastructures." In *Between
    Humanities and the Digital,* edited by Patrik Svensson and David Theo Goldberg,
    355–73. Cambridge, Mass.: MIT Press, 2015.

Salvo, Dalton. "Rhetorical Forms and Perceptual Realities: Form as Symbolic Action in
    William Blake's Poetry and Virtual Reality." Master's thesis. San Diego State Univer-
    sity, 2017. http://hdl.handle.net/20.500.11929/sdsu:21527.

Scholz, Trebor, ed. *Digital Labor: The Internet as Playground and Factory.* New York:
    Routledge, 2012.

Sklar, Debbie L. "SDSU Named Top College for LGBTQ Students," *Times of San Diego,*
    June 6, 2019. https://timesofsandiego.com/education/2019/06/06/sdsu-named-top
    -college-for-lgbtq-students/.

Star, Susan Leigh. "The Ethnography of Infrastructure." *American Behavioral Scientist* 43
    (November–December 1999): 377–91.

Svensson, Patrik. "The Humanistiscope—Exploring the Situatedness of Humanities Infra-
    structure." In *Between Humanities and the Digital,* edited by Patrik Svensson and
    David Theo Goldberg, 337–53. Cambridge, Mass.: MIT Press, 2015.

Building a DIY Community of Practice

ASHLEY SANDERS GARCIA, LYDIA BELLO, MADELYNN DICKERSON,
AND MARGARET HOGARTH

Both *hard* and *soft* infrastructure are necessary to offer centralized and sustainable support for the digital humanities.[1] Hard infrastructure includes technology, physical space, funding, and staff. Soft infrastructure is no less essential and includes an organizational culture that supports collaborative experimentation and organizational values that meaningfully reward the often-invisible labor of collaborators such as librarians. The Claremont Colleges have made a purposeful effort to develop soft infrastructure in order to sustain an intercollegiate digital humanities community of practice. This community supports digitally enabled research, teaching, and publication beyond the duration of a five-year Andrew W. Mellon Foundation grant. In partnership with the Claremont Colleges Library, the Claremont DH team seeks to foster an inclusive community of practice on campus that brings faculty, students, administrators, librarians, and staff together, simultaneously building the hard infrastructure with which this community can flourish. The Claremont Colleges' experience has shown that the library can take a leadership role in creating a community of practice, but for this DH program to be successful and sustainable, that community must reach across disciplines, positions, and ranks. A growing body of scholarship has shown that librarians are essential to building this community of practice, as facilitators and also as independent practitioners.[2] By centering the community of practice within the library, librarians raise their own status on campus as experts, as researchers in their own right, and therefore as partners in twenty-first-century scholarship.[3]

In a consortium, the centralization of support systems makes sense in order to prevent unnecessary duplication. At many institutions, including the Claremont Colleges, the library represents the largest shared resource on campus and provides a central space where all interested parties can gather and equitably access resources, expertise, and personalized support. These are precisely the ingredients needed to launch a digital humanities program. The Claremont DH team is not the first to discover this compatibility. There is an extensive literature describing how and why libraries often become the hub for digital scholarly activities.[4] At Claremont, a centralized model of DH support in the library building is appropriate and useful.[5] As highlighted in the new maturity framework for DH programs, there are a variety of organizational models that serve to support digital humanities work on college and university campuses.[6] Library-based digital scholarship centers are essential providers of hardware, software, tools, and expertise that many scholars in the humanities would otherwise struggle to find.[7] At Claremont, consortium-level infrastructural support includes introductory DH short courses for graduate students, faculty, and academic technologists, a course designed for librarians and library staff, and a variety of institutes, symposia, and reading groups that are open to all.

Developing the capacity for digital scholarship through community-building is an essential element in the creation of a DH program.[8] The establishment of a DH community of practice within the Claremont Colleges has meant an investment in the library as a partner in growing capacity-building initiatives and contributing to the sustainability of the program. Over the past three years, librarians, in addition to faculty and staff from across departments, have been learning more about digital humanities by directly engaging in their own DH research projects through a series of planned programs and designated project time. DH is not just a library "service" but an important part of the work that librarians engage in *alongside* and *in collaboration with* faculty and students.[9] Inspired by the changing nature of scholarship and a desire to best support the DH work of students and faculty, this project-based initiative has helped librarians and staff understand DH concepts. Additionally, it has contributed to deeper engagement with the highs and lows of DH research through firsthand experience, thereby enabling librarians to empathetically and knowledgeably support the digital research endeavors of other scholars and students.

Building a successful community of practice required an intentional focus on issues of inclusion and exclusion in DH, a hard infrastructure capable of handling a growing program, and the equitable availability of resources. This chapter highlights the organizational culture and infrastructural elements that contributed to this community's development, as well as the types of support it offers for members of the seven colleges regardless of position or rank. It unpacks the soft process through which the DH team cultivated an informal community of practice around digital humanities to support instruction, research, and the dissemination of scholarship by situating the development of a holistic learning community at Claremont in the context of a constructivist philosophy of learning through experimentation in DH.[10] This chapter describes the significance of equitable access and support across the disciplines, as well as across the seven institutions that comprise the Claremont Colleges, and the different roles that support can take in supporting DH in this environment.[11]

Institutional Culture

The Claremont Colleges are a consortium of five undergraduate liberal arts colleges—Claremont McKenna College, Harvey Mudd College, Pitzer College, Pomona College, and Scripps College—and two graduate institutions—Claremont Graduate University and Keck Graduate Institute. The Claremont Colleges consortium is a complicated but highly stimulating environment to work in, and presents many challenges for intercollegiate programs and a single library that serves all seven institutions. The complex organizational structure lends itself to some natural benefits. The Claremont Colleges Library, for instance, serves all seven colleges and lies at the physical heart of campus; as an institutionally neutral, shared, and central space, the library became the natural hub of the digital humanities. Likewise, the library has come to serve as the locus of other intercollegiate grants and scholarship beyond the Mellon DH grant.

In October 2014, the five undergraduate colleges received a five-year $1.5 million grant from the Andrew W. Mellon Foundation for an initiative entitled Digital Humanities at the Claremont Colleges: Developing Capacity and Community. The mission of the grant is to "expand the use of digital resources in scholarship and research in the humanities at the Claremont Colleges [and] . . . facilitate training and education of faculty members [to] support innovative projects to be undertaken by faculty and students."[12] The grant's administrative team originally consisted of a faculty director and a project manager in collaboration with a lead dean. In recognition of the evolving nature of scholarship and in support of the Mellon DH program, the Claremont Colleges Library also hired a digital scholarship librarian in January 2015. This position, filled by Ashley Sanders Garcia, played a key role in the initial phase of establishing a DH program at Claremont.[13]

The Mellon DH grant has four primary initiatives. These include a spring symposium to engage with DH practitioners outside of Claremont; a summer training institute for faculty, students, and staff; twenty-five course development grants for faculty; and a Digital Research Studio program that offers undergraduates an opportunity to work with faculty members on digital humanistic research projects. The first three years of the grant focused greater attention on pedagogy and the meaningful integration of technology in the classroom. In the final two years of the grant, the focus has expanded to include undergraduate engagement in academically and technologically sophisticated research projects. This grant launched a DH program founded on the principles of inclusivity, constructivism, experimentation, and play.[14]

The Mellon DH grant provided a catalyst for the Claremont Colleges Library to build on its existing scholarly communications initiatives and become actively involved in creating a community of practice around digital scholarship over the last three years. The library has become the center of digital humanities activities, but it is not just a container for DH events.[15] Claremont librarians have made it a vital center for fostering digital scholarship among librarians, faculty, and students interested in integrating digital technology in their research and instruction. Through planning and facilitating symposia, workshops, a summer institute, and an introductory short course for faculty, librarians have become an integral part of the DH community and digital skilling process at the Claremont Colleges.

Infrastructure, Power, and Resource Allocation

Initially, the Mellon DH grant proposal outlined a limited infrastructure to support the nascent community of DH practitioners, but it did not keep pace with the growing desire to learn digital skills and provide new opportunities for students. It took three years to determine the optimal size and composition of the team and steering committee—at least for the present and the foreseeable future. Along the way, the DH team experienced multiple transitions in its administrative home, leadership, and staffing, but its mission has remained the same: to foster an inclusive, welcoming, and affirming learning community.

When Sanders Garcia became director of the Digital Research Studio, she continued her efforts to grow and support the DH community of practice and was empowered to further develop the needed infrastructure. In this position she expanded the DH team to meet the increasing demand for workshops, support, and outreach in ways that she could not in her library roles. The administrative structure supporting the digital humanities initiative has grown commensurately with the needs and interests of the Claremont Colleges community. In addition to the original administrative structure, the DH team as of 2018 included four graduate student Digital Research Studio fellows and a reconstituted and active steering committee to provide additional support and guidance. Digital Research Studio fellows provide marketing, digital publishing, and teaching assistant support as well as consultations and workshops for faculty, student groups, and classes based on their various areas of expertise. A steering committee comprising faculty members, librarians, administrators, and other intercollegiate grant leaders assists with outreach, offers programming suggestions on the basis of their constituents' needs and interests, and provides guidance in navigating the complex social and political terrain of the various campuses and intercollegiate organizations. One person alone cannot build a community of practice or provide all the training, skills, and support required to advance digital scholarship—even on a small liberal arts campus.[16] Building a successful DH learning community takes many dedicated people in dedicated roles, with financial support. It also requires environmental and institutional knowledge with strategic, targeted outreach in order to achieve inclusiveness and maximize resource use and impact.[17]

One of the most challenging questions with which the DH team grapples is how to provide sustainable support for the consortium. As it turns out, the answer appears to lie in one of the most obvious of shared resources on campus—the library.

The Claremont Colleges Library offers an inclusive, equitable, supportive, and safe space for all members of the consortial community to learn and practice new skills. The organizational structure of DH at the Claremont Colleges Library most closely resembles a *network model*.[18] The library "is a more organic connection of services and resources on a campus, a connection that grows to meet other needs, but all the services have resources to contribute to the success of a Digital Humanities project."[19] The Claremont Colleges Library embodies this framework, as it provides a central point for all seven colleges to find interdisciplinary research support, including support for digital scholarship. Physically, the library houses the Digital Tool Shed, offices for the Mellon DH program team, and the Digital Research Studio.

Over the first three years of the grant, participation in the Claremont DH summer institutes has grown exponentially. In the summers of 2015 and 2016, the Mellon grant provided $1,000 stipends via an application process for ten faculty members each year to attend a week-long Digital Humanities training institute that the Claremont DH team hosted. The first summer saw eleven participants; one academic technologist audited the institute without a stipend. The second summer institute included eighteen participants, only ten of whom were funded by the grant; two graduate students, one undergraduate, and five other faculty members audited the institute. Given this success, the DH team enjoined the Mellon Foundation to reallocate the budget and continue both the spring symposium and the summer institute (without stipends) on an annual basis for the remaining years of the grant. The foundation approved this request, and forty-five faculty, graduate students, and IT staff signed up to attend the 2017 DH summer institute. The growth in participation, despite the lack of financial incentive to attend, demonstrates that professional development opportunities such as the summer institute are sustainable endeavors that have a high impact at a relatively low price point.[20]

The grant also provided minibursaries for faculty to develop new courses or redesign previously taught courses by infusing technology in order to improve student learning and engagement. For the first three years, the DH team issued a call for applications for the course development grants and convened a review committee composed of faculty and IT leaders from the various campuses to select each year's recipients. As the Mellon grant moves into its fourth year, it has awarded all twenty-five of the available minigrants to faculty who, upon accepting the funding, agree to teach their new or redesigned course at least twice. With an average of about ten students per class, this means that Mellon DH–funded courses will reach approximately five hundred students over the life of the grant and beyond, through this one initiative.[21]

To support faculty members who were interested in applying for this grant or launching other kinds of digital projects, Sanders Garcia, in her sequential roles as digital scholarship librarian, digital scholarship coordinator, and director of the Digital Research Studio, provided digital pedagogy workshops and numerous one-on-one course and assignment design consultations. This work was supported by

Mellon DH project manager Alexandra Margolin, who has expertise in digital storytelling and offers consultations and workshops as well. Through an in-house professional development series, Claremont Colleges librarians now have greater familiarity with digital humanities methods and approaches in research and teaching. As a result, librarians have begun to support faculty as they explore digital research and instructional tools. In addition, four graduate students from Claremont Graduate University serve as Digital Research Studio fellows and provide workshops and support for both grant-funded and nonfunded classes.

As a shared, centrally supported entity, equitably serving all faculty, students, and staff, DH finds a natural home in the library. Some campuses in the consortium have more support for emerging technology than others, so the library plays an important role in the impartial provision of services, resources, and technology. The Claremont Colleges' unique focus on undergraduate research broadens the potential scope of DH projects and collaborations between faculty, students, and librarians. Librarians' own experience with DH as fellow practitioners has positioned them to support the Claremont Colleges community through research partnerships and acquisition decisions informed by librarians' personal knowledge and experience. The library has historically supported DH professional development for librarians, faculty, staff, and students, as well as DH projects and instruction. Moving forward, there are signs that the library will continue this support through additional training in specific tools and methods for librarians, the technology lending program, and strategic partnerships with academic technologists.

The Challenge of Equitable Distribution of Resources

The library is committed to aligning resources and services to the colleges' teaching, learning, and research needs. In addition to creating new pathways to knowledge and empowering faculty, staff, and student information literacy and use of information resources, the library strives to be a vital center for academic and intellectual engagement for all stakeholders. The unique collaborative nature of the colleges is illustrated by the fact that 80 percent of funding for library resources comes from formula funding that is supported by all seven institutions. The remaining 20 percent comes from supplementary funding from endowments and gifts, as well as from consortial and departmental contributions. This is supported by memoranda of understanding with the campuses and with licenses for electronic resources. The library is poised to further support research and teaching with well-established policies and procedures (provided that funds are sufficient) for purchasing and making available additional print, electronic, and data resources requested by faculty, staff, and students.

Even though the library ceased funding her salary as a result of her move to a director role, Sanders Garcia remained an important advocate for digital humanities both in and outside of the library.[22] With the full support of library leadership,

Sanders Garcia and her team continued to facilitate requested staff and librarian training in digital humanities. She also continued to do extensive outreach, providing support to digital humanities initiatives across the campuses, and served as a crucial link connecting research and instruction needs to technical support and resources. This assistance is equitably available to all Claremont faculty, students, and staff.

Recent major renovations in the library have resulted in the creation of the Digital Tool Shed and Digital Research Studio, which are technologically enhanced facilities that provide space, digital tools, and support for research and media projects.[23] These spaces were funded in several ways. The Mellon DH grant paid for the technology; library operational reserves covered the furniture; and consortial delayed maintenance funds covered the rest. The Digital Tool Shed initially took advantage of graduate and undergraduate student workers' expertise to provide training to library users on the newly available specialized technology. Due to budgetary constraints, however, these positions were not renewed after the first year of operation. Research software and hardware, including GIS, R, Tableau, 2D/3D modeling software, and programming packages such as Python, are available on laptops as well as the workstations in the Research Studio. Media production and postproduction technology is available in the form of DSLR cameras, audio and video recording equipment, and the Adobe Creative Suite. This reflects the inclusive nature of library resources. Except in rare instances of provider-specified limitations, all students, faculty, and staff are welcome to use and reserve the facilities. If the Digital Tool Shed and the Digital Research Studio were housed in a department on one of the seven campuses, it would not be feasible to provide such broad access.

In addition to providing support for faculty and student research, the library also invests in its own staff. Librarians and library staff may request time and professional development funding in order to build out and share DH projects. Librarians and staff have requested time for DH-related projects. Professional development funding, also from seven-college-supported formula funding, is 1.4 percent of the total library budget. Much of the operations budget is predetermined by assessments. However, if the operations budget is limited to the portion that the library can actually control, the professional development funding is a significant 21.2 percent of the library operations budget. This translates to substantial support for librarians' presentation and publication opportunities for their DH projects, as evidenced by at least four librarians' taking advantage of this support. Through funding continuing education opportunities, the library is truly cultivating a "community of learners."[24]

Despite this funding support, it is worth noting some persistent challenges. Time for projects and outreach as well as knowledge of technical skills remain limiting factors for librarians, as does the cost of some specialized software not already provided by the library. Additionally, knowledge and experience extracting data, particularly from previous library systems, can be difficult to obtain on a deadline. IT resources remain a challenge in certain areas; individual campuses are working on several solutions, but the consortium has yet to resolve these issues for everyone. Server access and space in a consortial but centrally managed environment is scarce, particularly for web services. Progress on a solution for these issues has been institutionally slow. While the campuses work on a funding solution, grant applications for specific projects must address this need through outside sources. Last, staff laptops as well as campus broadband and storage networks may not be robust enough for uploading and manipulating large files.[25]

Checks and Balances for Equitable Access

An initial driving force for the library was developing better, more complete ways to support researchers, particularly in the areas of scholarly communication, digital humanities, big data, and data management. Librarians and staff studying DH through Sanders Garcia's workshops and project time quickly applied newly learned DH methodologies to projects that surface library resources to new or increased use and to analyze the library collections. A library staff member with an idea or project that aligns with library strategic initiatives is able to propose it for library leadership's consideration through their division's director. Experimentation and the pressing of traditionally perceived library and librarian boundaries is encouraged as long as it aligns with the mission of the library and funding obtained.

Under Sanders Garcia's leadership, a DH reading group for faculty and librarians formed to address continued education and training in text analysis and to discover faculty interests and needs. The text analysis working group continues through faculty participation and cofacilitation efforts. Currently, the members are developing a collaborative and interdisciplinary research project that utilizes text mining methods. They intend to apply for grant funding both for the project and for the support of continued digital and infrastructural improvements to advance digital scholarship at the Claremont Colleges.

Frequently, resource and technology connections are made between campuses and with the library. Faculty can find real-life DH projects for students to work on using library data sets. Students learn about the library's spaces and resources available to support their DH and media project work. Research appointments with subject and technology specialists, loanable tech, and room reservations are available for research and project needs.

Librarians, faculty, and staff are constantly challenged by the rapid development of technical advances. Knowing how to program is not appropriate for everyone, but seeking and developing expertise in new tools not only enhances library services and support: it grows the library's ability to adapt and benefit from change. Likewise, the nature of scholarship is quickly evolving, and there are new tools and research methods that make more effective use of scholars' time, raise new questions, and provide more efficient means of answering classic questions. Long-term staff need to develop new skills, and those early in their careers also benefit from training and experience in technical skills. All stakeholders find it difficult to strike a balance between the time it takes to learn transformational technology and fulfilling their daily responsibilities. Providing time and resources for technical training and rewarding its application is crucial for maximizing opportunities in DH, and building communities of practice is a way to provide a social infrastructure to meet those needs.

Inclusion and Exclusion in DH

The inclusive nature of the DH community at the Claremont Colleges is not unique in the world of digital humanities, but it is one of its most significant characteristics. Claremont DH is dedicated to welcoming all members of the Claremont Colleges community, "regardless of their status or position."[26] Claremont DH is a human-centric learning community rather than a project-centered service organization. The team supports all members of the Claremont Colleges community, regardless of project topic or faculty standing. The combination of libraries and digital humanities can be a contentious one, with many debates about whether the role of libraries (and librarians) in DH is of service or of collaboration. Trevor Muñoz posits that "libraries will be more successful at generating engagement with Digital Humanities if they focus on helping librarians lead their own DH initiatives and projects."[27] Muñoz's work, as is evident in this chapter, has been highly influential in shaping the approach to digital humanities at the Claremont Colleges, particularly its role in the library.

Within the first year of the Mellon DH grant, it became clear to the DH team that significant disparities in access and financial support were embedded in the original grant proposal. Funding to attend the first two summer institutes existed only for faculty members and only faculty members at the five undergraduate colleges. Furthermore, only faculty at the five undergraduate colleges were able to apply for the course development grants. This imbalance was unavoidable, however, as the Mellon grant was available only for undergraduate-serving liberal arts colleges. At the same time, in a consortium that includes two graduate institutions, the uneven distribution of support was painfully obvious. This inequity served as an additional incentive to create the short course for those left out of the grant proposal: faculty at all seven institutions, graduate students, and all the staff members, especially academic technologists and librarians who would be asked to support the integration of technology into classrooms and research projects. Additionally, in the first summer institute, the DH team welcomed anyone who was interested in learning more about the digital humanities to participate even though a stipend could not be provided for them. Consequently, the summer institute saw dramatic increases in attendance every year.

In its inclusiveness, Claremont DH adheres to a *big tent* philosophy but with a few caveats. Big tent DH argues for a broad disciplinary scope and developed out of the Digital Humanities 2011 conference at Stanford University. The danger of casting such a wide net, according to Patrik Svensson and Melissa Terras, is that it may result in a poorly defined field without a clear goal or sense of direction.[28] Johanna Drucker also argues that the value of the humanities and the way humanists see and understand the world is being lost and will be lost unless humanists carry their epistemology into the digital world and engage in it in a meaningful way.[29] Creating an all-inclusive definition of DH may obscure the *humanities* in favor of a sole focus on the *digital*. In the case of Claremont, a focus on the humanities in the creation and use of digital tools allows arts and humanities scholars to remain true to their disciplinary standpoints even as they employ innovative methodologies. In this way, Claremont DH seeks to create greater equity in accessibility across the disciplines, a goal that closely aligns with the purpose of libraries.

Creating a Library-Based DH Community of Practice

A "community of practice," according to anthropologist Jean Lave and computer scientist Etienne Wenger, is a group of learners united in their shared interest in a particular topic. The group comprises both newcomers and "old-timers" who learn together and from one another in a social context.[30] The work of Lave and Wenger extends the theory that knowledge is constructed and contends that learning takes place through one's interaction with other people, not just in the individual's mind. Through the process of learning in community, novices and mentors both undergo a shift in their identities, even as they cocreate a shared sense of identity within the community.[31]

The scholarship on library-facilitated professional learning communities for faculty in the area of scholarly communications, of which DH and digital scholarship are cousins, reveals several additional insights. Between 2011 and 2013, the Miami University librarians Jennifer W. Bazeley, Jen Waller, and Eric Resnis created and facilitated their own successful scholarly communication community of practice. Through institutional financial support and commendation, faculty felt empowered to participate in the community, committed to attending meetings every two to three weeks, shared their growing knowledge through public presentations, and developed an agreed-on deliverable—a website to disseminate knowledge about scholarly communications for their campus and the wider academic world.[32] Their innovative work has shown that with proper institutional support, faculty interest, and a small team to facilitate it, a librarian-run community of practice can be highly effective.

In order to meet Claremont's evolving needs for digital humanities support, Sanders Garcia, as digital scholarship coordinator, developed a customized Introduction to DH short course for Claremont Colleges librarians and staff. This five-week course covered definitions of digital humanities and digital literacy; concepts of data, spatial, and temporal pattern finding; network analysis; and topic modeling.

Starting in November 2015, librarians and library staff met weekly for seventy-five-minute scaffolded seminars covering topical readings, exemplar projects, and discussions about how that week's digital research method could be used in their own work as well as in that of faculty and students.

Four-member teams applied what they had learned in the short course by designing their own experimental pilot projects. The teams' proposals included a project description, justification of value statement, identification of audience, technical specifications, and a work plan that addressed sustainability. Short-course participants were then invited to build out their projects during a dedicated library DH Maker Week in July 2016. Library leadership agreed to give project team members half-days throughout the Maker Week to devote to their projects. The proposals drafted during and immediately after the short course served as road maps for cross-divisional project teams in the creation and successful launch of four DH projects. These included a collections-as-data project, a scalar book that features an eighteenth-century paper fan from the King's Theater, a WiFi mapping project, and digitally formed critical maps of biblical passages.[33] The projects were significant at the time they were developed, and after the library DH Maker Week, they have continued to evolve. The WiFi analysis project, for instance, has been used to communicate the value of the library to all seven campuses. The library uses the compelling data visualizations to demonstrate that there is representation from each one of the seven Claremont Colleges in the library every day of the week. Not only did these projects provide material for on-campus communication, conference presentations, and publications, the Maker Week also meant a great deal to the individuals involved. According to feedback provided in a post–Maker Week survey, all participants mentioned how much they appreciated the committed time to work on a research project they found meaningful. Over time, participants also reported that working on cross-divisional teams helped to create a greater sense of community and connection throughout the library.

Application, collaborative learning, and project-based experimentation contributed to participating librarians' understanding of new research methodologies and skills. By bringing their visions to life, they also embodied and enacted the heart of digital humanities, according to Stephen Ramsay's definition in his 2013 article, "On Building."[34] Participants did not just read maps; they *made* them. They did not simply imbibe written texts through traditional reading methods; they dismantled and reconfigured them as a database within which they could query, experiment, and generate new meanings. Librarians and library staff did not just learn how to support faculty projects in DH, they learned how to develop and launch their own.

Project-based learning in DH was, perhaps, most successful because it fostered a culture of process (rather than product) by building up the tentative confidence of participants and by focusing on play and experimentation.[35] In an otherwise ambitious and goal-oriented academic culture, the DH project teams were free to dream up ideas without fear of failure or punitive repercussions if a project was not actualized. The participants who did manage to design successful DH projects were, in fact, noted as having gone above and beyond expectations in contributing to the library's development as a center for DH. Furthermore, library leadership formally recognized individuals who wished to align their experimentation with professional goals through performance evaluations and the chance to present their findings at staff meetings. This freedom and flexibility made learning fun and empowered a community of motivated DIY DH learners and practitioners. A culture that allows for play and mistakes enables members to persist in their learning and motivates continued participation.

Although it is not unusual for a DH community to include librarians, their presence prompts several existential questions. Are librarians practitioners or theoreticians? Neither? Both? Digital Humanities scholarship depicts a divide between practitioners and theorists in the humanities and notes the tension between those with expertise in the *doing* versus the *knowing* of humanities.[36] There is power in both positions, and there are real repercussions in the academy when the two become competitive. In "Inclusion in the Digital Humanities," an article published alongside David Ramsay's "On Building," Geoffrey Rockwell contends that "the applied nature [of jobs in the digital humanities] will generally exclude those that have a strong critical understanding of information technology but little experience with implementation in computing environments."[37] In many ways, Claremont Colleges librarians now have one foot firmly rooted in each camp, enabling deeper connections and collaborations with both faculty and students.

The goal of the short course was not to transform librarians into solo researchers but to enable them to learn enough, and to be confident enough, to successfully handle a DH-focused research interview in the same way that they would approach a traditional reference interview. Through the seminars and personal experience conducting DH research and building projects, librarians now recognize when a traditional research project might benefit from digital exploration and are able to identify resources necessary for digital scholarship. What is more, librarians have reported that they feel more comfortable fielding questions and providing guidance as increasing numbers of digital project ideas emerge during interactions with faculty members.

Factors for Successful Communities of Practice

The DH community of practice at Claremont is notable for its inclusiveness. Through the aforementioned professional development offerings, librarians are equipped and empowered to participate in both library-specific and broader DH communities of practice. This section provides research-based suggestions for creating a community of practice that will help to sustain a DH program or center. According to the literature on successful communities of practice in higher education, there are six essential features. First and foremost is trust. Participants must trust themselves as learners who have much to contribute to the group, even as neophytes. Equally important, participants must trust each other, the facilitators, and the process. This can be a challenge in individualistic, competitive environments in which tenure and promotion hinge on individual research and publication rather than collaborative projects.[38]

At the Claremont Colleges, the DH community of practice seeks to foster trust by identifying and highlighting shared experiences, interests, and goals. Faculty, in particular, must trust the facilitator(s) and the community members enough to be vulnerable and admit when they do not know or understand something. The Claremont DH team members have found it most helpful to address this need by being transparent about their own learning process—their successes, but just as importantly, their failures. This level of transparency requires a safe and trusting environment in which such revelations do not diminish participants' perceptions of one another or the facilitators but rather bolster the confidence of all members. Success in DH hinges on participation rather than outcomes.

In order to create a safe environment, it is vital for facilitators to understand common barriers to adult learning. These include technology anxiety, library anxiety, a fear of looking incompetent, and adults' investment in their own prior knowledge. According to the literature on andragogy (instruction for adult learners), these barriers can be mitigated through consistent employment of the following practices.[39] First and foremost, facilitators need to be empathetic and remember their own struggles with difficult topics or skills. As a corollary, they should also be open, welcoming, and willing to answer any question, especially when the person asking states that the question might be obvious. The community must be a safe space where one is free to think out loud, make suggestions, and brainstorm. In addition, learning community leaders need to carefully scaffold knowledge and skills, in the same way that an instructor stages learning activities in classes and workshops for younger learners. Communities of practice should also create a flexible schedule to accommodate hectic academic schedules and the fact that many adult learners also shoulder child care and other family care-taking responsibilities. Finally, to help adult learners overcome preconceptions and potential biases from previous learning experiences, facilitators should assess participants' prior knowledge and ask them to reflect on how their learning compares to their former understanding of the concept(s) or skill(s).[40] Second, members of a successful community of practice share a commitment to their project and to mutual support structures put in place, both of which are necessary for the group to cohere.[41] Faculty attending the first summer institute and the second introduction to DH faculty course were asked to commit to attending most, if not all, of the meetings. In the summer institute, attendance was required for participants to receive the stipend from Mellon. However, the first time Sanders Garcia taught the short course, she did not ask for such a commitment. She had a rotating cast of four of the eight learners, and only two participants came to more than four meetings. In subsequent offerings, those registering for the short course have been asked to commit to attending at least five of the six classes to create a stronger sense of camaraderie.

The third feature of a successful community of practice is university and departmental support for faculty involvement. Most beneficial are tenure and review processes that take such involvement into consideration as professional development or service. Additionally, university or grant-funded financial support is a useful incentive, especially for new endeavors. Perhaps of even greater consequence, particularly at liberal arts colleges where teaching and service loads are often heavy, course or work release time allows community of practice members to explore, learn, collaborate, innovate, build, and write with greater freedom.[42]

Participation in Claremont's introductory short course, summer institute, and course development grant program has been entirely voluntary for faculty, which means that the DH program is reaching those with the most interest, motivation, and commitment. Although this seems self-evident, it is crucial to the development of a cohort of "old-timers" who can then serve as a pool from which to draw future mentors. Those who are most excited about DH also make the greatest ambassadors and advocates for DH on their home campuses and within their departments. Excitement tends to generate more interest, which then makes it easier to extend the community of practice to incorporate those who may have been hesitant to dive in right away.

The final three characteristics of successful communities of practice hinge on their voluntary nature. Learning communities are most collegial and productive when participants willingly join and contribute. Members are more likely to engage in the shared construction of skills, knowledge, and their respective identities when they have freely chosen to join the community and the practices are of interest.[43] Those willing to join and make a commitment to the community must also exhibit openness to change, especially to shifts within their own self-definition, and a willingness to embrace their transition from novice to an expert who can mentor others. Finally, participants are most likely to engage with the learning tasks and acquire expertise if they themselves shape the learning goals and define the desired outcomes.[44]

Nearly all of the faculty and graduate student participants in these early initiatives have been open to change but simply have not known how to go about it. The DH team offers various programs and activities to help them define the changes they would like to make in their own research, writing, publication, and instruction and then charts a course to those transformations. Again, beginning with volunteers makes this an easier objective to meet. However, the library confronts a slightly different scenario with librarians and staff who were required to attend the introductory five-week course on digital humanities. While some were excited about the new landscape of scholarship and teaching, others have been hesitant or resistant for many of the same reasons that a number of professors have been as well. It is frightening to feel less-than-knowledgeable when one's job requires expertise.

Some see little reason to change their practices; others simply have too many other commitments. Being empathetic, listening to concerns, understanding underlying fears, and addressing them is incredibly important for creating an environment that invites and encourages evolution.

In a large institution or a consortium of contiguously located smaller institutions, a centralized digital humanities program is one of the most efficient organizational models to cultivate the social and economic structures that enable and empower effective communities of practice. The library provides institutionally neutral, centrally located shared spaces and resources. Consequently, it is well-positioned to serve as a locus for developing technical skills, creating new digitally enabled research projects, and supporting digitally infused classes, thereby building capacity and community in the digital humanities. The library also offers a space that fosters an environment of play, experimentation, and missteps, through which the DH program builds trust and confidence among its members. Much of Claremont's success hinges on the expertise and experience of a DH specialist, the location of the DH program within the library, and the willingness of librarians, faculty, students, staff, and administrators to participate in the communities of practice. The broader DH community is generous, and leadership may be found within or outside the institution to facilitate learning communities that can launch a new DH program or bolster existing ones. A diverse leadership team drawn from invested stakeholders and champions that span the institution(s) is essential. Additionally, libraries make powerful partners when addressing the inequitable distribution of power, resources, knowledge, and expertise. Early projects, however modest they may be, can serve as illustrations of the kinds of scholarship that these tools and approaches enable. As such, they can lead to further collaborations within, and beyond, the library.

One of the main challenges that DH programs face is related to hard infrastructure: funding for technology and expertise. However, campuses and their libraries have proven that creativity yields dividends. Claremont drew upon professional development funds to send librarians, faculty, and staff to workshops and bring trainers to campus. Student employee budgets support skilled student workers who can provide technical support. Given that Claremont has multiple campuses and campus cultures, different campuses offer internal grants for course development or research that can be used for digital projects that bring together librarians, IT professionals, faculty, and students. Cultivating a sustainable program often requires the identification and integration of multiple funding sources.

In Claremont, the Mellon grant served as a catalyst, but the digital humanities program cultivated strong relationships among all members of the campus, including librarians, to form an inclusive, sustainable, and equitable support system for digital research, instruction, and scholarship. The "soft" social structures rooted in these communities of practice fostered the technological systems and processes that support digital humanities work. A centralized program radiating from the library provides equitable access to the information, resources, expertise, and the infrastructure necessary to build and maintain a strong learning community in the digital humanities. It is the soft infrastructure of community-building that informs a long-term organizational culture and, together with the hard infrastructure, can allow a DH program to survive and adapt to the inevitable future challenges it will face.

Notes

1. This idea of "hard" and "soft" infrastructure was inspired by Miriam Posner's use of the terms to describe the hard and soft skills needed by digital humanists. She emphasizes that these skills are "best learned through participation in actual DH projects," which is at the heart of the DH training program for librarians at the Claremont Colleges. Posner, "No Half Measures."

2. Posner, "No Half Measures"; Sula, "Digital Humanities and Libraries"; Vandergrift and Varner, "Evolving in Common"; and Cox, "Communicating New Library Roles."

3. Muñoz, "Digital Humanities in the Library."

4. Posner, "No Half Measures"; Sula, "Digital Humanities and Libraries"; Vandergrift and Varner, "Evolving in Common"; and Cox, "Communicating New Library Roles."

5. Schaffner and Erway describe many ways in which libraries support DH, including packaging services as a "virtual DH center"; coordinating support across the institution; consulting on preservation, copyright, and open access; configuring the institutional repository to accommodate DH objects and projects; consulting scholars at the beginning of digitization projects; and committing to a DH center. Schaffner and Erway, "Does Every Research Library Need?"

6. Anne et al., "Building Capacity."

7. Lippincott, "Libraries and the Digital University," 289.

8. Posner, "Here and There."

9. Muñoz, "Digital Humanities in the Library."

10. Constructivism is a theory of learning that suggests that "individuals create new knowledge through the interaction of what they already know or believe with new ideas." Richardson, *Constructivist Teacher Education*, 3. Compare Bevevino, Dengel, and Adams, "Constructivist Theory in the Classroom," 275–78.

11. For additional surveys, reports, and guidance on creating a DH center, see Nowviskie, "Too Small to Fail"; Vinopal and McCormick, "Scalability and Sustainability"; Lippincott and Goldenberg-Hart, *Digital Scholarship Centers;* Maron and Pickle, "Sustaining the Digital Humanities"; and Keener, "Arrival Fallacy."

12. Eugene M. Tobin, cover letter for grant proposal to Andrew W. Mellon Foundation, July 29, 2014: "Digital Humanities at the Claremont Colleges: Developing Capacity and Community."

13. This position evolved several times within the library. The positions of digital scholarship librarian (January–November 2015) and digital scholarship coordinator (November 2015–November 2016), both filled by Sanders Garcia, were located in the

library. When Sanders Garcia accepted a new position managing the Mellon DH grant as the Digital Research Studio director, the library used the available funding line to create a CLIR postdoc position and hired a two-year postdoc to serve as a data services librarian.

14. Each year, a fall DH Showcase is held to highlight recent Claremont DH projects. Project links and syllabi for DH courses can be found at http://claremontdh.omeka.net.

15. Lippincott, "Libraries and the Digital University"; and Sinclair, "University Library as Incubator."

16. Muñoz, "Digital Humanities in the Library."

17. This team has been funded by the Mellon DH grant. In the future, to continue this level of support the DH@CC team has partnered with librarians and academic technologists to train them to support specific technologies, such as Omeka and Voyant Tools. Additional funding will be needed for at least one person to lead these initiatives.

18. Gibson, Ladd, and Presnell, "Traversing the Gap."

19. Gibson, Ladd, and Presnell, "Traversing the Gap."

20. The summer institute at the Claremont Colleges costs $4,000 to $5,000 to run. This covers stipends for guest instructors and lodging for out-of-town instructors, and supplies. The Colleges offer classroom spaces free of charge, and the institute has been run by the Mellon DH project manager and the Digital Research Studio director or the Mellon DH faculty director. As a consequence, some additional money may need to be set aside to pay someone to plan and manage the institute if the director position is no longer funded after the grant ends.

21. For short descriptions of the course development grant recipient's proposed courses, see bit.ly/2015dhccCourses; bit.ly/2016dhccCourses; and bit.ly/2017dhccCourses.

22. Sanders Garcia's previous position within the library was repurposed to support a two-year CLIR postdoc to address emerging needs in data services.

23. For a description of the Digital Tool Shed and its design process, see http://ashleyrsanders.com/tag/digital-tool-shed/.

24. Nichols, Melo, and Dewland, "Unifying Space and Service," 363.

25. Miriam Posner has written on these challenges and more, and we have found her observations to be true in the Claremont Colleges setting as well. Posner, "No Half Measures."

26. For a graphic version of Claremont DH's vision statement and its mission statement, see http://dh.libraries.claremont.edu/.

27. Muñoz, "Digital Humanities in the Library."

28. Svensson, "Beyond the Big Tent"; and Terras, "Peering Inside."

29. Drucker, "Data as Capta"; and Drucker, "HTML and Structured Data."

30. Lave and Wenger, *Situated Learning*.

31. Smith, "Reconceptualizing Faculty Mentoring." There are two main forms of constructivism stemming from two leading learning theorists. One version is radical constructivism, which is based on Piaget's model of the *little scientist*. The students are faced with an idea or situation that conflicts with previously held beliefs, which forces them to

reexamine and reconstruct their worldview. The role of the teacher is to promote analytic or scientific thinking by presenting conflict-creating situations. In this model, students are actively constructing their own knowledge, but they generally work by themselves to do so. In another version, known as *social constructivism* (based on Vygotsky's social learning theory), the social context of learning is at least as important as what happens in the individual's mind. Groups of students along with their teacher construct knowledge and must come to an agreement about what is correct and incorrect. Compare Powell and Kalina, "Cognitive and Social Constructivism."

32. Bazeley, Waller, and Resnis, "Engaging Faculty."

33. Collections Analysis Project, http://madelynndickerson.wixsite.com/dh4collections; The King's Theater Fan Scalar Book, http://claremontdh.net/scalar/fan/index; WiFi mapping project, library's annual report, 2015–16, p. 19, http://libraries.claremont.edu/site/downloads/_annual-report/VITAL_Annual_Report_2015-2016.pdf. Graduate student project created from critical maps of biblical passages and a multimedia timeline that highlights events related to the composition history of 1 Enoch.

34. Ramsay, "On Building."

35. Coble, Potvin and Shiraz, "Process as Product."

36. Vanhoutte and Terras, *Defining Digital Humanities.*

37. Rockwell, "Inclusion in the Digital Humanities."

38. Smith, "Reconceptualizing Faculty Mentoring"; Maritz, Visagie, and Johnson, "External Group Coaching"; Nixon and Brown, "Community of Practice in Action"; and Posner, "Here and There."

39. Cooke, "Becoming an Andragogical Librarian."

40. Cannady, King, and Blendinger, "Proactive Outreach"; Ismail, "Getting Personal"; Knowles, *Adult Learner;* Knowles, Holton, and Swanson, *Adult Learner;* and Ruthven, "Training Needs and Preferences."

41. Cowan, "Strategies for Developing a Community of Practice."

42. Blanton and Stylianou, "Interpreting a Community of Practice Perspective."

43. Smith, "Reconceptualizing Faculty Mentoring."

44. Blanton and Stylianou, "Interpreting a Community of Practice Perspective," 88.

Bibliography

Anne, Kirk, Tara Carlisle, Quinn Dombrowski, Erin Glass, Tassie Gniady, Jason Jones, Joan Lippincott, John MacDermott, Megan Meredith-Lobay, Barbara Rockenbach, Annelie Rugg, Ashley Sanders, John Simpson, Bryan Sinclair, and Justin Sipher. "Building Capacity for Digital Humanities: A Framework for Institutional Planning." *EDUCAUSE Center for Analysis and Research/Coalition for Networked Information* (May 30, 2017). bit.ly/ECAR-DH.

Bazeley, Jennifer, Jen Waller, and Eric Resnis. "Engaging Faculty in Scholarly Communication Change: A Learning Community Approach." *Journal of Librarianship and Scholarly Communication* 2, no. 3 (August 4, 2015). https://doi.org/10.7710/2162-3309.1129.

Bevevino, Mary, Joan Dengel, and Kenneth Adams. "Constructivist Theory in the Classroom: Internalizing Concepts through Inquiry." *The Clearing House* 72, no. 5 (May/June 1999): 275–78.

Blanton, Maria L., and Despina A. Stylianou. "Interpreting a Community of Practice Perspective in Discipline-Specific Professional Development in Higher Education." *Innovative Higher Education* 34, no. 2 (2009): 79–80.

Cannady, Rachel E., Stephanie B. King, and Jack G. Blendinger. "Proactive Outreach to Adult Students: A Department and Library Collaborative Effort." *Reference Librarian* 53, no. 2 (April 2012): 156–69. https://doi.org/10.1080/02763877.2011.608603.

Coble, Zach, Sarah Potvin, and Roxanne Shiraz. "Process as Product: Scholarly Communication Experiments in the Digital Humanities." *Journal of Librarianship and Scholarly Communication* 2, no. 3 (2014): eP1137. http://dx.doi.org/10.7710/2162 -3309.1137.

Cooke, Nicole A. "Becoming an Andragogical Librarian: Using Library Instruction as a Tool to Combat Library Anxiety and Empower Adult Learners." *New Review of Academic Librarianship* 16, no. 2 (November 2010): 208–27. https://doi.org/10.1080/13 614533.2010.507388.

Cowan, John E. "Strategies for Developing a Community of Practice: Nine Years of Lessons Learned in a Hybrid Technology Education Master's Program." *TechTrends* 56, no. 1 (2012): 12–18.

Cox, John. "Communicating New Library Roles to Enable Digital Scholarship: A Review Article." *New Review of Academic Librarianship* 22, no. 2–3 (2016). https://doi.org /10.1080/13614533.2016.1181665.

Drucker, Johanna. "Data as Capta." *Digital Humanities Quarterly* 5, no. 1 (March 2011).

Drucker, Johanna. "HTML and Structured Data." DH 101, UCLA (September 2013). https://web.archive.org/web/20200511054705/http://dh101.humanities.ucla. edu/?page_id=20.

Gibson, Katie, Marcus Ladd, and Jenny Presnell. "Traversing the Gap: Subject Specialists Connecting Humanities Researchers and Digital Scholarship Centers." In *Digital Humanities in the Library: Challenges and Opportunities for Subject Specialists*, edited by Arianne Hartsell-Gundy, Laura Braunstein, and Liorah Golomb. Chicago: Association of College and Research Libraries, 2015.

Ismail, Lizah. "Getting Personal: Reaching Out to Adult Learners through a Course Management System." *Reference Librarian* 52, no. 3 (July 2011): 244–62. https://doi.org /10.1080/02763877.2011.556993.

Keener, Alix. "The Arrival Fallacy: Collaborative Research Relationships in the Digital Humanities." *Digital Humanities Quarterly* 9, no. 2 (2015). http://www.digitalhuman ities.org/dhq/vol/9/2/000213/000213.html.

Knowles, Malcolm S. *The Adult Learner: A Neglected Species.* Houston, Tex.: Gulf, 1973.

Knowles, Malcolm Shepherd, Ed Holton, and Richard A. Swanson. *The Adult Learner: The Definitive Classic in Adult Education and Human Resource Development.* 6th ed. Boston: Elsevier, 2005.

Lave, Jean, and Etienne Wenger. *Situated Learning: Legitimate Peripheral Participation, Learning in Doing.* Cambridge: Cambridge University Press, 1991.

Lippincott, Joan K. "Libraries and the Digital University." *College & Research Libraries* 75, no. 3 (March 2015): 289.

Lippincott, Joan K., and Diane Goldenberg-Hart. *Digital Scholarship Centers: Trends & Good Practice.* Report of the December 2014 CNI Workshop. https://www.cni.org /wp-content/uploads/2014/11/CNI-Digitial-Schol.-Centers-report-2014.web_.pdf.

Maritz, Jeannette, Retha Visagie, and Bernadette Johnson. "External Group Coaching and Mentoring: Building a Research Community of Practice at a University of Technology." *Perspectives in Education* 31, no. 4 (2013): 155–67.

Maron, Nancy L., and Sarah Pickle. "Sustaining the Digital Humanities: Host Institution Support Beyond the Start-Up Phase." *Ithaka S+R* (2014). http://www.sr.ithaka.org /wp-content/uploads/2015/08/SR_Supporting_Digital_Humanities_20140618f.pdf.

Muñoz, Trevor. "Digital Humanities in the Library Isn't a Service." August 19, 2012. http:// www.trevormunoz.com/notebook/2012/08/19/doing-dh-in-the-library.html.

Nichols, Jennifer, Marijel Melo, and Jason Dewland. "Unifying Space and Service for Makers, Entrepreneurs, and Digital Scholars." *Portal-Libraries and the Academy* 17, no. 2 (2017): 363–74. https://doi.org/10.1353/pla.2017.0022.

Nixon, Sarah, and Sally Brown. "A Community of Practice in Action: SEDA as a Learning Community for Educational Developers in Higher Education." *Innovations in Education and Teaching International* 50, no. 4 (2013): 357–65.

Nowviskie, Bethany. "Too Small to Fail." *Bethany Nowviskie* (blog), October 13, 2012. http://nowviskie.org/2012/too-small-to-fail/.

Posner, Miriam. "Here and There: Creating a DH Community." *Miriam Posner's Blog,* September 18, 2014. http://miriamposner.com/blog/here-and-there-creating-dh-community/.

Posner, Miriam. "No Half Measures: Overcoming Common Challenges to Doing Digital Humanities in the Library." *Journal of Library Administration* 53, no. 1 (2013). https:// doi.org/10.1080/01930826.2013.756694.

Powell, Katherine C., and Cody J. Kalina. "Cognitive and Social Constructivism: Developing Tools for an Effective Classroom." *Education* 130, no. 2 (2009): 241–50.

Ramsay, Stephen. "On Building." In *Defining Digital Humanities: A Reader,* edited by Edward Vanhoutte and Melissa Terras, 243–45. Surrey, U.K.: Ashgate, 2013.

Richardson, Virginia, ed. *Constructivist Teacher Education: Building New Understandings.* Washington, D.C.: Falmer Press, 1997.

Rockwell, Geoffrey. "Inclusion in the Digital Humanities." In *Defining Digital Humanities: A Reader,* edited by Edward Vanhoutte and Melissa Terras, 247–53. Surrey, U.K.: Ashgate, 2013.

Ruthven, Joan. "Training Needs and Preferences of Adult Public Library Clients in the Use of Online Resources." *Australian Library Journal* 59, no. 3 (August 2010): 108–17.

Schaffner, Jennifer, and Ricky Erway. "Does Every Research Library Need a Digital Humanities Center?" OCLC Online, 2014. https://www.oclc.org/content/dam/research/pub lications/library/2014/oclcresearch-digital-humanities-center-2014.pdf.

Sinclair, Bryan. "The University Library as Incubator for Digital Scholarship." *EDUCAUSE Review,* June 30, 2014. https://er.educause.edu/articles/2014/6/the-university-library-as-incubator-for-digital-scholarship.

Smith, Emily R. "Reconceptualizing Faculty Mentoring within a Community of Practice Model." *Mentoring & Tutoring: Partnership in Learning* 21, no. 2 (May 2013): 181–82. https://doi.org/10.1080/13611267.2013.813731.

Sula, Chris Alen. "Digital Humanities and Libraries: A Conceptual Model." *Journal of Library Administration* 53, no. 1 (2013). https://doi.org/10.1080/01930826.2013.756680.

Svensson, Patrik. "Beyond the Big Tent." In *Debates in the Digital Humanities* (2012). http://dhdebates.gc.cuny.edu/debates/text/22.

Terras, Melissa. "Peering Inside the Big Tent: Digital Humanities and the Crisis of Inclusion." Keynote at Interface 2011, University College London, July 2011.

Vandergrift, Micah, and Stewart Varner. "Evolving in Common: Creating Mutually Supportive Relationships between Libraries and the Digital Humanities." *Journal of Library Administration* 53, no. 1 (2013). https://doi.org/10.1080/01930826.2013.756699.

Vanhoutte, Edward, and Melissa Terras, eds. *Defining Digital Humanities: A Reader.* Surrey, U.K.: Ashgate, 2013.

Vinopal, Jennifer, and Monica McCormick. "Supporting Digital Scholarship in Research Libraries: Scalability and Sustainability." *Journal of Library Administration* 53, no. 1 (2013). https://doi.org/10.1080/01930826.2013.756689.

More Than Respecting Medium Specificity
An Argument for Web-Based Portfolios for Promotion and Tenure

JANA REMY

As important as it is that professional academic organizations such as the Modern Language Association (MLA) and American Historical Association (AHA) have created guidelines for tenure unit criteria for evaluating digital humanities scholarship, there remains a crucial element of administrative infrastructure to apply these guidelines for tenure and promotion candidates. That element is the institutional platform used for the tenure and promotion process. That faculty affairs staff and the campus IT department are unlikely to prioritize the need for a web-based digital evaluation platform to support DH work makes it unlikely that such scholarship can or will be evaluated according to the MLA/AHA guidelines. Thus scholars working in DH may continue to inhabit the margins, and the "exceptions" of the typical evaluation workflow are unlikely to have their work evaluated in a way that respects the "medium specificity" of their scholarship or guarantees the "procedural clarity and fairness" of the review process.[1]

In this article I offer my perspective as an alt-ac administrator who has grappled with the development and support of an online tenure and promotion (T&P) platform for nearly a decade. During that time I have not only supported my campus's platform but have spoken at dozens of academic conferences about my work and from those conversations have gained a solid understanding of the variety of ways universities are providing a T&P platform for their faculty. It is my hope that the lessons I have learned along the way can foster a dialogue between various institutions and their academic units, faculty affairs, and IT departments, to make wise choices about the platform that they adopt for T&P, and especially that they can do so in a way that supports (and encourages) all types of digital scholarly endeavors, including those in the digital humanities. On the basis of my experience I would urge institutions to adopt a platform for web-based portfolios. Here I list my reasons, along with explanations of why a web-based system is the best platform for tenure and promotion files.

My role in the T&P process is to mitigate any technological hurdles candidates might face in the process of uploading, embedding, or linking to the supporting materials in their digital portfolios. Not only do I support the candidates with the creation of their dossier but I also troubleshoot any issues that occur with the evaluators and the administrators who oversee the tenure and promotion process. While in this role I have seen hundreds of T&P dossiers, have examined numerous software packages promising to revolutionize the tenure process, and have seen very little progress toward applying the guidelines from the MLA (and other professional organizations) to evaluate digital scholarship. The reasons for this are varied, but they seem to stem largely from the fact that decisions about software adoptions are largely about the business processes of the university and are not made in consultation with faculty who have a stake in how their content is represented on the platform.

First, I offer a bit of background on why I became involved in the tenure process at my university. Years ago, when our chancellor became interested in a digital portfolio platform, I found myself consulting with campus leaders about their requirements for such a platform. At that time, the motivation for moving to digital was due mainly to the cost of shipping large boxes of private materials to external reviewers across the globe, but it also reflected the concerns about paper dossiers' inability to represent the creative and scholarly activities of faculty working in the arts. The faculty in our film school and in the college of performing arts were not able to adequately represent their work in the pages of a binder. Moreover, there were logistical challenges to shipping DVDs of films or of performances to each reviewer, and to reproducing high-quality prints of the studio art produced by our faculty. At that time I was aware of the MLA's then-new guidelines about evaluating the scholarly output of faculty working in digital media, and I added their guidelines to the growing list of requirements for our ideal digital portfolio platform.

That took place in 2010, and as we surveyed the landscape of various vendors who provided ePortfolio software, we found none that met the requirements of being able to stream multimedia content, nor were they easy to use or customizable to adapt to the variety of disciplines found on our campus. Following the precedents of a variety of popular digital humanities projects such as *CommentPress, Anthologize,* and *PressForward,* we settled on an in-house installation of WordPress MultiSite to support our dossiers. WordPress seemed a wise direction to move because of its flexibility and ease of use. There was also a robust local developer community that we could draw from, should the need for customizations arise.

In our pilot year, a dozen faculty tried the WordPress platform. The next year we doubled that number. And in the third year the chancellor mandated the platform for all faculty for their critical year reviews and their tenure and promotion files. The reason for the mandate was the high level of satisfaction on the part of the evaluators. No longer did they have to go to our administration building during business hours and pore over reams of materials piled into banker's boxes. Instead, they could peruse the candidate's ePortfolio from anywhere with a web browser and an internet connection. Additionally, committees could pull up a candidate's portfolio on a screen in a conference room and discuss the materials together without having to pass around hard copies of documents. They also could collaboratively author a recommendation letter online as they moved seamlessly back and forth from portfolio to Word. In short, the success of the endeavor was due primarily to the ease of use for the evaluators and the evaluation committees. This was nearly the opposite of what was expected when we first launched the platform, as deans were grumbling about changing the age-old pattern of file review. They quickly became the most enthusiastic champions of our ePortfolios. That the buy-in came from the top down meant that candidates with digital scholarship were on a level playing field with their colleagues who had more traditional forms of research output, rather than having to vie for exceptions and alternatives to the standard process.

On the basis of my experience with selecting and supporting a campus platform for ePortfolios, I have learned the following about the benefits and challenges of using digital portfolios for T&P review:

Avoid platforms that are web forms with PDF output. Whether building an in-house web form or purchasing a product with web form capabilities, using this style of ePortfolio for digital dossiers will limit faculty in expressing the full range of their creative and scholarly endeavors. Even a well-designed web form will not adapt to the multiplicity of ways that faculty create and publish content. Rather, a web form–based template generally adheres to and reinforces the notion that scholarship occurs in journals and in books rather than opening the possibilities for a variety of scholarly expressions that do not necessarily fit into an author / title / publication date style of format.

The move toward the PDF output of an ePortfolio file is also problematic for the most obvious reason: it creates a static document that is often over five hundred pages long. Those gigantic PDFs are tedious for evaluators to peruse, and unless care is taken to create hyperlinks between sections and to materials outside of the dossier, it replicates the same problems as paper in that large PDFs do not allow faculty working in a digital realm to feature their work in the platform for which it was intended to be accessed and viewed.

Adopting a platform that allows faculty to create a hyperlinked, interactive, and dynamic site for their portfolio facilitates an ease of navigation for the evaluator in addition to allowing the embedding and linking of materials.

Require the platform to stream multimedia. While most ePortfolio platforms allow the upload and attachment of multimedia files to faculty dossiers, few allow the content to be hosted and streamed directly from the platform. Streaming is necessary because if the media files are merely attached, evaluators must download each file before listening to or viewing the media. Given that faculty on our campus produce feature-length films and hours-long musical scores, it is simply not acceptable to put the burden of file download on the evaluators, for reasons of both time and space. In some cases, attaching and downloading the media files to the evaluator's local computer also might violate copyright or intellectual property rules about that media.

Consider whether to integrate with other campus platforms. On our campus we wanted scholarship held in our institutional repository, the Digital Commons (DC), to be linked to the candidates' T&P dossier. Doing so would allow faculty to upload their materials in only one place, to a location with a persistent URL/DOI. However, we encountered two obstacles with that plan: the first was that our DC uses Bepress software that does not stream multimedia (see my previous point about why this is necessary), and the second was that some teaching materials are not appropriate for public access, such as videos of students in the classroom, and our DC defaults to making all materials publicly accessible. Thus, an integration with the DC was useful only for a subset of materials.

There is an emerging trend in the landscape of digital dossiers to have the web form data fields integrate with an institutional data repository to facilitate the tracking of faculty productivity according to algorithms that count the number of publications correlated with their impact factor. This is a concerning practice, especially within the humanities, because it relies on formulas for measuring and valuing the research and creative output of faculty. In short, it can place a higher value on quantity over quality and might diminish the visibility of publications in "nontraditional venues such as new open access journals, blogs or articles written and posted on a personal website or institutional repository, or non-narrative digital projects."[2] I would encourage any campus that is exploring this integration to be cautious about how such metrics would be used to represent faculty productivity.

Other on-campus platforms that one could consider integrating with the ePortfolios include the Learning Management System, course evaluation system, and faculty websites. In each case, the integrations allow for faculty to link to their work on those platforms rather than needing to upload or re-represent that work separately in their T&P dossier.

Be wary of platforms that mandate disciplinary homogeneity. In the last decade I have seen hundreds of ePortfolios, ranging the gamut from pharmacy faculty to poetry faculty. I have yet to see any that were identical in tone, structure, or form. Even though we use the same fairly vanilla WordPress theme for each dossier, faculty have a remarkable amount of latitude about how they present their materials. Some like outlines with bullet points, others prefer long narratives broken up with page breaks, and yet others feature visualizations more than text. This wide variety allows faculty to reflect their unique career trajectory in the manner that most suits their sense of aesthetics and discipline-specific expression.

Moreover, it allows for candidates to present materials in a multitude of formats, which is as important in their discussion of their research as it is in their teaching folio. For example, in their teaching materials section a faculty member can include a written statement on their teaching philosophy, images showing them in their classroom, videos of students doing in-class presentations, and PDFs of syllabi and course assignments. Together, all those items offer a much deeper view into the candidates' classrooms than any of those alone would provide, and they feature a look at the many ways that faculty engage with their students rather than offering only a static repository of syllabi and course evaluations. That candidates can order, emphasize, and feature different aspects of their teaching practice, as well as link to student materials hosted on the web, allows them to tell the story of their teaching as dynamic, evolving, and multimodal.

Understand the good, bad, and the ugly of the user experience. For the most part, creating an online portfolio ought to be easy for a candidate who has basic digital fluency. If she can attach a document to an email and buy a book on Amazon, she is likely to have the skills necessary to create an ePortfolio. For some candidates the work of attaching and uploading files can feel tedious, especially when they are locating, renaming, and uploading more than a decade's worth of teaching evaluations or a similar number of syllabi. Additionally, there is a small subset of users who struggle with making the leap from print to digital, and this hurdle impacts their confidence in an already stressful process. With a web-based platform the greatest challenge for faculty is often that web pages are dynamic and responsive to the device and platform where they are accessed. This means that the line breaks and images do not fall in exactly the same spot as they would in a Word document and that they can vary significantly from desktop to tablet. For the faculty member who is used to the static nature of a PDF or a word document, this can be frustrating and can contribute to that candidate's feeling a lack of control over the process of creating their dossier. Although training can help to ameliorate this issue, it remains frustrating to many candidates that the text and layout of their dossier varies from one computer to another. On my campus I held quarterly workshops to train faculty on using the ePortfolio platform and also scheduled one-on-one consultations upon request. This level of support tended to assure candidates that their materials were well represented in their digital dossiers.

But these small user issues aside, using WordPress—a platform with millions of users and a responsive development community—provides a fairly straightforward interface for our faculty. Most have used WordPress at least once before, so it feels intuitive to use it for their ePortfolio. For most it feels open and customizable: they can alter the size, color, and style of the text; they can embed a wide variety of media including tables and images; and they can hyperlink to other sections of their ePortfolio as well as to content on the web.

Hands down, the user group that is most enthusiastic about using the web-based ePortfolio platform are the evaluators. The ease of login and viewing the materials far outweighs the logistical challenges of working with hard-copy or PDF dossiers.

Resolve concerns about archiving the materials. Sustainability is a concern for all DH scholarship, with the long-term access and function of online resources in question for all born-digital materials. The concerns about long-term preservation of ePortfolios are no different. On my campus, for example, there is a mandate that tenure dossiers must be kept for the entire career of that faculty member. That is certainly a tall order for junior faculty who may be employed for three, or even four, decades at our institution. To address this problem we store periodic backup snapshots of our WordPress server, and we use a web crawler to copy the HTML of each portfolio at the close of each review cycle, which is then added to the digital file kept on each faculty member at our institution.

In conclusion, the most significant lesson emerging from my years of supporting ePortfolios is that a web-based platform for creating and evaluating content allows all faculty, not just DH practitioners, to build customized media-rich dossiers that feature both print-based and digital content. I have observed that having a web-based platform ensures that evaluators are familiar with evaluating digital materials, which has been a concern for those working in DH who have struggled to represent their work in a process that used to be almost exclusively on paper. Using online ePortfolios minimizes the leap from traditional forms of scholarship to those of the digital. Moreover, I have seen that even the most traditional scholars have an increasing amount of born-digital material for their dossiers, which might include ePubs, online data sets, webinars, podcasts, or online-only journal articles. Thus for all T&P candidates, having a web-based ePortfolio platform on which digital content can be easily linked to and embedded features the growing range of ways that they now teach and work, and of course it familiarizes evaluators with the wide variety of materials that are created by twenty-first-century faculty.

There is some irony in my advocacy for a web-based platform for ePortfolios, because at my institution we will soon conduct an evaluation of our platform to determine whether we can continue to support it. In the past few years our IT department has moved away from in-house development and has adopted more out-of-the-box and cloud-based services. The reason is that it is too costly to maintain and support systems that are unique to our campus. Simultaneously, several for-profit IT companies are promoting ePortfolio software packages for T&P that feed higher ed's growing desire for data metrics about faculty productivity and that may well come at a cost for faculty whose work is not easily measured according to those standard metrics. While I am sensitive to my campus's needs to conserve resources and make wise decisions about IT services, it is with some concern about the future that I close this article. I suspect that decisions about my campus's T&P platform will not be made with the needs of digital humanities faculty in mind, nor even with an eye to the benefits that all faculty enjoy with our current platform. I fear that a move to a standard software solution may introduce more roadblocks into the tenure and promotion process for digital humanities faculty. Thus I would encourage the MLA and other similar organizations to advocate for a web-based platform for candidates, a platform that respects medium specificity, allows for the embedding and streaming of multimedia, supports hyperlinks to online materials, and fosters the creative expression of all candidates. Because it is not enough to have guidelines for evaluation, there also needs to be advocacy for the infrastructure necessary to support those guidelines for evaluating faculty with digital scholarship.

Appendix

PROFESSIONAL ORGANIZATIONS WITH STATEMENTS ABOUT EVALUATING DIGITAL SCHOLARSHIP

Modern Language Association

Guidelines for Evaluating Work in Digital Humanities and Digital Media

Respect Medium Specificity When Reviewing Work. Since scholarly work is always designed for presentation in a specific medium, evaluative bodies should foreground medium specificity by reviewing faculty members' work in the medium for which it was produced. For example, born-digital and Web-based projects are often spatial, interactive, iterative, and networked. If possible, they should be viewed in electronic form, not in print or as snapshots of dynamic behavior.

https://www.mla.org/About-Us/Governance/Committees/Committee-Listings/Professional-Issues/Committee-on-Information-Technology/Guidelines-for-Evaluating-Work-in-Digital-Humanities-and-Digital-Media

American Historical Association

Guidelines for the Professional Evaluation of Digital Scholarship by Historians

Digital scholarship should be evaluated in its native digital medium, not printed out for inclusion in review materials. Evaluators need to understand how a project works, what capacities it possesses, and how well those capacities perform. This can only be done by actually using the interface.

https://www.historians.org/teaching-and-learning/digital-history-resources/evaluation-of-digital-scholarship-in-history/guidelines-for-the-professional-evaluation-of-digital-scholarship-by-historians

College Art Association and the Society of Architectural Historians

Guidelines for the Evaluation of Digital Scholarship in Art and Architectural History

Evaluate the work in its native environment. Many institutions and scholarly societies have determined that it is crucial that digital work be seen in the environment for which it was designed. Scholars deserve to have their work taken seriously, including the digital contribution. Hence, all work of digital scholarship must be evaluated in its appropriate environment.

http://www.collegeart.org/pdf/evaluating-digital-scholarship-in-art-and -architectural-history.pdf

Notes

1. See the Modern Language Association's *Guidelines for Evaluating Work in Digital Humanities and Digital Media.* Accessed August 1, 2017. https://www.mla.org /About-Us/Governance/Committees/Committee-Listings/Professional-Issues/Committee -on-Information-Technology/Guidelines-for-Evaluating-Work-in-Digital-Humanities -and-Digital-Media.

2. From Dan Cohen's blog post "Open Access Publishing and Scholarly Values," May 27, 2010. http://www.dancohen.org/2010/05/27/open-access-publishing-and-schol arly-values/.

Is Digital Humanities Adjuncting Infrastructurally Significant?

KATHI INMAN BERENS

Adjuncts and "Digital" Humanities

The question of when *digital humanities* will drop the *digital* modifier and become *humanities* has special resonance for adjunct instructors. Stuart Varner, in his 2013 talk "Digital Humanities or Just Humanities," concludes, "I don't think it really matters if you want to say digital humanities or something else. What will matter is whether or not you are doing good work, ethical work and work that makes effective and rigorous use of the tools and methods that are available whether they be digital or not." Varner cites Josh Honn's declaration, "what I am advocating for is a more central role in DH for this skeptical digital work, both embedded in and existing outside of the digital projects and tools we use and build." I open with these remarks because they frame how and why digital humanities tenured and tenurable scholars might bridge the gap between tenured working conditions and adjunct working conditions in crafting field infrastructures, not just because adjuncts merit both employment protections and what I call *microbenefactions* (more on that below) but because adjuncts are the invisible mass of humanities faculty buttressing every kind of institution, from community college to elite research-1 university. Adjuncts shoulder the humanities enterprise, teaching the general education classes that free researchers to pursue critical questions that advance the field.

From 1975 to 2015, non-tenure-track positions of all types grew to account for over 70 percent of all instructional staff appointments in American higher education, according to data from the U.S. Department of Education.[1] The American Association of University Professors notes that "the turn towards cheaper contingent labor is largely a matter of priorities rather than economic necessity," observing that "the greatest growth in contingent appointments occurred during times of economic prosperity" ("Background Facts"). Faculty have seen how funding for technologies, tools, and edu-tech has sharply increased during the attrition of tenure lines and the growth of alt-ac (alternative academic) positions, defined as academic employment off the tenure track in places such as academic libraries, writing centers, university-affiliated research groups, and cultural heritage organizations.[2] In terms of employment security, alt-ac and non-tenure-track fixed-term (NTTF) positions are a middle ground between the insecurity of adjuncting and the security of tenure-track employment. Alt-acs and NTTFs usually can apply for professional development resources (such as travel funding) and qualify for health and other employment benefits if their appointments are full-time.[3]

Field scholarship about adjunct DH is sparse. The first scholarly article is mine, "Want to Save the Humanities? Pay Adjuncts to Learn Digital Tools" (*Disrupting Digital Humanities,* Digital Edition, 2015); the second is "The New Itinerancy: Digital Pedagogy and the Adjunct Instructor in the Modern Academy" by Andrew Bretz (*Digital Humanities Quarterly,* 2017). Lee Skallerup Bessette made a witty game, *Adjunct Run,* and is a longtime commenter on precarious higher education employment. Acknowledgment of DH adjunct status in talk bios on university websites is a new phenomenon; an example is Dr. Erin Warford's StoryTelling with Digital Maps workshop using ARCGIS at the Digital Humanities Summer Workshop series at Canisius University, a regional Catholic institution in western New York (2017). One hopes such traces in field literature and university websites might be the beginning of increased visibility of DH adjuncts who, for reasons this essay discloses, are hard to reach and count.

This essay examines the infrastructural causes of DH adjunct invisibility and proposes two remedies: to motivate DH adjunct self-identification by convening DH adjunct-specific prizes and bursaries; and to invite senior DH faculty to perform microbenefactions that cost little effort and can give adjuncts access to prize-worthy work opportunities or other benefits, such as renewable funding. First, a word about background and method. I have occupied all three classes of faculty employment: NTTF, adjunct, and now tenured. I wrote this essay because many people have asked me: how can I help adjuncts? While adjunct working and living conditions have been remarked upon extensively in the popular press (for example, *The Atlantic* did a very good occasional series), there is scant documentation about DH and adjuncting. The unspoken assumption is that DH skills are so much in demand that people with these skills are protected from adjuncting. As I informally interviewed seven DH adjuncts (more on that process subsequently), their heterogeneous responses to standard questions reminded me that happy families are all alike; unhappy families are unhappy in their own particular ways. Tenure-track employment conditions are alike; adjunct employment conditions are unhappy in their own particular ways. They vary from state to state and from institution to institution. This essay seeks to situate such heterogeneity in overlapping employment contexts (TT, alt-ac, and temporary) and recommends two practical, simple-to-perform interventions that tenured and tenurable DHers could do to materially improve the prospects and daily working experiences of DH adjuncts.

DH Adjuncts in the Gig Economy

The McKinsey Global Institute estimates that "up to 162 million people in North America and Europe—20% to 30% of the working age population—engage in some kind of independent work" without the protections or benefits of employment status.[4] Humanities gigging is one facet of this global trend. In just forty years, "adjunctification" has flipped the ratio of tenure-track faculty to non-tenure-track faculty. Tenured and tenure-track faculty now comprise just 24 percent of humanities faculty.[5] Of the 76 percent of faculty working off the tenure track, slightly more than 50 percent of those (approximately 700,000 faculty) are adjunct, according to the New Faculty Majority's "Facts about Adjuncts." Income insecurity is a well-documented feature of this flip. It is less known that 25 percent of all part-time faculty are enrolled in public assistance programs alongside fast food workers, child care workers, and home care workers (UC Berkeley Center for Labor Research).[6]

During the fall 2017 hiring season, I saw the first national job advertisement I recall having seen recruiting a DH adjunct in the United States. The hiring institution was Molloy College in Rockville, New York, which educates about 5,000 students and confers undergraduate and graduate degrees. The ad called for an adjunct to teach "advanced digital media courses." There is a slippage here between *digital humanities* and *online content production* that I recognize as characteristic of organizations whose teaching charge is more general than that of organizations vested with R-1 priorities and funding. As an adjunct in 2013–14, I performed almost exactly the work described in the Molloy job ad at a Portland, Oregon-area private university, which at the time teetered on the brink of insolvency. It has since closed, citing a sharply declining enrollment.[7] Molloy College did not fill the adjunct job for which they advertised. In 2021, their digital humanities and new media program employs three full-time faculty at the assistant professor rank.

As DH becomes not just a course offering but a certificate program at R-2s, SLACs, small private universities, and community colleges, it is hard to imagine that demand for *DH adjuncts,* variously defined, will not increase. "The institutional structure of digital humanities threatens to intensify (both within DH itself and among the humanities more broadly) the proliferation of temporary, insecure labor that is rampant not only in the academy but throughout twenty-first-century capitalism," noted Richard Grusin in his presentation on the "Dark Side of the Digital Humanities" roundtable at the 2013 Modern Language Association convention.[8] Grusin names the push for DH by "university administrators, foundation officers, and government agencies" a "neoliberal instrumentalism [that] reproduces within the academy (both in traditional humanities and in digital humanities alike) the precaritization of labor that marks the dark side of information capitalism in the twenty-first century." Matthew Kirschenbaum, in a longer essay version of his "Dark Side of DH" roundtable talk, shifts the focus of instrumentalism from something done *to faculty* to something done *by faculty,* in which "galvanized" DH practitioners "wield the label 'digital humanities' instrumentally amid an increasingly monstrous institutional terrain defined by declining public support for higher education, rising tuitions, shrinking endowments, the proliferation of distance education and the for-profit university, and, underlying it all, the conversion of full-time, tenure-track academic labor to a part-time adjunct workforce."[9] However, even an adjunct actively "wielding" DH remains vulnerable to systemic procedures that are normative and functional for most full-time faculty. Emails circulating on a department listserv are not a site of disenfranchisement until adjunct employment status restricts access to them.

In the gig economy, DH adjuncts pay an additional tithe in the now-typical university requirement to create digital course shells using proprietary course management software (such as Canvas, Blackboard, or Desire2Learn) rather than equivalent free and open tools that would enable the adjunct to port courses from one university to another. Such a requirement is onerous, similar to asking a temporary ride-sharing provider to use a different vehicle depending on whether the referring service is Uber, Lyft, or Via. When I adjuncted, I solved the portability-and-intellectual-property problem by hosting almost everything on my own website and server and instructing students how to use freely accessible tools mostly in the Google suite; but in the years since then, as Bretz has noted, universities are more insistent that coursework transpire within the proprietary software. "At the present moment [2017], the sessional instructor and the course are both subject to the curriculum of an individual university and department, despite the fact that courses with a heavy DH component tend towards portability, interoperability, and modularity that renders such boundaries largely incoherent."[10] I would add that this requirement also disenfranchises students who do not learn to make, share, and navigate the open web and who stand to lose access to university work if it is locked within proprietary systems. FERPA laws protecting student privacy must be accommodated in designing digital humanities pedagogy, and this argues against the open web. However, many DH pedagogy practitioners have found ways both to protect student privacy and to permit them to work in public-facing digital projects.[11]

How Many Adjuncts Teach Digital Humanities?

The DH adjuncts with whom I have spoken are typically hired not to teach DH-specific courses but general education or introductory classes that are not marked in the course catalog as digital humanities. They simply teach their assigned classes using DH methods. This makes their DH work infrastructurally invisible. The pedagogy is DH, but its replicability as a DH course is contingent on several factors, such as whether or not DH methods facilitate general education course learning objectives; whether or not the hiring department has capacity to offer access to computers; and whether or not the adjunct is rehired by the institution. Adjunct

DH scholars have no travel support and so are unlikely to present work at or even attend DH conferences, and therefore their DH work is less likely to get telegraphed through DH listservs. These factors impede discovery of DH adjuncts.[12]

The challenge of tallying DH adjuncts is exacerbated by unreliable communication systems. Some adjuncts lose access to faculty listservs if they are not employed by that university or college. Some are on adjunct-only listservs. Some work several jobs and open only the mail that is directly related to the classes they teach. Twitter, once a reliable DH meeting place circa 2009–12, is decentralized in 2020. In preparation for this article, my tweets to reach adjunct DHers were retweeted by prominent DH pedagogues, reaching hundreds of thousands of potential viewers, but that yielded just two new practitioners I had not previously met. I had better luck finding adjunct DHers by scouring conference hashtags for people I did not know and participating in discussion threads on my friends' Facebook walls with people whose work sounded like it might be adjunct DH. Still another challenge to quantifying DH adjuncting originates in the blurred lines between DH project work and teaching. Some people working full-time alt-ac jobs are occasionally tapped to teach a DH course. Such teaching is not part of their contract; it is additional work that they take on for a fee. Such adjuncts' relationships to the hiring institutions are not precarious, but neither are such adjuncts integrated into faculty meetings and department listservs. They are frequently overworked. Their offices may be located offsite or across campus from the department in which they are adjuncting.

Adjuncting is the apogee of the *lone wolf* phenomenon observed by Elena Pierazzo in her 2017 keynote at the Digital Humanities Summer Institute in Victoria, British Columbia. The lone wolf is the DHer whose community is not embodied in a department but is virtual in online DH venues.[13] However, many adjuncts have scant time to participate in online conversations because most are working several piecemeal jobs. In one case, in which student access to campus computers was impossible, the adjunct designed assignments around cell phone network access. I identify this technique as "micro DH," a term Roopika Risam coined to account for DH work done in impoverished environments and "at small scale."[14] Such conditions of computer scarcity can apply to adjunct professors as well. Most of the seven DH adjuncts that I interviewed for this essay do not necessarily identify their teaching as digital humanities because they are not hired specifically to teach DH, although their methods are consistent with DH pedagogical practices. *Imposter syndrome* is intensified by employment insecurity and DH definitional heterogeneity.[15]

In its mentoring, promotion, and awards structures, the humanities professoriate is legacy bound, oriented to a tenure system that now pertains to only one quarter of the people working in the field. Travel bursaries and other awards for "young" scholars (under age 35), such as the Paul Fortier Prize conferred by the Alliance of Digital Humanities Organizations, elevate and support the work of junior scholars. There is no equivalent support for the DH adjuncts I talked with, more than half of whom were too old to qualify for existing awards. If, as James English contends in

The Economy of Prestige, the key indicator of any contemporary cultural phenomenon's entering the mainstream is the creation of a prize, then perhaps it is time for digital humanists to create criteria of DH excellence specific to DH adjunct working conditions because adjuncting is now the humanities instructional mainstream.[16] Doing so would motivate adjunct DHers to identify their work as DH and contribute recognizably toward DH research and pedagogy development.

Adjuncts and the "Hot" DH Job Market

DH senior scholars may not recognize that adjunctification is a DH problem. Tenured and tenure-track DHers may not know that adjuncts working at their own institution are using DH methods in the classroom, because these courses are introductory or general education and rarely are singled out for special attention or accolade. Some of the challenges adjuncts face are exacerbated versions of problems caused by state defunding and faced by all workers in higher education. As lines for tenured or tenurable humanities faculty are eliminated after retirement and replaced with adjunct, NTT, or nothing, more service work falls onto the shoulders of remaining faculty. When I began my career in 2000, NTT faculty hired in teaching lines were not expected to do university service, but that is no longer the case. Some adjuncts volunteer to do service labor, some of which is compensated and some of which is not. Job advertisements for new DH hires are issued pervasively by research-1 institutions, regional comprehensive universities, small liberal arts colleges, and community colleges.[17] This prompts some people to see DH as a ballast against dwindling tenure lines. But DH is, like any other humanities subfield, subject to boom/bust cycles that respond to enrollment trends.

Miriam Posner notes that DH's "sexiness" today obscures the "widespread understaffing" of many fledgling DH initiatives. "Launching a program with a two-year postdoc is clearly absurd and shortsighted, but it's nevertheless become standard operating procedure for many places looking to get a program going. So, in a way, many of these conditions are just typical of our corner of academia at our current moment."[18] This is an analog to adjunctification, the shortsighted boom/bust cycles of soft money quickly depleted that then require maintenance funded by a precarious budget. Amy Earhart has documented the unsustainability of early DH passion projects, websites whose hand-built archives decay when the faculty author retires or moves institutions.[19] Start-ups are sexy, but maintenance is not. When today's senior DH faculty retire in ten or twenty years, what infrastructures of care will be in place to stop those vacated tenure lines from converting to untenurable positions?

In 2012, Stephen Ramsay problematized DH as "the hot thing." It's a skepticism shared by many in the field, including panelists of the DH 2017 Conference panel "Challenges for New Infrastructures and Paradigms in DH Curricular Program Development," which openly wondered whether graduate students were well served by DH certificate programs.[20] The hot thing prompts graduate students to craft their careers along paths mostly likely to result in hiring and future support. So long as digital humanities remains hot and traditional humanities hiring remains implicitly cold, DH would seem less vulnerable to the adjunctification that has decimated humanities tenure lines.[21] But it is just a matter of time until the *digital* drops from view and *DH* becomes no longer specifically referential to using computers for organizing, displaying, and searching for patterns within digitized texts. Such field diversification is already well underway.

There are no adjunct administrators, as Laura E. Sanders and I observe in our essay about DH adjuncting and social justice.[22] Job security for managers but not teachers is a key feature of the neoliberal university. One female adjunct I interviewed became an interim dean at a community college at which for seven years she had cobbled together several part-time teaching and grant-writing jobs. "I had to get out of teaching," she told me. "I feel terrible for saying it, but it just doesn't pay." Some of the arts-based DH adjuncts I interviewed combine freelance arts work (graphic design or website building) with teaching, whereas others teach full time. One just-graduated male DH master's graduate in his twenties took a DH programming job at an Ivy League school, where he is now earning the equivalent of a generously paid assistant professor. Two female DH adjuncts in their forties left teaching and moved into full-time instructional design (alt-ac) work. The gender politics of *sexy, hot* DH summons gendered implications of youth and desirability that actually obscure the realities of labor conditions for anyone off the tenure track. "As a woman of color," Liana M. Silva has wondered, "I am especially interested to know what the women in contingent ranks look like. According to the U.S. Education Department's 2009 report, 81.9 percent of contingent faculty are white. To what extent is contingent labor a problem for white women? Or, from another angle, to what extent is [adjuncting] a white labor issue, where class is meant to trump race?"[23] These questions about contingent labor, gender, race, and age are digital humanities variables that the field has yet to measure.

In my interviews I observed that no two institutions construe the adjunct employment relationship the same way. At some institutions, adjuncts could buy into health care proportionally to their percentage of full-time employment. At others, health care was off the table entirely, no matter how close to full-time was the adjunct's contract. One institution hosts a "sick bank," a crowdsourced pool of unused sick hours from which all employees including adjuncts can draw. Some adjuncts did not even know whom to ask about such benefits. Access to server space, office space, on-campus computers, and technical support varied. The implications of the California Assembly Bill 1690 and Senate Bill 1379, which Governor Jerry Brown signed into law in 2016, mandating that the state's community college districts "come to the negotiating table with part-time instructors to discuss reemployment and termination rules," are still being measured. For example, an April 14, 2021, a legislative panel heard about costs associated with AB 375, which increases the maximum number of instructional hours that a California Community College (CCC) faculty member may teach at any single community college district and still be classified as a part-time employee from 67 percent to 85 percent.[24]

An adjunct is a chameleon that changes color to fit the local needs of the temporarily hiring institution. To a certain extent, this is true of anybody applying for grants and framing their skill sets to increase their chances of winning funding. But when such shifts are the baseline of one's professional identity, the cost of frame-shifting can tax energy, capacity, and confidence. From 2011 to 2014, I was publicly a DH adjunct, blogging about what I was doing in the classroom (blog title: *Face-to-Face in the Mediated Classroom*), convening national conference panels about digital pedagogy, and occasionally posting about my challenges finding sustainable work ("Day of DH 2012"). I recognized that I was doing DH work because I measured my pedagogy and the work my students produced alongside what faculty hired to teach DH were posting about their teaching on Twitter and on their blogs. In some interviews for adjunct jobs, I declared myself a digital humanist. In others, I kept it to myself. My work was consistent, but how I positioned it varied depending on local needs. I felt sometimes like Harry Nash in Kurt Vonnegut's short story "Who Am I This Time?": the quiet guy who becomes whatever role he plays on stage.

I told myself—many adjuncts tell themselves—that adjuncting is an audition for full-time work. The hint at the possibility of full-time employment entices adjuncts to perform unpaid labor. It never came to pass that a job where I adjuncted converted to a full-time line; nor did it convert for any other adjunct I interviewed. It was not uncommon in the early 2000s at the regional comprehensive university where I am now tenured for adjunct and fixed-term positions to convert to TT lines. That was laudable. Recently, however, I have observed the obverse, where one- or two-year fixed-term appointments expire and the fixed-term professor converts to adjunct status.

Perversely, standout "star" adjuncts may have a harder time landing full-time work at the institutions where they excel than they might at an institution with no direct experience of their excellence. A star adjunct promoted to a TT line creates an adjunct vacancy which may or may not be filled by an equivalently good adjunct. The prudent administrative move is thus to keep the star adjunct and hire the TT line externally, even though the adjunct has institutional expertise that may take years for the newly hired external candidate to develop. This scenario happened to a star adjunct in biology (not DH) who had been teaching 80 percent of full time at a community college. Her department awarded her curricular innovation grants, praised her teaching, and encouraged her to apply for the job. After making it through three rounds of cuts—there were over three hundred applicants for the job—it was down to her and an external candidate with equivalent qualifications. The dean gave the job to the external candidate. The adjunct's loss of the TT job demoralized the department, which is 75 percent adjunct labor and has only one tenure-track position. The lost job was equivalent to a once-in-a-lifetime opportunity. Losing that tenure line tallies to about $250,000 in lost wages and sabbaticals over the adjunct's remaining years of employment. "It is a wrenching battle between doing my job in a way I am proud, a way that brings me joy, and the sick feeling of being undervalued, or taken advantage of," she said. She continues to teach there because she has built her life around the job, but she now must restrict her impulse to perform unpaid work. "I find it infuriating that there is a huge push for student equity and inclusion, and I have secured small grants to determine student achievement gaps and design course content and pedagogy to reduce gaps—all the while knowing that these same principles do not apply to me [as part-time faculty]."

When I was hired in a tenure-track line, it was by a department that had never employed me as an adjunct. Some of the work I'd done for free collaborating with tenured DHers fortified my expertise and made me a valuable potential colleague who could build things. Performing free labor had connected me meaningfully to senior scholars with whom I collaborated, some of whom wrote me letters of recommendation. This is where DH adjuncting has an advantage over non-DH adjuncting. Building projects together also builds respect, trust, and admiration: qualities that can foster strong advocacy in letters of recommendation. It creates a body of work that is medially distinct from the essays that a search committee typically reads from applicants, and it demonstrates initiative because adjuncts are frequently paid only to teach and not to build publicly visible projects.

In a labor context in which most of the humanities professoriate is insecurely employed and in which the academic publisher Elsevier wins a U.S. patent for an online peer review system, DH should build infrastructure to safeguard and foster status-agnostic collaboration and collegiality.[25] Elsevier's successful effort to put online peer review behind a paywall has been compared to a "restaurant where the customers bring the ingredients, find volunteers to do all the cooking, and then get hit with a $10,000 bill."[26] Elsevier was denied its first two applications for the patent on online peer review. The third, successful patent application makes narrow claims that the Electronic Frontier Foundation surmises will be "hard to enforce." The larger matter of trying to put collegial service behind a paywall is ominous and, I argue, of a piece with adjunctification. Both reduce the branching, expansive shape of collegiality to mere transactions, like the biology adjunct who now must refuse collegial work she wants to do unless she is paid for it. Digital humanities led open-access publishing that loosened academic publishers' control over how readers digitally access published research. So, too, DH should imagine infrastructures of support to safeguard collegial service and working conditions of all teachers, including temporary ones.

DH adjuncting is not a new phenomenon. The problem is that DH's cresting wave did not lift all boats to tenure lines. In the electronic literature community, for example, many adjuncts and non-tenure-track faculty have made and taught digital literature for decades, building generative poems, experimental hypertexts, and multimodal Flash poetry around the same time that Jerome McGann and others built the Rossetti Archive and Julia Flanders and others built the Women Writer's Project. But unlike archival DH, arts-based DH is populated by individual practitioners making one-off projects that do not require (or even if they require it, do not command) interdisciplinary teams and shared institutional stakeholders evident in some of the larger DH team-based projects. The institutional insecurity of arts-based DH practitioners is beginning to change as organizations like the Electronic Literature Organization advocate for institutional support (NEH and Mellon grants, sustained archives of work, integration into syllabi, preservation efforts, and swelling membership ranks). Rita Raley and Matthew Kirschenbaum, in separate keynotes at the 2017 Electronic Literature Organization conference, noted those attributes of institutional support as testament to electronic literature's field stability. One hopes that field stability might confer employment stability to the many adjuncts making electronic literature, though there's no necessary correlation between field stability and employment stability, as the broader history of adjuncting has taught us. To the *alternative histories* of digital humanities articulated by Tara McPherson, Amy Earhart, Steven Jones, Padmini Ray Murray, and Roger Whitson in their DH 2017 conference panel in Montreal, I would add arts-based DH adjuncts as a group with a varied and rich alternate DH field history.[27]

Structural Changes and Microbenefactions: A Call to Tenured Faculty

Microbenefaction is a term I invented. A microbenefaction is a small action that shifts the balance of power and gives an adjunct access to prestige or information otherwise inaccessible to them. Note that I use the singular here: *an* adjunct. These acts of inclusion are doable as one-offs or limited to the course of a given term; they are not the Herculean efforts of adjunct advocacy groups such as New Faculty Majority, Adjunct Nation, and the PrecariCorps collective, who publish PrecariTales, 300–500-word anonymously authored adjunct stories.[28] Then there is the wonderful example of Chicana literature professor Karen Mary Davalos, whose mentorship of then-adjunct Annemarie Perez equipped Perez to win her "dream job," a tenure-track position in Los Angeles teaching interdisciplinary studies to a "student population I love." Perez's 2018 blog post "A Radical Idea about Adjuncting: Written for Those with Tenure (or on the Tenure Track)" extols Davalos's generous treatment, in which Davalos, as department chair where Perez adjuncted for six years, treated Perez "basically like a post-doc . . . mak[ing] sure I had office space with a working computer, access to printing, and work-study student support. She read my research and gave me comments on articles I was working on. And, perhaps the most important act of all, she told me she was doing this so she could write a strong and knowledgeable letter of recommendation." Davalos mentored a young colleague: actions typical of a tenure line, but so atypical of adjuncting as to be "radical." (Even more so, because Davalos mentored other adjuncts in her department with similar care and attention.) Perez's blog post "went academic viral," inspiring people with Davalos's example and Perez's message of status-blind collegiality.

Perez's story is terrific, and the world needs more chairs like Davalos. But not every person feels the ethical commitment to personally repair the shattering effects caused by adjuncting. Why is scholarly mentorship of adjuncts so unusual? It is because of the massive scale of adjuncting. For every Perez who lands her dream job in her home city (and I myself am one of those extraordinarily lucky people!) there are thousands of adjuncts with no clear path out of adjuncting. There is not enough time for all adjuncts to be cared for the way Perez was cared for. Microbenefactions are small and structural. They do not depend upon personal investment, such as when a compassionate chair mentors a promising scholar fresh out of graduate school, as Perez was. Microbenefactions are designed to be temporary and achievable at scale.

What is a microbenefaction? It is action by a tenured or tenure-track scholar who does one or more of the following:

- Gives adjuncts access to information;
- Writes funding for adjunct salary into grant proposals;
- Advises and mentors adjuncts;
- Seeks input from adjuncts about student-centered pedagogy;
- Aids adjuncts in finding university resources or paid extra work;
- Invites adjuncts to meetings;
- Coauthors with adjuncts;
- Does not eliminate adjunct applications when deciding awards and honors;
- Authorizes support for adjunct professional development, such as paid time for mandatory CMS software training;
- Pays to license adjunct-authored course materials after the adjunct leaves the institution;
- Writes letters of recommendation supporting the adjunct's full-time job prospects.

Microbenefactions enact DH's ethical ambit, which the Global Outlook::Digital Humanities special interest group articulates as recognition "that excellent work is being done around the world [and] that students, researchers, and institutions in all geographic regions and types of economies all have much to contribute to the development of digitally enabled work in the arts, humanities, and cultural heritage sector."[29] Although focused on the global dimensions of DH work, GO::DH, with its emphasis on local conditions, also provides an important frame for understanding how adjuncts and their students in the United States practice DH under constraint.

Senior scholars are key to giving adjuncts prizeworthy work opportunities. Microbenefactions given to me by senior scholars when I adjuncted (2011–2014) positioned me to win awards that validated my bid for the tenure-track job I now occupy. Katherine Harris, Dene Grigar, Bethany Nowviskie, Stuart Moulthrop, Elizabeth Losh, and Henry Jenkins all invited me to join labs, make projects, curate shows, publish in essay collections, and attend conferences. Those invitations gave me access to nationally visible projects in which I trained myself in techniques that are now a core part of my tenured job. I am grateful to those scholars. Senior scholars using soft influence, often in benign ways that are impact-neutral to their own careers, can make or break an adjunct's career trajectory. Adjuncts are usually cut adrift from decision-making processes, learning of them only when it is time to implement decisions others have made. The most basic microbenefaction is to give adjuncts access to information. Further, it takes almost no effort: forward an email, or better yet, add your department's adjunct list to department-wide communications.

This is human-centered DH infrastructure. We acknowledge that humans are not widgets. DH teaching is not a dissemination of knowledge but is a production of value and values. If the medium is adjuncting, then the message is that learning is transactional. Is that really what digital humanities should impart?

Mutual Win: A Microbenefaction Case Study

A microbenefaction is more likely to make its way through an approval chain if everybody gets something good from the exchange.

I aimed to solve a problem caused by the imminent departure of an adjunct in our book publishing program at Portland State. Like all adjuncts teaching in our program, this book industry professional teaches one class in her specialization, in this case ebook production. Having audited the class, I knew firsthand that the best way to ensure course continuity for our master's students would be to arrange for my department to buy permanent access to her excellent course materials. A replacement adjunct with a solid knowledge of ebook production could, using those course materials, teach a master's class. Licensing the adjunct's ebook production course materials involved consultations with

- A senior scholar in my department, who became an advisor and advocate;
- The adjunct;
- Our department chair;
- Our English department faculty executive committee;
- The Office of Academic Innovation;
- A humanities librarian; and
- Staff overseeing contracts.

It took several months for the various stakeholders to deliberate and confer. I was Hermes, relaying information between the parties. I made the case for why the course materials merited licensing and conveyed how the loss of ebook production would diminish the professional readiness of our master's students. The senior scholar, Michael Clark, was the microbenefactor. He moved the process along when it stalled. Other actors in the network each represented a gateway at which the licensing effort could pass or fail: those people balanced the licensing request alongside other claims on scarce resources. This is where the senior scholar's stewardship was most beneficial. Involved advocacy cost him very little time—less than two hours altogether, I speculate. And yet his expertise was invaluable, delivering a win for graduate students, the book publishing program, and the adjunct.

In a migrant labor force, getting adjuncts paid for pedagogical resources they leave behind after their university contracts expire is an ethical issue.[30] Adjuncts need TT or tenured faculty to advocate for such payment, because adjuncts lack access to the approval chain in which such decisions are made by deliberation and consensus. In the end, everybody won: the adjunct earned money licensing her course materials, students got course continuity, the book publishing program retained a core competency, and the university fortified its reputation for innovation. (*U.S. News & World Report* named Portland State University a "Most Innovative" campus in 2016 and 2017.)

Awarding Adjuncts

DH adjuncts should be squarely in view when TT faculty organize panels and workshops about DH infrastructure. How to involve adjuncts who are hard to talk to or even identify?

If ADHO (or ACH, the Association for Computer and the Humanities) were to award a prize specifically designed to recognize adjunct DH work, then some adjuncts would be motivated to put themselves forward. It might make sense also to offer adjunct-specific bursaries to the annual digital humanities conference. My DH adjunct work became visible when DH awards and other honors validated it. In 2012, I was nominated for a digital humanities award (Best DH Project for a Public Audience: "Avenues of Access Exhibit of Electronic Literature," cocurated with Grigar). In 2014, I won a midcareer, year-long Fulbright and was the Fulbright Scholar of Digital Culture to Norway. One can measure the boost those awards gave my career if we consider that the universities where I adjuncted when I won the awards did not publicize or even acknowledge them. (Not even an email!) But when I went on the job market during my Fulbright year, I landed a tenure-track job and other campus interviews. Such a stark difference in responses to my DH awards demonstrates how adjunct status can overshadow other qualifications. Disconnected from infrastructures of support, such as faculty department meetings or faculty-only listservs, my awards were invisible to the communities that might have been my best advocates for full-time work.

An adjunct winning an award typically reserved for tenured or tenure-track faculty prompts uncomfortable questions about merit. There is growing acknowledgment that access to the tenure system is influenced by luck or chance. "I adjuncted twice, each time the year before I got a t-t job—will never forget the experience," tenured Victorianist Talia Schaffer noted in a Facebook comment. "Anyone who was hired within the last 30 years is one step from adjuncting and anyone who has a t-t job just got incredibly lucky, and should never assume it's anything more than luck, imho."[31] Schaffer, along with professors Carolyn Betensky and Seth Kahn, authored a letter urging *U.S. News & World Report* to consider adjusting the "faculty resources" section of the America's Best Colleges rankings to more accurately reflect current academic realities. "Currently you allocate only 5% of this category to part-time vs full-time faculty, while you give 35% to faculty salaries," they write. "However, those faculty salary numbers do not reflect the majority of college instructors, who are contingent faculty: underpaid temporary workers."[32] The letter garnered over 1,200 signatures, about 75 percent of which were tenured or tenure-track faculty. In response, *U.S. News* met with the Tenure for a Common Good delegation (Betensky, Kahn, Schaffer, and New Faculty Majority president and executive director Maria Maisto) on June 14, 2018. In a Facebook post on the Tenure for a Common Good page, Betensky noted that the magazine is willing to consider "a) refining their definitions for part-time/full-time faculty to reflect the real conditions in higher education today; b) refining the questions they ask of colleges and universities to get institutions to report information about part-time/full-time/contingent/tenure-track instructors more accurately; and c) adding a specific request for colleges/universities to report full-time NTT instructor salaries in addition to the TT/T salaries they currently ask for."[33] *U.S. News* decided not to adjust their metrics. Such data collection would benefit students, tuition-paying parents, and faculty because an accurate disclosure of professorial working conditions and remuneration should factor into rankings of university prestige.

Prizes like a Fulbright or a *U.S. News & World Report* American Best Colleges designation are flags that locate a person or institution in a vast relational field of symbolic and cultural capital. James English calls prizes "a uniquely contemporary form of cultural biography. It is almost as though winning a prize is the only truly newsworthy thing a cultural worker can do, the one thing that really counts in a lifetime of more or less nonassessable, indescribable, or at least unreportable cultural accomplishments."[34] If prizes become one's biography, then adjuncts' lack of access to prizes reinforces their invisibility, making it highly unlikely that even very good research will attain the recognition necessary to vault out of adjuncting.

Does *hot* DH inoculate practitioners against the viral decay of stable humanities employment? No, it does not. When DH infrastructure supplies award incentives for adjuncts to proclaim their work and self-identify, the field will be better able to measure how many DH faculty are working precariously. Such visibility will enable the field to assess the extent to which DH adjuncting is a significant or growing phenomenon. It will also give tenured and tenurable faculty more opportunity to practice collegiality with the full range of faculty who grow and advance the field.

Notes

1. Knapp et al., *Employees in Postsecondary Institutions, Fall 2009, and Salaries of Full-Time Instructional Staff, 2009–10.*

2. Bethany Nowviskie observed in a 2010 blog post ("#alt-ac") that "we started using the term [alt-ac] in 2009" as "a pointed push-back against the predominant phrase, 'non-academic careers.'"

3. Nowviskie ("#alt-ac") explains that the origin of the term *alt-ac* links to *#Alt-Academy,* an early and digital-born edited collection of essays hosted on Media Commons. The hashtag is an important feature of the title because the movement was facilitated by conversations and shared posts on DH Twitter. Nowviskie launched an ebook version of #Alt-Academy in 2011.

4. Manyika et al., "Independent Work," para. 3.

5. American Association of University Professors, "Here's the News," Annual Report on the Economic Status of the Profession 2012–13. Adjunctification is well documented by adjunct advocacy organizations such as New Faculty Majority and Adjunct Nation; professional groups such as the American Association of University Professors and the Modern Language Association (2014); intrauniversity studies such as George Mason's, which surveyed 240 GMU adjuncts and "has been hailed as the most comprehensive study of a university's contingent faculty working conditions to date" (2014); trade journals like *Inside Higher Education* and *The Chronicle of Higher Education;* and the popular press. I am struck by *The Atlantic Monthly's* occasional series (2013–present) that features titles like "There's No Excuse for How Universities Treat Adjuncts" and "The Cost of an Adjunct."

6. Jacobs, Perry, and MacGillvary, "The High Public Cost of Low Wages."

7. Marylhurst University in Lake Oswego, Oregon, which had been in operation for 125 years, announced its closure on May 18, 2018 (https://www.marylhurst.edu/closure/). This decision was contested by students and faculty, to no avail. It is worth noting that since then, two more local Portland colleges and universities have shut or declared their intention to shut: Oregon College of Arts and Crafts (founded in 1907) closed in spring 2019, and Concordia University (founded in 1905) ceased operations in spring 2020.

8. "The Dark Side of DH" roundtable presentations were published in *Debates in Digital Humanities 2016* and also expanded into a full-length essay in a special issue of *differences* 25, no. 1 (2014) entitled "In the Shadows of the Digital Humanities," edited by Ellen Rooney and Elizabeth Weed.

9. Kirschenbaum, "What Is 'Digital Humanities'?," 3–4.

10. Bretz, "New Itinerancy," para. 21.

11. For more on best open-web DH pedagogy practices, see *Digital Pedagogy in the Humanities,* a field guide containing fifty-nine curated keywords, each featuring ten ready-to-use assignments that include assignment prompts, syllabi, and faculty reflections on

student results (edited by Davis, Gold, Harris, and Sayers). See also Cohen and Scheinfeldt, *Hacking the Academy;* and Batterskill and Ross, *Using Digital Humanities.*

12. This essay was composed before the COVID-19 pandemic and the shift in 2020–21 to virtual-only conferencing. Whether virtual access to conferences will persist beyond pandemic conditions remains to be seen.

13. Pierazzo, "Disciplinary Impact of the Digital."

14. See Berens's *Debates in Digital Humanities 2019* essay, "Digital Humanities Adjuncts"; and Risam and Edwards's 2017 Digital Humanities Conference talk "Micro DH."

15. The authors of the "Alternate Histories of the Digital Humanities" panel note in their abstract, "Matthew Kirschenbaum's identification of the digital humanities in 2014 as a 'discursive construction' that ignores the 'actually existing projects' of the field set the stage for scholars to rethink how the digital humanities conceptualizes its work and its history ("What Is 'Digital Humanities,'" 48). More recently, in the introduction to *Debates in the Digital Humanities 2016,* Matthew Gold and Lauren Klein use the scholarship of Rosalind Krauss who, in 1979, described art history as emerging as "only one term on the periphery of a field in which there are other, differently structured possibilities." Krauss, "Sculpture in the Expanded Field," 30.

16. English, *Economy of Prestige,* 2.

17. Adjuncts are not mentioned in Anne McGrail's essay "Whole Game." It is the first overview of DH in community colleges.

18. Posner, "Money and Time."

19. Earhart, *Traces of the Old.*

20. Cordell pointedly observed in the published version of his DH 2017 talk that "completing the hours required for our robust [DH graduate] certificate program requires students to decide their path almost immediately upon admission, and the decision to pursue the certificate dictates very particular routes through the larger Ph.D. program." See his "Abundance and Usurpation."

21. Jasnik, "Humanities Job Woes."

22. Berens and Sanders, "Putting the Human Back in the Humanities."

23. Liana M. Silva cites the National Center for Education Statistics 2009 report at https://nces.ed.gov/pubs2011/2011150.pdf. See also "Women as Contingent Faculty," published by the American Association of University Professors, http://archive.aacu.org/ocww/volume37_3/feature.cfm?section=1; and New Faculty Majority's "Women and Contingency" project at http://www.newfacultymajority.info/women-and-contingency-project/.

24. The provisions of the law requiring California community colleges to negotiate employment protections with adjunct professors:

> Part-time, temporary faculty would be evaluated regularly.
> After six semesters or nine quarters of service, part-time, temporary faculty members with good evaluations would be placed on a seniority list, and assignments would be offered in seniority order.

> In cases where adjunct faculty receive a less-than-satisfactory evaluation, a writ-
> ten plan of remediation with concrete suggestions for improvement would be
> provided, and a system of due process would be followed in cases of possible
> termination.

Reported in Koseff, "Part-Time Community College Instructors." See also the compen-
dious "Resources for Organizing" at https://contingentworld.com/, which gathers state of
California legislative reports and data related to contingent higher education employment.

25. Sara Catherine Stanley, in a blog post responding to a faux-provocative tweet
("It's 2017 and still nobody knows what Digital Humanities is"), shifts the "*What* is DH?"
question to "*Why* is DH?" She concludes, "To me, all [DH] means is that we are addressing the needs and concerns of our community and engaging in a bottom-up approach
to knowledge-making." Stanley's third maxim is particularly applicable to adjuncts: "DH
is a response to an environment where the hierarchical structures of the academy don't
always map onto the actual expertise held by various members of the community." Stanley's focus in that paragraph is to make visible the work of "librarians, archivists, developers, technologists, and many other actors [who] have played into the formation of DH."
As DH adjuncting becomes more visible, particularly in teaching-intensive institutions, it
may warrant being added to that list.

26. The quip is from Parker Higgins's tweet, "I'm opening an academic-publishing-
themed restaurant."

27. For the disproportional gender distribution of early e-literature women authors
as adjuncts and men as tenure track, see my article "Judy Malloy's Seat at the (Database)
Table." Just one generation later, as I note in the essay, women e-lit artists made inroads
to tenure lines and now run programs at R-1 institutions. But the lack of tenure and other
forms of institutional support for many e-literature artists persists.

28. https://precaricorps.org/about/true-stories/. The pinned story at time of writing
details an adjunct who has taught at the same university for ten years and has been hired
to revise materials for a large-enrollment course. One chair made sure she got paid the
first lump sum; the replacement chair didn't with the second, and she's still waiting with
"no recourse except to wait." The Twitter hashtags #AdjunctLife and #RealAcademicBios
also gather adjunct stories but do not curate them.

29. Global Outlook::Digital Humanities is a special interest group of the Alliance of
Digital Humanities Organization. Quotation drawn from the "About" page.

30. See also the section "Copyright, Adjuncts & Intellectual Property" in Bretz, "The
New Itinerancy."

31. See Schaffer's comment at 7:11AM, October 28, 2017, in this publicly accessible
thread: https://www.facebook.com/talia.schaffer/posts/10212355234688778?comment
_id=10212359303950507&reply_comment_id=10212366775697296&comment_tracking
=%7B%22tn%22%3A%22R9%22%7D&pnref=story.

32. The letter is viewable but no longer accepting signatures: https://docs.google.com
/document/d/1ILg0QaMrhzQLQvfPbOrE4BClsWfw_pLNPAUAB4yVR7w/edit.

33. See the publicly accessible post by Carolyn Betensky ("Last week, a TCG delega-tion") to the Tenure for a Common Good Facebook page, June 19, 2018.

34. English, *Economy of Prestige*, 21.

Bibliography

American Association of University Professors. "Background Facts on Contingent Faculty." Accessed June 5, 2018. https://www.aaup.org/issues/contingency/background-facts.

American Association of University Professors. "Here's the News." Annual Report on the Economic Status of the Profession 2012–13. https://www.aaup.org/sites/default/files /files/2013%20Salary%20Survey%20Tables%20and%20Figures/report.pdf.

American Association of University Professors Research Office. "Trends in the Academic Labor Force, 1975–2015." Chart produced March 2017 using data from the Integrated Postsecondary Education Data System. https://www.aaup.org/sites/default/files/Aca demic_Labor_Force_Trends_1975-2015.pdf.

Batterskill, Claire, and Shawna Ross. *Using Digital Humanities in the Classroom: A Prac-tical Introduction for Teachers, Lecturers, and Students.* New York: Bloomsbury Aca-demic Press, 2017.

Berens, Kathi Inman. "DH Adjuncts: Social Justice and Care." In *Debates in Digital Human-ities 2019,* edited by Matthew K. Gold and Lauren F. Klein. Minneapolis: University of Minnesota Press, 2019. https://dhdebates.gc.cuny.edu/read/untitled-f2acf72c-a469 -49d8-be35-67f9ac1e3a60/section/4f3663db-3967-4f02-8516-44bf00d945b8#ch41.

Berens, Kathi Inman. "Judy Malloy's Seat at the (Database) Table: A Feminist Reception History of Early Electronic Literature Hypertext." *Literary and Linguistic Computing* 29, no. 3 (2014): 340–48. https://doi.org/10.1093/llc/fqu037.

Berens, Kathi Inman. "Want to Save the Humanities? Pay Adjuncts to Learn Digital Tools." In *Disrupting the Humanities: Digital Edition,* January 5, 2015. http://www. disruptingdh.com/want-to-save-the-humanities-pay-adjuncts-to-learn-digital -tools/.

Berens, Kathi Inman, and Laura E. Sanders. "Putting the Human Back in the Humanities: Adjuncts and Digital Humanities." In *Disrupting Digital Humanities,* edited by Dor-othy Kim and Jesse Stommel. New York: Punctum Press, 2018.

Bessette, Lee Skallerup. *Adjunct Run.* Accessed November 27, 2017. https://adjunctrun. readywriting.org/.

Betensky, Carolyn. "Last week, a TCG delegation (Talia Schaffer, Seth Kahn, Maria Maisto, and Carolyn Betensky) met at the offices of USNWR in Washington, DC, with their chief data strategist, Robert Morse, and his team of analysts." Facebook, June 19, 2018, 11:35 AM. https://www.facebook.com/groups/163317600885815/permalink /249545328929708/.

Bretz, Andrew. "The New Itinerancy: Digital Pedagogy and the Adjunct Instructor in the Modern Academy." *Digital Humanities Quarterly* 11, no. 3 (2017). http://www.digit alhumanities.org/dhq/vol/11/3/000304/000304.html.

Clement, Tanya, Alison Booth, Ryan Cordell, Miriam Posner, and Maria Sachiko Cecire. "Challenges for New Infrastructures and Paradigms in DH Curricular Program Development." Panel (chair: Tanya Clement) at the 2017 Digital Humanities Conference in Montreal, Quebec, August 8–11, 2017. https://dh2017.adho.org/abstracts/176/176.pdf.

Cohen, Daniel, and Joseph Thomas Scheinfeldt. *Hacking the Academy: New Approaches to Scholarship and Teaching from Digital Humanities*. Ann Arbor: University of Michigan Digital Culture Books, 2013.

Contingent World. https://contingentworld.com/. Accessed May 30, 2021.

Cordell, Ryan. "Abundance and Usurpation while Building a DH Curriculum." August 23, 2017. http://ryancordell.org/research/abundance/.

Davis, Rebecca Frost, Matthew K. Gold, Katherine D. Harris, and Jentery Sayers, eds. *Digital Pedagogy in the Humanities*. New York: Modern Language Association, 2021. https://digitalpedagogy.hcommons.org/.

Earhart, Amy E. *Traces of the Old, Uses of the New: The Emergence of Digital Literary Studies*. Ann Arbor: University of Michigan Press, 2015.

English, James F. *The Economy of Prestige: Prizes, Awards, and the Circulation of Cultural Value*. Cambridge, Mass.: Harvard University Press. 2008.

Finley, Ashley. "Women as Contingent Faculty: The Glass Wall." Featured article of the Association of American Colleges and Universities, *On Campus with Women* 37, no. 3 (Winter 2009). https://go.gale.com/ps/anonymous?id=GALE%7CA197802547&sid =googleScholar&v=2.1&it=r&linkaccess=abs&issn=07340141&p=AONE&sw=w.

Grusin, Richard. "The Dark Side of Digital Humanities: Dispatches from Two Recent MLA Conventions." In special issue, "In the Shadows of the Digital Humanities," edited by Ellen Rooney and Elizabeth Weed. *differences* 25, no. 1 (2014): 79–92. https://read .dukeupress.edu/differences/article-abstract/25/1/79/60682/The-Dark-Side-of-Dig ital-Humanities-Dispatches?redirectedFrom=fulltext.

Higgins, Parker. "I'm opening an academic-publishing-themed restaurant. You bring the ingredients and get volunteers to cook and serve. Now pay me $10,000." Twitter, January 6, 2015. https://twitter.com/xor/status/552456370629672960.

Honn, Joshua. "Never Neutral: Critical Approaches to Digital Tools Culture in the Humanities." Accessed November 21, 2017. https://figshare.com/articles/Never_Neutral _Critical_Approaches_to_Digital_Tools_Culture_in_the_Humanities/1101385.

Jacobs, Ken, Ian Perry, and Jenifer MacGillvary. "The High Public Cost of Low Wages: Poverty-Level Wages Cost U.S. Taxpayers $152.8 Billion Each Year in Public Support for Working Families." UC Berkeley Center for Labor Research and Education, April 13, 2015. https://laborcenter.berkeley.edu/the-high-public-cost-of-low-wages/.

Jasnik, Scott. "Humanities Job Woes." *Inside Higher Ed*, January 4, 2016. https://www .insidehighered.com/news/2016/01/04/job-market-tight-many-humanities-fields -healthy-economics.

Kirschenbaum, Matthew. "What Is 'Digital Humanities,' and Why Are They Saying Such Terrible Things about It?" https://mkirschenbaum.files.wordpress.com/2014/04/dh terriblethingskirschenbaum.pdf.

Knapp, Laura G., Janice E. Kelly-Reid, and Scott A. Ginder. *Employees in Postsecondary Institutions, Fall 2009, and Salaries of Full-Time Instructional Staff, 2009–10*. Report, U.S. Department of Education, November 2010. https://nces.ed.gov/pubs2011/2011150 .pdf.

Koseff, Alexei. "Part-Time Community College Instructors to Get Job Protections." *Sacramento Bee*, September 30, 2016. http://www.sacbee.com/news/politics-government /capitol-alert/article105301086.html.

Krauss, Rosalind. "Sculpture in the Expanded Field." *October* 8 (Spring 1979): 30–44.

Manyika, James, Susan Lund, Jacques Bughin, Kelsey Robinson, Jan Mischke, and Deepa Mahajan. "Independent Work: Choice, Necessity, and the Gig Economy." McKinsey Global Institute, October 2016. https://www.mckinsey.com/global-themes/employ ment-and-growth/independent-work-choice-necessity-and-the-gig-economy.

McGrail, Anne B. "Whole Game: Digital Humanities at Community Colleges." In *Debates in Digital Humanities 2016*, edited by Lauren F. Klein and Matthew K. Gold. Minneapolis: University of Minnesota Press, 2016. http://dhdebates.gc.cuny.edu/debates /text/53.

McPherson, Tara. "Theory/Practice: Lessons Learned from Feminist Film Studies." On the panel "Alternate Histories of the Digital Humanities: A Short Paper Panel Proposal," convened by Roger Whitson and featuring Whitson, Amy Earhart, Steven Jones, and Padmini Ray Murray at the 2017 Digital Humanities Conference in Montreal, Quebec, August 8–11, 2017. https://dh2017.adho.org/abstracts/115/115.pdf.

Molloy College. DH adjunct job advertisement posted to the Higher Education Recruiting Consortium, fall 2017. Accessed November 18, 2017. https://main.hercjobs.org /jobs/10389448/new-media-and-digital-humanities-adjunct (link has expired).

Nazer, Daniel, and Elliot Harmon. "Stupid Patent of the Month: Elsevier Patents Online Peer Review." *EFF: Electronic Frontier Foundation*, August 31, 2016. https://www.eff .org/deeplinks/2016/08/stupid-patent-month-elsevier-patents-online-peer-review.

New Faculty Majority. "Facts about Adjuncts." Accessed June 5, 2018. http://www.newfac ultymajority.info/facts-about-adjuncts/.

New Faculty Majority. "Women and Contingency Project." Accessed November 27, 2017. http://www.newfacultymajority.info/women-and-contingency-project/.

Nowviskie, Bethany. "#alt-ac: Alternate Academic Careers for Humanities Scholars." *Bethany Nowviskie* (blog), January 2010. http://nowviskie.org/2010/alt-ac/.

Pérez, Annemarie. "A Radical Idea about Adjuncting: Written for Those with Tenure (or on the Tenure Track)." *Annemarie Pérez* (blog), April 1, 2018. http://citedatthecross roads.net/blog/2018/04/01/a-radical-idea-about-adjuncting-written-for-those -with-tenure-or-on-the-tenure-track/.

Pierazzo, Elena. "The Disciplinary Impact of the Digital: DH and 'The Others.'" Keynote at the Digital Humanities Summer Institute 2017, Victoria, B.C., June 2017. https:// hal.archives-ouvertes.fr/cel-01544594.

Posner, Miriam. "Money and Time." *Miriam Posner's Blog*, March 14, 2016. http://miri amposner.com/blog/money-and-time/.

Precaricorps. "True Stories." Accessed November 27, 2017. https://precaricorps.org/about /true-stories/.

Ramsay, Stephen. "The Hot Thing." Accessed November 27, 2017. https://github.com /sramsay/sramsay.github.com/blob/master/_posts/2012-04-09-hot-thing.markdown.

Risam, Roopika, and Susan Edwards. "Micro DH: Digital Humanities at the Small Scale." Conference talk at the 2017 Digital Humanities Conference in Montreal, Quebec, August 8–11, 2017. https://dh2017.adho.org/abstracts/196/196.pdf .

Silva, Liana. "How Many Women Are Adjuncts Out There?" *Chronicle of Higher Education,* May 27, 2015. https://chroniclevitae.com/news/1017-how-many-women-are -adjuncts-out-there.

Stanley, Sara Catherine. "Why Is Digital Humanities?" *Sara Catherine Stanley* (blog), June 21, 2017. http://scatherinestanley.us/2017/06/why-is-dh.

Varner, Stuart. "Digital Humanities or Just Humanities?" *Stewart Varner* (blog). Accessed November 21, 2017. https://stewartvarner.com/2013/11/digital-humanities-or-just -humanities/.

Warford, Erin. "StoryTelling with Digital Maps." Workshop at the 2017 Summer Digital Humanities Workshop Series at Canisius College. Accessed November 27, 2017. https://blogs.canisius.edu/digital-humanities/gis2017/.

PART III

PEDAGOGY

Vulnerability, Collaboration, and Resilience

Access, Touch, and Human Infrastructures in Digital Pedagogy

MARGARET SIMON

Today's media and technology landscape has created two related conundrums for scholars and teachers of premodern texts. The first taps into a concern of digital humanities broadly. How can teachers and scholars recognize and encourage digital pedagogies that do not rely on or derive from traditional resource-heavy models?[1] In other words, how can less resourced institutions access digital tools and develop pedagogies not as *apprentice* or *aspiring* to more well-resourced models but as recognized innovations in their own right?[2] The second conundrum is more field specific: digital remediations of premodern print and manuscript texts do not just offer increased access to rare cultural materials; they present "complex technological translations" that reframe the codex within a new media environment and extend the interpretive landscape of archival research.[3] In short, the question of access emerges both as a pragmatic concern and as a theoretical, methodological juggernaut.[4] This essay uses my experience teaching the transcription of digitized manuscripts as a way to connect these questions of access with the less well-defined ways that scholars themselves access institutional infrastructures and professional networks. Jesse Stommel notes the hybridity of digital pedagogy, asserting that "it is important to engage the digital selves of our students. And, in online pedagogy, it is equally important to engage their physical selves."[5] Infrastructures for faculty that enable such pedagogies are likewise hybrid, comprising both concrete resources and less quantifiable interpersonal economies; faculty (often exclusively those on the tenure track) at well-resourced schools not only can access the hardware useful to digital humanities projects but also have the time and support to pursue the networking and professional development that facilitate classroom innovation. These crucial yet often less apparent or quantifiable supports can enable instructors to develop the course modules that are frequently the first point of contact for students with digital projects and methodologies.

Using student reflections on transcribing digitized manuscripts and considering the scholarly connections and specialized training that can make these class modules possible, this essay both conveys what such assignments offer to students and brings attention to the human networks of support that enable digital pedagogies. This seemingly basic course module and the surprising insights it elicited demonstrate how access to such materials and practices creates luminous, even haptic encounters for students and in turn how such student experiences rely on assignment design itself as a digital humanities tool. This digital transcription project not only manifests the rewards for students of working with relatively straightforward digitized archives but also reveals how user-friendly technologies in the classroom can belie the complex professional networks and institutional hierarchies that can determine how and if teachers undertake digital humanities work.

The notion of "minimal computing," which undergirds the coursework discussed in this essay, has from its inception been less a definition than a touchstone for discussing the networks of human, hardware, and computing resources activated by digital humanities projects. Like the term *access, minimal* means more than it seems to mean. In presenting the term, Alex Gil immediately considers its limits, noting how stripped-down hardware, like a Raspberry Pi, while compact and minimalist, still requires "more than minimum effort" to use. Likewise, he notes that an uncluttered interface design like Google's may still use "an enormous amount of code and data in the back end, needing enormous computing power in turn."[6] Jentery Sayers, as a proponent of minimal computing, also extends this critique, bringing attention to the aesthetic and political assumptions that emerge from the "legacies of elegance in programming."[7] The term is useful precisely for reflecting on increasingly common digital tools, as well as for fine-grained explorations of digital projects and pedagogies undertaken from different positionalities within academe. In a conference paper given at the 2017 MLA conference and now available on the go-dh website, Anne B. McGrail, a community college professor and coeditor of this volume, points out more assumptions within minimal computing, particularly the sense that even the minimal requires a great deal of know-how, the ability to bootstrap projects, time for development, and, in the classroom, a student group who perceives the landscape of DH as open to them. McGrail asserts that DH tools, whether maximal or minimal, are ultimately moot if the students using them do not conceptualize their own space and agency within a digital learning environment.[8] This essay works to unpack certain ideological aspects of access and of "minimal computing" through a fine-grained look at a seemingly uncomplicated course module.

Haptic Encounters with Digitized Texts

As brick-and-mortar archives digitize their collections, improved access is often widely celebrated as the primary goal of such projects. To take one recent example, an article in *Forbes* touts the British Museum's new 3D archive as "creating access to cultural heritage for the millions of people who can't afford a ticket to London."[9]

Increasingly high-quality digital scans and models of texts and objects seemingly open to a much broader public what was once relegated to scholars with a travel budget. Such archives serve "a mediating and immediating function in bringing the thoughts and actions of an earlier time into closer contact."[10] That contact can come at an immediate cost, with certain digitized archives defended by paywalls, as is the case with the Early English Books Online database. By contrast, open-access collections, such as the Folger Shakespeare Library's digitized materials, are free to use. But beyond costs, access means much more than the ability to simply view rare materials.

What exactly does an accessible digital object give us access to? Scholars have sometimes criticized certain manuscript digitization projects as "window dressing" for major collections, while lacking a clear mode of engagement for users. Meg Twycross continues: "There is nothing wrong with advertising the attractions of our national treasures and making the general public and indeed students aware of and enthused about them; but one would like evidence that their audience is expected to proceed to the next stage of appreciation, which is to do something with them."[11] The question of exactly what is to be done with digitized manuscripts has been variously addressed. Twycross herself reports on her work in digital restoration of delicate materials. This critique sets up a more far-ranging inquiry into how digital archives balance the mimetic with the interpretive and, further, how those decisions effect scholarly engagements with digitized texts.[12] Scholars, in turn, have to evaluate the extent to which digitizations are useful facsimiles or independent artifacts. The digital medium further informs the document's bibliographic and cultural radiance, demonstrating digital materiality as "technology in practice," wherein a text's "phenomenological existence is inseparable from the process of interpretation."[13]

Questions surrounding the access and uses of digitized manuscripts have also emerged within the context of the senses. Jonathan Wilcox, in the introduction to the edited collection *Scraped, Stroked, and Bound,* complains that while the "visual access that such productions provide is often stunningly good . . . digital facsimiles fail to engage senses other than sight." How then, he asks, "can responsible scholars overcome the disadvantages of digital reproductions and more fully engage with the physicality of the book?"[14] For Wilcox, the answer lies in "craft scholarship," which opposes itself to digitized archives with an emphasis on physical experiences. For example, Wilcox gives a small group of scholars the experience of making book components such as parchment. He reports, "What got amplified was precisely what is lacking in digital reproductions. Rather than relating to the eyes alone, the hands proved utterly central to the crafting of books and this accentuates an awareness of the tactile. Books involve a touching of the past in the most literal of senses."[15] Certainly experiences like this can convey information about craft labor and offer a different sensory landscape. However, this perspective presumes a sharp binary between the tactile and visual, mapped on to the other sharp binary of material and digital, neither of which holds up to scrutiny.

The senses are never so distinct as they are in our linguistic taxonomies, and the digital may unexpectedly extend their historical entwinement. In Western culture, touch and vision have long been imbricated. In the Catholic mass of the early sixteenth century, for example, congregants experienced a mediated form of touch by viewing the consecrated host while its handling was limited to priests.[16] Touch was highly regulated in a way that, when combined with the visual dramaturgy of the mass, developed a complex dynamic of involvement and exclusion.[17] Jonathan Crary looks to the seventeenth and eighteenth centuries as a period when vision was particularly apt to be "conceived in analogies to touch." He notes in particular how Denis Diderot "resisted treating any phenomenon in terms of a single sense."[18] These early insights are borne out in history of the senses research that challenges "the platitude that there are five senses, as well as the presupposition that we know what we are counting when we count them as five (or more)."[19] The senses all operate and mingle in the experience of a page, including, as Bonnie Mak asserts, digitized pages: "Like their analogue counterparts, these pages communicate verbally, graphically, aurally, and tactilely and are constructed in a material way that influences how they are read and understood."[20]

Remediation shapes the sensual affordances of the digital interface as well as "the ontology of digital artefacts," a phrase that pushes against the seeming neutrality or solely mimetic function of digitized materials.[21] The papyrologist Ségolène Tarte recommends that, beyond highlighting the "purely visual aspects of the original artefact, the acts of digitization and visualization can choose to explicitly imitate the actions and procedures the experts adopt when handling an artefact."[22] Tarte imagines translating onto the screen the "kinesthetic approach" common in reading papyri, drawing the text as it is seen: "papyrologists establish a feedback loop . . . Their minds oscillate between the text as a shape and the text as a meaning. And a continuous negotiation takes place between the two . . . It is the embodied act of drawing the text that serves as a negotiation tool." Tarte explains this approach as "an embodied model of cognition, where it is a physical interaction with the world that prompts a state of knowledge."[23] If scholars habitually engage in such sensed cognition when handling and interpreting historical materials, then digitization practices might similarly strive for such a model to help students and scholars explore the unique interpretive potentials of digital objects.

Colin Reeves-Fortney, a filmmaker and artist, likewise envisions the digital realm as rife with embodied-interpretive potential. Reeves-Fortney helped to create Stanford University's Digging Deeper series, a pair of online classes that introduced the study of codicology and paleography primarily through online video instruction. Faced with the perhaps paradoxical challenge of conveying material experiences through an online course format, Reeves-Fortney attempted to reimagine the affective encounter that many researchers have with rare materials in the archive. Reeves-Fortney wanted to explore how film might cultivate a similar frisson, creating empathy between viewer/user and textual object. His films of rare materials avoid the idealized visual presentation of an archival object. As he points out, humans do not generally encounter books completely head on, nor are we, in many cases, able to use our own eyes, or even a loupe, to get as close as some high-quality digital scans allow us to get. And certainly if we want to get close to an object, we have to move toward it, not simply zoom on a screen. It was important to Fortney, in creating an immersive classroom environment, to balance the affordances of extreme visuality with the need to keep the sense of human scale and proximity to texts. In so doing, Fortney also reveals the aesthetics and intervention of the filmmaker, resisting the type of neutrality that the digital image can convey. From Fortney's experience, these filmic encounters can cultivate empathy in physically distant students for their objects of study. This work tacitly suggests that the ontology of digital artifacts allows them not just to be interpreted but also, as Tarte claims, to "influence the real."[24]

The Phenomenality of Digital Transcription

My course module did not begin with such ambitions. Rather, it sought to take advantage of open-access manuscript collections and available digital tools to teach students about paleography, transcription, and early modern culture. However, the experience of the module brought into focus all these questions of access, empathy, and their institutional preconditions. We used a transcription portal developed by the Folger to access the 267-page medical recipe book compiled by a Mrs. Corlyon across the first half of the seventeenth century.[25] One of the two period handwritten copies of this manuscript is digitized and held at the Wellcome Library while the other is held at the Folger; a third is not digitized and is held at Arundel Castle. Researchers can thus bring together historically dispersed manuscripts for comparative study and can likewise perceive both distances and gaps in digitization by understanding which archives have not made their materials available in this way. Being able to access simultaneously two versions of this manuscript held in geographically disparate archives also better conveys the amount and significance of materials largely compiled by women, depicting on the screen the volume of such texts and better witnessing the extent of knowledge produced or disseminated by women during this historical period, a contribution that has long been neglected. This is one goal of the Early Modern Recipes Online Collective (EMROC), which works with a number of different repositories to transcribe and make searchable sixteenth- and seventeenth-century medical and culinary recipe books and through which our class was able to transcribe portions of Mrs. Corlyon's collection.

It is surprising that the simple practice of transcribing from a digitized manuscript can offer insights into broad concerns about the interpretive potentials of remediation, the sensory aspects of the digital-material, and the role of digitized texts in embodied cognition. But transcription is all at once an editorial, constructivist, and kinesthetic project. Digital transcription involves rewriting a manuscript according to certain conventions and tagging it according to Text Encoding Initiative (TEI) standards. Transcribing handwriting often necessitates building an alphabet for a given writer's hand, typing and correcting a draft transcription, and then adding tags. The process requires extensive attention to the linguistic and material features of a textual object, and given the number of text technologies involved in the transcription's production, creates a mindset attuned to media specificity and change. It presents an opportunity for students to connect the practices of traditional manuscript scholarship with an interpretive posture toward the text technologies they employ. Transcribing from digitized texts can give users the opportunity to consider the theoretical questions raised by such remediations while also experiencing the embodied act of working with such materials. To access the Corlyon manuscript students could use the Folger Library's LUNA image database or view the same images loaded into the library's transcription portal. LUNA's image archive sometimes presents openings of manuscripts, displaying both recto and verso in the visual context familiar to manuscript readers. In other cases, single pages are presented alone, a denatured view of the text possible only in the digital realm, where, as Andrew Piper has quipped, "all is recto."[26] In either case the viewer's line of sight is unrealistically perpendicular to the page. The archive is not trying to replicate a physical encounter with the book. Students worked experientially to accomplish their task, becoming aware of the affordances and constraints of remediation. Several students articulated a critical resistance to this mode of research; nonetheless, the project encouraged them to wrestle with methodological and interpretive challenges of the digital artifact. The particular historical and material value of an early manuscript invited students to consider the sensory imbrications, particularly of vision and touch, of the screen itself. My students' reactions demonstrate how an engaged digital pedagogy can facilitate a luminous, yet still critical, encounter with a rare historical object.[27] Rather than privileging an auratic original document, digital transcription technologies can let students experience what Jerome McGann calls the "phenomenal event" of textuality.[28]

For nonspecialists encountering the period and its textual traces, the concept of *presence* becomes crucial. Its significance for the early modern period gets reanimated in thinking about how the visual and tactile combine in encountering digitized texts. If, as Hans Ulricht Gumbrecht has claimed, presence is more spatial than temporal, digitally navigating a manuscript display gives students an experience of presence different from their print anthology.[29] These print editions, with lines sometimes broken infelicitously to accommodate a two-column imposition, are not material touchstones for understanding the period and its written culture. Working with manuscript recipe books accomplishes two things in terms of creating a sense of textual presence for students. First, just seeing the page as it was written in its period evokes from students words like "connection," a feeling of contextually "knowing" and even having a sense of "intimacy" with the writer. Second, the mere encounter with the digitized manuscript page is surprisingly haptic. Students even sometimes described this in the slippery terms of "feeling." One student reported that after having worked with the manuscript transcription "the texts seem more approachable and tangible." Struggling to articulate the experience as both affective and even tactile, one student writes, "The handwritten documents definitely added a new feel to the texts and made them feel much more personal." They find themselves looking for traces of the author's own body—thumbprints or other signs of wear.

The process of reading becomes actively embodied as it moves from the eyes to the hands which render the words. One student wrote, "I read Corlyon's writing and felt as if those words were being written right next to me." Transcription accomplished in the student imaginary what my previous efforts to convey through example, lecture, and discussion never quite could: the beautiful and crucial insight that "the material dimension of the assignment—the high definition yet at times difficult-to-read images of real manuscripts—allowed me to consider the material nature of knowledge production and transmittance, and the role that this materiality plays in the history of language and knowledge as it is tied to language."

That said, students do not generally conflate the experiences of reading a book and reading on the screen either. Some reported a range of frustrations with the distance they sometimes sensed from the scanned object. One student noted that "Having the manuscript online made it hard to connect even with the ability to view the handwriting closely. The digital medium almost cancels out the humanness of the writing." The student echoes how given text technologies mediate certain differences between vision and touch: "vision is the experience of spatial separation, touch the experience of colocation."[30] At the same time, both sense perception and interpretation are, to varying degrees, about integrating body and environment through proximity (consider the metaphor of "close reading"), an imperfect process, and the recognition of which is a surprising byproduct of this form of digital pedagogy. Encountering manuscripts online involves a form of "mediate touch" that partakes of changes in medium, changes which create an amplified synesthesia of the visual and tactile as students use pencils, paper, keyboards, touchscreens, or the mouse to navigate, approach, and transcribe the digitized object, sometimes in ways that would be impossible in the nondigital realm.[31]

When we allow textual tools to display their constraints and encourage students to articulate them, students become reflective and, more importantly, comparative, users of media. Jessica Pressman and N. Katharine Hayles theorize what student comments imply: that comparative media studies can "break the transparency of cultural sets and denaturalize assumptions and presuppositions, bringing into view their ideological underpinnings."[32] By having students read a manuscript embedded in a digital interface, they address the friction between the technologies of the codex and of the screen, the different ways these technologies activate, and imbricate, touch and vision. They are forced to encounter and address their own embodied reading practices, moving toward the sort of critical disposition that Roger Chartier advocates for the history of reading: "Recognizing its diverse modalities and multiple variations is the first aim of a history of reading that strives to grasp—in all their differences—communities of readers and their 'arts of reading.'"[33]

Transcribing digitized texts not only challenged students' theoretical and physical perceptions of the media they use each day but also shifted their typical bodily habitus within the classroom. Students worked in pairs, sitting close together, eyes bouncing from computer screen, to overhead projection, to page, hands moving from pencils to keyboards to touchscreens. Their own voices formed part of the productive textual melee as they compared readings or enlisted the help of the whole group on a particularly tricky word. We used a large projection of a manuscript page, not so different from massive antiphonals (manuscript musical scores that guided group singing centuries ago) to support group reading and the type of public insights that define the intellectual standard and space of a classroom. One student took apart the benefits of this process: "Collaboration was a strong motivator for me in completing the transcription . . . because we discussed our thought processes and reached a consensus based on our experiences with the text." This collaborative structure may likewise elevate the strengths of certain student groups. For example, Jamila Moore Pewu and Annelise Hanson Shrout, in their essay in this volume, discuss how first-generation college students are often particularly adept at working in teams. In so doing, the students themselves become a necessary "infrastructure" for the success of the project.[34]

Students were also compelled by the transcription portal that the Folger's software offers, as they could more or less see their transcriptions joining the many other keyings of pages for the same manuscript. One student spoke to this sense of immediacy and community: "The process of reading a handwritten work and immediately producing a more usable document with the potential to share newfound information for research and analysis felt very satisfying."

This sense of research accomplishment was not universal. One outcome of researching at a physical distance from archives or scholars doing interpretive work is difficulty in connecting the task at hand to broader research goals, something students noted. This disconnect is perhaps also enhanced by the Folger's transcription portal, which sort of absorbs students' transcriptions without giving them a sense of where they end up on the back end or, indeed, of what scholars might plan to do with them. This concern highlights a warrant of this volume, particularly explored in the chapter "Manifesto for Student-Driven Research and Learning,"[35] that we need better thinking about the research communities that grow and change around given projects as they develop, giving particular consideration to diverse student constituencies and institutional and regional differences.

Working in the classroom with digitized manuscripts has helped me to reassess the connection between digital text technologies and critical reading. In the first iteration of this transcription module I was surprised to see the way the process of transcription benefits from the potential diversions of the internet. While students did use the OED online or Google to look up unfamiliar words, these resources supported rather than interrupted the focus and engagement both transcribing and tagging materials requires. Students noted reading the author's work "so intently and closely." In this case, the readerly demands of the seventeenth-century text reframe the affordances of its remediation. As one student put it, "There was a discipline involved in paying meticulous attention to the details of each word, each phrase, that brought about new habits in me as I approached these texts—a discipline that I think will stick with me." Transcription also became for students not a mechanical but a creative process, offering them a sense of their own discoveries. Many times, as students interpret canonical texts in class discussion or critical essays, they model the insights of other scholars or their professors. The moment of transcription offered to at least one student an experience of actual archival discovery. He wrote that "there is a unique sense of accomplishment in deriving your own evidence from transcription. It grants you a different kind of authority in your research since it's your own work at play, rather than just citing a scholarly source." A focus on student abilities works to rectify what Roopika Risam in the chapter in this volume titled "Stewarding Place: Digital Humanities at the Regional Comprehensive University"[36] identifies as students being trained through high-stakes testing to be "consumers, not creators, of knowledge."

Importantly, students even began to move beyond the initial fascination with contributing to a scholarly domain to a critical awareness of the broader assumptions that underlie the Folger and EMROC's research protocols. One student reflected,

> I personally wonder about the security of such a system—with increasingly crowdsourced, semi-anonymous, lay participation comes an almost inevitable decrease in accountability and quality of work . . . To entrust any archive, digitally hosted or no, to people who have only just learned the word "manuscript" . . . seems perhaps a bit less than desirable.

This student's unease may be warranted. In looking at the pages of the manuscript we transcribed, it is easy to see that many transcriptions have been abandoned mid-page, while others have keyings into the double digits. At what point does what is useful for students become an impediment to quality research?[37] This student's experience sparked metareflections on research practices in tune with current scholarly debates about how to most productively scaffold crowdsourced research.[38]

In all these reflections, students are engaging with and profiting from the nuances of access; calling up a digitized manuscript offers far more than a performed proximity to an object. And the majority of my students have never visited, and may never visit, an archive; they do not come to the exercise with prejudices about authentic or surrogate encounters with rare materials. Students experienced the primarily visual dynamic of the digital display as conceptually haptic and material. Their experiences translated into a broader awareness of the inscriptive, material, and contingent ways that texts were produced and circulated across our syllabus.

Furthermore, especially for newcomers to early modern literature, this activity helped students to, as one reflection put it,

> appreciate how our understanding of different historical periods stems from readings of historical documents that are both interpretive and material. By this, I mean that our reading of certain non-literary manuscripts like recipe books, miscellanies, etc., requires that we physically engage with the document, and grapple with it as a complexly formulated technology, even at the same time as we assess the content of the document with respect to our understanding of the social, political, economic, philosophical, and religious orders of a given time period.

We should perhaps not question but rather foster the sort of synesthesia or visual touch that digitized manuscripts enable for students, not seeing it as a degradation of presence, but as an important version of presence itself.

Scholarly Networks as Digital Humanities Infrastructures

Anne McGrail, in her pointed assessment of "minimal computing," brings careful attention to how critical DH pedagogy needs to see the conceptual and interpersonal as deeply embedded within the pragmatic and instrumental, another version of hybridity within these teaching approaches. Emily Isaacson, a teacher and scholar working at a small, non-elite liberal arts college, recently brought similar attention to the financial and institutional pressures that profoundly limit the ability of professors and students to undertake work in DH even at many small, private institutions. Isaacson points out that small, non-elite liberal arts colleges enroll a significantly larger proportion of students who are first-generation college students and/ or have lower academic achievement in high school than many public institutions.[39] Isaacson and McGrail focus on the psychosocial barriers that might keep students at non-elite schools disenfranchised from DH's vaunted experimentation and "productive failure," and the same barriers can hinder professors. I work on the tenure track at a large, public, STEM-focused institution. We have many resources for work in digital humanities and a teaching load that enables our faculty to apply for, and often be awarded, large grants to pursue international DH projects. The spotlight on such resources for research, however, can overlook the economic foundations on which critical DH pedagogy is built. I have come to see my digital pedagogy in the context of how we might reconceive the role of large, resource-rich cultural institutions in improving not just access but also instructors' sense of digital agency.

As an early modernist, I generally teach undergraduate and graduate surveys of pre-1800 literatures, often in classes that have both upper-level undergraduates and master's-level students. Undertaking transcription of women's manuscripts in my combined graduate-undergraduate seventeenth-century nondramatic literature class aims to expose students to not just canonical authors but also to texts and writers outside of the strictly literary. In reflecting on three years of teaching digital transcription supported by the Folger and EMROC, I have tended to focus more on student outcomes, soliciting the anonymous feedback on their experiences detailed above. Increasingly, however, I have come to recognize this extremely simple assignment design, which relies only on a computer and an internet connection, as surprisingly resource heavy, although not in the ways that we might initially expect. Recognizing the back-end work and resources that go into even minimal DH teaching can help practitioners better realize how well-funded, open-access institutions and less easily accessible professional networks are crucial forces in bringing DH methodologies to non-elite classrooms.[40] Human connections are an unseen DH resource essential to many "minimal computing" projects in the classroom, recognition of which might help scholars and institutions dismantle the barriers that can sometimes make it difficult to bring DH approaches to a broader faculty and student community.[41] In offering open-access materials, cultural institutions—whose missions are often quite different from for-profit tech companies—create a way around McGrail's concern that "minimal computing" might inadvertently lead students to rely only on "overprocessed commercial platforms."[42] At the same time, the elite scholarly networks such institutions and universities cultivate can be harder to plug into.

My course's module is relatively uncomplicated from a technical perspective but relies extensively on a well-resourced professional network. In the case study of my class, in order to set this technologically straightforward transcription module in motion, I first had to myself learn paleography. I had sufficient time to research and apply for a summer institute in paleography funded by the Mellon Foundation and run by the Folger. Such professional development would have been unthinkable in my previous position as a contingent faculty member at a large state school. I then needed to forge the professional networks that would open the way for my students to contribute to the EMROC/Folger transcription project. After meeting scholars at the Folger, I was able to follow up and request to be made part of the project. Again, my tenure-track status and institutional affiliation helped me gain access to these research networks.

It is important to recognize that higher education labor practices have downstream effects in the classrooms in both pragmatic and conceptual ways. Course loads, pay inequity, and poor contracts rightly dominate discussions of labor conditions in the academy. Relatedly, the challenges presented to scholarly networking by institutional inequity is an important component to considering how and why certain types of innovations do or do not occur in the classroom. When I was working off the tenure track it would have been impossible for me to have the time or the level of professional confidence and self-perceived credibility to pursue such collaborations. It is slippery and anecdotal to try to bring individual psychologies and their great variety into conversations about digital resources and critical pedagogy;

certainly many scholars might not have had this same set of situational anxieties. Yet if "Seeing the research process both as it is for oneself and as it might be for someone else—what we might think of as a sympathetic research imagination—also lies at the core of archive-centric digital humanities," we might consider how this affective disposition, facilitated by archival research, could lead into a better understanding of the human elements that make such archive-centric DH pedagogies possible.[43] Students evidence this affective investment in the tools and terms of their research when they find, through transcription, a sense of contribution to a domain and a feeling of coexistence with the authors whose hands they study. Analyzing what we might broadly call the human within digital humanities pedagogy can reveal not just the haptic and interpretive possibilities such classroom approaches hold for students but the market-driven economies of professional connection and prestige that function as shadow infrastructures in fostering digital learning and research.

Notes

I am grateful to the students of ENG 530 who have generously offered to share their insights and experiences for inclusion in this essay. I would like to thank Colin Reeves-Fortney for his insightful conversation regarding filming of rare materials for online instruction. Thank you also to the team at the Early Modern Recipes Online Collective whose time and generosity made this experience possible for our class. I am likewise indebted to participants in the Folger Library's 2017 symposium "The Embodied Senses" who broadened my understanding of sense history and to participants and audience members in the Renaissance Society of America 2017 conference panel "New Technologies and Renaissance Studies V: Texts and Code" who provided feedback on an earlier version of this essay.

1. This conversation pertains both to inequities among America's institutions of higher learning and to global networks of digital humanities inquiry. Alex Gil and Érika Ortega discuss the latter, assessing how insular networks of scholarly communications emerge among countries with similar economic statuses.

2. Gil and Ortega discuss this as a feature of new thinking in global DH, but it also has resonance for America's educational hierarchies. For more on this topic, see the other essays in this part of this volume, all of which address the way conventional understandings of infrastructure leave out digital projects and pedagogies at less conventionally resourced institutions.

3. The "complex technological translations" observation is from Mak, *How the Page Matters*, 63. For a cogent summary of some of the opportunities and pitfalls of digitization projects see Nelson and Terras, "Introduction," 8–9.

4. Although this piece does not take up the vital access questions raised by scholars of disability studies, in bringing attention to the nuances of our sensory taxonomies, aspects of this essay contribute to George H. Williams's call to "broaden our understanding of the ways in which people use digital resources." Digitized archives, with their emphasis on the visual, require far more work to create interfaces that do not, as Williams suggests

many technologies do, "assume everyone approaches information with the same abilities" (Williams, "Disability, Universal Design"). At the same time, the hypervisuality enabled by high-resolution scans and zooming technology holds the promise of better access for certain users.

5. Stommel, "What Is Hybrid Pedagogy?"

6. Gil, "User, the Learner and the Machines We Make."

7. Sayers, "Minimal Definitions."

8. McGrail, "Open Source in Open Access Environments."

9. Bond, "Five New 3D Models of Ancient Artifacts."

10. Nelson and Terras, "Introduction," 8.

11. Twycross, "Virtual Restoration and Manuscript Archaeology," 23.

12. I borrow the paired terms *mimetic* and *interpretive* from Tarte, "Digital Visual Representations in Papyrology: Implications on the Nature of Digital Artefacts." Ian Gadd, in "The Use and Misuse of Early English Books Online," discusses how Early English Books Online reshapes sensory dynamics, extending to its use of black-and-white scans, which even degrade the visual remediation for which digitized materials are so often vaunted.

13. Shep, "Digital Materiality," 323.

14. Wilcox, "Introduction: The Philology of Smell," 3.

15. Wilcox, "Introduction: The Philology of Smell," 7.

16. Moshenska, *Feeling Pleasures,* 35.

17. Moshenska, *Feeling Pleasures,* 34.

18. Crary, *Techniques of the Observer,* 58.

19. Macpherson, "Introduction," 3.

20. Mak, *How the Page Matters,* 62.

21. Tarte, "Digital Visual Representations in Papyrology," 7.

22. Tarte, "Digital Visual Representations in Papyrology," 4.

23. Tarte, "Digital Visual Representations in Papyrology," 3.

24. Tarte, "Digital Visual Representations in Papyrology," 1.

25. The Folger's open-source transcription tool is called Dromio and is available on GitHub.

26. Piper, *Book Was There,* 45. The photography department at the Folger uses many criteria for determining how a textual object is photographed, guided mostly by conservation goals.

27. I sought and received permission from my students to share their anonymous reflections on this assignment in this article.

28. McGann, *The Textual Condition,* 5.

29. Gumbrecht, *Production of Presence,* xv.

30. Hopkins, "Re-Imagining, Re-Viewing, and Re-Touching," 264.

31. The phrase "mediate touch" is from Moshenska, *Feeling Pleasures,* 33.

32. Pressman, *Digital Modernism,* viii.

33. Chartier, *The Order of Books,* viii.

34. See pages 236 and 263.

35. Miya et al., "Manifesto for Student-Driven Research and Learning."

36. Risam, "Stewarding Place."

37. EMROC addresses this issue by grant-funding paleographers or recruiting volunteer scholars to vet the initial transcriptions. Transcribers are recognized by their user names. The means by which to credit crowdsourced work is evolving. *Transcribe Bentham* (http://blogs.ucl.ac.uk/transcribe-bentham/), for example, pledges to acknowledge transcribers in volumes created from the transcriptions of Bentham's manuscripts.

38. Melissa Terras, for example, discusses the need for crowdsourced transcription projects to be structured in such a way that "complex representational issues are preserved" as one step to assure that the project will be "useful over a longer term and for a variety of research," 23.

39. Isaacson, "'[V]Olumes That/ I Prize above My Dukedome': The Archive, Digital Projects," 10.

40. For a slightly different take on the substance and benefits of minimal computing, see chapters 9 and especially 19 in this volume.

41. Sarah Catherine Stanley addresses these hidden infrastructures as she notes how digital humanists have "been deeply engaged in discussions about sustainable labor practices in the academy." A recent conference at Florida State University takes up "Invisible Work in the Digital Humanities," exploring how different participants in digital collaborations have shared or divergent goals based on often overlooked factors including "unequal labor" (iwdh.cci.fsu.edu).

42. McGrail, "Open Source in Open Access Environments."

43. The quotation is from Burma and Levine, "Sympathetic Research Imagination."

Bibliography

Bond, Sarah. "Five New 3D Models of Ancient Artifacts That Are Changing How We Interact With Museums." Accessed June 19, 2017. https://www.forbes.com/sites/drsarahbond/2017/05/19/five-new-3d-models-of-ancient-artifacts-that-are-changing-how-we-interact-with-museums/#3cf6b3ec1e30.

Burma, Rachel Sagner, and Anna Tione Levine. "The Sympathetic Research Imagination: Digital Humanities and the Liberal Arts." In *Debates in the Digital Humanities 2016*. Accessed January 21, 2020. http://dhdebates.gc.cuny.edu/debates/text/74.

Chartier, Roger. *The Order of Books: Readers, Authors and Libraries in Europe between the Fourteenth and Eighteenth Centuries*. Stanford, Calif.: Stanford University Press, 1994.

Crary, Jonathan. *Techniques of the Observer: On Vision and Modernity in the Nineteenth Century*. Cambridge, Mass.: MIT Press, 1992.

Gadd, Ian. "The Use and Misuse of Early English Books Online." *Literature Compass* 6, no. 3 (May 1, 2009): 680–92.

Gil, Alex. "The User, the Learner and the Machines We Make," *Minimal Computing*. Accessed May 18, 2017. http://go-dh.github.io/mincomp/thoughts/2015/05/21/user-vs-learner/.

Gil, Alex, and Élika Ortega. "Multilingual Practices and Minimal Computing." In *Doing Digital Humanities*, edited by Constance Crompton, Richard J. Lane, and Ray Siemens, 22–34. London: Routledge, 2016.

Gumbrecht, Hans Ulrich. *Production of Presence: What Meaning Cannot Convey.* Stanford, Calif.: Stanford University Press, 2004.

Hopkins, Robert. "Re-Imagining, Re-Viewing, and Re-Touching." In *The Senses: Classic and Contemporary Perspectives,* edited by Fiona Macpherson, 261–84. New York: Oxford University Press, 2011.

Isaacson, Emily. "'[V]Olumes That/ I Prize above My Dukedome': The Archive, Digital Projects, and the Democratization of Knowledge Creation." Paper presented at the Shakespeare Association of America Annual Meeting. Atlanta, Ga., April 2017.

Macpherson, Fiona. "Introduction." In *The Senses: Classic and Contemporary Philosophical Perspectives,* 3–43. New York: Oxford University Press, 2011.

Mak, Bonnie. *How the Page Matters.* Studies in Book and Print Culture Series. Toronto: University of Toronto Press, 2011.

McGann, Jerome J. *The Textual Condition.* Princeton Studies in Culture/Power/History. Princeton, N.J.: Princeton University Press, 1991.

McGrail, Anne B. "Open Source in Open Access Environments: Choices and Necessities." *Minimal Computing: A Working Group of Go::DH.* February, 2017. Accessed January 21, 2020. http://go-dh.github.io/mincomp/thoughts/2017/02/17/mcgrail-choices/.

Miya, Chelsea, Laura Gerlitz, Kaitlyn Grant, Maryse Ndilu Kiese, Mengchi Sun, and Christina Boyles. "Manifesto for Student-Driven Research and Learning." In *People, Practice, Power: Digital Humanities outside the Center,* edited by Anne B. McGrail, Angel David Nieves, and Siobhan Senier. Minneapolis: University of Minnesota Press, 2021.

Moshenska, Joseph. *Feeling Pleasures: The Sense of Touch in Renaissance England.* 1st ed. Oxford: Oxford University Press, 2014.

Nelson, Brent, and Melissa Terras. "Introduction." In *Digitizing Medieval and Early Modern Material Culture,* 1–20. Toronto and Tempe, Ariz.: Iter: Gateway to the Middle Ages and Renaissance with Arizona Center for Medieval and Renaissance Studies, 2012.

Piper, Andrew. *Book Was There.* Chicago: University of Chicago Press, 2012.

Pressman, Jessica. *Digital Modernism: Making It New in New Media.* Modernist Literature & Culture. New York: Oxford University Press, 2014.

Risam, Roopika. "Stewarding Place: Digital Humanities at the Regional Comprehensive University." In *People, Practice, Power: Digital Humanities outside the Center,* edited by Anne B. McGrail, Angel David Nieves, and Siobhan Senier. Minneapolis: University of Minnesota Press, 2021.

Sayers, Jentery. "Minimal Definitions · Minimal Computing." *Global Outlook::Digital Humanities.* Accessed June 27, 2017. http://go-dh.github.io/mincomp/thoughts/2016/10/02/minimal-definitions/.

Shep, Sydney J. "Digital Materiality." In *A New Companion to Digital Humanities,* 322–30. Online: Wiley-Blackwell, 2015.

Stanley, Sarah Catherine. "Why Is Digital Humanities?" *Sarah Catherine Stanley* (blog), June 21, 2017. http://scatherinestanley.us/2017/06/why-is-dh.

Stommel, Jesse. "What Is Hybrid Pedagogy?" In *An Urgency of Teachers: The Work of Critical Digital Pedagogy.* Pressbooks, n.d. Accessed January 21, 2020. https://criticaldigitalpedagogy.pressbooks.com/chapter/what-is-hybrid-pedagogy/.

Tarte, Segolene M. "Digital Visual Representations in Papyrology: Implications on the Nature of Digital Artefacts." *Academia.Edu,* 2011. Accessed January 21, 2020. https://www.academia.edu/776645/Digital_Visual_Representations_in_Papyrology_Implications_on_the_Nature_of_Digital_Artefacts?auto=download.

Terras, Melissa. "Crowdsourcing in the Digital Humanities." In *A New Companion to Digital Humanities*, edited by Susan Schreibman, Ray Siemens, and John Unsworth. Malden, Mass.: John Wiley & Sons, Ltd., 2016.

Twycross, Meg. "Virtual Restoration and Manuscript Archaeology." In *The Virtual Representation of the Past,* edited by Mark Greengrass and Lorna M. Hughes, 23–47. Burlington, Vt.: Ashgate, 2008.

Wilcox, Jonathan. "Introduction: The Philology of Smell." In *Scraped, Stroked, and Bound: Materially Engaged Readings of Medieval Manuscripts,* 1–13. Turnhout, Belgium: Brepols, 2013.

Williams, George H. "Disability, Universal Design, and the Digital Humanities." In *Debates in the Digital Humanities.* Minneapolis: University of Minnesota Press, 2012. Accessed January 21, 2020. http://dhdebates.gc.cuny.edu/debates/text/44.

Manifesto for Student-Driven Research and Learning

CHELSEA MIYA, LAURA GERLITZ, KAITLYN GRANT,
MARYSE NDILU KIESE, MENGCHI SUN, AND CHRISTINA BOYLES

How do we train, support, and embolden the next generation of digital humanists?

Many departments housed within the arts and humanities engage with digital tools and technologies. Yet, not all students within the humanities have access to computational training or physical space to experiment with tools. Are focused digital humanities programs the only answer, or is there an alternative learning model that can better support students and encourage collaboration and experimentation? Students seeking digital training often gain hands-on experience through research assistantships. While there are certainly benefits to working on faculty-led digital projects, it also has its drawbacks. A recent study on "Student Labour and Training in the Digital Humanities" by Anderson et al. drew attention to how hierarchies of power become replicated within DH. The study found that faculty often perceive digital projects to be far more inclusive and collaborative than students, who reported feeling only minimally involved in the overall direction of the projects.[1]

Tanya Clement, whose work is cited in the cited study, notes that part of the problem is that students recruited to digital projects are often relegated to "tedious" and labor-intensive processing tasks and are excluded from the more intellectually involved work. For this reason, students become "unseen collaborators" whose contributions are not fully recognized.[2] As Anderson et al. point out, the problem of invisible labor is particularly acute in the digital humanities in which student work is buried under an additional layer of "hidden coding and programming."[3] The study also found that lack of formal training and unpaid work were other issues that contributed to student researchers feeling "frustrated" and "overload[ed]."[4] One of the chief recommendations of the study was to provide more opportunities for student-led DH projects.[5]

How then can institutions better support students engaged in digital research? In what ways can we encourage grassroots, self-directed learning?

To address these issues, graduate students from diverse backgrounds have come together to coauthor a manifesto on supporting student-driven research in the digital humanities. The document was initially drafted by graduate students and junior scholars at the New Scholars Seminar at DH 2016, an event that was jointly organized by centerNet, the Consortium of Humanities Centres and Institutes (CHCI), and the Kule Institute for Advanced Study (KIAS). The manifesto has since been reworked and expanded upon by the digital scholars student group at the University of Alberta.

Our manifesto draws attention to gaps in the current academic model and offers new approaches. While this manifesto was written with graduate students in mind, its central tenets apply to students at any stage of academia. Our concerns include access to and provision of shared spaces, access to training and technology, data preservation, and student organization.

Background

Manifestos are about self-definition, and the digital humanities' preoccupation with this subject is perhaps reflected in the many notable works produced in this genre, which include Digital Humanities Manifesto 2.0 (2008), The Paris Digital Humanities Manifesto (2011), A [S]creed for Digital Fiction (2010), and The Critical Engineering Manifesto (2011, 2016), among others. In different ways, these documents seek to announce, provoke, unsettle, and probe who we are as digital humanists.

As emerging digital scholars, we believe that the time to be bold and to be political is not over, particularly as key issues regarding student labor and learning have yet to be addressed satisfactorily. In fact, we argue that the precarious position of students within the digital humanities has largely been overlooked.

There is a precedent for student-authored digital humanities manifestos. In 2015, a group of graduate students at UCLA published A Student Collaborators' Bill of Rights. The document provides guidelines for the proper compensation and accreditation of student work. While A Student Collaborators' Bill of Rights drew much needed attention to the issue of labor inequality in the digital humanities, this speaks only to part of the problem. As emerging digital scholars, we are calling for grassroots institutional change that addresses not just how we work but how we learn.

We believe that students in the digital humanities should be given the opportunity to take charge of our own learning. In fact, we argue that the integrity of the digital humanities depends on it.

Program Development and Training

✊ We call for

Reconfiguring and rethinking the design of traditional humanities programs to create opportunities for digital training that combine practical, hands-on skills and theory.

Skills is a vexed word in the humanities. Daniel Allington, Sarah Brouillette, and David Golumbia argue that to talk about skills is to "sell out" to the neoliberal machine.[6] Others such as Alan Liu, while distancing themselves from Allington, Brouillette, and Golumbia, have also warned against losing sight of the humanities' true mission.[7] As students, we share their concerns that the humanities (digital and otherwise) needs to remain self-critical. However, we also find their position to be an insular one. What about those not served by the current system? What, furthermore, are we talking about when we talk about skills? Where do students fit within this debate?

The primary concerns of Allington, Brouillette, and Golumbia feel disconnected from the material realities of those entering the workforce. Practical skills might be looked down upon by tenured scholars. However, this is a position that we, as students, cannot afford to take.

Let us not forget that preparing for a job after graduation is many students' top priority. One might argue that hands-on skills, unlike theory, run the risk of becoming outmoded. Yet, what students seek is not necessarily specific programming languages like Python or Java but rather a general fluency, in other words, the ability to translate between humanities and computing. Our dynamism is part of what makes digital humanities grads valuable.

Yet, we also pursue DH for the pure joy of it. Contrary to Allington, Brouillette, and Golumbia, *skills* are more than a means-end to developing a *product*.[8] Skills signify play, experimentation, and teamwork. *To have skills* is a form of praise: to do the extraordinary and the unexpected.

We furthermore question the claim that the digital humanities places technical skills on a pedestal at the expense of other forms of knowledge. Proponents of critical tool theory such as Stephen Ramsay and Geoffrey Rockwell, among others, have pointed out the ways that theory and practice are naturally compatible.[9] Each furthers the understanding of the other, and together they can teach us how to think *both* critically and computationally.

We are likewise not advocating for skills over theory but instead for a better balance between the two. Our reason is that for all the fears of traditional scholarship's being displaced, as students we have experienced the opposite. If students doing DH work are under added "pressure," as Allington, Brouillette, and Golumbia claim, it is not due to an overemphasis on skills but to their neglect.

With regard to program development, we believe that the absence of skills training actively discourages technically innovative research, particularly for students outside of DH-focused programs. In a 2012 editorial for *The Chronicle of Higher Education*, Kathleen Fitzpatrick wrote of feeling hesitant to advise a graduate student to take the plunge and do a digital dissertation. Fitzpatrick's conflict arose from the knowledge that students in this position are at "risk of burnout from having to produce twice as much—traditional scholarship and digital projects—as their counterparts do."[10] "Real innovation requires risk," wrote Fitzpatrick, and yet students cannot afford to "do the risky thing" without support from their faculty and administration.[11]

Not all humanities students with an interest in computing should necessarily incorporate a digital project into their dissertation. Paige Morgan makes the point that there is value in being able to play with technology without the pressure of getting "serious."[12] Yet, even the privilege to "mess around" with computers is *just that,* and it requires that certain infrastructure such as the allocation of software, lab space, and training already be in place.

For many students, *practice* comes at a price.

The Anderson et al. study found that students in the digital humanities often feel the need to do "double duty." As the authors pointed out, even free online workshops require dedicated time and mental (and emotional) energy.[13] Thus, while students might desire additional training, they may find themselves unable to cope with the additional demands.

In downplaying skills in favor of traditional scholarship, students are also closed off from the possibility of non-ac and alt-ac careers. A 2013 survey by the University of Virginia Library's Scholarly Communication Institute found that not nearly enough is being done to promote opportunities outside of academia. Even though tenure-track jobs are on the decline, the survey participants reported receiving "very little advice or training for any other career."[14] We are in agreement with the study authors that students in the humanities are underinformed and undersupported with regard to pursuing alt-ac and alt-research (and non-ac/research) positions. As such, we assert the need for DH programs to partner with alt-ac professionals, particularly libraries, during their digital humanities training. Doing so will provide students with a hands-on understanding of alt-ac work, create stronger bonds between humanities departments and libraries, and emphasize the value of alt-ac scholarship.[15] We also strongly concur that the impact of programs cannot be measured without a more rigorous effort to "track the career outcomes" of former students and that, moreover, such data needs to be made open and accessible to students.[16] However, program design also plays a crucial role: when we devalue skills, we miss the manifold ways that scholarship translates into practice and vice versa.

Policy changes regarding digital dissertations continue to lag behind. Jentery Sayers has brought up the practical challenges of supervising digital thesis work, asking how "drafts" of a digital project might be stored, "circulated," and "commented upon"?[17] The wide range of areas of expertise encompassed by the digital humanities also creates unique complications.[18]

The new guidelines for evaluating digital scholarship produced by the Modern Language Association were rightly praised as a step forward in the right direction; the American Historical Association and the Canadian Society for Digital Humanities have released similar lists of recommendations.[19] Yet, disappointingly, these documents exclude any mention of graduate research.

The omission speaks volumes: when it comes to institutional supports for digital research, students are often treated as an afterthought.

In order to shift this line of thinking, we need to embrace practice and, above all, *build digital training into existing programs of study*. In addition to diversifying career streams and establishing guidelines for digital dissertations, other strategies to consider include making it easier for students in the humanities to take computer courses for credit; establishing practicum courses in partnership with organizations like libraries and digital centers; establishing more diverse types of degrees, such as certificate programs; and giving students the option to use programming skills to fulfill language requirements.

If we are to meet these challenges, students need to be part of the dialogue.

Just as importantly, we need to stop treating *skills* like a dirty word and realize that positing practice as incompatible with other types of scholarship often does students a disservice.

Data Management and Organization

✊ We call for

> Increased training and resources so students can engage in good research data management practices to allow for more student-created sustainable data in the scholarly sphere.

One of the foundations of sustainable research, which has yet to be discussed from the student perspective, is the practice of data management and organization. Institutions, typically through their libraries, play an important role in the gathering, analysis, dissemination, preservation, and showcasing of academic data and research, particularly for student researchers. Through research data management (RDM) a scholar documents how "data are collected, formatted, preserved and shared, as well as how existing datasets will be used and what new data will be created. These guidelines assist researchers in determining the costs, benefits and challenges of managing data."[20] Without high-quality management, data can be lost through hardware failure or technological obsolescence, sensitive information may not be stored or anonymized securely, and the research resulting from the data may be difficult to replicate. Additionally, a growing number of funding agencies require researchers to comply with their data management planning policies.[21] These challenges are not exclusive to students. However, as the main support system available to students, it is crucial that universities provide them with the education and skills necessary to properly manage their data.

RDM offers many necessary benefits to student researchers. It allows them to build skills and experience in documenting the step-by-step process of gathering and analyzing data, helping them to gain a better understanding of the research practices and methodologies that they are using. This act of documentation improves the overall organization of a study and allows for future replicability to confirm that the results were reached. This in turn is a way for students (new researchers) lacking the legitimacy that comes with having been published to prove that their study is sound. RDM also serves to protect their intellectual property and ensure that they receive proper accreditation through citations. Students can learn valuable methods for ensuring that their data is secure and anonymized, if necessary, and how to document the methods that they use. Discussions of security and anonymity encourage a student to consider the ethics surrounding their data, a complex issue in itself, and practical skills such as understanding how to acquire data through Freedom of Information Act (FOIA) requests are also cultivated. Finally, RDM plans that are open access help promote student research to the academic community at large.

Training for all facets of RDM, including facets such as data visualization, processing, and cleanup, needs to occur for student researchers; but what form should it take? Consultations with RDM staff offer face-to-face assistance with the added benefit of one-on-one time with someone who is trained to handle unique RDM issues. Online guides, although not offering the in-person training of courses or workshops, can be useful as quick references or as an aid to students who may lack the time to dedicate to scheduled arrangements. Institutional courses offer the most structure, whereas workshops are more flexible, require less time to complete, and are administratively easier to arrange than a class that requires registration. Currently, libraries are the most common place to find such training and expertise, often with the added benefit of librarians who are strong advocates for students and student research. However, with the growing use of digital data sets in research and the importance of following RDM best practices, universities on the whole need to take a more prominent role in supporting students in this field.[22]

Universities should work to encourage student participation in workshops by being explicit in their registration language; a workshop may appear to be geared toward staff or to be staff-focused but in reality allows students to attend. If a university does not organize workshops on RDM, they need to make external training opportunities known. Training opportunities for faculty and staff need to be expanded to support students as well. As supervisors and professors, faculty need to be aware of new and developing trends in DH to provide an additional academic support system. Students must be free to independently pursue their own projects, and faculty need to be reliable and approachable for seeking assistance and advice in DH training and research. In the absence of university support, students need to be able to seek training through other avenues, such as by finding external opportunities through other educational programs or by organizing their peers to share their knowledge via workshops, unconferences, and clubs.

Digital storage space is another aspect of data management in which students require support of their institution. Some may offer their own hosted server space or have cross-institutional or federal support with external organizations that provide these services, such as (for Canadian institutions) Compute Canada or (for American institutions) the Extreme Science and Engineering Discovery Environment (XSEDE), but students are not often given explicit access. Students may not be mentioned in the policies and guidelines; they may require faculty sponsorship regardless of the legitimacy of the data; or they simply might not be aware of any organizations that could assist in data storage. Universities must make their affiliations known to students and handle student usage of these services in a manner that does not force them to rely on faculty sponsorship. Otherwise, they are promoting a culture of dependence, in which student research is not considered important.

Repositories are digital spaces provided by an organization, normally the organization's library system, for the purpose of preserving and showcasing the intellectual output of those affiliated with it. Student involvement in a repository is often limited to the student's institution, and often only in the long-term, secure archival storage of theses and dissertations. This kind of secure storage and display for students is an absolute necessity for research beyond this category in order to step into the role of a professional academic. If a student's only interaction with a repository is the depositing of his or her thesis, the student loses out on making that research used in both academia and professional development capacities known; remains one step removed from the preservation of that research; and will develop poor preservation habits as that person steps further into his or her professional career. The benefits of using a repository are massive for students: they offer permanent identifiers for research and discoverability in search engines, a legitimate space for long-term preservation, and an increase in citations and credibility.

Consider the following: a student spends years on professional development, making presentations at conferences, engaging in poster sessions, and running workshops for fellow students. What happens to this material after the conference or workshop ends? In many cases the only indication of the student's efforts is a note in a program which may or may not be available online. If the student is lucky, the abstract may be searchable. Those physical presentations, be they slideshows, posters, recordings or other forms of media, are lost to the academic ether. Repositories therefore have an obligation to save this research and make it discoverable to the academic community at large.

This call to action extends beyond the university to grant agencies and even to governments. We may be students, but the archiving of our data does not have to be tethered to our academic institution.[23] We demand that our research and data be recognized as important and significant and that the organizations in place to provide these services to professional scholars support us in the same manner.

Digital Centers

✊ We call for

> Digital centers to be made more democratic and inclusive by making them more accessible and open to students.

Often digital centers are created with the needs of established scholars in mind. However, we argue that emerging digital scholars—a group that includes undergraduates, graduates, and postdocs—need a space of our own. In other words, we would like students to become more involved in how digital centers are designed and how they are run.

Collaboration is a necessity in the digital humanities, and this has opened up new opportunities for graduate students who are often recruited as research assistants. The problem, as Amy Earhart, Tanya Clement, and Anderson et al. have all pointed out, is that the relationship between the team members is more hierarchical and less symbiotic than one might hope.[24]

We want to shift this dynamic by rethinking the uses of these spaces. Amy Earhart and Richard Lane have each used the scientific space of the laboratory as a model for "imagining new forms of practices."[25] But another way to think of centers is as *communal* spaces that shape and are shaped by certain social structures. One might consider to what various uses are digital centers put and how these spaces are perceived differently by the multiple communities they serve, including the student community.

One possible model is to envision digital centers as adaptable spaces designed to meet a variety of students' digital scholarship needs. At Trinity College in Hartford, Connecticut, the Digital Scholarship Studio is a reservable space that hosts a variety of events for students and the public, including mapathons, transcribe-a-thons, and edit-a-thons. This model encourages students to take ownership of the space both by allowing them to utilize it as a study space, meeting room, or alternate classroom, and by inviting them into the space for events that appeal to the digital humanities community at large.

Developing centers and policies that focus on care-based practices would also encourage grassroots movements and community engagement between digital scholarship centers and those who utilize them. As Bethany Nowviskie points out, care-based practices are "meant to reorient the practitioner's understanding in two ways. The first is toward an appreciation of context, interdependence, and vulnerability—of fragile, little things and their interrelation. The second is an orientation . . . toward personal, worldly action and response."[26] Incorporating care into our regular vocabulary in DH would encourage equal collaboration in projects and ensure that those who require, or want, skills and professional development have opportunities to do just that. There are many ways to become more care focused, including the writing of manifestos, an activity that helps groups such as ours "articulate its shared values and understand its individual members' needs" and creates the opportunity for action by facilitating "real peer-to-peer collaboration" that transcends the "boundaries of academic status and rank."[27]

In this spirit of encouraging collaborative, care-based practice, we call on scholars, librarians, and administrators in digital centers to involve students in the strategic planning of digital centers. Digital centers and labs act as pipelines for the formal and informal negotiation processes that exist between junior digital scholars and faculty members, in relation to the activities of learning new skills, building networks, and gaining leadership and professional experience.[28] Consulting with students in the design and development of a center can help create spaces that better meet the needs of those they service. Julie Friddell makes the point that with regard to cultivating an environment that is conducive to collaboration, "enhancing human interoperability is just as important as technical interoperability."[29] Opening up a dialogue between students and administration helps build the mutual trust and familiarity on which digital research is built.

Allowing students to have more use of these facilities, whether as a makerspace or for hosting students' clubs, can help to integrate digital centers more fully into the campus community. Showcasing student projects, both onsite and online, can likewise inspire future digital scholars. Digital centers can also benefit students by opening up information channels. Departments are not always effective at sharing news and events that might have cross-disciplinary appeal. Digital centers can help overcome the silo effect by serving as a billboard for digital humanities-related news and events.

Some institutions are already taking steps in these directions. The Digital Scholarship Commons at the University of Victoria is one of a growing number of student-centered spaces. One of its stated aims is to "act as a hub for students to come together to share knowledge and to collaborate."[30] The University of Virginia Scholars' Lab, home to the Praxis program for graduate students, is another example.[31]

We argue that digital centers as "public" or communal spaces are also inherently political. These shared spaces give students from multiple fields the opportunity to exchange ideas and build relationships. This sense of community is especially important for students from departments that may not have a strong digital presence and, as a result, might be in need of additional mentorship and support in addition to tools and training. Furthermore, as we found with the Digital Scholars student group, having a central space can be essential in mobilizing students across multiple departments, which in turn puts us in a stronger position to articulate demands for change. Institutions with a dedicated center are likewise better placed to acknowledge and listen to those demands and administer supports where needed. Finally, digital centers can help academic institutions to become less insular by modeling open scholarship practices at the student level, creating opportunities for emerging scholars to communicate their research to the larger public.

Student Organization

✊ We call for

> Students to work together to make our learning experience more encouraging and
> less daunting.

Although we hope that this manifesto can help to better inform institutional practices, we are also aware that top-down change is often slow to come. Therefore, in this section we speak directly to our peers.

Grassroots initiatives, organized and led by students, are one way that we, as the next generation of digital scholars, can take charge of our learning and experiment with new organizational structures. In recent years, there have been notable student-run research projects. UBC's From Stone to Screen is a digitization project that is run entirely by graduate students in the history and classics department.[32] On the publishing side, Inciting Sparks is a multimedia platform developed by graduate students for posting blogs, videos, and online exhibits related to arts and humanities research.[33] There is also a growing number of student-run maker spaces, such as Five College Digital Humanities' GlowLime Games student game development studio and the University of North Carolina's Student Maker Network MakNet.[34] These projects are examples of how the mobilization of students can play a crucial role in the future of the digital humanities.

At our own institution, we have had considerable success with the Digital Scholars student group (DSUA). The University of Alberta is unique in that it has one of the oldest digital humanities-focused masters programs. Yet, when we started the DSUA, our university did not have a digital center. As such, we had the opportunity and the impetus to create a "space of our own," which came to be centered on student-led training.

Students have never been more interested in doing digital dissertations and projects. In our experience, this is true in arts departments across the board. Our own student group is fiercely interdisciplinary, and our diverse membership includes students from humanities computing, linguistics, the School of Library and Information Science, English and film studies, and many more. We have also found many unexpected allies including faculty, library staff, and administration.

Much of our efforts are put into connecting students with resources both on and off campus. A growing number of organizations, for instance, offer computing workshops free of charge or at heavily subsidized cost and we have worked with Ladies Learning Code, Compute Canada, and Edmonton Media Hive to promote their events to students. Last year, we also appealed to the Digital Humanities Summer Institute to create a special scholarship for student members of our group. Through these efforts, we have been able to cultivate relationships and share information and skills across disciplinary and institutional bounds.

By stepping into leadership roles, students build skills in areas like project management, communication, business, and graphic design, as well as gain the opportunity to network with faculty, instructors, and staff. As teacher-mentors in training, we learn how to identify key concepts, break challenging material into layperson's terms, and troubleshoot unexpected issues.

Building supportive networks that extend beyond the classroom helps students to maintain and deepen computational knowledge over the long term, particularly as students can feel more comfortable coming to peers for help. Some institutions run summer camp–style training sessions just for students with upper-level graduate students involved as counselors and organizers.[35] Digital centers could follow the example of campus writing centers and hire students to act as mentors and tutors, or at least designate space for study groups and student-run code-along sessions.[36]

Despite the benefits of grassroots, student-led initiatives, this strategy has its limitations. The success of an organization like the DSUA depends on the energy and enthusiasm of student members and on the support of faculty and instructors, and we are cautious of demanding too much from those whose time and labor are already stretched.[37] Thus, while we hope this manifesto can inspire students in the digital humanities to form organizations of their own, such grassroots efforts must be sustained and supported by institutional reform.

The blind spot of university administration can be partly attributed to how students are viewed in relation to the larger academic community. Ray Siemens has often spoken about DH as a "community of practice" defined by shared methodologies. Yet, past attempts to *map* the digital humanities, such as Willard McCarty and Harold Short's often-cited Methodological Commons, are limited in that they tend to be oriented toward disciplines and to overlook communities that are not defined by field and yet are still distinct.

What organizations like the DSUA, From Stone to Screen, Inciting Sparks, GlowLime Games, and MakNet demonstrate is that students indeed operate as a distinct community within the digital humanities with its own unique practices, goals, and perspectives. Ray Siemens has spoken about the need for "self determination" in the digital humanities: in other words, the need to "grow our own" and "learn to do our own stunts."[38] As students, we too need to develop our own ways of doing things and in the process revolutionize and reimagine the field from the bottom up.

Notes

This chapter was written with contributions from Monika Biesaga, Paul Gifford, and Greg Whistance-Smith.

1. Anderson et al., "Student Labour and Training," para. 24. http://www.digitalhu manities.org/dhq/vol/10/1/000233/000233.html.

2. Clement, "Text Analysis, Data Mining, and Visualizations," para. 29.

3. Anderson et al., "Student Labour and Training," para. 25.

4. Anderson et al., "Student Labour and Training," para. 14–15, 19.

5. Anderson et al., "Student Labour and Training," para. 32–33.

6. Allington, Brouillette, and Golumbia, "Neoliberal Tools (and Archives)," https://lareviewofbooks.org/article/neoliberal-tools-archives-political-history-digital-humanities/#.

7. Regarding distancing himself from Allington, Brouillette, and Golumbia, see Liu's post (@alanyliu), Twitter, "in working inside the neoliberal university as way to differentiate it from other kinds of neoliberalism, such difference-making", May 2, 2016, https://twitter.com/alanyliu/status/727293053006802944. Regarding his warning, see Liu, "State of Digital Humanities: A Report and a Critique," http://journals.sagepub.com/doi/pdf/10.1177/1474022211427364.

8. Allington, Brouillette, and Golumbia, "Neoliberal Tools (and Archives)."

9. Ramsay and Rockwell, "Developing Things."

10. Kathleen Fitzpatrick, "Do 'The Risky Thing' in Digital Humanities." http://www.chronicle.com/article/Do-the-Risky-Thing-in/129132.

11. Fitzpatrick, "Do 'The Risky Thing' in Digital Humanities."

12. Paige Morgan, "How to Get a Digital Humanities Project off the Ground." http://www.paigemorgan.net/how-to-get-a-digital-humanities-project-off-the-ground/.

13. Anderson et al., "Student Labour and Training," para. 14–15.

14. Rogers, "Humanities Unbound." https://libraopen.lib.virginia.edu/public_view/fb4948446.

15. For a more in-depth discussion of alt-act professionals as allies and collaborators, see the chapter in this volume by Christina Boyles, "Intersectionality and Infrastructure: Toward a Critical Digital Humanities."

16. Rogers, "Humanities Unbound," 4.

17. Jentery Sayers, "Digital Humanities (DH) and/in the Dissertation." For further discussion of digital dissertations, also see Visconti, "Evaluating Non-Traditional Digital Humanities Dissertations."

18. For a discussion of the complications of hiring and promotion in DH, see Cosgrave et al., "Evaluating Digital Scholarship."

19. Modern Language Association, "Guidelines for Evaluating Work"; American Historical Association, "Guidelines for the Professional Evaluation"; and Canadian Society for Digital Humanities, "Evaluating DH Scholarship: Guidelines."

20. Government of Canada, "Tri-Agency Statement of Principles," para. 10.

21. Cox and Pinfield, "Research Data Management and Libraries," para. 1.

22. One university-wide method is to enact open access mandates, such as Simon Fraser University's Open Access Policy (https://www.lib.sfu.ca/help/publish/scholarly-publishing/open-access-policy). However, such mandates are most impactful when researchers are on board with the message before it becomes a requirement.

23. SocArXiv (https://socopen.org/) is an example of a subject repository aiming to make social science research, regardless of the institution from which it originates, open access.

24. See Clement, "Text Analysis"; Earhart, "Digital Humanities as a Laboratory; and Anderson et al., "Student Labour and Training."

25. Earhart, "Digital Humanities as a Laboratory," 399. See also Lane, *Big Humanities.*

26. Bethany Nowviskie, blog post "On Capacity and Care," October 4, 2015, http://nowviskie.org/2015/on-capacity-and-care/.

27. Nowviskie, "On Capacity and Care."

28. Joan Lippincott, Harriette Hemmasi, and Viv Lewis, "Trends in Digital Scholarship Centers," http://er.educause.edu/articles/2014/6/trends-in-digital-scholarship-centers.

29. Friddell, "How Do We Support Collaboration?" See also Dana L. Church, et al., "The Northern Voice: Listening to Indigenous and Northern Perspectives on Management of Data in Canada"; and Holly Handley, "A Network Model for Human Interoperability."

30. See the University of Victoria's Digital Scholarship Commons' Makerspace, https://onlineacademiccommunity.uvic.ca/dsc/about/.

31. See the University of Virginia's Praxis Program, http://praxis.scholarslab.org/.

32. See UBC's From Stone to Screen, https://cnrs.ubc.ca/research/stone-to-screen -project/.

33. See Inciting Sparks, https://incitingsparks.org/.

34. See Five College Digital Humanities' GlowLime Games and UNC's MakNet, http://glowlime.com/; http://maknet.web.unc.edu/.

35. See Cornell University's Summer Graduate Fellowship (https://blogs.cornell.edu /sgfdh/) and Illinois Tech's Digital Humanities Summer Camp for high school students cotaught by graduate students (https://blogs.illinois.edu/view/7822/598952).

36. For instance, the Digital Scholarship Studio at Trinity College recruits Student Technology Assistants (STAs) to provide technical support for their peers.

37. See Spencer Keralis, who points out in "Milking the Deficit Internship" that students can be pressured into giving away their labor with exploitive practices disguised as "engagement" and "collaboration."

38. Ray Siemens, "Communities of Practice, the Methodological Commons, and Digital Self-Determination in the Humanities," para. 29, http://doi.org/10.16995/ dscn.31.

Bibliography

Allington, Daniel, Sarah Brouillette, and David Golumbia. "Neoliberal Tools (and Archives): A Political History of Digital Humanities." *Los Angeles Review of Books,* May 1, 2016. https://lareviewofbooks.org/article/neoliberal-tools-archives-political -history-digital-humanities/#.

American Academy of Arts and Sciences. "Advanced Degrees in the Humanities." *Humanities Indicators.* August 2017. https://humanitiesindicators.org/content/indicatordoc .aspx?i=44.

Anderson, Katrina, Lindsey Bannister, Janey Dodd, Deanna Fong, Michelle Levy, and Lindsey Seatter. "Student Labour and Training in Digital Humanities." *Digital Humanities Quarterly* 10, no. 1 (2016). http://www.digitalhumanities.org/dhq/vol/10/1/000233/000233.html.

Bell, Alice, Astrid Ensslin, Dave Ciccoricco, Hans Rustad, Jess Laccetti, and Jessica Pressman. "A [S]creed for Digital Fiction." *Electronic Book Review,* March 7, 2010. https://electronicbookreview.com/essay/a-screed-for-digital-fiction/.

Canadian Society for Digital Humanities. "Evaluating DH Scholarship: Guidelines." December 31, 2015. https://csdh-schn.org/296-2/.

Church, Dana L., Julie E. Friddell, Ellsworth F. LeDrew, Gabrielle Alix, and Garret Reid. "The Northern Voice: Listening to Indigenous and Northern Perspectives on Management of Data in Canada." *Data Science Journal,* 16 (2017): 48. https://doi.org/10.5334/dsj-2017-048.

Clement, Tanya. "Text Analysis, Data Mining, and Visualizations in Literary Scholarship." In *Literary Studies in the Digital Age: An Evolving Anthology.* New York: Modern Language Association, 2013.

Cordell, Ryan. "How Not to Teach Digital Humanities." *Ryan Cordell* (blog), February 1, 2015. http://ryancordell.org/teaching/how-not-to-teach-digital-humanities/.

Cosgrave, Michael, Anna Dowling, Lynn Harding, Róisín O'Brien, and Olivia Rohan. "Evaluating Digital Scholarship: Experiences in New Programmes at an Irish University." *Journal of Digital Humanities* 1, no. 4 (2012). http://journalofdigitalhumanities.org/1-4/evaluating-digital-scholarship-experiences-in-new-programmes-at-an-irish-university/.

Cox, Andrew M., and Stephen Pinfield. "Research Data Management and Libraries: Current Activities and Future Priorities." *Journal of Librarianship And Information Science* 46, no. 4 (2013): 299–316.

Dacos, Marin. "Manifesto for the Digital Humanities." *THATCamp Paris,* March 26, 2011. Updated January 25, 2012. http://tcp.hypotheses.org/411.

Di Pressi, Haley, Stephanie Gorman, Miriam Posner, Raphael Sasayama, and Tori Schmitt, with contributions from Roderic Crooks, Megan Driscoll, Amy Earhart, Spencer Keralis, Tiffany Naiman, and Todd Presner. "A Student Collaborators' Bill of Rights." UCLA Digital Humanities, 2015. https://humtech.ucla.edu/news/a-student-collaborators-bill-of-rights/.

Earhart, Amy. "The Digital Humanities as a Laboratory." In *Between Humanities and the Digital,* edited by Patrik Svensson and David Theo Goldberg, 391–400. Cambridge, Mass.: MIT, 2015. https://dhtoph.files.wordpress.com/2015/07/earhartdhaslaboratory.pdf.

Fitzpatrick, Kathleen. "Do 'The Risky Thing' in Digital Humanities." *The Chronicle of Higher Education,* September 25, 2011. http://www.chronicle.com/article/Do-the-Risky-Thing-in/129132.

Friddell, Julie. "How Do We Support Collaboration and Strong DRI User Communities?" (breakaway session). The Leadership Council for Digital Research Infrastructure Summit. Chestnut Conference Centre, June 27, 2017.

GC Digital Fellows. "What Is a Digital Dissertation?" *CUNY Academic Commons.* Updated December 2020. https://digitalfellows.commons.gc.cuny.edu/digital-dissertations/.

George Mason University. "Digital Dissertation Guidelines." *History and Art History, College of Humanities and Social Sciences.* http://historyarthistory.gmu.edu/graduate /phd-history/digital-dissertation-guidelines.

Government of Canada. "Tri-Agency Statement of Principles on Digital Data Management." 2016. http://www.science.gc.ca/eic/site/063.nsf/eng/h_83F7624E.html?OpenDocument.

Handley, Holly A. H. "A Network Model for Human Interoperability." *Human Factors* 56, no. 2 (2014): 349–360. https://doi.org/10.1177/0018720813493640.

Keralis, Spencer. "Milking the Deficit Internship." *Disrupting the Digital Humanities,* January 6, 2016. http://www.disruptingdh.com/milking-the-deficit-internship/.

Lane, Richard J. *The Big Humanities: Digital Humanities/Digital Laboratories.* London: Routledge, 2017.

Lave, Jean, and Etienne Wenger. *Situated Learning: Legitimate Peripheral Participation.* Cambridge: Cambridge University Press, 1991.

Liu, Alan. "The State of the Digital Humanities: A Report and a Critique." *Arts & Humanities in Higher Education* 11: 8–41. http://journals.sagepub.com/doi/pdf/10.1177 /1474022211427364.

Modern Language Association. "Guidelines for Evaluating Work in Digital Humanities and Digital Media." *MLA,* 2012. https://www.mla.org/About-Us/Governance/Committees /Committee-Listings/Professional-Issues/Committee-on-Information-Technology /Guidelines-for-Evaluating-Work-in-Digital-Humanities-and-Digital-Media.

Modern Language Association. *Report on the MLA Job Information List, 2015–16.* MLA Office of Research, January 2017. https://www.mla.org/content/download/58256 /1846498/RptJIL15_16.pdf.

Morgan, Paige. "How to Get a Digital Humanities Project off the Ground." *Paige Morgan* (blog), June 5, 2014. http://www.paigemorgan.net/how-to-get-a-digital-humanities -project-off-the-ground/.

Oliver, Julian, Gordan Savičić, and Danja Vasiliev. "The Critical Engineering Manifesto." The Critical Engineering Working Group, October 2011. http://conceptlab.com/criti calmaking/PDFs/CriticalMaking2012Hertz-Manifestos-pp41-OliverSavicicVasiliev -TheCriticalEngineeringManifesto.pdf.

Ramsay, Stephen, and Geoffrey Rockwell, "Developing Things: Notes toward an Epistemology of Building in the Digital Humanities." *Debates in the Digital Humanities* (2012), 75–84. https://dhdebates.gc.cuny.edu/read/untitled-88c11800-9446-469b -a3be-3fdb36bfbd1e/section/c733786e-5787-454e-8f12-e1b7a85cac72#ch05.

Rogers, Katina. "Humanities Unbound: Supporting Careers and Scholarship beyond the Tenure Track." *Scholarly Communication Institute,* 2013. https://libraopen.lib.virginia .edu/public_view/fb4948446.

Sayers, Jentery. "DH and/in the Dissertation." Jentery Sayers, Annotation of Opening Remarks. MLA Convention, January 7, 2016. https://github.com/jentery/mla16/blob /master/dhsiDissertationOpeningRemarks.md.

Schnapp, Jeffrey, Todd Presner, Peter Lunenfeld, and Johanna Drucker. "Digital Humanities Manifesto 2.0." *Multitudes* 59, no. 2 (2015): 181–95.

Siemens, Ray. "Communities of Practice, the Methodological Commons, and Digital Self-Determination in the Humanities." *Digital Studies/Le champ numérique* (2014). http://doi.org/10.16995/dscn.31.

Sula, Chris Alen, and S. E. Hackney. "A Survey of Digital Humanities Programs." *The Journal of Interactive Technology and Pedagogy* 11 (May 2017). https://jitp.commons.gc.cuny.edu/a-survey-of-digital-humanities-programs/.

Visconti, Amanda. "Evaluating Non-Traditional Digital Humanities Dissertations." *Amanda Visconti* (blog), September 30, 2014. http://literaturegeek.com/2014/09/30/evaluating-non-traditional-digital-humanities-dissertations.

Warwick, Claire. "Institutional Models for the Digital Humanities." In *Digital Humanities in Practice,* edited by Claire Warwick, Melissa Terras, and Julianne Nyhan, 193–216. London: Facet, 2012.

Centering First-Generation Students in the Digital Humanities

JAMILA MOORE PEWU AND ANELISE HANSON SHROUT

Digital humanities pedagogy has been heralded as a way to undercut the *digital divide* and combat structural inequality within the academy.[1] However, when we imagine *typical* college-level DH students, or at least the DH students who are conjured by much of the writing on DH pedagogy, they are overwhelmingly beneficiaries of structural privilege.[2] We expect these students to be enrolled in school full time and to finish a BA, BS, or BFA in four years. We expect them to be familiar with academic norms and to be fluent in cutting-edge technologies. We expect them to be conversant in the vernaculars of online communication. We also imagine that they are eager to use these digital tools to "disrupt" the academy.[3] These characteristics are typical of American students who possess significant social capital, who inherited educational expertise from their parents, who come from privileged backgrounds, and who are neurotypical. These are not characteristics shared by all graduate or undergraduate students.

Typical DH students are also often assumed to attend elite institutions that are equipped with makerspaces, academic programmers, and the funding needed to execute large-scale research projects. This might include DH programs housed at large research universities or infrastructurally rich small liberal arts colleges. In either of these educational environments, students benefit from DH courses with lower student-to-faculty ratios and bespoke seminars run by faculty experts with access to intensive training that allows them to support nontraditional academic projects.[4] These characteristics are typical of institutions with access to sufficient capital to offer robust infrastructural support for DH. They are not, however, characteristics shared by all U.S. institutions of higher education.

In fact, most United States–based college students do not attend institutions that fit these *typical* DH models. As Roopika Risam reminds us in her essay in this volume, the growing plurality of students enrolled in U.S. colleges and universities attend for-profit colleges, community colleges, regional public comprehensive universities, and minority-serving institutions (MSIs). Most of these students enter college without the social capital that comes from having college-educated parents. The majority of college-enrolled students in the United States are the first in their families to attend college. This means that most U.S. college students do not occupy educational spaces that are assumed to be infrastructurally conducive to DH pedagogy.

This essay explores what this distance between assumption and reality means for DH pedagogy. We argue that the actual (rather than imagined) DH educational landscape requires new infrastructures including curricula and pedagogical theories that center, rather than merely accommodate, first-generation and minority students at *nontraditional* DH institutions. We contend that as practitioners of DH pedagogy, we must rethink our understanding of infrastructure and institutional capital. Namely, we should not allow infrastructural scarcity to drive pedagogy and prevent us from teaching DH theory when there is a lack of IT support. Likewise, programs and institutions facing infrastructural scarcity should not focus on replicating the DH structures of more privileged institutions, because such an approach negates the rich cultural and technological capital that first-generation and other marginalized students bring to our institutions. It also risks, as Sasha Costanza-Chock recently articulated in her call for design justice, reproducing a "matrix of domination (white supremacy, heteropatriarchy, capitalism and settler colonialism)."[5] Instead, we must embrace alternative understandings of access to infrastructure.

We begin this work by describing the demographic profile of higher education in the United States and sketching how our own institution fits within that profile. We then discuss the implications of this landscape for DH pedagogy, infrastructure, and theory. In particular we focus on first-generation learning practices, the digital divide and digital "nativity," and decolonized histories of DH. We close with some concrete solutions and best practices derived from our experiences administering DH pedagogy at our own minority-serving institution. We hope that these approaches will help both to integrate first-generation students and their diverse experiences into the extant DH community and to push that community toward a more expansive and less infrastructurally limited conception of DH.

Our DH Students: A Demographic Snapshot

In 2012, Matt Gold provocatively asked:

> What can digital humanities mean for cash-poor colleges with underserved student populations that have neither the staffing nor the expertise to complete DH projects on their own? What responsibilities do funders have to attempt to achieve a more equitable distribution of funding? Most importantly, what is the digital humanities missing when its professional discourse does not include the voices of the institutionally subaltern?[6]

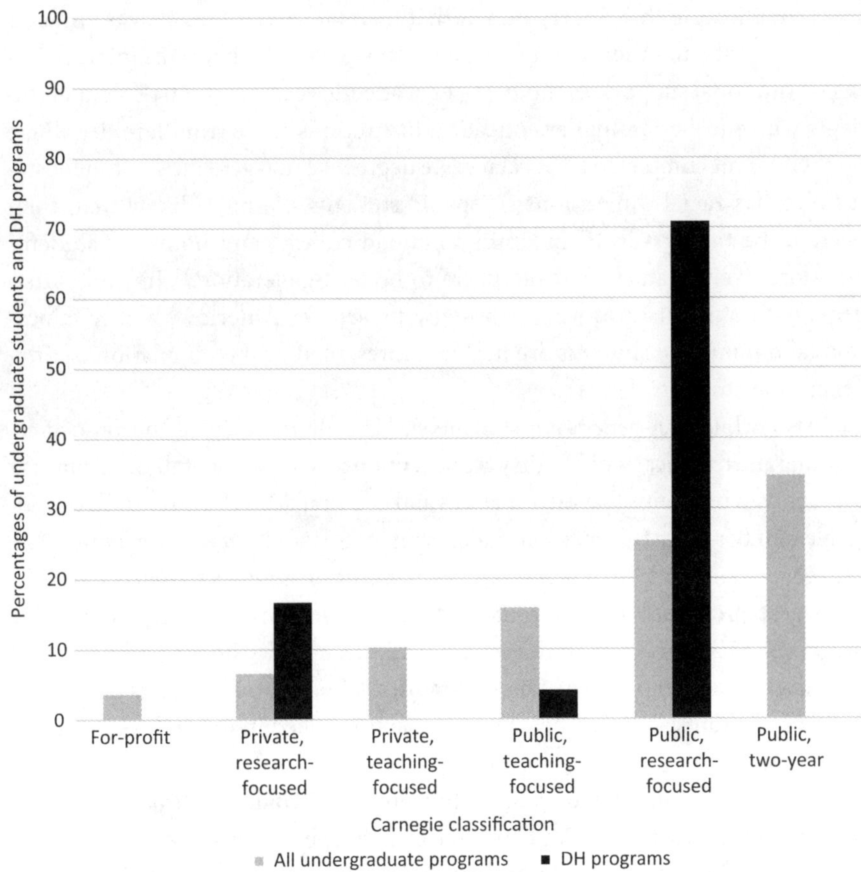

Figure 19.1. Percentage of students enrolled in various Carnegie Classifications of Institutions and percentage of digital humanities programs housed in each classification category. This data represents institutions in the United States. Source: Data compiled from *Carnegie Classifications 2018 Public Data File,* http://carnegieclassifications.iu.edu/downloads/CCIHE2018-PublicData File.xlsx, March 10, 2020; and Hackney, Cunningham, and Sula, "A Survey of Digital Humanities Programs."

The majority of college students in the United States fall under Gold's rubric of "institutional subalternity."[7] For instance (see figure 19.1), in 2015, 36 percent of U.S. undergraduates attended public two-year colleges; 15 percent attended public institutions with a teaching focus; and 27 percent attended public or private research-intensive universities.[8] A 2017 survey of DH programs found that the vast majority of American institutions offering digital humanities degrees, certificates, minors, and concentrations were housed either at research-focused universities or private liberal arts colleges.[9] In sum, the distribution of U.S. undergraduates does not reflect the distribution of American DH programs; and institutions that serve the majority of our students do not offer learning experiences that might enhance digital literacy and combat the digital divide.

Complicating this discrepancy is that the majority of U.S. college students do not inherit from their parents the educational capital that is useful in claiming institutional support. In the 2011–12 academic year, nearly 60 percent of students who enrolled in higher education institutions came from families where neither parent completed a baccalaureate degree.[10] First-generation student status also has racial dimensions. Hispanic students are more likely than their peers to be the first in their family to attend college, and nonwhite students are more likely than their white peers to be first-generation.[11] In short, first-generation students are overwhelmingly present in American higher education, and nonwhite students are heavily represented in the population of first-generation students.

Also, while first-generation students are heavily represented in non-degree-granting and technical schools, they are not confined to those institutions. Four-year colleges with programs that offer master's and doctoral degrees also enroll a considerable number of first-generation students. In the 2011–12 survey (see figure 19.2), first-generation students represented 69.1 percent of students enrolled in associate degree programs; 75.8 percent of students enrolled in non-degree-granting programs; 65.3 percent of students enrolled in technical schools; 50.4 percent of students enrolled in baccalaureate programs; 48.8 percent of students enrolled in master's programs; and 36.2 percent of students enrolled in research and doctoral programs.

The growing majority of college students in the United States are also overwhelmingly represented at MSIs, which include tribal colleges and universities, historically Black colleges and universities (HBCUs), Asian American and Pacific Islander serving institutions (AAPISIs), and Hispanic-Serving Institutions (HSIs). While HBCUs have received varying levels of private and federal support since the late nineteenth century, some Tribal Colleges and Universities (TCUs), HSIs, and AAPISIs are less than thirty years old and were born from demographic changes within certain regions, shifts in job needs, and increased access to higher education.[12] Collectively, these schools educate 40 percent of currently enrolled underrepresented students.[13] Beginning in 2020, "approximately 43% of the U.S. population will be comprised of minority populations."[14] These statistics reflect that institutions serving minority and first-generation college students already numerically dominate the higher-education landscape in the United States.[15]

Many of the students who attend these institutions have received little parental knowledge about what to expect when completing their degrees. As a result, they lack access to the technological capital that we assume of first-time DH students. Thus, just as higher education is teeming with initiatives and efforts to *diversify the professoriate*, so too must we think critically about how to mobilize the cultural capital of this incumbent generation to ensure long-term diversity within DH. This means developing pedagogical practices that increasingly center the students that MSI and nontraditional institutions serve.

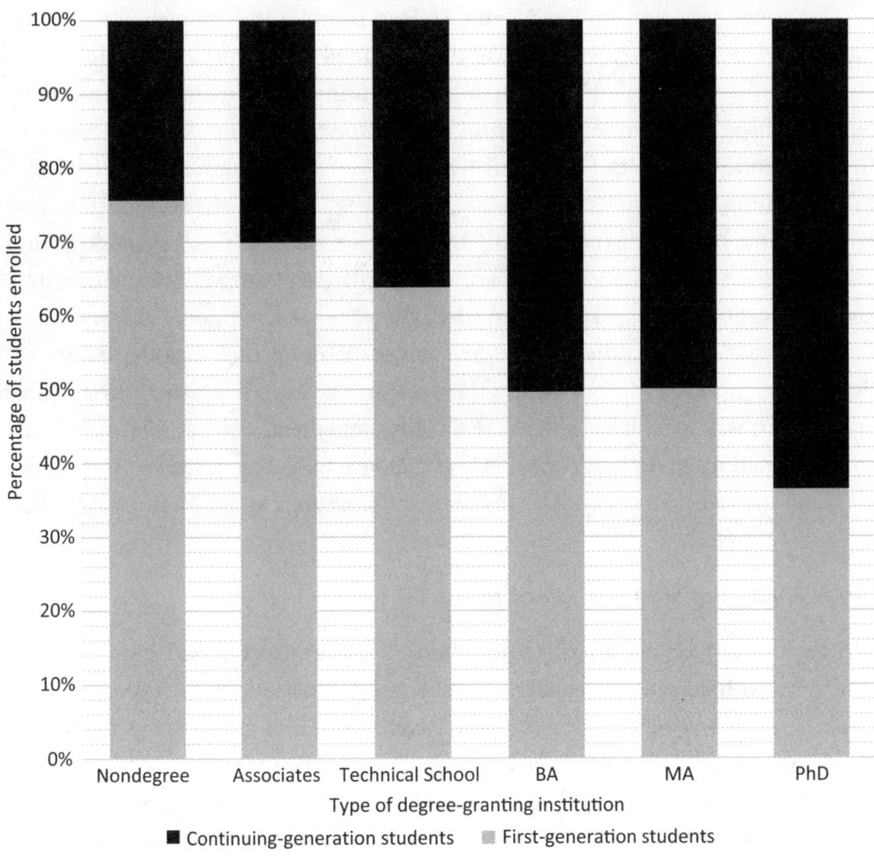

Figure 19.2. Proportion of first- and continuing-generation students in different categories of degree-granting programs in the United States. Source: Data compiled from U.S. Department of Education, National Center for Education Statistics, *2012/17 Beginning Postsecondary Students Longitudinal Study (BPS:12/17).*

At California State University Fullerton (CSUF) in the 2016–17 academic year, of the over forty thousand students, more than twelve thousand (about 30 percent) of all enrolled students were first generation. In the College of Humanities and Social Sciences where the CSUF DH Initiative currently resides, that number is a bit higher—nearly 40 percent of all of our students come from families where neither parent went to college. CSUF is also an MSI and, more specifically, an HSI. CSUF's Hispanic student enrollment regularly exceeds 40 percent (institutions must have at least 25 percent total full-time enrollment of Hispanic undergraduate students to be considered an HSI). Consequently, the institution continues to rank number one in the state of California and number two in the nation for the number of bachelor's degrees awarded to Hispanic students. Thus, our approach to DH pedagogy is substantially influenced by the demographic profile of CSUF's student body.[16]

Yet, what does it mean for DH at CSUF and similar institutions, in which the majority of students neither look like the imagined prototypical DH student nor attend the prototypical DH-supporting institution? The remainder of this essay outlines three frameworks for rethinking DH pedagogy: (1) learning styles of first-generation students; (2) technical expertise of first-generation students; and (3) integrating the long history of marginalized people into our understanding of DH. We close by arguing that building DH programs around this capital, skills, and history will result in curricula that are necessarily decolonized, globally oriented, and anti-neoliberal. Instead of focusing on (often absent) institutional infrastructural support, these curricula draw on human infrastructure, which includes collaboration among groups and actors with different kinds of expertise, as well as the tools and systems within which students are already embedded.[17] Hence, these curricula are not imitations or replications of DH education at more resourced institutions but are innovative ways to engage DH research and pedagogy at nontraditional MSIs.

First-Generation Students' Learning Styles

Writing on first-generation students often adopts a deficit-based model. When compared with continuing-generation students' graduation rates, GPAs, and overall success integrating into postsecondary education, first-generation students are at a disadvantage.[18] This reason is that their continuing-generation peers often have ample familial knowledge and social capital to prepare them for higher education. These findings pose a challenge for traditional approaches to teaching DH, which have tended to emphasize strategies that can be anathema to the ways in which first-generation students learn.

For instance, students enrolled in DH classes are often presumed to have some level of technological expertise (otherwise, we might ask, why are they in DH classes?), but first-generation students are among the least likely to have the time and resources to develop those skills. Furthermore, DH classes often require skills that fall outside of the traditional humanities practices, but we know that first-generation students are among the least likely to seek out institutional support. This means that students enrolled in these classes are asked to explore new terrain but are ill equipped to find help in traversing it. Finally, DH classes tend not to be part of general education courses and are often elective, so they do not fall within a prescribed career path, and they often require students to take a risk on material that might not come naturally to them or might unsettle a student's carefully planned academic career. A central principle of our approach to DH pedagogy is that it is unfair to ask students to take risks without providing them with support.

An asset-based model (exemplified by Eduard Arriaga's and Margaret Simon's work in this volume) centers the skills, practices, and knowledge that first-generation students bring to DH classrooms. For instance, research shows that first-generation students are significantly better at some learning tasks than their continuing-generation peers. In contrast to a prevailing postsecondary education context that privileges independence and individual motivations, first-generation college students are more likely to succeed in interdependent, collaborative work environments.[19] Strengths in collaboration are particularly conducive to DH pedagogy. Much recent work has called for a greater emphasis on collaboration—both within and across disciplinary boundaries.[20] In sum, while first-generation students are less likely to seek institutional support or experiment with new subjects, they are more likely to excel at collaboration than their continuing-generation peers—a skill that has the potential to make them more adept digital practitioners.

Students' Digital Expertise

Much of the writing on minority and/or first-generation students and DH has been vexed by assumptions about *digital "natives"* and their ability to engage with educationally appropriate technologies. Marc Prensky originally coined *digital "native"* as a metaphor to describe why many people in some generations, whom Prensky calls *digital immigrants,* feel "at sea" when faced with digital technologies.[21] Usually, *digital "native"* is used to signal a discrepancy between what instructors expect of students and what the students themselves know.[22] There are some very real problems with this model. *Digital "native"* is often used to criticize students who belong to a "native" generation, but who are less conversant with the workings of technology than their teachers and mentors. These critiques invoke students who might know how to manipulate an iPhone but do not know what file structures signify or cannot conceptualize the difference between print and born-digital publications. This model also presumes a homogeneous digital experience and that students coming from this metaphorical "digital country" all have the same access to technology and expertise.[23] It also has the potential to undervalue skills that students have developed on their own but that are not emphasized in classrooms.

Alongside anxieties about how digitally "native" students are somehow unknowable by digitally immigrant faculty is a concern that some groups, inclusive of some students, are separated from their more privileged peers by a *digital divide.* The idea of a digital divide or even a series of digital divides premised on educational background is not new. Sociologists and education scholars note that this divide takes two forms. The first-level digital divide is occasioned by different degrees of access to new technologies. The second-level digital divide is occasioned by different degrees of experience or proficiency. Though these divides have different origins, both are the product of social and economic inequalities.[24] These digital divides have obviously global dimensions; inequalities in internet infrastructure around the world are well documented. However, the concept also has implications within national spaces and, for the purposes of this essay, within the United States.[25]

For our purposes, concerns about the digital divides between students and about the degree to which students are digital "natives" both point to a set of troubling assumptions about who DH students are and how much they have in common. For instance, first-generation students often have trouble navigating the unspoken technical norms of bourgeoisie higher educational spaces, which has the potential to reinforce assumptions about digital "nativity."[26] Additionally, compared with peers from families with college or professional education, first-generation students are less likely to use digital tools for "capital-enhancing online activities."[27] Put another way, students from more privileged backgrounds are more likely to reap the economic benefits of the internet. Finally, first-generation college students are less likely to have more developed "internet user skills," which is mostly related to information-seeking activities on the internet but is also correlated with owning laptops, having multiple spaces to access the internet, and having the time to access the internet.[28] Students from households where neither parent attended college are more likely to rely on smartphones for their internet access, and many more households have access to smartphones than have access to personal computers.[29] These characteristics should not lead us to lament the degree to which students do not live up to our (often bourgeois) technical values but should instead cause us to question whether these values are necessary for DH education.

Expanding the History of DH

Finally, we need to adopt Roopika Risam's call to tell "alternate histories of the digital humanities . . . through intersectional lenses" and keep in mind the ways in which structural inequality has already conditioned the development of DH.[30] This also makes manifest the ways in which DH does not always need to be nor has been entirely the purview of people who are white, privileged, and male. After all, the earlier works of Anna Everett, Tyrone Taborn, and Chela Sandoval remind us that digital humanists and their proponents have always been multidimensional and have long grappled with questions of race, identity, and access in the digital realm. Everett argued in 2002 that 1995 was the "watershed moment in the transformation of the Internet from a predominantly elite, white masculinist domain to a more egalitarian public sphere."[31] This transformation was ushered in by *Yahoo*'s creation of a separate category for Afrocentric content on the web. By championing an increased African diasporic consciousness in what was then termed cyberspace, while interrogating its absence, Everett and other early scholars of race and digital technology/digital media helped to usher in the problem spaces we know today as the Digital Black Atlantic, Black DH, critical DH, and postcolonial DH.[32]

Similarly, in 2008 publisher and communications CEO Tyrone Taborn recognized that simply providing historically marginalized students with access to computers and other technology would do little to close the digital divide or increase minority participation in computing and technology fields, because these issues were related more to the narratives and mythologies that surround these fields rather than just the socioeconomic position of the student. More specifically, he advanced the idea that minority representation within narratives of America's technological history are scarce and often hidden and that "The lack of visible role models in science and digital media technologies represents an enormous problem for closing the technology gap."[33] Taborn calls for the (re)insertion of racial and ethnic minorities into founding narratives on science, technology, invention, and innovation in America. He also advanced more structural solutions including providing students in science, technology, and in this case, DH courses, with living and nonliving role models to whom they can relate, thus helping to increase feelings of self-confidence, belonging, and inclusion within the discipline. To this end Taborn relocated race within narratives on technological innovation through the stories of racial and ethnic minorities such as Katherine Johnson, Edson de Castro, and Tianna Shaw, to name a few.[34]

Early digital humanists rightfully perceived that the issue of scarcity and lack was not simply the burden of the historically marginalized digital public sphere, but that it was representative of a rather anemic technological infrastructure predicated on espousing incomplete histories, engaging fragmented publics, and creating limited spaces (both physically and theoretically) for innovation. As such, we want to close by offering some concrete solutions for building DH pedagogy that centers first-generation college students at minority-serving institutions. These solutions focus on how to develop programs that support students; how to build assignments that foster DH skills; and how to reframe our understanding of DH in response to critiques of neoliberalism, globalization, and colonialism.

Concrete Solutions

Rather than designing DH programs that *fix* the problem of first-generation students' not learning or using the internet in ways that researchers expect of them or not fitting the traditional notions of digital practitioners, we argue that DH courses and programs should embrace the ways in which students are already using the digital to explore humanistic questions. This shifts the focus away from lamenting underresourced institutional infrastructure to utilizing students' own human infrastructure. In doing so, we support the model outlined in the chapter "Manifesto for Student-Driven Research and Learning," which centers student voices and builds on student needs and expertise.[35]

More than their continuing-generation peers, first-generation students engage in augmented reality through smartphones and mobile devices. They are adept practitioners of flexible and collaborative work, both because they are generally more proficient in collaborative work and because many work across multiple desktops or mobile devices instead of a single dedicated computer. Many first-generation students are also already engaging with the long history of nonwhite DH. For example, first-generation students of Hispanic descent are more adept with the Spanish-language internet than they are with the English-language inter-net.[36] Similarly, indigenous digital practitioners have been developing DH projects that speak to the unique needs of indigenous communities.[37] The suggestions that follow emerged in response to students in DH classes at California State University Fullerton. This means that they sometimes emphasize the specific needs of students who are both first-generation and Hispanic. However, we anticipate that many of them will be generalizable to first-generation populations at other institutions and, more broadly, to other student populations.

In order to address the disparities between first- and continuing-generation students' familiarity with DH as a field, institutions that serve minority and first-generation students should work to introduce DH modules in lower-division general education courses, so that students develop early familiarity with DH concepts, tools, and practices such as experiential learning. In so doing, students can "test drive" DH without the risk of committing to an entire course, and yet these modules can act as a bridge for students who want to engage in more robust DH courses and pedagogy in the future.

Several strategies will help to ensure that students' access to tools matches pedagogical expectations. This includes incorporating Global Outlook::DH's call "to help break down barriers that hinder communication and collaboration among researchers and students of the Digital Arts, Humanities, and Cultural Heritage sectors in high, mid, and low income economies."[38] As part of this approach, we need to explore the possibilities of minimal computing, which interrogates the "dichotomy of choice vs. necessity and focuses the group on computing that is decidedly not high-performance and importantly not first-world desktop computing."[39] As several of the chapters in this volume on infrastructure demonstrate, not all DH projects require complicated and expensive tools. In fact, we may do our students a better service by talking about the structure of digital tools and introducing them to tools that they will be able to access for free when they leave our campuses. For example, in our DH practicum we ask students to explore a number of low-stakes and free or low-cost tools, such as Voyant, Palladio, Google Earth Web, and With-Known, which allow them to participate in DH practices without committing funds or hours to mastering technology for the sake of mastery.

Another approach should include carving out physical spaces for DH on MSI campuses. This means labs with hours that extend beyond the 9 a.m.–5 p.m. work day, computers loaded with required software, and the ability to check out machines for home use. We cannot assume that all students have access to all technology at all times and must give them space to explore in institutionally supported arenas. We must also consider developing assignments that make use of hardware with which students are already proficient. This might mean assignments that foreground work that can be done on smartphones. These kinds of assignments might build on recent studies that have shown that increased smartphone usage can help develop users' abilities to master tasks that demand sustained attention and multitasking.[40] These kinds of assignments also decenter institutional infrastructure in favor of the human infrastructure in which students are already embedded.

In order to capitalize on students' connection with nonwhite DH in classrooms, faculty should begin by designing projects and assignments that introduce students not only to DH, but also to new ways of looking at themselves or their communities by using digital storytelling or personal mapping modules. It is not surprising that Gina Garcia and Otgonjargal Okhidoi's 2015 study underscores the powerful role that culturally relevant curricula play in shaping academic engagement and achievement, particularly at HSIs. They argue that for minority and first-generation students culturally relevant curricula are essential for fomenting a sense of belonging within the institution and also for "affirm[ing] the existence [of] Latina/o and other underrepresented groups, while validating their experiences.[41] Although their study focuses specifically on Chicana/o studies programs and Latina/o support services, their claim can and should be applied to DH courses that provide new tools for engaging diverse perspectives within new and old problem spaces.

Another strategy involves meeting students in their own digital vernacular spaces. Many students are already engaging with DH through social media, and pretending that TEI is real DH whereas tumblr archives are not real DH does a disservice both to the profession and to our students. In fact, the need for students to critically engage with social media was recently underscored by the African American History, Culture and Digital Humanities (AADHum) Initiative's inaugural Social Media Corps Fellowship, which trains undergraduate and graduate students to produce digital content or artifacts specifically for social media. One way to discover which web 2.0 tools and technologies students are already working with, as well as assess their fears and/or expectations for the course, is to administer a prelearning self-assessment during the first week of class. This does not have to be a major assignment but rather a "lite" opportunity to learn more about your students and their interest in DH. The prelearning self-assessment is typically four hundred words maximum and asks students to (1) provide brief background on how they came to take this course and how it fits into their overall academic plans for this semester/school year or beyond; (2) detail any prior academic background or life experiences that have allowed them to interact with digital history; and (3) describe what they hope to learn throughout the semester and how they plan to meet the learning objectives outlined on page 1 of the syllabus.

Although we complete ice-breakers and "get to know you" exercises in class, we often discover more about our students and their personal and academic lives in this short exercise than in face-to-face exercises. Instructors can also use this assignment to help troubleshoot potential areas of concern that students may have. This assessment can also be followed up with a postlearning self-assessment at the end of the class, but it is not required.

In the first five weeks of our Intro to Digital History course, students were asked to prepare a two-minute script for a podcast or multimedia blog post that shared the history of an object. The objective of this assignment was for students to weave a compelling historical narrative around an artifact using digital tools that they had never accessed before. Not surprisingly, many students chose objects that had personal significance, including a great-uncle's postcard sent home from the front lines during World War II, which gave a glimpse of a young soldier's experience in war. Another student featured a guitar used to play Mexican corridos in her home, which also disclosed personal stories of migration, and another student selected a "joint," which symbolized a friend's arrest for possession of marijuana and his subsequent introduction to U.S. drug policy and the historical disparities within the "war on drugs." All these "Two Minutes in History" submissions, as they were called, served to acclimate students to new digital tools and methods for moving historical work off the printed page and also to contextualize and disseminate important local and family histories to a wider public.

As we design new assignments, we need to think about how to assess both those students who prefer individualistic, independent work and those who work better in collaborative environments. This might mean scaffolding assignments. It might also mean borrowing the *paired programming* model from computer science, which requires students to collaboratively tackle new skills, and adopting lab time for experimentation with new tools. It also requires an explicit discussion about how to work in academic groups, mechanisms for dividing labor, and rules of engagement for collaboration. After all, assuming that collaboration looks the same for students and for instructors, or even for all students, would be a mistake.

To this end we find that pairing collaborative assignments with reflexive writing exercises helps to build comprehension and alleviate some of the fear that students have that group work will not adequately reflect their individual contributions or, worse, that a lack of participation from other group members will ruin the quality of the assignment and thereby bring down their course grade. For this reason, we make collaboration itself a unit of study within the Intro to Digital History course by analyzing critical readings and examples of collaborative and participatory research. Throughout this unit, students learn that the value of collaborative design is not simply in the final product that it produces but is also in the process itself. Following the completion of the collaborative assignment, all students are asked to assess their experience in two ways. First they are required to submit an online peer-evaluation and self-evaluation form, which serves as a brief "report" disclosing the quality and frequency of individual engagement with the team during the completion of the project. This form asks students to evaluate on a scale of 1 to 3, with 3 being the highest, each group member's cooperation, availability for communication, and contribution to the overall success of the project including their own. The second assessment asks students to write a blog post that earnestly reflects upon their collaboration process.

Finally, we who are building DH programs at MSIs must remember that it is not necessary to automatically adopt a neoliberal framework that says that the digital is an avenue to better jobs but also not to assume that our students are not interested in the economic value of their labor. Rather, we should make clear that some DH labor is highly valued and may help students navigate the labor market. For instance, students might be interested in learning GIS as a way to get into state and county jobs that require spatial analysis. These students should not be discouraged from learning ArcGIS simply because it is a valued skill but should also not be encouraged to learn it *only* because it is valued. Rather, DH classes should discuss the analytical payoff of these tools and introduce students to ways of thinking with digital humanities. As potential and future DH practitioners, students should have the opportunity to reframe traditional discussions about DH pedagogy and in the process make the digital more open and accessible to all.

Notes

1. See Allington, Brouillette, and Golumbia, "Neoliberal Tools (and Archives)"; and Litvack, "In Harlem, a Digital Renaissance Takes Shape."

2. Bailey, "All the Digital Humanists Are White."

3. See, for example, the work published by EdSurge Independent: https://edsurgeindependent.com/.

4. See Gold, "Whose Revolution?"; and Hackney, Cunningham, and Sula, "A Survey of Digital Humanities Programs."

5. Costanza-Chock, "Design Justice," 5.

6. Gold, "Whose Revolution?"

7. McGrail, "The Whole Game"; and Cottom, *Lower Ed.*

8. Carnegie Foundation for the Advancement of Teaching, Carnegie Classification.

9. The findings from Hackney, Cunningham, and Sula's study were correlated with Carnegie Classification of Institutions (http://carnegieclassifications.iu.edu) by the authors.

10. National Center for Education Statistics, "Beginning Postsecondary Students Longitudinal Study".

11. Saenz et al., *First in My Family.*

12. For this reason Executive Orders 13592, 13555, and 13515 are aimed at increasing and strengthening the participation of American Indian and Alaskan Native, Hispanic, and Asian Americans, respectively, within higher education (U.S. Department of the Interior, "Minority Serving Institutions Program").

13. Institute for Higher Education Policy, *Supporting First Generation College Students.*

14. Montenegro and Jankowski, *Focused on What Matters.*

15. Between 2013 and 2017 the Penn Center for MSIs released over twenty publications and research reports on MSIs and awarded "$1.3 million in capacity-building grants to 26 different MSIs to support innovation, retention, and degree attainment for over 180,000 students."

16. Though the figures mentioned here reflect data from the 2016–2017 academic year, they are consistent with the most recent Fall 2020 Institutional Profile for CSUF, which reported that 48.5 percent of enrolled students were from underrepresented minority groups, and first-generation students made up 31.5 percent of the undergraduate population.

17. Lee, Dourish, and Mark, "The Human Infrastructure of Cyberinfrastructure."

18. National Center for Education Statistics, "Status and Trends."

19. Stephens et al., "Unseen Disadvantage."

20. Chan et al., "Interdisciplinary Collaboration."

21. Prensky, "Digital Natives."

22. Shrout and Christian-Lamb, " 'Starting from Scratch'?"

23. See Helsper and Eynon, "Digital Natives"; and Margaryan, Littlejohn, and Vojt, "Are Digital Natives a Myth or Reality?"

24. See Stern, "Inequality in the Internet Age"; Tsatsou, "Digital Divides Revisited"; and Trültzch, Kõuts-Klemm, and Aroldi, "Transforming Digital Divides."

25. Robison and Crenshaw, "Reevaluating the Global Digital Divide."

26. Stephens, Hamedani, and Destin, "Closing the Social Class Achievement Gap."

27. Hargittai, "Digital Na(t)ives?"

28. Chen, *First-Generation Students in Postsecondary Education.*

29. Pew Research Center, "Mobile Fact Sheet."

30. Risam, "Beyond the Margins."

31. Everett, "The Revolution Will Be Digitized," 126.

32. For more on any of these concentrations see the *Digital Black Atlantic* volume in the Debates in DH Series and other works by Kim Gallon, Alan Lui, and/or Roopika Risam.

33. Taborn, "Separating Race from Technology," 40.

34. Taborn, "Separating Race from Technology."

35. Miya et al., "Manifesto for Student-Driven Research and Learning."

36. Torrent, "Edición Digital."

37. LaPensée, "Games as Enduring Presence."

38. Global Outlook::Digital Humanities, "About."

39. Global Outlook::Digital Humanities, "Minimal Computing."

40. Wilmer, Sherman, and Chein, "Smartphones and Cognition."

41. Garcia and Okhidoi, "Culturally Relevant Practices."

Bibliography

Allington, Daniel, Sarah Brouillette, and David Golumbia. "Neoliberal Tools (and Archives): A Political History of Digital Humanities." *Los Angeles Review of Books,* May 1, 2016. https://lareviewofbooks.org/article/neoliberal-tools-archives-political -history-digital-humanities/.

Bailey, Moya Z. "All the Digital Humanists Are White, All the Nerds Are Men, but Some of Us Are Brave." *Journal of Digital Humanities* 1, no. 1 (Winter 2011). http://

journalofdigitalhumanities.org/1-1/all-the-digital-humanists-are-white-all-the
-nerds-are-men-but-some-of-us-are-brave-by-moya-z-bailey/.

Carnegie Foundation for the Advancement of Teaching. *The Carnegie Classification of Institutions of Higher Education.* 2015 editions. https://carnegieclassifications.iu.edu/.

Center for Minority Serving Institutions. "Supporting Minority Serving Institutions (MSIs) by the Numbers." Accessed August 2, 2017. https://cmsi.gse.rutgers.edu/content/supporting-minority-serving-institutions-numbers-2017.

Chan, Anela, Richard Chenhall, Tamara Kohn, and Carolyn Stevens. "Interdisciplinary Collaboration and Brokerage in the Digital Humanities." *Digital Humanities Quarterly* 11, no. 3 (2017). http://www.digitalhumanities.org/dhq/vol/11/3/000336/000336.html.

Chen, X. *First Generation Students in Postsecondary Education: A Look at Their College Transcripts.* U.S. Department of Education, National Center for Education Statistics. Washington, D.C.: U.S. Government Printing Office, 2005.

Costanza-Chock, Sasha. "Design Justice: Towards an Intersectional Feminist Framework for Design Theory and Practice." SSRN Scholarly Paper ID 3189696. Rochester, N.Y.: Social Science Research Network, 2018. https://papers.ssrn.com/abstract=3189696.

Cottom, Tressie McMillan. *Lower Ed: The Troubling Rise of For-Profit Colleges in the New Economy.* New York: New Press, 2017.

Everett, Anna. "The Revolution Will Be Digitized: Afrocentricity and the Digital Public Sphere." *Social Text* 20, no. 2 (2002): 125–46.

Garcia, Gina A., and Otgonjargal Okhidoi. "Culturally Relevant Practices That 'Serve' Students at a Hispanic Serving Institution." *Innovative Higher Education* 40, no. 4 (2015): 345–57.

Global Outlook::Digital Humanities. "About." *Global Outlook::Digital Humanities.* Accessed August 2, 2017. http://www.globaloutlookdh.org/.

Global Outlook::Digital Humanities. "Minimal Computing." *Global Outlook::Digital Humanities* (blog), April 15, 2013. http://www.globaloutlookdh.org/minimal-computing/.

Gold, Matt. "Whose Revolution? Towards a More Equitable Digital Humanities." *The Lapland Chronicles* (blog), January 10, 2012. http://blog.mkgold.net/2012/01/10/whose-revolution-toward-a-more-equitable-digital-humanities/.

Hackney, S. E., Phillip Cunningham, and Chris Alen Sula. "A Survey of Digital Humanities Programs." *The Journal of Interactive Technology & Pedagogy,* no. 11 (May 24, 2017). https://jitp.commons.gc.cuny.edu/a-survey-of-digital-humanities-programs/.

Hargittai, Eszter. "Digital Na(t)ives? Variation in Internet Skills and Uses among Members of the 'Net Generation'". *Sociological Inquiry* 80, no. 1 (February 2010): 92–113. https://doi.org/10.1111/j.1475-682X.2009.00317.x.

Helsper, Ellen Johanna, and Rebecca Eynon. "Digital Natives: Where Is the Evidence?" *British Educational Research Journal* 36, no. 3 (2010): 503–20. https://doi.org/10.1080/01411920902989227.

Institute for Higher Education Policy. *Supporting First-Generation College Students through Classroom-Based Practices: Issue Brief.* Washington, D.C.: IHEP, 2012.

LaPensée, Elizabeth. "Games as Enduring Presence." *Public* 27, no. 54 (2016): 178–86.

Lee, Charlotte P., Paul Dourish, and Gloria Mark. "The Human Infrastructure of Cyberinfrastructure." In *Proceedings of the 2006 20th Anniversary Conference on Computer Supported Cooperative Work, CSCW '06*, 483–92. New York: ACM, 2006. https://doi.org/10.1145/1180875.1180950.

Litvack, Emily. "In Harlem, a Digital Renaissance Takes Shape." *University of Arizona News*, November 27, 2017. https://uanews.arizona.edu/story/harlem-digital-renaissance-takes-shape.

Margaryan, Anoush, Allison Littlejohn, and Gabrielle Vojt. "Are Digital Natives a Myth or Reality? University Students' Use of Digital Technologies." *Computers & Education* 56, no. 2 (2011): 429–40.

McGlynn, Terry, Amy Parachnowitsch, and Catherine Scott, eds. "What Do Students Call You? Professor, Ms., Mrs., Mr., Dr., Sir?" *Small Pond Science* (blog), May 21, 2013. https://smallpondscience.com/2013/05/21/what-do-students-call-you-professor-ms-mrs-mr-dr-sir/.

McGrail, Anne B. "The 'Whole Game': Digital Humanities at Community Colleges." In *Debates in the Digital Humanities.* Minneapolis: University of Minnesota Press, 2016.

Miya, Chelsea, Laura Gerlitz, Kaitlyn Grant, Maryse Ndilu Kiese, Mengchi Sun, and Christina Boyles. "Manifesto for Student-Driven Research and Learning." In *People, Practice, Power: Digital Humanities outside the Center*, edited by Anne B. McGrail, Angel David Nieves, and Siobhan Senier. Minneapolis: University of Minnesota Press, 2021.

Montenegro, Eric, and Natasha A. Jankowski. *Focused on What Matters: Assessment of Student Learning Outcomes at Minority-Serving Institutions.* Urbana: University of Illinois and Indiana University, National Institute for Learning Outcomes Assessment (NILOA).

National Center for Education Statistics. "Beginning Postsecondary Students Longitudinal Study, First Follow-up (BPS:12/14)." U.S. Department of Education, 2011.

National Center for Education Statistics. "Status and Trends in the Education of Racial and Ethnic Minorities." 2010. Accessed March 30, 2017. https://nces.ed.gov/pubs2010/2010015/indicator1_5.asp.

Pew Research Center. "Mobile Fact Sheet." *Internet and Technology*, 2018.

Prensky, Marc. "Digital Natives, Digital Immigrants Part 1." *On the Horizon* 9, no. 5 (2001): 1–6. https://doi.org/10.1108/10748120110424816.

Risam, Roopika. "Beyond the Margins: Intersectionality and the Digital Humanities." *Digital Humanities Quarterly* 9, no. 2 (2015). http://www.digitalhumanities.org/dhq/vol/9/2/000208/000208.html.

Robison, Kristopher K., and Edward M. Crenshaw. "Reevaluating the Global Digital Divide: Socio-Demographic and Conflict Barriers to the Internet Revolution." *Sociological Inquiry* 80, no. 1 (2010): 34–62. https://doi.org/10.1111/j.1475-682X.2009.00315.x.

Saenz, Victor B., Sylvia Hurtado, Doug Barrera, De'Sha Wolf, and Fanny Yeung. *First in My Family: A Profile of First-Generation College Students at Four-Year Institutions since 1971.* Los Angeles, Calif.: Higher Education Research Institute, 2007.

Shrout, Anelise Hanson, and Caitlin Christian-Lamb. "'Starting From Scratch'? Workshopping New Directions in Undergraduate Digital Humanities." *Digital Humanities Quarterly* 11, no. 3 (2017). http://www.digitalhumanities.org/dhq/vol/11/3.

Stephens, Nicole M., Stephanie A. Fryberg, Hazel Rose Markus, Camille S. Johnson, and Rebecca Covarrubias. "Unseen Disadvantage: How American Universities' Focus on Independence Undermines the Academic Performance of First-Generation College Students." *Journal of Personality and Social Psychology* 102, no. 6 (2012): 1178–97. https://doi.org/10.1037/a0027143.

Stephens, Nicole M., MarYam G. Hamedani, and Mesmin Destin. "Closing the Social-Class Achievement Gap: A Difference-Education Intervention Improves First-Generation Students' Academic Performance and All Students' College Transition." *Psychological Science* 25, no. 4 (2014): 943–53. https://doi.org/10.1177/0956797613518349.

Stern, Michael J. "Inequality in the Internet Age: A Twenty-First Century Dilemma." *Sociological Inquiry* 80, no. 1(2010): 28–33. https://doi.org/10.1111/j.1475-682X.2009.00314.x.

Taborn, Tyrone D. "Separating Race from Technology: Finding Tomorrow's IT Progress in the Past." In *Learning Race and Ethnicity: Youth and Digital Media,* edited by Anna Everett. John D. and Catherine T. MacArthur Foundation Series on Digital Media and Learning. Cambridge, Mass.: MIT Press, 2008.

Torrent, Susanna Alles. "Edición Digital y Algunas Tecnologías Aliadas." *Insula* 822 (June 2015): 18–21.

Trültzch, Sascha, Ragne Kõuts-Klemm, and Piermarco Aroldi. "Transforming Digital Divides in Different National Contexts." In *Audience Transformations: Late Modernity's Shifting Audience Positions,* edited by Nico Carpentier, Kim Christian Schrøder, and Lawrie Hallett. London: Routledge, 2013.

Tsatsou, Panayiota. "Digital Divides Revisited: What Is New about Divides and Their Research?" *Media, Culture & Society* 33, no. 2 (2011): 317–31. https://doi.org/10.1177/0163443710393865.

U.S. Department of the Interior. "Minority Serving Institutions Program." *Office of Civil Rights,* July 1, 2015. https://www.doi.gov/pmb/eeo/doi-minority-serving-institutions-program.

Wilmer, Henry H., Lauren E. Sherman, and Jason M. Chein. "Smartphones and Cognition: A Review of Research Exploring the Links between Mobile Technology Habits and Cognitive Functioning." *Frontiers in Psychology* 8 (2017): 605.

Stewarding Place

Digital Humanities at the Regional Comprehensive University

ROOPIKA RISAM

One of the stories told about digital humanities is how it looks in particular contexts, such as research-intensive universities or elite small liberal arts colleges. However, this impulse toward classification elides the variety of work that is being undertaken in other contexts. Currently, the lion's share of digital humanities scholarship in the United States emerges from Carnegie-classified R1: Doctoral Universities—Highest Research Activity, or R1s. Given that these universities are focused on research, this is not unusual. As a result, however, the scholarship that attends to the infrastructural dimensions of digital humanities does so with these universities and their libraries in mind. In fact, this particular context for digital humanities is presumed. This work is important, and scholarly and institutional investment from these institutions has led to the creation of important tools and platforms that facilitate digital humanities scholarship in other contexts with access to fewer resources; however, the flip side is that digital humanities production from R1 institutions overdetermines the practices of digital humanities scholarship, without acknowledging both the privileged position from which it emerges and its admittedly limited context. This raises the question of how can academic institutions support digital humanities scholarship without major infrastructure and how, in turn, does that redefine approaches to digital humanities for such institutions?

Digital Humanities in (Other) Contexts

The vast majority of colleges and universities in the United States operate in other contexts, and the majority of students are not educated at these elite institutions. That digital humanities at R1 institutions is taken as the model of digital humanities in the United States poses a challenge for universities and colleges in other contexts in which digital humanities is practiced, such as small liberal arts colleges, community colleges, regional comprehensives, and other non-flagship public universities. Within this group, digital humanities has gained the most traction at elite small liberal arts colleges, which have produced models for digital humanities at these institutions. For example, Hamilton College's Digital Humanities Initiative has developed a model for collaborative research and teaching that engages undergraduate students in digital humanities. Another excellent example is Bard College's Experimental Humanities, which offers an intervention in liberal arts–focused digital humanities that is interdisciplinary and multimedia. More recently, digital humanities has begun flourishing at community colleges, due to the work of Anne McGrail and funding from the National Endowment for the Humanities. What these initiatives have made clear is that the types of institutions in which digital humanities is practiced merits attention. The practices that are effective at small liberal arts college are not easily translatable to community colleges, and the needs of community college students are different from those at residential, elite liberal arts colleges.

However, another type of institution is largely ignored: the regional comprehensive university. Regional comprehensive universities are neither research universities nor liberal arts colleges. They are typically Carnegie-classified as Master's Colleges and Universities, although some do offer applied PhD programs in health and human services areas (education, nursing, social work, and occupational therapy). In these contexts, the value of arts and sciences degrees is endangered, as university resources and student enrollments favor "professional" degrees that lead students toward more obvious career trajectories. This is a reflection of the student populations that regional comprehensive universities serve: their immediate, local, geographical communities. More specifically, these are neighboring middle- and working-class communities. Consequently, regional comprehensive universities have populations that include significant numbers of students on Pell Grants, veterans on the GI Bill, and first-generation college students.

Regional comprehensives in proximity to urban areas often have significant populations of students of color. These universities also accept significant numbers of transfer students from community colleges, in-state and out-of-state public universities, and small liberal arts colleges. Often, students at regional comprehensive universities come from underserved public school districts and are working their way through college. These are, in many ways, some of the most vulnerable students in higher education: the ones less likely to have advantages, such as financial or emotional family support; more likely to be in need of remedial education, which increases the time to and cost of receiving a degree; and less likely to complete a bachelor's degree (the average Massachusetts state university graduation rate is 53 percent). For many of these students, these institutions, which are often open access or nearly open access, are their only feasible option for receiving a bachelor's degree. Despite the high need of this student population, regional comprehensive universities are short-changed financially in competition with state research universities and flagships. They receive less funding than the flagship systems, relying on enrollments and endowments that are already small because they are educating an underserved student population, primarily in professions like nursing, social work, and education that tend to not generate a wealthy alumni base.

These institutional constraints create significant challenges for the development of digital humanities programs. Foundations like Mellon are not especially interested in funding initiatives for these universities, which fall between the cracks of available funding. While there are a number of great initiatives that intend to bring together digital humanities practitioners across types of institutions, like the Institute for Digital Liberal Arts Scholarship (Illiads) or the Digital Liberal Arts Exchange (DLAx), they do not include regional comprehensive universities. Thus, they fail to take into account the unique characteristics and needs of these institutions.

With funding heavily invested in student success initiatives, there is little left to fund digital humanities research. Faculty and librarian time is at a premium as well. Because the mission of these universities is teaching rather than research, faculty have high teaching loads (typically 4/4), while librarian roles are primarily instructional. Service demands on faculty and librarians are significant as well, with rising research expectations. However, these demands are not offset by increased research support, such as course releases, adjusted job descriptions, or research budgets, which poses a logistical and financial barrier for starting digital humanities initiatives. Because evaluating digital humanities projects for tenure and promotion remains a challenge, faculty and librarians are less likely to invest their rare research time in digital humanities projects when their value in evaluation is unclear. Even the idea of using digital humanities to incorporate students into faculty and librarian research is a daunting one because of time constraints and lack of funds.

Salem State University is a typical case for universities that fit this profile. One of the Massachusetts state universities—the tier below the flagship University of Massachusetts system—Salem State is a regional comprehensive university in Salem, Massachusetts, a small city 15 miles north of Boston on the North Shore of Massachusetts. Institutions like Salem State primarily serve undergraduate student populations through degree programs that include health and human services as well as arts and sciences. The digital humanities initiatives at Salem State respond to these obstacles. They are structured around the Digital Scholars Program, an undergraduate digital humanities research program that university archivist Susan Edwards and I developed and that we now run along with digital initiatives librarian Justin Snow. Students apply to the program through a competitive process and are mentored through the process of creating small-scale digital humanities projects over the course of a semester. We introduce students to the university's archives and special collections, teach them how to conduct archival research, guide their inquiry as they identify topics of interest and develop research questions, and mentor them through project development. The program connects students to local history, equips them with digital literacy, strengthens their research skills, and offers them professional development for translating their experiences for employers. Students who wish to do so may submit their small projects for inclusion in *Digital Salem,* the institution-wide umbrella digital humanities project we have developed to bring together digital humanities projects at the university. Throughout this work, we have drawn on the specific nature and positioning of regional comprehensive universities to identify how to build an infrastructure that allows digital humanities programs to flourish at these types of institutions to serve our students and intervene in the gaps where they have been underserved by public education.

The Regional as Local

The theoretical underpinnings of Salem State's digital humanities initiatives emerge from my research interest in global digital humanities. In this work, I have made the case for close attention to the local dimensions of global practices. For example, I have suggested that digital humanities practices be framed as a series of "accents."[1] Just as languages share common vocabularies and linguistic structures but are articulated differently depending on context, so too are digital humanities practices diverse and varied. While a common set of distinguishable features unite digital humanities practices, they have developed in their own ways, deeply inflected by the local circumstances that surround their production. This is an idea that has been emphasized through the work of Global Outlook::Digital Humanities and its insistence on the "local self-determination of what constitutes DH work and where its value resides."[2] As such, the attention to the local in global digital humanities provides a way of thinking through the nuances of practice that exist within national contexts, where we can find tremendous variability in access to resources and infrastructures. From the outside, it may appear that because we are undertaking digital humanities in the United States, the large-scale contexts such as digital humanities centers that are more visible in digital humanities practice are the frames in which we operate. However, despite the significant amount of privilege that we have because we are working in the United States, this is simply not the case for our work. Instead, we have had to focus on our local, institutional context to build our programs and identify which practices work for universities like ours.

Initiatives at Salem State have been further influenced by the Minimal Computing Working Group of Global Outlook::Digital Humanities. Jentery Sayers has identified key components of minimal computing, including minimal design, maximum justice, and minimal technical language.[3] These principles privilege access and openness for stakeholders across economic and technical barriers, as well as design choices made by necessity. As Gil and Ortega note, "We prefer to (un-)define minimal computing around the question, 'What do we need?'"[4] The question of what we need has been essential to the development of digital humanities at Salem State. So too is the focus on what we have, as we draw on Ernesto Oroza's "architecture of necessity," which Gil and Ortega define as, "A cleverness that can make-do with available materials; and a constant care for our social surroundings."[5]

Thus, we have attended to both what we do not have and what we have, as we built a model for digital humanities at regional comprehensive universities. We have done this work in spite of our lack of access to resources, adopting Gil's proposition that, "We need not wait for the affordances of infrastructure."[6] At Salem State and other regional comprehensive universities, if we were to, as Gil writes, "Wait for a grant to hire developers to carry out their visions, others for a fully funded DH center at their universities to 'support' them," we would be waiting forever.[7] However, the model we have designed for our digital humanities initiatives is a useful case for how digital humanities can be made accessible to vulnerable student populations with few resources.

We do this work without a center or other institutional entity to support digital humanities work. Digital humanities initiatives, often in the form of centers, at R1 institutions in the United States are driven by interests that are less relevant to regional comprehensive universities. As Neil Fraistat suggests, these institutions are research focused, emphasize faculty and graduate student collaboration, and emerge from bottom-up research initiatives.[8] Naturally, there are exceptions and variations, such as centers that focus on pedagogy. Yet, as Mark Sample notes:

> Most of us working in the digital humanities will never have the opportunity to collaborate with a dedicated center or institute. We'll never have the chance to work with programmers who speak the language of the humanities as well as Perl, Python, or PH. We'll never be able to turn to colleagues who routinely navigate grant applications and budget deadlines, who are paid to know about the latest digital tools and trends–but who'd know about them and share their knowledge even if they weren't paid a dime. We'll never have an institutional advocate on campus who can speak with a single voice to administrators, to students, to donors, to publishers, to communities about the value of digital humanities.[9]

This is the condition of digital humanities at Salem State, where we do not—and will not—have digital humanities infrastructure of this nature because it is largely irrelevant to the conditions under which we work. Despite a lack of institutionally supported infrastructure that resembles models, such as centers, that are not feasible in our institutional context, we have envisioned a digital humanities infrastructure based on our undergraduate research program, supported by a working group of interested faculty and librarians to foster collaborative conversations about digital humanities.

Additionally, we do not have students who come to us well prepared to undertake digital humanities work. Rather, we have an underserved student population that struggles with digital literacy and undertakes coursework with woefully insufficient computing access. In Massachusetts public schools, like others around the country, computer classes have been eliminated due to budget cuts and the presumption that students are "digital natives" and thus do not need instruction. This is a troubling assumption because, as instructors find, students struggle with basic computer use. Only recently, in 2016, Massachusetts unveiled new digital literacy standards, although they have only begun to be implemented in school districts because the roll-out has not been accompanied by professional development opportunities for teachers. Salem State eliminated its own computer competency requirement in 2015 because the test was outdated, and yet there has been no initiative to replace it or integrate digital literacy into the curriculum. Despite ramifications for students in all majors, this is particularly important for students in the humanities, where they are unlikely to receive discipline-specific training in technologies. Without facility with technology, they are at a disadvantage in the employment market. Consequently, we specifically use these gaps to make the case for the value of our digital humanities initiatives for our student population.

The circumstances of our students' lives factor prominently, as well. Because they are working to support themselves (and often, their families) and are predominantly commuter students, their time on campus is constrained and they must use it efficiently to complete their degrees. They also do not have the disposable time or income to devote to multiple extracurricular activities, unpaid internships, or other uncompensated opportunities that their peers with more means can pursue more easily. The majority who live off campus tend to be disconnected from campus culture, institutional histories, and even the local community. These students, however, benefit from access to experience with digital humanities. At Salem State, we have leveraged these particularities of institutional life and student experience to design a digital humanities program that suits their needs and have tapped into our institutional strategic plan priority for *student success* to gain departmental and administrative support for the program.

In spite of what we do not have, we do have students who know what they want and need, and designing digital humanities initiatives to meet these requests underscores the role of social justice in our work. In surveys undertaken by Salem State's English department, students report the need for more opportunities for internships and cocurricular experiences to complement their bachelor's degrees. They also seek career preparation and advice, which they want to receive as part of their English majors. Because they tend to lack forms of cultural capital that are rewarded in job searches, they have difficulty imagining career options or translating marketable skills from humanities majors into employment. These students are also not convinced that they can be creators of knowledge; rather, they see themselves as consumers only. This is, in large part, due to the nature of public education in the underserved Massachusetts communities from which Salem State draws. In those districts, emphasis on the MCAS, the state's high-stakes testing apparatus, has sacrificed curiosity, inquiry, and instructional time to success on standardized tests. The Digital Scholars Program has provided one such option for remediating these challenges. As a result, we have drawn on our knowledge of our student population and our institution with a growth mindset that emphasizes what we do have. We situated the focus of our work in our university's archives and special collections, a diverse and free but untapped source of material that we have at the university.

This also led us to think about the role of digital humanities at regional comprehensive universities like ours in relation to the American State Colleges and Universities' mission that universities like ours be *stewards of place*, given our strong connections to our local regions and commitment to civic engagement.[10] We have positioned our work as a digital stewarding of place, with the goal of shedding light on the unheard stories of Salem, Massachusetts. Salem is perhaps best known for the Witch Trials of 1692 and the literature of Nathaniel Hawthorne. However, Salem State's archives do not hold material on those subjects. We also share a sense of frustration that these narratives have become the defining ones for Salem. This is a result of the strategic way Salem as a city has revived itself from decades of economic depression through a tourist industry that focuses on witches and Hawthorne. What has happened, as a result, is that other, rich histories of Salem have been obscured, such as the city's history of immigration and activism. Because we do have material on these subjects in Salem State's archives, we have positioned the work of students in the Digital Scholars Program as diversifying the digital cultural record by giving voice to the ordinary and everyday, shedding light on the hidden histories that shape Salem today.

Our undergraduate students and our local archives, therefore, are driving the practices of our digital humanities program. Therefore, we have reframed the limitations of a regional comprehensive university—student profile, unique untapped resources, and emphasis on student success—as affordances for our local approach to digital humanities. We approach design from this perspective, recognizing that there would not be need for digital humanities at the university if not for its value to our students. There is simply not enough time or money available to invest in projects based on faculty research alone, and digital humanities experiences are especially valuable to our students. Moreover, we are bringing attention to our underused archives and leveraging them to challenge foregoing narratives of Salem. In doing so, we engage our students in the digital stewarding of place.

The Salem State Playbook

This model has been a successful one and is replicable for those working at other regional comprehensive universities. What follows is a list of suggestions for those who wish to adopt or adapt our model in their institutions.

Our first recommendation is to find existing resources to repurpose toward assembling a digital humanities community. We considered existing structures and professional development opportunities that could be used to develop digital humanities programs. We began with creating a faculty learning community, which I ran during 2014–15. The intention of starting a faculty learning community on digital humanities was to find faculty and librarians who were engaged in or interested in digital humanities. At Salem State, faculty can apply to facilitate a learning community on a topic of their choice related to pedagogy. The communities meet every other week over the course of an academic year to read and discuss the topic and to plan, implement, and assess an activity, assignment, or project based on the topic.

The digital humanities learning community that I proposed yielded a group of nine participants from the English and history departments and the library. From this experience, I recognized that the only way we could effectively make the case for digital humanities and take advantage of existing resources would be to appeal to its use for *student success*, a mandate of our strategic plan. This included supporting retention by mentoring student research; cultivating students' connections to Salem and to the university by immersing them in our archives; helping humanities students understand applications of humanities knowledge outside the classroom; and exposing students to career opportunities with which they were unfamiliar, such as in libraries, archives, and museums. The faculty learning community proved to be an effective way of taking advantage of existing resources to build the digital humanities presence at the university by bringing together colleagues most inclined to be advocates for it. We subsequently ran another faculty learning community, during 2016–17, to build shared expectations around digital humanities pedagogy and labor practices.

We also suggest thinking outside of departments and units to leverage expertise across the university. This can be difficult at teaching institutions, where faculty are siloed in teaching areas and instructional librarians are responsible for particular departments. Through our first faculty learning community, however, I began collaborating with university archivist Susan Edwards, who had experience with our institutional repository and had experience with digitizing materials from our archives and special collections. Edwards and I recognized that we shared similar interests and had complementary knowledge that would be valuable for building digital humanities initiatives at the university.

Our initiatives have also been successful because we have tailored them to our university's strategic plan and to the funding attached to the strategic plan. Underfunded universities are often under pressure to improve retention and graduation rates, as well as employment outcomes. Quite often, there are funds attached to these initiatives. In the case of Salem State, an annual Strategic Innovation Grants competition supports cross-unit collaboration and creative approaches to strategic plan goals. Based on our experience in the 2014–15 faculty learning community, Edwards and I recognized that we had to position our digital humanities initiative as pedagogical, interdisciplinary, and directly engaged in meeting the needs of our student population. By receiving one of these grants, we were able to pilot the Digital Scholars Program that we developed.

With pedagogically oriented digital humanities initiatives, it is also important to attend to the ethics of using student labor for digital humanities. Students in the Digital Scholars Program receive course credit for their participation, so we designed the program to be research based instead of an internship. As a result, students set their own research agendas based on the library's collections. This has had the added benefit of allowing them to gain appreciation and love for the process of inquiry in research, to find materials that strike a chord for them, make them curious, and help them develop their own research questions and create their own projects

Without access to resources to develop a large digital humanities project, we have also had to think modularly about how projects can be built. To navigate this challenge, Edwards and I created the university's digital humanities umbrella project *Digital Salem,* which we envisioned as a portal that would aggregate the small digital humanities projects our students created. Even though the projects within *Digital Salem* are small, together they add up to a vibrant collection of material on the untold stories of Salem. Students are fully credited for their projects, which become part of their portfolio, while we provide ongoing maintenance for the projects on our server.

We also learned that we had to be flexible in response to student needs. The first year of the Digital Scholars Program was a process of trial and error. We had not realized our students were so ill-equipped for research, but we realized that they were approaching archival materials with preconceived ideas about what they would find and arguments that they wanted to make. The experience also demonstrated that our students needed significantly more structure for their research than we had anticipated. Consequently, we redesigned the process to provide more formal constraints on the students, which improved their experience significantly.

Building a digital humanities program that puts an underserved student population at its center also meant having to sacrifice our own vision to put our students' needs first. By choosing to focus on the untold stories of Salem, we have designed a program that fits our shared interests in storytelling and community engagement. Beyond that, however, we let go and let students engage with the particular topics and narratives that interest them and use the digital research methods that are most intriguing for them. We have also drawn on existing student support services to emphasize the cocurricular nature of our initiatives. For example, we have facilitated workshops for Digital Scholars Program participants with Career Services. Through these workshops, students have learned how to talk about their experiences for cover letters, resumes, and job searches. We are exploring partnerships with relevant initiatives on campus, such as the Office of Multicultural Student Affairs and the Center for Civic Engagement, as well. In doing so, we have discovered the resources that exist within the broader underresourced environment of the university.

Through our experience, we have come to realize that we have valuable skill sets for digital humanities precisely because of the institutional context in which we work. We are able to build programs with few resources, involve with underprepared undergraduate students, and work with local archives and communities. Our work with the Digital Scholars Program and *Digital Salem* has been the basis of our NEH grant, Networking the Regional Comprehensives, an initiative intended to bring together other digital humanities practitioners at regional comprehensive universities. Those of us at these types of universities face the same challenges—the lack of funding, a focus on teaching over research, and the imperative to provide experiential learning for student success initiatives.

The initiatives that I have outlined offer a model for developing digital humanities at scales appropriate for regional comprehensive university institutional contexts and strategic planning. Perhaps more importantly, they offer a vision of digital humanities with learning curves and barriers to entry that do not require affiliation with centers, access to expensive technologies, or resources beyond what we have available to us. This approach is essential to the development of an inclusive digital humanities community that includes teaching-intensive public universities.

Notes

1. Risam, "Other Worlds, Other DHs," 377.

2. Gil and Ortega, "Global Outlooks in Digital Humanities," 27.

3. Sayers, "Minimal Definitions."

4. Gil and Ortega, "Global Outlooks in Digital Humanities," 27.

5. Gil and Ortega, "Global Outlooks in Digital Humanities," 29.

6. Gil, "Interview with Ernesto Oroza," 184.

7. Gil, "Interview with Ernesto Oroza," 184.

8. Fraistat, "The Function of Digital Humanities Centers at the Present Time," 281.

9. Sample, "On the Death of the Digital Humanities Center."

10. American Association of State Colleges and Universities, "Stepping Forward as Stewards of Place."

Bibliography

American Association of State Colleges and Universities. "Stepping Forward as Stewards of Place." *American Association of State Colleges and Universities,* 2002.

Fraistat, Neil. "The Function of Digital Humanities Centers at the Present Time." In *Debates in the Digital Humanities,* edited by Matthew K. Gold, 281–91. Minneapolis: University of Minnesota Press, 2012.

Gil, Alex. "Interview with Ernesto Oroza." In *Debates in the Digital Humanities 2016,* edited by Matthew K. Gold and Lauren Klein, 184–93. Minneapolis: University of Minnesota Press, 2016.

Gil, Alex, and Élika Ortega. "Global Outlooks in Digital Humanities: Multilingual Practices and Minimal Computing." In *Doing Digital Humanities,* edited by Constance Crompton, Richard J. Lane, and Ray Siemens, 22–34. London: Routledge, 2016.

Risam, Roopika. "Other Worlds, Other DHs: Notes towards a DH Accent." *Digital Scholarship in the Humanities* 32, no. 2 (2017): 377–84.

Sample, Mark. "On the Death of the Digital Humanities Center." *@samplereality* (blog), March 26, 2010.

Sayers, Jentery. "Minimal Definitions." *Minimal Computing,* October 2, 2016.

Digital Humanities as Critical University Studies
Three Provocations

MATTHEW APPLEGATE

The United States may have embraced knowledge capitalism, but it has not embraced post*capitalism.*

—Christopher Newfield, *Unmaking the Public University*

Digital humanists have heard numerous recent calls for the field to interrogate race, gender, and other structures of power [. . .] To truly engage in this kind of critical work, I contend, would be much more difficult and fascinating than anything we have previously imagined for the future of DH; in fact, it would require dismantling and rebuilding much of the organizing logic that underlies our work.

—Miriam Posner, "What's Next: The Radical, Unrealized Potential of
   Digital Humanities"

In these pages, I combine critical digital humanities (DH) work with selected arguments from critical university studies (CUS). I do so in order to further articulate what makes DH critical for our present moment, particularly our present academic-corporate circumstances, in which intellectual labor is often precarious, competitive, and reducible to acts of "accumulation and acquisition."[1] If DH is "an active form of resistance to traditional academic hierarchies," ideally sensitive to how power "replicate[s] privilege," then CUS might be best described as a sustained discourse of resistance to the university's neoliberalization via local and globalized forms of educational autonomy, predicated on conflict in knowledge production and "the construction of the common."[2] Both approaches, necessarily so, go hand in hand.

The argument I forward is simple: DH and CUS need each other. They need each other for three, interrelated reasons. Coarticulating the rhetoric and method of both discourses would broaden the awareness and need to refuse the university's continued neoliberalization. DH and CUS's political cohesion would better ground egalitarian visions of the university's future. Finally, developing common organizational models would better oppose institutional and disciplinary inequities. The infrastructural imperatives of both discourses demand their connection. Yet, for all our focus on critical infrastructures in DH and for all the radical evocations that CUS forwards to combat neoliberal directives, both are still grasping at the collective labor that might integrate CUS's postcapitalist propositions with DH's focus on infrastructural development. The provocations that this chapter forwards are an explicit attempt to do so.

Against Scarcity

Writing on his blog, *The Pinocchio Theory,* literary and cultural critic Steven Shaviro argues that "scarcity is equivalent, in theological terms, to original sin." "We can never know abundance," Shaviro continues, "because we have been expelled from the Garden of Eden." Shaviro is not speaking literally here, nor does he invoke a biblical utopia in order to lament a lost state of perfection. His invocation is rather meant to describe our neoliberal present: a Darwinian/Malthusian state in which "producers must always battle over limited resources" and "consumers must always decide how to allocate limited means."[3] The efficacy of this logic is plain in our contemporary world. However, the import of Shaviro's argument lies in the fact that our "sin" is self-imposed. We live and adapt to scarcity because we make it a material reality.

For those of us who are able to call it an intellectual home, the university is among the most intimate sites within which logics of scarcity affect us. We know scarcity because its imposition defines the scope of our labor. More fundamentally, it threatens what the university represents. Chandra Talpade Mohanty identifies this precise problem in her 2003 *Feminism without Borders,* writing, "[The university] is that contradictory place where knowledges are colonized but also contested—a place that engenders mobilizations and progressive movements of various kinds. It is one of the few remaining spaces in a rapidly privatized world that offers some semblance of a public arena for dialogue, engagement, and visioning of democracy and justice."[4] The privatized world that she invokes is here, and its effects on the university are manifest.

Consider the stark statistical realities of the recent downturn in humanities work from the "Preliminary Report on the MLA *Job Information List,* 2016–2017" as an illustration of this point:

> In 2016–17, the downturn in jobs advertised in the MLA *Job Information List* (JIL) continued for a fifth consecutive year. [. . .] The declines of the past five years bring the number of advertised jobs to yet another new low, below the level reached after the severe drop between 2007–08 and 2009–10. The 851 jobs

in the English edition for 2016–17 are 249 (22.6%) below the 1,100 advertised in 2009–10. The 808 jobs in the foreign language edition are 214 (20.9%) below the 1,022 advertised in 2009–10.[5]

Consider also Ryan Cordell's anecdotal interpretation of such data: "There are no assistant professorships because administrators can't replace positions in English departments because English majors are down because English classes do not sufficiently enroll."[6] Taken together, this bleak state of American higher education clarifies Shaviro's argument. Attributing loss to a lack of enrollment gives it coherence. However, not all disciplines are affected equally. As Matthew K. Gold has acknowledged, DH's late rise to prominence is predicated on austerity measures that, at least in recent history, belie such anecdotal interpretations:

> At a time when many academic institutions are facing austerity budgets, department closings, and staffing shortages, the digital humanities experienced a banner year that saw cluster hires at multiple universities, the establishment of new digital humanities centers and initiatives across the globe, and multimillion-dollar grants distributed by federal agencies and charitable foundations [. . .] Clearly, this is a significant moment of growth and opportunity for the field, but it has arrived amid larger questions concerning the nature and purpose of the university system.[7]

The truth of Gold's statement is indisputable. DH's growth arrived amid a wave of austerity, a wave that has continued to reshape the humanities. The questions that follow Gold's statement are worth paraphrasing. Is DH meant to redefine the nature and purpose of humanistic practice? Is it meant to reshape the university system? Does DH need theory and politics in order to accurately assess its rapid growth? Any response to these questions is already situated within the material contrast between scarcity and abundance and thus within a larger political frame.

What, then, of abundance? The difficulty of conceptualizing abundance beyond its narrow contrast to scarcity looms large in this discourse. DH in particular has fashioned itself as a humanistic discipline best positioned to obtain scarce resources. DH is a "tactical term," Matthew Kirschenbaum argues, which functions as "a rare vector for jujitsu" at "a moment when the academy in general and the humanities in particular are the objects of massive and wrenching changes."[8] DH's ability to attract and obtain funding is "simultaneously serving to position the humanities at the very forefront of certain value-laden agendas [. . .] while at the same time allowing for various forms of intrainstitutional mobility as new courses are approved, new colleagues are hired, new resources are allotted, and old resources are reallocated."[9] These gains are certainly a first step toward securing DH's disciplinary influence but are now perhaps prototypical of more radical approaches. The draw to manage scarcity is alluring but is not yet abundant under Shaviro's figuration of economic thinking.[10] CUS and CUS-related work shows us just how difficult overcoming logics of scarcity actually is.

In his 2008 *Unmaking the Public University,* for example, Christopher Newfield traced how our concepts of merit and competition are racialized from legislature down to university infrastructure, disallowing egalitarian modes of distribution to operate.[11] Kristen Monroe et al.'s study and subsequent 2008 article, "Gender Equality in Academia: Bad News from the Trenches, and Some Possible Solutions" show how merit and competition are discriminatory via processes of gendered devaluation, equally limiting egalitarian modes of distribution within institutional infrastructures.[12] CUS collectives like the Edu-factory Collective have gone as far as to liken the university to a factory in which knowledge is automated, commodified, and made precarious, thus demanding autonomous control over its oppressive modulation.[13] Finally, Mohanty turns facts like these into rallying points, arguing that feminist literacy in particular "necessitates learning to see (and theorize) differently—to identify and challenge the politics of knowledge that naturalizes global capitalism and business-as-usual in North American higher education."[14] These brief references are only a starting point but all presuppose a similar argument: the university *already has* resources that it does not distribute equitably. The point is to compel equity for all as new modes of organization and forms of knowledge are pursued.

Abundance is thus something other than a perspectival shift regarding our finances. Abundance, we might conclude, begins with refusal. Abundant thinking demands a politics of knowledge that refuses scarcity at its moment of departure *and* its horizon. It is, as Shaviro would have it, a site of conflict, but also the movement toward the common: "Scarcity is never a problem for capitalism; only abundance is." "For once scarcity has been overcome," he argues, "there's nothing left to drive competition."[15] Which varieties of DH refuse scarcity's imposition? What formation of DH/CUS might create the work of the common?

Differential Infrastructures

CUS, like DH, often imagines its work to be that of transforming academic institutions. It claims to be an insurgent disciplinary force positioned against technocratic influence and neoliberal demand. To quote Jeffrey J. Williams, CUS "focuses on the consequences of corporate methods and goals, like corrupting research and increasing managerial (as opposed to academic) control, cutting labor through reducing regular faculty positions (while increasing adjunct positions), and exploiting students by requiring them to work more and take on more debt."[16] CUS does so with abandonment, not from an ideal position but from a material one, recasting our present academic-corporate situation at the divide between abundance and scarcity.

Of the CUS work that forwards this logic, the conclusion to Newfield's *Unmaking the Public University* is perhaps the most accessible. After a sustained exegesis of the UC system's acquiescence to austerity and conservative cultural politics over the 1980s, 1990s, and 2000s, Newfield positions CUS as a transformative method-ological operation at the infrastructural level, advocating for numerous institutional remedies to the cultural and economic interests that undermine higher education. Newfield's intervention is vital because of the concrete rallying points it provides from which to act. Akin to Mohanty's argument, Newfield pairs the managerial demand placed on humanistic disciplines in particular with a liberatory politics that refuses the university's continuous contour toward corporate directives. The most pertinent imperatives of the five that Newfield proposes are the following: "First, racial equality needs to be reaffirmed as a value and as a goal." "Third, the univer-sity needs to be understood as an engagement in forms of individual and collective development that cannot be captured in economic terms." "Fifth, public universities need to insist on the value of understanding societies beyond their status as com-mercial markets."[17]

Newfield's imperatives are, parallel to DH concerns, a realization of transforma-tive critique. His fifth imperative embodies this in particular. Conceptualizing uni-versities beyond their status as commercial markets is certainly something that DH can assist in, and his first imperative is already apparent in movements like #trans-formDH and #DisruptDH. Think of Moya Bailey et al.'s "Reflections on a Move-ment: #transformDH, Growing Up." The piece opens with an apposite quote from Fiona Barnett: "*What happens when we shift difference away from a deficit that must be managed and amended (with nods in the direction of diversity).*" What happens when we shift difference "*toward understanding difference as our oper-ating system, our thesis, our inspiration, our goal*"?[18] The type of refusal that Bar-nett forwards is predicated on a conceptualization of value that cannot be captured economically. When she redirects the question of difference away from deficit and management, she moves toward a kind of heterogeneity that opposes business as usual in North American higher education. This is affirmed by Bailey et al. when they expand their call for politics' centrality in DH work: "Higher education in the United States is in a moment of simultaneous hope and despair. While individual actors recognize the need for a deeper commitment to social justice in the acad-emy, universities have fired professors at the behest of powerful trustees and donors, threatening academic freedom."[19] When value is conceptualized politically, beyond the problem of its management, its abundance is perhaps more threatening but is also liberatory. "Getting things done" from this position demands that we protect those most vulnerable to the university's inequities while building alternatives to scarcity. Abundance is shifting difference toward our goal.

In the introduction to their coedited anthology *Disrupting the Digital Human-ities,* Dorothy Kim and Jesse Stommel have also taken a stand against neoliberal imperatives informing DH praxis, affirming many points made here,

> we take for this volume [. . .] to decenter the digital humanities narrative vis-à-vis new critical voices, new languages, new locations, and new methodologies

that reimagine DH as not the seamless products of neoliberal governments and non-profit capitalism, but the work of people, labor, and voices at the margins creating friction and fantasy, mapping edges and new locations, playing slanted and in glitches with distributed resources and global communities.[20]

Stommel and Kim locate abundance in the interdisciplinary alliances that we make rather than in resource accrual or managerial logics. It is a simple inversion of imposed scarcity but a concrete point of reorganization from which refusal is prioritized alongside egalitarian models for intellectual labor. The concrete realities of nurturing this position, however, are much more difficult to implement.

Before analyzing arguments over infrastructure in more detail, I briefly explore two examples that forward the commitment to differential infrastructural work, one from DH and one from CUS. Both speak to the needs identified by the abundant thinkers mentioned here.

Consider first Roopika Risam's argument in "Navigating the Global Digital Humanities: Insights from Black Feminism" that DH is simultaneously global and local—a complex of intersecting methods, tools, and interests that frame the discipline:

> As the field of digital humanities has grown in size and scope, the question of how to navigate a scholarly community that is diverse in geography, language, and participant demographics has become pressing. [. . .] From the work of GO::DH in particular, an important perspective has emerged: digital humanities, as a field, can only be inclusive and its diversity can only thrive in an environment in which local specificity—the unique concerns that influence and define digital humanities at regional and national levels—is positioned at its center and its global dimensions are outlined through an assemblage of the local.[21]

Risam's description of DH organization fulfills all three of Newfield's criteria discussed previously and also adds a fourth: global scaffolding based on local needs. This insight is vital for DH's infrastructural turn and vital for DH's articulation of difference. Risam's model is relational, needs-based, and diverse without any compulsion toward homogeneity. "The challenge," Risam has argued, "is not to let hegemonic local forms—such as practices or debates taken for granted in the United States—overdetermine the definition of digital humanities globally."[22] Indeed, this argument is reaffirmed in her chapter in this volume, "Stewarding Place."[23] When she writes of DH work outside of R1 models, Risam affirms a radically contingent mode of DH organization and infrastructure in the pursuit of common goals.

This concept is reaffirmed in a second CUS example that operates between local and global iterations of its politics. Writing of their work with CAFA (Committee for Academic Freedom in Africa), George Caffentzis and Silvia Federici comment on

institutional formations like those that Risam identifies. On Caffentzis and Federici's view, a globalized vision of the university requires that we see "the continuity
of our struggle through the difference of our places in the international division of
labor, and to articulate our demands and strategies in accordance to these differences
and the need to overcome them."[24] Scarcity is further refused in their figuration of
common labor. Where the majority of "Africans do not have access to the Internet or
for that matter even the telephone; even the miniscule minority who does, has access
to it only for limited periods of time," conceptualizing value—particularly the value
of education—beyond commercial markets is neither easy nor universal.[25] In their
view, there isn't a digital cure-all to the current imposition of scarcity in the African
communities they work with. They go on to argue that "We cannot cast the 'cognitive' net so widely that almost every kind of work becomes 'cognitive' labor, short of
making arbitrary social equations and obfuscating our understanding of what is new
about 'cognitive labor' in the present phase of capitalism."[26] To do so would undermine both global and local efforts, disallowing common goals to emerge.

If local needs are to be taken seriously, if infrastructure is tactical and contingent, this cited work begins to outline a coalitional standard for educational infrastructure that forefronts difference in its refusal of scarcity. Abundance is present in
localized sites of knowledge production whose material conditions shape the character of their labor and thus the possibility of its participation in global initiatives
focused on collective development. Both are a question of infrastructure. Both are
radical expressions of the common. What infrastructure signifies—how it came to
be DH's horizon of disciplinary development—contours the DH/CUS connection.

There is perhaps no better place to explore DH's contemporary focus on infrastructure than Alan Liu's now infamous blog post, "Drafts for *Against the Cultural
Singularity*." There, Liu summarizes his interest in critical infrastructure studies as a
"call for digital humanities research and development informed by, and able to influence, the way scholarship, teaching, administration, support services, labor practices, and even development and investment strategies in higher education intersect with society."[27] Where Liu goes so far to say that most, *if not the whole of our
lives,* are organized through institutional mechanisms formative of a "social-cum-
technological milieu," "the word 'infrastructure' give[s] us the same kind of general purchase on social complexity that Stuart Hall, Raymond Williams, and others
sought when they reached for their all-purpose word, 'culture.'"

This claim is motivated by three logical moments on Liu's view, paralleling
James Smithies' claim to a *postfoundationalist* approach to DH praxis. His logical
moments proceed as follows: (1) "critique recognizes that the 'real,' 'true,' or 'law-
ful' groundwork (i.e., infrastructure) for anything, especially the things that matter most to people, such as the allocation of goods or the assignation of identity,
is ungrounded"; (2) "critique then goes antifoundationalist to the second degree
by criticizing its own standing in the political-economic system—a recursion
effect attested in now familiar, post-May-1968 worries that critics themselves are

complicit in elitism, 'embourgeoisment,' 'recuperation,' 'containment,' and majoritarian identity, not to mention tenure" and (3) "critique seeks to turn its complicity to advantage—for example, by positioning critics as what Foucault called embedded or 'specific intellectuals' acting on a particular institutional scene to steer social forces."[28]

Here, Liu has offered a mode of infrastructural critique that preserves the radical possibilities inherent to cultural critique as it places them within DH praxis. This argument is shored up in his reliance on Michel Foucault's *specific intellectual*. To remind, Foucault's consideration of this figure in "Truth and Power" does not situate her as "the master of truth and justice" but rather as a radically contingent political actor.[29] The figure is situated at "points where their own conditions of life or work situate them (housing, the hospital, the asylum, the laboratory, the university, family and sexual relations)."[30] The point then is to interrogate the conditions under which the subject is determined, to understand their structural formation, and further "to develop lateral connections across different forms of knowledge and from one focus of politicisation to another."[31] Following Foucault, Liu's argument culminates in a critical DH method that signifies our "ability to treat infrastructure not as a foundation, a given, but instead as a tactical medium that opens the possibility of critical infrastructure studies as a mode of cultural studies."[32]

Paired with Risam's work, Liu's post draws us closer to a profound DH/CUS pairing. Two features of Liu's and Risam's arguments draw out this point. First, Liu's argument offers a strategic intervention in DH's complicity with neoliberal educational imperatives. His antifoundationalism makes space for self-critique as DH extends into new arenas of influence. Second, Risam's work formalizes a global/local concept within DH praxis at the same time that she considers the question of diversity as an imbalance of power—an imbalance that implies socioeconomic difference. This feature of Risam's work dovetails with Mohanty's concern for a transformative concept of feminist literacy, especially where Mohanty claims that "Perhaps the only way to fight the corporatization of the university [. . .] is to link this struggle with other anti-corporatization struggle (e.g., the anti-World Trade Organization movement)."[33] The global/local focus in contemporary DH is thus a tactical opening to rework Liu's remarks on thinking critical infrastructure as a form of cultural studies, complicating the kinds of partnerships we make with noneducational entities.

Paired with Federici and Caffentzis's work, Liu's arguments are problematized. Federici and Caffentzis prioritize autonomy over strategic complicities in their egalitarian vision of the university's future. The university's alliances are thus far more tactical and perhaps far more wary of technocratic influence. This further outlines a problem of difference. To reaffirm the abundant political DH thinkers mentioned previously, if difference is our thesis, it demands the reconstruction of merit, the valorization of plurality, and the support of these irreducible to economic rationalization. This extends to the character of our labor, including a skepticism of the digital, and thus to the strategic alliances that we make. The tension between the demand for autonomy and the need for infrastructural longevity is thus productive of any DH/CUS pairing moving forward.

Autonomous Institutionality

This essay concludes by prioritizing a model that forefronts political consensus building, prior to any act of "thinking big," from within the university. Opposing institutional inequities requires such work, and our political goals are not always transparent or neatly aligned. This concluding section is therefore the most provocative. What would it mean for DH to situate itself within a lineage of political autonomy rather than its own technological and infrastructural development? How might we begin the process?

In her article "Digital Humanities for the Next Five Minutes," Rita Raley has argued that "the digital humanities should not, and cannot, bear the burden of transforming technocracy, the academic-corporate situation in which we are all mired."[34] What Raley ultimately proposed radically departs from large-scale infrastructure projects and tool-building. She has proposed a kind of dialectical inversion of DH's protected status. The abundance that DH has garnered demands its alignment with critical approaches that also interrogate the material realities of university infrastructure. "Perhaps more than other academic professional communities," Raley has written,

> digital humanists need continually to work to perceive and negotiate the institutional imaginary of informational technology so as not to fall into the trap of unconsciously adopting its optics. This institutional imaginary informs the conditions of our labor. It shapes intellectual rhythms according to administrative calendars and asks that we adopt the habit of innovating for the next grant cycle [. . .] We ought, in my view, to be marshalling the full critical, philosophical, and rhetorical resources at our disposal in order to think about the very universities in which we are embedded, their organizational structures, instrumentalities, and governing ideas.[35]

Raley's tactics are not so much a matter of preserving DH's permanence in any of its current iterations. Raley positions DH's alignment with resource accrual as a necessary site of CUS intervention as she demonstrates the tactical application of her politics: embrace the scarcity that surrounds DH in order to strengthen disciplinary and institutional bodies holistically. The politics of Raley's position demand contingent applications—and the applications also demand small-scale beginnings.

But what of the common? The common is simply another name for tactical acts of refusal that redefine our educational infrastructures. Indeed, Raley's work establishes a political rearticulation of DH's abundance and reclamation of the tactical as a mode of refusal. It does so at the height of DH's interest in large-scale infrastructural development. CUS's emphasis on postcapitalist modes of relation, organization, and knowledge production is the radical prefiguration of the critical engagements that Raley names. Consequently, the common cannot be conceived as "a good to be defended or protected," as the Edu-Factory Collective has written.[36] It rather defines "the affirmation of social cooperation's autonomy and self-organization."[37] Under this figuration of the common, we are not limited to a choice between the corporate logic of the contemporary university (privatization) and the total rejection of its infrastructure (public utopia). Rather, the common maximizes our embeddedness and our complicity in the imposition of scarcity as it also demands that we radically depart from market logics and corporate values.

Articulating the collective feature of DH's political character in this way is perhaps the weightiest wager made by the DH/CUS pairing. It demands that we conceptualize infrastructure as a constellation of autonomous institutional incursions, both local and global, that refuses the imposition of scarcity. To adopt CUS terminology, the political demand that thinking DH and CUS together results in a "global geography of autonomous institutionality."[38] This position valorizes differential infrastructures—beginning with difference as our thesis—as it also places a limit on the institutional alliances we make. A global geography of autonomous institutionality is a first iteration of what DH and CUS might accomplish together if difference and refusal are coarticulated on the infrastructural level.

To conclude, coarticulating Raley's work with tactical iterations of CUS addresses three political needs. First, it offers a structure that seriously thinks beyond our academic-corporate situation. Second, it better grounds egalitarian visions of the university's future. Third, it assists in conceptualizing common organizational models that would better oppose institutional and disciplinary inequities. The final challenge that the DH/CUS pairing forwards is thus a precarious challenge: how do we mobilize our global geography of autonomous institutionality toward an equitable distribution of resources for all?

Notes

1. In "Digital Humanities for the Next Five Minutes," Rita Raley draws on a broad body of scholarship to describe how the contemporary university has succumbed to explicitly neoliberal objectives. Relying on Shelia Slaughter and Gary Rhoades's work in particular, Raley argues that "Knowledge production has been administratively captured, as is evinced by patent deals, copyright disputes, measurable impact, pay-to-publish schemes, and corporate sponsorship of facilities and research processes alike," 33. This is what she terms our academic-corporate milieu.

2. Earhart, *Traces of the Old*, 121–23; and Edu-factory Collective, *Toward a Global Autonomous University*, 2.

3. Shaviro, "Scarcity and Abundance."

4. Mohanty, *Feminism without Borders*, 170.

5. Modern Language Association, "Preliminary Report on the MLA *Job Information List.*"

6. Cordell, "Humorless Man."

7. Gold, "Digital Humanities Moment," ix.

8. Kirschenbaum, "Digital Humanities As/Is a Tactical Term," 415.

9. Kirschenbaum, "Digital Humanities," 415–16.

10. Kirschenbaum argues that DH is a populist term because it is self-identified and self-perpetuated "through algorithmic structures of contemporary social media," particularly Twitter. This has led to the formation of journals (*DHQ*) and infrastructures (ADHO), but it does not fundamentally challenge the economic situation on which DH capitalizes.

11. Part 2 of Newfield's book, "Inventing PC: The War on Equality," charts a robust history of racialized exclusions in law and university policy that prefigures his consideration of finance within university structures.

12. Monroe, et al. interviewed eighty women faculty at UC Irvine between 2002 and 2006 and found that, "In part, discrimination occurs through a process of gender devaluation, whereby the status and power of an authoritative position is downplayed when that position is held by a woman. The UCI women find legal mechanisms and overt, direct political action of limited utility. As a result, they increasingly turn to more understated forms of incremental collective action, revealing an adaptive response to discrimination and a keen sense of the power dynamics within the university," 216. The narrative that the authors provide demonstrates that women do not feel the institution respects their needs, especially leading up to evaluation.

13. See Edu-factory Collective, *Toward a Global Autonomous University.*

14. Mohanty, *Feminism without Borders,* 171.

15. Shaviro, "Scarcity and Abundance."

16. Williams, "Deconstructing Academe."

17. Newfield, *Unmaking the Public University,* 272–74.

18. Barnett, "The Brave Side," 76.

19. Bailey et al. "#transformDH, Growing Up," 76.

20. Kim and Stommel, "Introduction."

21. Risam, "Navigating the Global Digital Humanities," 359.

22. Risam, "Navigating the Global Digital Humanities," 362.

23. Risam, "Stewarding Place."

24. Caffentzis and Federici, "Notes on the Edu-factory," 129.

25. Caffentzis and Federici, "Notes," 129.

26. Caffentzis and Federici, "Notes," 129.

27. Liu, "Drafts for *Against the Cultural Singularity.*"

28. Liu, "Drafts for *Against the Cultural Singularity.*"

29. Foucault, "Truth and Power," 126.

30. Foucault, "Truth and Power," 126.

31. Foucault, "Truth and Power," 127.

32. Liu, "Drafts for *Against the Cultural Singularity.*"

33. Mohanty, *Feminism without Borders,* 177.

34. Raley, "Digital Humanities for the Next Five Minutes," 35.

35. Raley, "Digital Humanities for the Next Five Minutes," 35.

36. Edu-factory Collective, *Toward a Global Autonomous University,* 11.

37. Edu-factory Collective, *Toward a Global Autonomous University,* 11.

38. Edu-factory Collective, *Toward a Global Autonomous University,* 11.

Bibliography

Bailey, Moya, Anne Cong-Huyen, Alexis Lothian, and Amanda Phillips. "Reflections on a Movement: #transformDH, Growing Up." In *Debates in Digital Humanities: 2016,* edited by Matthew K. Gold and Lauren F. Klein, 71–82. Minneapolis: University of Minnesota Press, 2016.

Barnett, Fiona. "The Brave Side of Digital Humanities." *Differences* 25, no. 1 (2014): 64–78.

Caffentzis, George, and Silvia Federici. "Notes on the Edu-factory and Cognitive Capitalism." In *Toward a Global Autonomous University,* edited by the Edu-factory Collective, 125–31. New York: Autonomedia, 2009.

Cordell, Ryan. "Humorless Man Yells at English Major Jokes." *Ryan Cordell* (blog), December 5, 2017. http://ryancordell.org/personal/english-major-jokes/.

Earhart, Amy. *Traces of the Old, Uses of the New: The Emergence of Digital Literary Studies.* Ann Arbor: University of Michigan Press, 2015.

Edu-factory Collective. *Toward a Global Autonomous University: Cognitive Labor, the Production of Knowledge, and Exodus from the Education Factory.* New York: Autonomedia, 2009.

Foucault, Michel. "Truth and Power." In *Power/Knowledge: Selected Writings and Other Interviews 1972–1977,* edited by Colin Gordon. Translated by Colin Gordon, Leo Marshall, John Mepham, and Kate Soper, 109–33. New York: Pantheon Books, 1980.

Gold, Matthew K. "The Digital Humanities Moment." In *Debates in the Digital Humanities: 2012,* edited by Matthew K. Gold, ix-xvi. Minnesota: University of Minnesota Press, 2012.

Kim, Dorothy, and Jesse Stommel. "Introduction: Disrupting the Digital Humanities." In *Disrupting the Digital Humanities,* edited by Dorothy Kim and Jesse Stommel, Online, June 15, 2017.

Kirschenbaum, Matthew. "Digital Humanities As/Is a Tactical Term." In *Debates in the Digital Humanities,* edited by Matthew K. Gold, 415–28. Minneapolis: University of Minnesota Press, 2012.

Liu, Alan. "Drafts for *Against the Singularity* (Book in Progress)." *Alan Liu* (blog), May 2, 2016. https://liu.english.ucsb.edu/drafts-for-against-the-cultural-singularity/.

Modern Language Association. "Preliminary Report on the MLA Job Information List, 2016–17." *The Trend: The Blog of the MLA Office of Research,* October 17, 2017. http://mlaresearch.mla.hcommons.org/2017/10/17/preliminary-report-on-the-mla-job-information-list-2016-17/.

Mohanty, Chandra Talpade. *Feminism without Borders: Decolonizing Theory, Practicing Solidarity*. Durham, N.C.: Duke University Press, 2003.

Monroe, Kristen, Saba Ozyurt, Ted Wrigley, and Amy Alexander. "Gender Equality in Academia: Bad News from the Trenches, and Some Possible Solutions." *Perspectives on Politics* 6, no. 2 (2008): 215–33. https://doi.org/10.1017/S1537592708080572.

Newfield, Christopher. *Unmaking the Public University*. Cambridge, Mass.: Harvard University Press, 2008.

Posner, Miriam. "What's Next: The Radical, Unrealized Potential of Digital Humanities." In *Debates in the Digital Humanities: 2016*, edited by Matthew K. Gold and Laura F. Klein, 32–41. Minnesota: University of Minnesota Press, 2016.

Raley, Rita. "Digital Humanities for the Next Five Minutes." *Differences: A Journal of Feminist Cultural Studies* 1, no. 25 (2014): 26–45.

Risam, Roopika. "Navigating the Global Digital Humanities: Insights from Black Feminism." In *Debates in the Digital Humanities: 2016*, edited by Matthew K. Gold and Laura F. Klein, 359–67. Minneapolis: University of Minnesota Press, 2016.

Risam, Roopika. "Stewarding Place: Digital Humanities at the Regional Comprehensive University." In *People, Practice, Power: Digital Humanities outside the Center*, edited by Anne B. McGrail, Angel David Nieves, and Siobhan Senier. Minneapolis: University of Minnesota Press, 2021.

Shaviro, Steven. "Scarcity and Abundance." *The Pinocchio Theory* (blog), June 3, 2005. http://www.shaviro.com.

Williams, Jeffrey J. "Deconstructing Academe." *The Chronicle of Higher Education*. 58.25. http://www.chronicle.com/article/An-Emerging-Field-Deconstructs/130791.

MATTHEW APPLEGATE is assistant professor of English and digital humanities at Molloy College. He is the author of *Guerrilla Theory: Political Concepts, Critical Digital Humanities*.

TAYLOR ARNOLD is assistant professor of statistics in the Department of Math and Computer Science and director of the Distant Viewing Lab at the University of Richmond. He is coauthor of *Humanities Data in R* and *A Computational Approach to Statistical Learning*.

EDUARD ARRIAGA is assistant professor of global languages and cross-cultural studies at the University of Indianapolis. He is the author of *Afro-Latinx Digital Connections*.

LYDIA BELLO is research services librarian for science and engineering at the Lemieux Library and McGoldrick Learning Commons at Seattle University.

KATHI INMAN BERENS is associate professor of English at Portland State University.

CHRISTINA BOYLES is assistant professor of culturally engaged digital humanities at Michigan State University.

LAURA R. BRAUNSTEIN is the digital humanities librarian and colead of Digital by Dartmouth Library at Dartmouth College. She is coeditor of *Digital Humanities in the Library: Challenges and Opportunities for Subject Specialists*.

ABBY R. BROUGHTON is lecturer in French in the Department of World Languages, Literatures, and Cultures at Middle Tennessee State University.

MARIA SACHIKO CECIRE is associate professor of literature and founding director of the Center for Experimental Humanities at Bard College. She is the author of *Re-Enchanted: The Rise of Children's Fantasy Literature in the Twentieth Century* (Minnesota, 2019) and coeditor of *Space and Place in Children's Literature, 1789–Present*.

BRENNAN COLLINS is a senior academic professional in the Department of English and associate director of the Digital Pedagogy, Atlanta Studies, and Writing Across the Curriculum Program of the Center for Excellence in Teaching, Learning, and Online Education at Georgia State University.

KELSEY CORLETT-RIVERA is a federal librarian in Washington, D.C. Her work on this project was completed while she was a librarian for the School of Language, Literatures, and Cultures at the University of Maryland.

BRITTANY DE GAIL completed work on this project while she was an administrative assistant in the office of the dean of the libraries at the University of Maryland. She is currently a technical writer for the software company Atlas Systems.

MADELYNN DICKERSON is research librarian for digital humanities and history at UC Irvine Libraries. Her previous publications include *The Handy Art History Answer Book*.

NATHAN H. DIZE is visiting assistant professor of French at Oberlin College.

QUINN DOMBROWSKI supports digitally facilitated research in the Division of Literatures, Cultures and Languages at Stanford University, where she coleads Stanford's Textile Makerspace. She is coeditor of the *Coding for Humanists* series and the author of *Drupal for Humanists* and *Crescat Graffiti, Vita Excolatur: Confessions of the University of Chicago*.

LAURA GERLITZ is a metadata librarian at the Bank of Canada.

ERIN ROSE GLASS is cofounder of the online learning community Ethical EdTech; cofounder of Social Paper, a networked platform for student writing and feedback; and founder of KNIT, a noncommercial digital commons for higher education in San Diego.

KAITLYN GRANT is former copresident of the Digital Scholars UA.

MARGARET HOGARTH is electronic resources and licenses librarian at the Claremont Colleges. Her books include *Game Theory and Water Resources: Critical Review of Its Contributions, Progress, and Remaining Challenges* (with Arial Dinar) and *Foundations and Trends in Microeconomics* and *Data Clean-Up and Presentation: A Practical Guide for Librarians* (with Kenneth Furuta).

MARYSE NDILU KIESE is a graduate student at the University of Alberta.

PAMELLA R. LACH is digital humanities librarian at San Diego State University.

JAMES MALAZITA is assistant professor of science and technology studies and of games and simulation arts and sciences at Rensselaer Polytechnic Institute.

ANNE MCGRAIL is on the English faculty at Lane Community College in Eugene, Oregon.

SUSAN MERRIAM is associate professor at Bard College, where she teaches in the art history and human rights program; she also runs the Mobile History Van, a public history project. She is the author of *Seventeenth-Century Flemish Floral Garland Paintings: Still Life, Vision, and the Devotional Image.*

CHELSEA MIYA is a PhD candidate and CGS SSHRC fellow in English and film studies at the University of Alberta. She is cofounder of the University of Alberta's digital scholars student group.

ANGEL DAVID NIEVES is professor of cultures, societies, and global studies (CSGS), professor of history, adjunct professor of English, and director of public history and public humanities at Northeastern University. He is author of *An Architecture of Education: African American Women Design the New South* and coeditor (with Leslie Alexander) of *"We Shall Independent Be": African American Place Making and the Struggle to Claim Space in the United States.*

URSZULA PAWLICKA-DEGER is a postdoctoral researcher in the Department of Media at Aalto University, Finland. She is the author of *Literatura cyfrowa. W stronę podejścia procesualnego* (Electronic literature: Toward processual approach).

JAMILA MOORE PEWU is assistant professor of digital humanities and new media in history at California State University, Fullerton.

JESSICA PRESSMAN is associate professor of English and comparative literature at San Diego State University. She is the author of *Bookishness: Loving Books in a Digital Age* and *Digital Modernism: Making It New in New Media*; coauthor of *Reading Project: A Collaborative Analysis of William Poundstone's Project for Tachistoscope*; and coeditor of *Comparative Textual Media: Transforming the Humanities in the Postprint Era* (Minnesota, 2013) and *Book Presence in a Digital Age.*

JANA REMY is director of educational technology and codirector of the Institute for Teaching and Learning at Chapman University.

ROOPIKA RISAM is associate professor of secondary and higher education and English at Salem State University. She is the author of *New Digital Worlds: Postcolonial Digital Humanities in Theory, Praxis, and Pedagogy* and coeditor of *Intersectionality in Digital Humanities* and *The Digital Black Atlantic* (Minnesota, 2021).

ELIZABETH RODRIGUES is assistant professor of humanities and digital scholarship librarian at Grinnell College.

DYLAN RUEDIGER is an analyst at Ithaka S + R. His research on settler colonialism and political subordination in the early modern Chesapeake has been published in *Early American Studies*; in Danielle Moretti-Langholtz and Buck Woodard, eds., *Building the Brafferton: The Founding, Funding and Legacy of America's Indian School;* and in Michael Goode and John Smolenski, eds., *The Specter of Peace: Rethinking Violence and Power in the Colonial Atlantic.*

ASHLEY SANDERS GARCIA is vice chair of the digital humanities program at UCLA.

RACHEL SCHNEPPER is director of academic technology at Wesleyan University.

SIOBHAN SENIER is chair of the Department of Women's and Gender Studies at the University of New Hampshire. Her publications include *Sovereignty and Sustainability: Indigenous Literary Stewardship in New England* and *Dawnland Voices: An Anthology of Indigenous Writing from New England* with its companion website, dawnlandvoices.org.

ANELISE HANSON SHROUT is assistant professor of digital and computational studies at Bates College.

MARGARET SIMON is associate professor of English at North Carolina State University. She is coeditor of *Forming Sleep: Representing Lost Consciousness in the English Renaissance.*

MENGCHI SUN is a graduate student in the digital humanities program at the University of Alberta.

LAUREN TILTON is assistant professor of digital humanities in the Department of Rhetoric and Communication Studies and director of the Distant Viewing Lab at the University of Richmond. She is coauthor of *Humanities Data in R.*

MICHELLE R. WARREN is professor of comparative literature at Dartmouth College. She is the author of *Creole Medievalism: Colonial France and Joseph Bédier's Middle Ages* and *History on the Edge: Excalibur and the Borders of Britain (1100–1300)*, both published by Minnesota.